Raspberry Pi Hacks

Ruth Suehle and Tom Callaway

Beijing · Cambridge · Farnham · Köln · Sebastopol · Tokyo

Raspberry Pi Hacks

by Ruth Suehle and Tom Callaway

Published by O'Reilly Media, Inc., 1005 Gravenstein Highway North, Sebastopol, CA 95472.

O'Reilly books may be purchased for educational, business, or sales promotional use. Online editions are also available for most titles (*http://my.safaribooksonline.com*). For more information, contact our corporate/institutional sales department: 800-998-9938 or *corporate@oreilly.com*.

Editors: Brian Sawyer and Rachel Roumeliotis
Production Editor: Christopher Hearse
Copyeditor: Amanda Kersey
Proofreader: Jasmine Kwityn

Indexer: Ellen Troutman
Cover Designer: Mark Paglietti
Interior Designer: David Futato
Illustrator: Rebecca Demarest

December 2013:   First Edition

Revision History for the First Edition:

2013-12-06:   First release

2014-01-24:   Second release

See *http://oreilly.com/catalog/errata.csp?isbn=9781449362348* for release details.

ISBN: 978-1-449-36234-8

[LSI]

This book is dedicated to Seth Vidal. Seth didn't live long enough to see this book finished, but within it, a little piece of his hacker spirit will live on forever.

Table of Contents

Foreword . . . . **ix**

Preface . . . . **xi**

1. Configuration Hacks **1**

Hack 01. Choose and Format the Right SD Card   1

Hack 02. Mount the SD Card   3

Hack 03. Decode the LEDs   7

Hack 04. Update the Firmware   8

Hack 05. Monitor the Raspberry Pi Hardware   13

Hack 06. Overclock Your Pi   17

Hack 07. Overvolt for Higher Performance   20

Hack 08. Get More USB Ports   22

Hack 09. Troubleshoot Power Problems   24

Hack 10. Unbreak Your Raspberry Pi   29

Hack 11. Go Headless   31

Hack 12. Connect with SSH   32

Hack 13. Give Your Pi a Static IP Address   34

Hack 14. Learn to Speak GPIO   36

Hack 15. Connect GPIO Pins to a Breadboard   39

Hack 16. Add a USB Serial Console   47

Hack 17. Add a Reset Button   54

Hack 18. Get Power to the Pi on the Move   56

Hack 19. Test Your Might (in Volts)   57

Hack 20. Add Additional Memory with Swap   61

2. Hacking Linux for the Raspberry Pi **63**

Hack 21. Build a Cross-Compiler Toolchain   63

Hack 22. Build a Custom Kernel   76

Hack 23. Update to the Latest Prebuilt Kernel   87

Hack 24. Split Memory Between the GPU and Linux Userspace   91

Hack 25. Update the Firmware and Prebuilt Binary Kernel the Easy Way   96
Hack 26. Emulate the Pi   97
Hack 27. Try Occidentalis: The Raspberry Pi Distro for (Advanced)
    Education   99
Hack 28. Monitor the Pi's IP Address   102
Hack 29. Run Android on the Raspberry Pi   107

3. Raspberry Pi Around the House **111**
Hack 30. Share Files with Samba   111
Hack 31. Use Your Raspberry Pi as a Remote Print Server   117
Hack 32. Make Calls with a Raspberry Pi Asterisk Telephone System   121
Hack 33. Build Your Own Web Server   127
Hack 34. Control a LEGO Robot   134
Hack 35. (Appear to) Survive a Gaping Chest Wound   150
Hack 36. Look for Aliens   158

4. Hacking the Outdoors **165**
Hack 37. Tell the Temperature Outside (Without Going Out There)   165
Hack 38. Check on Your Plants   172
Hack 39. Make Your Pi Water-Resistant (with a Case)   176
Hack 40. Make Your Pi Water-Resistant (Without a Case)   178
Hack 41. Find Geocaches from Your Car   182
Hack 42. See the Light   189
Hack 43. Listen to Aircraft Transponders   198
Hack 44. Control Aerial Photography   204
Hack 45. Have the Best Holiday Lights Display   219

5. Multimedia Hacks **227**
Hack 46. Play Video Files   227
Hack 47. Enable Additional Video Codecs   231
Hack 48. Build a Pi MusicBox   232
Hack 49. Turn Your Pi into a Radio   244
Hack 50. Control the Pi via Touchscreen   247
Hack 51. Emulate Classic Video Game Consoles   255
Hack 52. Connect a DSLR   258
Hack 53. Set Up a Photobooth   262
Hack 54. Turn Your Pi into a Tiny Media Center   269
Hack 55. Watch Movies in the Backseat of Your Car   277

6. Extend Your Pi **287**
Hack 56. Control GPIO from a Web Browser   287
Hack 57. Add a Tiny Screen   290
Hack 58. Connect Arduino Shields to Your Raspberry Pi   292
Hack 59. Control a 3D Printer   312
Hack 60. Add a Numeric Keypad   316

Hack 61. Add a Heat Sink   322
Hack 62. Enable the Raspberry Pi Camera on Pidora   325
Hack 63. Build a Solar-Powered Lab   326
Hack 64. Build a MIDI Controller (on the Cheap!)   329
Hack 65. Build a Raspberry Pi Supercomputer   337

Index **345**

Foreword

In April 2011 I was coming to the end of an executive MBA program at Cambridge and looking forward to spending some quality time with my wife, Liz. The old joke is that MBA stands for married but absent, and after two years of barely seeing each other, the last thing on our minds was jumping straight into another startup.

But after our accidental announcement of the Raspberry Pi educational computer project the following month (see "Funny Story..." sidebar), we had little choice but to knuckle down and make it happen. Liz, a freelance journalist by background, dropped everything to run our nascent community at *www.raspberrypi.org*. I, along with my colleagues at Broadcom and my fellow Raspberry Pi Foundation trustee Pete Lomas, started to figure out how to actually deliver the $25 ARM/Linux box that we'd so rashly promised to build.

Funny Story...

We went to see Rory Cellan-Jones at the BBC, in the hope that we might be able to use the dormant "BBC Micro" brand. He put a video of our prototype on his blog and got 600,000 YouTube views in two days. There's nothing quite like accidentally promising over half a million people that you'll make them a $25 computer to focus the mind.

Nine months later, we launched the Model B Raspberry Pi, taking 100,000 orders on the first day and knocking out both our distributors' websites for a period of several hours. In the 18 months since then, we've sold nearly two million Raspberry Pis in over 80 countries.

So, how did our little educational computer, conceived as a way of getting a few hundred more applicants to the Computer Science Tripos at Cambridge, get so out of control? Without a doubt, the explosive growth of the Pi community has been thanks to the creativity and enthusiasm of hobbyists, who see the Pi as an easy way to connect sensors, actuators, displays, and the network to build cool new things. Where for the first year of the project Liz's blog posts described work that was being done by us as we struggled first to design the Pi and then to build enough of them to keep up with demand, today the vast majority of her posts are about what you have been doing with the Pi.

It's hard to pick favorites from the vast number of projects that we've seen and featured on the website. As an unreformed space cadet, the ones that stand out most in my mind are Dave Akerman's high-altitude ballooning and Cristos Vasilas's astrophotography experiments. Dave's work in particular promises to put a space program within the budgetary reach of every primary school in the developed world and is part of a broader trend toward using the Pi to teach young people not just about computer programming, but about the whole range of STEM (science, technology, engineering, and mathematics) subjects. Another great development in this area was Mojang's decision at the end of 2012 to port Minecraft to the Pi, creating the scriptable Minecraft Pi Edition and spawning a large range of educational software projects.

As we head into 2014 and toward the second anniversary of the launch, we're looking forward to seeing what you all get up to with the Pi. One thing is certain: it won't be anything I can imagine today.

—Eben Upton
Founder and Trustee, Raspberry Pi Foundation

Preface

The inspiration for the Raspberry Pi was born when Eben Upton was working with computer science students at Cambridge University (see the Foreword for his own account). He saw a need for incoming students to have greater opportunities to obtain programming experience before they got to the university level. The first concept designs for what would become the Pi we know now were born in 2006. Alpha boards were demonstrated in late 2011, and the first 10 boards were auctioned off at the beginning of 2012, raising £16,000.

The first batch of 10,000 Raspberry Pis went on sale February 29, 2012. Toward the end of 2011, the SD card image for it had already been downloaded more than 50,000 times, hinting at its impending popularity. The two UK sellers at the time, Premier Farnell and RS Components, sold out within minutes, with the latter reporting more than 100,000 orders that day. Upton designed them for education—specifically Python, hence the "Pi" part of the name. But the tiny board caught the eye of already-experienced programmers and electronics hackers. As of this writing, a year and a half after that first day of sale, more than two million have been sold.

And then roughly 1.95 million of them got stuck in an office drawer while their owners gathered with hackerspace friends over beer and collectively lamented, "Yeah, I bought a Pi, but I haven't figured out what to do with it yet. I was thinking I might use it to build a time machine and try to study the K-Pg event in person, but I'll probably just put XBMC on it."

We wrote this book for you, the ones who haven't decided what to do with your languishing Pis yet. Of course, if you do just want to install XBMC, you can refer to Hack #54 and then read the rest of the book to see the fun you're missing. Alas, we haven't perfected the time machine hack yet, but follow *@suehle* (*https://twitter.com/suehle*) and *@spotrh* (*https://twitter.com/spotrh*) on Twitter, and we'll let you know if we find a good source for flux capacitors.

We're in what we hope is still the early stages of a return to a DIY culture. Those of you deeply embroiled in it already, who have been to every Maker Faire and joined your local hackerspace the day it opened, might insist that, on the contrary, we are deep in the midst of said return. But it hasn't gone far enough yet. Beyond our little maker/hacker/builder/doer niche is still a wide world of disposable goods and electronics consumption and dump-tion. Our devices are increasingly designed to do what the designer intended without the flexibility to do what the owner intends, needs, or wants. Further, they often are sealed up boxes, keeping prying fingers from ripping them apart and rebuilding them to suit new visions.

The acceptance of closed, unhackable, unfixable goods is relatively new in the course of human culture. It's not so long ago—perhaps even your own childhood if you're over 30 or so—in which we were happily building our computers from kits and taking the TV to the repair shop instead of buying a new one. Devices like the Raspberry Pi help bring us back to that better time when we knew (or could find out) what was happening inside the things that we owned, when we could change them for the better and give them new life when they broke down.

The first chapter of this book is for everyone with a Raspberry Pi; it gives you a basis on which to build all of the hacks. From there, we move on to the larger projects that implement all of those smaller hack needs. And in the spirit of the Pi's original purpose, we hope you learn a lot.

Who This Book Is For

Despite the potentially intimdating word "hacks" in the title, we don't expect you to be a Linux kernel developer or electrical engineer to be able to use this book. Hacks and hacking—not in the sense you hear those words used on the six o'clock news—are how many of us learn best. Hands on, trying something new, possibly frying electronics in the process.

We've tried to write these hacks so that even the novice can follow along and become a Raspberry Pi hacker. It will help greatly if you have at least a rudimentary understanding of how to use the Linux command line. For the most part, we walk you through those steps, too, but in places where we haven't, a quick look to Google or to the man pages of a command should catch you up.

As to the electronics half of the hacking, we've tried to spell as much out in detail as possible. For those who already have a workroom filled with jumper wires and strange parts you picked up out of the electronics store clearance bin "because they might be handy someday," this level of detail might feel belabored. Just skip ahead to the parts that are useful to you and be thankful that your less-knowledgeable friends will be getting help from the book instead of calling you to ask if "GND" is really that important, based on the assumption that it's an amusing nod to their childhood and stands for "Goonies Never (say) Die."

How to Use This Book

Although you can read this book cover to cover, each hack should stand alone, so feel free to browse and jump to the different sections that interest you most. If there's a prerequisite you need to know about, a cross-reference will guide you to the right hack.

The hacks in the book are organized into the following chapters:

Chapter 1, Configuration Hacks

The first chapter introduces you to the common needs of Raspberry Pi users, like making sure you have the right SD card for the project. It deals with the assorted parts and issues you're likely to encounter with any Raspberry Pi project, such as power problems and getting aquainted with the GPIO pins. You'll also find tips and tricks for dealing with some of its more finicky aspects.

Chapter 2, Hacking Linux for the Raspberry Pi

The most basic description you can give of the Raspberry Pi is "small Linux computer," which means a lot of the things you'll want to do will require some knowledge of Linux, working from the command line, and getting into the system. Even if you're relatively new to Linux, we'll help you walk through processes—like building a custom kernel and updating the firmware—that might sound challenging to the novice but don't have to be.

Chapter 3, Raspberry Pi Around the House

Now that you've gotten the hardware and operating system under control, you can start looking for bigger projects. In this chapter, you'll find some ways to use it around the house, including in really useful projects that make your home computing setup a little smoother.

Chapter 4, Hacking the Outdoors

Why should all the Pi fun be inside your house? You can use it to help out in the garden, take it geocaching, or run an animated holiday lights display from it. And that's just the beginning. What if you could (nearly) waterproof it?

Chapter 5, Multimedia Hacks

Back inside (mostly), this chapter presents the many ways you can use your Pi for entertainment. You can play music in a few ways, including by turning the Pi itself into an FM radio or by using it to set up a home theater. Then you can take it on the road and let the kids watch movies from the backseat by integrating a touchscreen.

Chapter 6, Extend Your Pi

This final chapter addresses some larger projects (not that launching an aerial photography rig isn't big!). Use the hacks in this chapter to attach more things to your Pi, get more control over the GPIO, and even build your own cluster of Raspberry Pis with up to 64 nodes.

Hardware Requirements

Most of the hacks in this book use the Raspberry Pi Model B, version 2. Here is a little information for you to consult and compare to the needs of your intended project before deciding whether the board you have will serve your purpose.

Why "Model A" and "Model B"?

In keeping with the educational goals, these names are a nod to the inspiration for the Raspberry Pi, the BBC Micro computer released with the same model names in 1981.

The Broadcom BCM2835 chip, 700 MHz CPU, and GPU are the same across the boards. All of them offer HDMI, composite RAC (PAL and NTSC), and a 3.5 mm audio jack. They all also have the same SD card slot. The Model A sells for $25, while the Model B sells for $35. See Table P-1 for a description of notable differences.

Table P-1. Differences between Model A and Model B

FEATURE	MODEL A	MODEL B
Memory	256 MB SDRAM	512 MB SDRAM
USB ports	1	2
Ethernet	none	10/100 Ehternet RJ45

There are also two revisions of the Model B board, as shown in Figure P-1.

Figure P-1.
For visual comparison, the two Model B boards: revision 1 (top) and revision 2 (bottom)

Changes made for rev 2 include:

- 2 2.5 mm nonplated mounting holes added
- LED labeling: D9 (yellow) corrects 10 label to 100, and D5 (green) says ACT for "Activity" instead of OK.
- Reset circuit added (see Hack #17 for how to use it)
- USB fuses removed (this helps with USB hubs that backfeed power, as long it's no more than 2.5A under fault conditions)
- GPIO pin changes:
  - CAM_GPIO: GPIO27 now GPIO21 routed to S5 pin 11 (S5 is the camera interface)
  - GPIO_GEN2: GPIO21 now GPIO27 routed to P1 pin 13 (P1 is the main, long strip of GPIO pins)
  - Additional GPIO added on P5 (see Figure P-2), which maps as follows:
    - P1 - 5V0
    - P2 - 3.3V
    - P3 - GPIO28
    - P4 - GPIO29
    - P5 - GPIO30
    - P6 - GPIO31
    - P7 - GND
    - P8 - GND
- Primary and secondary I²C channels switched (see Table P-2)

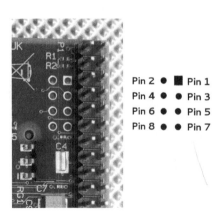

Pin 2 ● ■ Pin 1
Pin 4 ● ● Pin 3
Pin 6 ● ● Pin 5
Pin 8 ● ● Pin 7

Figure P-2.
P5 pin order (Note that "P5" label is on bottom of the board)

Table P-2. I^{2}C channels in Rev 1 and Rev 2

	REV 1	REV 2
SCL0 (GPIO 1)	routed to P1 pin 5	routed to S5 pin 13
SDA0 (GPIO 0)	routed to P1 pin 3	routed to S5 pin 14
SCL1 (GPIO 3)	routed to S5 pin 13	routed to P1 pin 5

This information is applicable for most of the hacks in the book. But, of course, just because they were tested (and possibly designed for) the Model B, it doesn't mean that the hacks won't work with a different model or revision (unless otherwise specified). Feel free to use what you have, but know you might need to refer to additional information online about older boards.

Conventions Used in This Book

The following typographical conventions are used in this book:

Italic

> Indicates new terms, URLs, and email addresses.

`Constant width`

> Used for program listings, as well as within paragraphs to refer to program elements such as variable or function names, databases, data types, environment variables, statements, filenames, file extensions, and keywords.

`Constant width bold`

> Shows commands or other text that should be typed literally by the user.

`Constant width italic`

> Shows text that should be replaced with user-supplied values or by values determined by context.

> *This element signifies a tip, suggestion, warning, caution or general note.*

Using Code Examples

All code listings are also available at the book's *GitHub repository* (*https://github.com/spotrh/rpihacks*).

This book is here to help you get your job done. In general, if example code is offered with this book, you may use it in your programs and documentation. You do not need to contact us for permission unless you're reproducing a significant portion of the code. For example, writing a program that uses several chunks of code from this book does not require permission. Selling or distributing a CD-ROM of examples from O'Reilly books does require permission. Answering a question by citing this book and quoting example code does not require permission. Incorporating a significant amount of example code from this book into your product's documentation does require permission.

We appreciate, but do not require, attribution. An attribution usually includes the title, author, publisher, and ISBN. For example: For example: "*Raspberry Pi Hacks* by Ruth Suehle and Tom Callaway (O'Reilly). Copyright 2014 Ruth Suehle and Tom Callaway, 978-1-449-36234-8."

If you feel your use of code examples falls outside fair use or the permission given above, feel free to contact us at *permissions@oreilly.com*.

Safari® Books Online

Safari Safari Books Online is an on-demand digital library that delivers
Books Online expert *content* in both book and video form from the world's leading authors in technology and business.

Technology professionals, software developers, web designers, and business and creative professionals use Safari Books Online as their primary resource for research, problem solving, learning, and certification training.

Safari Books Online offers a range of *product mixes* and pricing programs for *organizations*, *government agencies*, and *individuals*. Subscribers have access to thousands of books, training videos, and prepublication manuscripts in one fully searchable database from publishers like O'Reilly Media, Prentice Hall Professional, Addison-Wesley Professional, Microsoft Press, Sams, Que, Peachpit Press, Focal Press, Cisco Press, John Wiley & Sons, Syngress, Morgan Kaufmann, IBM Redbooks, Packt, Adobe Press, FT Press, Apress, Manning, New Riders, McGraw-Hill, Jones & Bartlett, Course Technology, and dozens *more*. For more information about Safari Books Online, please visit us *online*.

How to Contact Us

Please address comments and questions concerning this book to the publisher:

O'Reilly Media, Inc.
1005 Gravenstein Highway North
Sebastopol, CA 95472
800-998-9938 (in the United States or Canada)
707-829-0515 (international or local)
707-829-0104 (fax)

We have a web page for this book, where we list errata, examples, and any additional information. You can access this page at *http://oreil.ly/Raspberry-Pi-Hacks*.

To comment or ask technical questions about this book, send email to *bookques tions@oreilly.com*.

For more information about our books, courses, conferences, and news, see our website at *http://www.oreilly.com*.

Find us on Facebook: *http://facebook.com/oreilly*

Follow us on Twitter: *http://twitter.com/oreillymedia*

Watch us on YouTube: *http://www.youtube.com/oreillymedia*

Acknowledgments

Ruth and Tom would like to thank the following people for their inspiration, ideas, help, and support:

- Le Dernier Bar Avant Le Fin Du Monde, which we affectionately refer to as "the greatest bar in the world," where this book's initial hack list was born with the help of Josh Boyer, Dennis Gilmore, a few pitchers of French beer, and a Pan Galactic Gargle Blaster

- Every Fedora contributor, as one of the *four foundations* (*http://fedorapro ject.org/wiki/Foundations*) is *friends* and so many of you friends have helped us along the way

- Rodney Radford, both contributor and new friend, for tirelessly answering what he no doubt thought were absurd questions, driving many miles to tinker in person, and for trying to help moderately dangerous X-Men costume ideas come true without harm to the wearer or to the book's deadline

Ruth thanks Scott, for being the kind of husband who understands when she runs off to places with nicknames like "the greatest bar in the world" and events like Maker

Faire while he stays home with two awesome kids, who, while awesome, neither serve Pan Galactic Gargle Blasters nor build massive fire-based art installations (yet). Those awesome kids are the ones this is really for—the next generation of hackers and makers—so even greater thanks to Hannah, who QAed the XBMC instructions in this book (proving they're easy enough for a seven-year-old) and Ian, who can always say he learned to spell his first word during the writing of this book: a 12-character login password.

Tom would like to thank his wife Pam for putting up with him. He was writing this book in the midst of traveling the world, presenting at conferences, having a second child, and moving across the United States. He'd also like to dedicate his parts of this book to his sons, Jimmy (3) and Danny (0.5), who will hopefully read this book one day and think, "Dad, this stuff is so old, it doesn't even respond to my brain WiFi signals."

Contributors

Emmanuel Ackerman is a retired computer programmer who now spends his time doing Sufi meditation and exercises, making pottery, and doing volunteer work for Powering Potential and related groups. Ackerman contributed Hack #63.

David Bordonada works for *Libelium* (*http://www.libelium.com*), which runs *Cooking Hacks* (*http://www.cooking-hacks.com*), a site full of both tutorials and parts for your Raspberry Pi and other hardware projects. Bordonada contributed Hack #58.

Simon Cox is professor of computational methods and head of the Computational Engineering Design Research Group (CED) Group within the Faculty of Engineering and the Environment (FEE) at the *University of Southampton* (*http://www.southampton.ac.uk/*). He is also the associate dean for enterprise in engineering and the environment. Cox contributed Hack #65.

Lori Easterly is currently an information security engineer with a background in Linux and systems administration, currently residing in central Florida. Among numerous hacky interests, she is a shortwave and radio-listening enthusiast with a passion for technology, tinkering, and discovery. Easterly contributed Hack #43.

Oliver Mattos is a search engine mechanic at Google by day and a Pi hacker by night who loves to make anything do something it wasn't made for. Mattos contributed Hack #49 with Oskar Weigl.

Joe Ottinger is a principal engineer on the Open Source and Standards team at Red Hat. Ottinger contributed Hack #64.

Rodney Radford is an embedded software developer and collector of hobbies, bouncing between hardware tinkering, nearspace telemetry, high altitude rocketry, geocaching, SCUBA diving, woodworking, time travel, and robotics as time (and time travel) permits. Radford contributed Hack #44 and Hack #45.

Jared Smith is an open source enthusiast. He enjoys programming, systems administration, documentation, VoIP, and teaching others how to use open source software. Smith contributed Hack #32.

Wouter van Wijk (*www.woutervanwijk.nl*) is the creator of Pi MusicBox. He combines being a journalist for the second biggest newspaper in the Netherlands with being a techie who is fascinated by the interaction of people and computers. He enjoys designing user interfaces and experimenting, and likes to make computers and services easier to use. van Wijk contributed Hack #48.

Oskar Weigl is a master's student at Imperial College and ARM engineer whose greatest passions are playing with hardware and software (and building robots)—a true forward- and reverse-engineer. Weigl contributed Hack #49 with Oliver Mattos.

1

Configuration Hacks

They say the beginning is usually a good place to start anything, but this is a *Hacks* book. You're likely to skip around to things with interesting titles, or perhaps the one that starts in Old English because you were flipping through the pages and it looked like the book had some terrible printing errors.

That said, there are some things that it's nice to keep in the back of your head before you start building things, and the Raspberry Pi has a few unexpected quirks that it's good to be aware of. If you're entirely new to Linux, electronics hacking, or both, it's a good idea to give this chapter a read-through before proceeding with any of the other hacks. You just might learn something that will save your Pi (and the $35 of having to replace it).

`HACK 01` Choose and Format the Right SD Card

> The Raspberry Pi does not have any built-in flash storage; it needs an SD card to do anything. Picking the right one might seem simple, but we're here to help you make the right choice.

Your SD card choice is an important one. After all, when it comes to the Raspberry Pi, it's the equivalent of choosing a hard drive. Being able to change the entire system quickly by inserting a new SD card is also one of the Pi's most interesting strengths, especially when it comes to education. A few factors should weigh into your card selection, though, and even if you think you've chosen well, you might still need to troubleshoot minor problems.

SD cards are sold with a class number (e.g., 4, 6, 10), in which a higher class number equates to a faster card. Most high-quality, Class-4-or-greater SDHC cards (i.e., a recognized name brand) should work for most purposes. Vendors that sell cards with a Linux distribution meant for the Raspberry Pi largely use SanDisk or Kingston brand SDHC Class 4 cards. You can find a thorough list of known, tested cards (as well as cards that don't work) at *http://elinux.org/RPi_VerifiedPeripherals*. That said, a faster card can as much as double your transfer rate (in terms of MB/sec), so if speed is critical to your use, you should go with a higher class card.

Class 10 Too Classy?

The early Raspberry Pi firmware and bootloader didn't like Class 10 SD cards. This problem is supposed to have been fixed, but you'll still see people occasionally running into problems with Class 10 cards, so just be aware that it's a potential issue. If you have your heart set on a Class 10 card and the first one doesn't work, try a different brand. In addition, overclocking has been found to cause errors with Class 6 and Class 10 SD cards, regardless of size or brand, and the errors might not appear for a few days or weeks. Keep this in mind if you plan to overclock your Pi.

If decision making isn't your strong suit, you can also keep multiple cards around, each with a different purpose, for a single Raspberry Pi. If you'd like easy peace of mind, several vendors sell SD cards preloaded with Linux distributions for the Raspberry Pi, including a card containing NOOBS (New Out-Of-Box Software), which has several distro options on it. RS Components and element14 offer a card preloaded with NOOBS as an add-on when you purchase a Raspberry Pi.

NOOBS

NOOBS was designed to make setting up a Raspberry Pi super easy. It supports multiple OS installations and re-installations, as well as config file editing and web browsing (to research answers to boot problems) in a pre-boot environment. After all, this thing was designed for education, and you're not going to learn much if you can't even get started. It fits on a 4 GB card and gives you multiple choices about which distro you'd like to set up. After you've chosen, you can always return to the menu and make a different selection by holding down Shift during boot, either to try something new or to get a mulligan on a corrupted card. If you don't buy it on a preloaded card, you can download it from http://www.raspberrypi.org/down loads.

If you used one of the SD cards that's known to work and you're still having problems, you should check a few other things. Be sure that you've updated the firmware on the Pi (see Hack #04). If it was not a new SD card, be sure you fully formatted it first, and make sure you do so for the whole card and not just a partition.

First, find the card's device name:

```
$ su -c 'fdisk -ls'
```

or:

```
$ df -h
```

You're looking for something like /dev/sdd or /dev/mmcblk0 with the size of your SD card. To format, run the mkdosfs command, replacing /dev/mmcblk0 with the location of your card:

```
$ mkdosfs -I -F32 /dev/mmcblk0
```

This will make a single FAT formatted partition on the SD card. To be honest, it really doesn't matter very much how you format or partition the SD card in most cases, because when installing any of the system images for Raspberry Pi OS distributions that include partitions (such as Pidora or Raspbian), the partition table on the SD card will be completely overwritten by the installed OS image. The exception to that is NOOBS. By partitioning the disk with a single FAT partition, it is possible to install NOOBS to the SD card by simply copying the NOOBS files directly onto the SD card.

If you find that you have, say, an 8 GB card, and your computer thinks it's only 2 GB, you need to "grow" it to match. Or you might have found that your card's device name ends in p1 (followed by p2 and so forth):

```
/dev/mmcblk0p2      1.6G  1.5G   54M  97% /run/media/wwatson/rootfs
/dev/mmcblk0p1       50M   18M   33M  35% /run/media/wwatson/boot
```

This means your card is partitioned, and you should get down to one partition before formatting. Adjusting partitions and their sizes is most easily accomplished with a GUI tool called *Gparted* (*http://gparted.sourceforge.net/*), a visual version of the command-line parted.

HACK 02 Mount the SD Card

> While you can certainly access the files on the Raspberry Pi directly from within a running instance, mounting the SD card on a separate computer with an SD card reader makes many tasks (such as adding or editing files) easier.

The Raspberry Pi is a standalone Linux computer, but it really helps to have another computer on hand. In some cases, it might even be necessary. Fortunately, many computers now come with SD card readers built in, and if yours didn't, they're inexpensive and easy to come by. So, even if you buy your SD cards preloaded, you should probably still have an SD card reader and a second computer for interacting with your Raspberry Pi build.

Most Linux distributions for the Raspberry Pi create at least two partitions on the SD card. The first partition is always /boot, because the Raspberry Pi GPU reads its firmware from the beginning of the SD card. The second partition is usually / (also known as the *root partition*).

Modern Linux distributions (on your separate computer), such as Fedora or Ubuntu, will auto-mount the partitions on the SD card when it is inserted and provide some sort of notification of this event. However, if you're not sure, running the mount command should list all mounted partitions on the system. You are looking for something like /dev/mmcblk0p1, which means the first partition (p1) on the MMC block (mmcblk) device:

```
[spot@wolverine ~]$ mount
proc on /proc type proc (rw,nosuid,nodev,noexec,relatime)
sysfs on /sys type sysfs (rw,nosuid,nodev,noexec,relatime)
...
/dev/sda3 on / type ext4 (rw,relatime,data=ordered)
/dev/sda1 on /boot type ext4 (rw,relatime,data=ordered)
/dev/mmcblk0p1 on /run/media/spot/boot type vfat
(rw,nosuid,nodev,relatime,uid=1000,gid=1000,fmask=0022,dmask=0077,codepage=4
37,iocharset=ascii,shortname=mixed,showexec,utf8,flush,errors=remount-
ro,uhelper=udisks2)
/dev/mmcblk0p2 on /run/media/spot/rootfs type ext4 (rw,nosuid,nodev,rela
time,data=ordered,uhelper=udisks2)
```

The last two lines in the output identify the MMC block device partitions mounted in /run/media/spot/boot and /run/media/spot/rootfs, respectively.

If your SD card is not mounted automatically, make sure it's inserted and look at the output from the dmesg command. You do not need to pass any options to dmesg (although piping it through less is always a good idea). When you run it, it will print out quite a bit of stuff, but the output is in order from the last time you have booted your Linux system.

You'll want to look at the end of the output. Specifically, you look toward the end of the output to figure out the name of the MMC block device. Figure 1-1 shows an example of the sort of messages you are looking for.

Figure 1-1.
Output from dmesg on Fedora 19, with the MMC block device messages highlighted

In Figure 1-1, the MMC block device name is mmcblk0, and it has two partitions, p0 and p1. This gives you enough information to determine the Linux device names for these partitions: /dev/mmcblk0p0 and /dev/mmcblk0p1. You can confirm these are the correct device names by running:

```
brw-rw---- 1 root disk 179, 1 Aug 20 20:42 /dev/mmcblk0p1
brw-rw---- 1 root disk 179, 2 Aug 20 20:42 /dev/mmcblk0p2
```

If they exist, they're probably the ones you want (unless you have multiple SD cards inserted into your system somehow).

SD card readers connected via SPI interfaces are generally designated /dev/ mmc*, but SD card readers connected via USB are designated /dev/sd* (and some laptops' internal SD card readers are connected via USB). Be careful when accessing a /dev/sd* device, as it's then much easier to accidentally specify a hard disk drive instead.

Once you've identified the Linux device names for the MMC block device partitions on your system, you should be able to manually mount them by creating two mount point directories (as root):

```
$ su -c 'mkdir /mnt/raspi-boot'
$ su -c 'mkdir /mnt/raspi-root'
```

These directories will serve as anchors for mounting the partitions from the MMC block device.

Then, use the mount command to mount the boot and root partitions:

```
$ su -c 'mount /dev/mmcblk0p1 /mnt/raspi-boot'
$ su -c 'mount /dev/mmcblk0p2 /mnt/raspi-root'
```

If these mount commands return without errors, it means they have mounted successfully. You can confirm they have mounted by running mount again and piping the output through a grep for the MMC block device name (mmcblk0):

```
$ mount | grep mmcblk0
/dev/mmcblk0p1 on /mnt/raspi-boot type vfat
(rw,relatime,fmask=0022,dmask=0022,codepage=437,iocharset=ascii,shortname=mi
xed,errors=remount-ro)
/dev/mmcblk0p2 on /mnt/raspi-root type ext4 (rw,relatime,data=ordered)
```

You should also now be able to see files in the /mnt/raspi-boot and /mnt/raspi-root directories.

It is also possible to mount the /boot partition inside the mounted / partition, but we recommend keeping them separate. That way, if you forget to mount the boot partition, it is more obvious, and you avoid the problem of accidentally copying files into the /boot directory on the *root* partition. Remember, Linux mounts the boot partition on top of that /boot directory, and any files that get copied into that directory when the boot partition is not mounted are not visible!

Mounting the SD card is especially useful to make quick changes to the config.txt file that lives in the Raspberry Pi Linux /boot partition. If you need to change the ouput display settings for a new monitor (or an old HDMI TV with less than amusing quirks), it's a lot easier to do it from a mounted SD card than from a headless Raspberry Pi.

Just make sure the boot partition is mounted, and then change into that directory (/mnt/raspi-boot) and directly edit config.txt (as root). Save your changes, and then run sync to make sure the buffers get written back to the SD card.

When that finishes, change out of the directory (if you do not, Linux will not let you cleanly unmount the partition) and unmount both of the partitions (as root) with the umount command:

```
$ cd /mnt/raspi-boot/
$ su -c 'vi config.txt'
$ sync;sync;sync;
$ cd /mnt
```

```
$ su -c 'umount /mnt/raspi-boot'
$ su -c 'umount /mnt/raspi-root'
```

If the umount commands both return without any errors, it is now safe to remove your SD card. Just put it back in your Raspberry Pi, power it on, and hope for the best.

HACK 03 Decode the LEDs

Each Raspberry Pi has a set of LEDs in one corner that give you clues about what's happening (or not happening!) with the device. The Model A had only two lights, but the Model B offers a lot more insight and valuable troubleshooting information.

The Raspberry Pi Model B has five status LEDs (shown in Figure 1-2 and described in Table 1-1) that will help you troubleshoot problems when it won't boot or other problems arise. Since the Pi has no BIOS, the screen won't show you anything at all until the Pi successfully boots. That's where these little lights come in handy.

Figure 1-2.
Model B LEDs

Table 1-1. Status LEDs on the Raspberry Pi Model B

NUMBER	LABEL	COLOR	FUNCTION
D5	OK (Rev 1.0) ACT (Rev 2.0)	Green	SD card access, connected to GPIO 16
D6	PWR	Red	3.3 V Power, connected to 3.3 V
D7	FDX	Green	Full Duplex LAN
D8	LNK	Green	Link/Activity LAN
D9	10M (Rev 1.0) 100 (Rev 2.0)	Yellow	10/100Mbit LAN

The first two lights (D5 and D6) are the most important pair when you want to make sure that your problem isn't as simple as "it's not plugged in." Table 1-2 describes the most common indicators you'll see on these lights.

Table 1-2. Common LED Error Codes

LIGHT INDICATION	MOST LIKELY PROBLEM
Red PWR light off	No power
Red PWR light on, green OK light off	The Pi can't read the image on the card. The voltage is below 5V.
Green OK light blinks 3 times*	start.elf was not found
Green OK light blinks 4 times*	start.elf did not launch
Green OK light blinks 7 times*	kernel.img was not found

Note that the flash patterns identified with an asterisk in Table 1-2 are accurate for the firmware available since October 20, 2012. Earlier firmware used different patterns, and later firmware may change these indicators as well.

The two files it's looking for, start.elf and kernel.img, absolutely must be on the boot partition. The first, start.elf, is the GPU binary firmware image, and kernel.img, as its name implies, is the Linux kernel. If the red PWR light is on, you know have power; then it's up to the green light to tell you what's gone wrong.

If the green light doesn't flash at all, the first thing you shuld do is check your SD card in another computer. Make sure that the image is written correctly. If all of the filenames look like somebody leaned on the keyboard, it did not write correctly! Format it and start again. If it does look OK, plug in nothing but the power and the SD card, then each of your other peripherals one at a time to see which is causing the problem.

If the green light does blink, refer to Table 1-2 for information about what has gone wrong. Note that once start.elf has loaded, you'll see "the rainbow" (four large squares of color bleeding together). It should quickly go away as your Linux distro continues to boot, but if it doesn't, your problem is in the kernel.img file.

Blink Your IP Address Through the LEDs

Pidora offers some features specifically for running in headless mode, including the use of the LEDs to communicate your IP address. See Hack #11 *to learn how.*

HACK 04 ## Update the Firmware

The firmware your Raspberry Pi requires comes with any Linux distribution you choose, but it's frequently updated upstream, and your project might benefit from (or require) a more recent version.

The Raspberry Pi is a little different from your laptop, and even different from a lot of traditional embedded computers. The heart of the Raspberry Pi is the Broadcom BCM2835 system-on-chip, which is the CPU, GPU, and memory all combined in a single component. This detail is important, because the Raspberry Pi actually boots from the BCM2835 GPU. When you provide power to the Raspberry Pi, the CPU in the BCM2835 system-on-chip is actually disabled!

The Raspberry Pi boots like this:

1. **First-stage bootloader:** A bootloader programmed into the BCM2835 system-on-chip hardware mounts the FAT32 boot partition from the Linux distribution on the SD card. Note that this first-stage bootloader is programmed at manufacture time and is not modifiable or replaceable. A small, dedicated RISC core on the Raspberry Pi GPU starts this process.

2. **Second-stage bootloader:** Read off the boot partition on the SD card, this firmware (`bootcode.bin`) accesses the additional GPU firmware files, programs those firmware files into the Raspberry Pi GPU, and then starts it.

3. **GPU firmware:** This firmware (`start.elf`) allows the GPU to enable the CPU. An additional file, `fixup.dat`, configures the SDRAM partition between the GPU and the CPU. At this point, the CPU is released, and execution is transferred to it from the GPU.

4. **User code:** The CPU boots any supported binary, but the Linux kernel is the default. It assumes the filename is `kernel.img`, but you can be override the default in `config.txt`.

Versions of the Raspberry Pi firmware prior to October 19, 2012 contained an additional third-stage bootloader (`loader.bin`), but this is no longer required or used. Previous builds also had different versions of the GPU firmware that had to be swapped in and out to enable different memory splits between the ARM CPU and GPU, but this is now configured in `config.txt`.

Because of how the Raspberry Pi boots, you must use an SD card to boot the Raspberry Pi; you cannot boot it from any other device (such as network or USB storage) alone. But this is a good thing. It prevents you from rendering the device unusable, because you cannot override the first-stage bootloader. If you end up with damaged, broken, or incomplete firmware, you can simply start over with a clean SD card.

The Raspberry Pi Foundation provides the firmware files that the GPU loads, which then enable the Raspberry Pi to boot a specially formatted Linux kernel image. All the Linux distribution images intended for use on the Raspberry Pi come with a copy of this firmware, but it is constantly updated upstream. To enable new functionality (or boot newer Linux kernels), you will want to make sure you are running the latest revision of the firmware.

The upstream home for the Raspberry Pi firmware is *https://github.com/raspberrypi/firmware/*. There is currently no source code available for these firmware files, so this repository contains only binary versions. Because the Raspberry Pi is so slow (especially for Git operations), we strongly recommend that you check out these files to your x86 laptop.

First, you need to make sure you have a Git client installed by running the following command on Fedora:

```
$ yum install git
```

or this command on Debian/Ubuntu:

```
$ apt-get install git-core
```

Next, create a working directory for Raspberry Pi related files, such as ~/raspi:

```
$ mkdir ~/raspi
```

Go into the raspi directory:

```
$ cd ~/raspi
```

Use Git to get a local copy of the firmware files:

```
$ git clone https://github.com/raspberrypi/firmware.git
```

This will create a checkout in a new directory, named firmware. By default, this checks out the master branch, which at the time of this writing was synced up to the version of the firmware currently used by the Raspbian Linux kernel (3.2). If you are using a 3.2 kernel, this is the firmware you want to use. Another branch (named next) enables the updated drivers in the 3.6 Linux kernel. If you want to use this branch, change into the firmware directory and enter:

```
$ git checkout next
```

To switch back to the master branch, enter:

```
$ git checkout master
```

If you want to update your firmware again later, you don't need to check out this tree again. Simply go to the top-level checkout directory (~/raspi/firmware) and enter:

```
$ git pull
```

Remember, this will pull changes for the current branch only. If you want to pull changes for the other branch, you will need to switch to the other branch with the Git checkout command and run git pull there as well.

Now that you have checked out the repository and chosen your branch, your next step is to copy the boot firmware onto the SD card that has the Raspberry Pi Linux distribution image. To do this, you'll need to make sure the partitions on that SD card are properly mounted (covered in detail in Hack #02).

From here on, we will assume that the boot partition from your SD card with the Raspberry Pi Linux distribution image is mounted at `/mnt/raspbi-boot`. Current versions of Fedora (including Pidora) will automount it to `/run/media/$USERNAME/boot`, where `$USERNAME` is your username, so if you have it mounted somewhere else, substitute that mount point in the next set of instructions.

To update the firmware on the boot partition, all you need to do is copy the right files from the `firmware/boot` directory into the mounted boot partition (as root).

You probably do not want to copy all *of the files from this directory.*

You're looking for these critical firmware files in the `firmware/boot` directory:

- `bootcode.bin`
- `fixup.dat`
- `start.elf`

We strongly recommend that you back up the existing (and presumably) working copies of these files at this point. You can accomplish this by renaming these files (as root) in the mounted boot partition first:

```
$ su -c 'mv /mnt/raspi-boot/bootcode.bin /mnt/raspi-boot/bootcode.bin.back
up'
$ su -c 'mv /mnt/raspi-boot/fixup.dat /mnt/raspi-boot/fixup.dat.backup'
$ su -c 'mv /mnt/raspi-boot/start.elf /mnt/raspi-boot/start.elf.backup'
```

Copy each of these firmware files (as root) into the mounted boot partition:

```
$ cd ~/raspi/firmware/boot/
$ su -c 'cp -a bootcode.bin fixup.dat start.elf /mnt/raspi-boot/'
```

---

su versus sudo

The command example used here for copying firmware files (along with most other command examples in this book) use su. The su command will prompt you for the root password of your Linux laptop. If you have configured sudo for use on your Linux laptop, you can replace the su -c command with sudo and the command to copy the firmware files (as root) will look like this instead:

```
$ sudo cp -a bootcode.bin fixup.dat start.elf /mnt/raspi-boot/
```

Whichever method you prefer is fine, as they are both valid methods for Linux operations as the root user. We use the su -c syntax in most examples throughout the book for all root operations because it will work in all cases, whereas sudo works only if it is configured for your user on that Linux distribution. If you an encounter instructions prefaced with sudo, know that su is an option when you don't have sudo configured.

When the new Raspberry Pi firmware finishes copying onto the boot partition, run the sync command to ensure the data has all arrived onto the SD card:

```
$ sync
```

Then it should be safe to unmount the SD card partition(s) and eject the SD card. You can unmount these partitions from the GUI interface of your Linux laptop, or you can manually unmount them from the terminal by changing into a directory that is not in either of the mounted partitions and then enter:

```
$ cd ~
$ su -c 'umount /mnt/raspi-boot'
$ su -c 'umount /mnt/raspi-root'
```

At this point, the SD card will contain the new firmware. You'll know that the update worked if the Raspberry Pi still boots into the Linux image, but at a minimum, the firmware will draw a multicolored "rainbow" box (see "Somewhere Over the Rainbow..." sidebar) to the configured output device (usually an HDMI connected one) as its first step in the boot process (unless you have explicitly disabled this behavior in config.txt). If that occurs, the firmware is properly installed onto the SD card.

Somewhere Over the Rainbow...

Hopefully, if everything goes well with your Raspberry Pi, you'll never have to see the "rainbow" screen (shown in Figure 1-3) for more than a fraction of a second when it boots up. The screen is generated by the Raspberry Pi firmware as it initializes the GPU component of the BCM2835 system-on-chip.

To test that the output works successfully, the GPU draws four pixels on the screen and then scales those pixels to be very large, resulting in the multicolor screen. If your Raspberry Pi ever refuses to go over the rainbow and into a proper Linux boot, it means that the configured Linux kernel image (default: kernel.img) was not able to boot.

Figure 1-3.
The "rainbow" screen (uploaded to *http://elinux.org/File:Debug-screen.jpg* by user Popcorn-mix and shared under the terms of the Creative Commons Attribution-ShareAlike 3.0 Unported License)

Some optional versions exist for some of the Raspberry Pi firmware files. It is possible to configure the Raspberry Pi to dedicate the minimum amount of memory to the GPU (16 MB). When this is done, the Raspberry Pi Second Stage Bootloader looks for `start_cd.elf` and `fixup_cd.dat` instead of `start.elf` and `fixup.dat`. Hack #24 provides a longer discussion on GPU/CPU memory splitting.

`HACK 05` Monitor the Raspberry Pi Hardware

> Worried that your Pi is throwing wild parties while you're out of the house? Here's how to point a webcam at it and stream the video to the Internet. Just kidding! These tools can monitor the physical state of your tiny hardware.

A "normal" Linux computer would likely include onboard health monitoring sensors. Quite a few monitoring chips and components are used in various systems, but on the Raspberry Pi, all of that hardware is entirely hidden inside the Broadcom system-on-chip, so you can't access it with those usual methods.

To reach those components to monitor your Pi's health, you need to use the `vcgencmd` utility. It should be preinstalled with any of the general-purpose Raspberry Pi Linux distributions available, but if it's not, you can get a copy from the firmware tree at *https://github.com/raspberrypi*. If your distribution is compiled for ARM hardware floating point, look in the `hardfp/` subdirectory; otherwise, look in the `opt/` subdirectory.

Checking for Hard Float

At the time of this writing, most Linux distributions (including Pidora, Raspbian, Occidentalis, OpenELEC, and RaspBMC) are built for the ARMv6 hard-float architecture, because that gives the best possible performance on the Raspberry Pi. However, some older releases of these targets (and other OS platforms) were built with optimization for ARMv6 soft-float. These two op-

---

timization levels are not compatible with each other. On Linux, there is a good way to check for support for ARMv6 hard-float, using the `readelf` command:

```
$ readelf -a /usr/lib/libc.so.6 | grep FP
```

You can run this command directly on the Raspberry Pi Linux distribution (you might need to install the `elfutils` package first), or you can copy a binary or library from within the Raspberry Pi Linux distribution and onto another system with `readelf` handy.

If the binary has support for ARMv6 hard-float optimization, you will get output that looks like this:

```
Tag_FP_arch: VFPv2
Tag_ABI_FP_rounding: Needed
Tag_ABI_FP_denormal: Needed
Tag_ABI_FP_exceptions: Needed
Tag_ABI_FP_number_model: IEEE 754
Tag_ABI_HardFP_use: SP and DP
Tag_ABI_VFP_args: VFP registers
```

The important line is the last one, `Tag_ABI_VFP_args: VFP registers`. It will show up only if the binary being checked is built with ARMv6 hard-float optimization.

Once you've installed it (if necessary), look at the options that vcgencmd offers:

```
$ vcgencmd commands
```

This will output a list of all the commands that you can pass to the vcgencmd tool:

```
commands="vcos, ap_output_control, ap_output_post_processing,
vchi_test_init, vchi_test_exit, pm_set_policy, pm_get_status,
pm_show_stats, pm_start_logging, pm_stop_logging, version, commands,
set_vll_dir, led_control, set_backlight, set_logging, get_lcd_info,
set_bus_arbiter_mode, cache_flush, otp_dump, codec_enabled, get_camera,
get_mem, measure_clock, measure_volts, measure_temp, get_config,
hdmi_ntsc_freqs, hdmi_status_show, render_bar, disk_notify, inuse_notify,
sus_suspend, sus_status, sus_is_enabled, sus_stop_test_thread, egl_plat
form_switch, mem_validate, mem_oom, mem_reloc_stats, file, vctest_memmap,
vctest_start, vctest_stop, vctest_set, vctest_get"
```

Unfortunately, it doesn't actually tell you anything about those commands or what they do. Some of them seem obvious, but then when you run them, they return things like this:

```
error=2 error_msg="Invalid arguments"
```

The tool is poorly documented, but the Raspberry Pi community has come together and figured some of them out.

Measure Component Voltage

The `vcgencmd measure_volts` command shows the voltage for some of the key Raspberry Pi components, specifically:

core
> The GPU processor core

sdram_c
> The SDRAM controller

sdram_i
> The SDRAM input/output (I/O)

sdram_p
> The SDRAM physical memory

Each of these components can be passed as an option to the `vcgencmd measure_volts` command (if you don't specify one, it will return the value for `core`).

You might be wondering why you'd care about measuring these voltages, and in most cases, you probably don't. They'll sit happily as shown in Table 1-3.

Table 1-3. Components voltage

COMPONENT	VOLTAGE
core	1.20
sdram_c	1.20
sdram_i	1.20
sdram_p	1.23

The only time you might care about the component voltages is if you decide you want to overclock your Raspberry Pi. All of these voltages are configurable (as covered in detail in Hack #06).

You might expect this command to return the system board voltage (which varies between 4.75V and 5.25V under normal conditions), but it doesn't. See Hack #09 for how to do that manually.

Measure Temperature

The `vcgencmd measure_temp` command reports the core temperature of the BCM2835 system-on-chip on your Raspberry Pi (in Celsius):

```
temp=44.4'C
```

Alternatively, you can get the same temperature reading by reading this value directly from `/sys/class/thermal/thermal_zone0/temp`:

```
$ cat /sys/class/thermal/thermal_zone0/temp
44388
```

Fun with Math and Science

To convert that value to the Celsius temperature, simply divide it by 1,000. To get Fahrenheit, multiply the Celsius temperature by 1.8 and add 32. To get Kelvin, add 273.15 to the Celsius temperature. Is it getting hot in here, or is it just us?

From the perspective of monitoring the Raspberry Pi hardware, this reading is probably sufficient. Since there is really no separation of the CPU/GPU (at least not from a physical or heating perspective), this gives you an idea of how hot the board is running. That said, if you want a more detailed (or just an additional) temperature reading, you can wire in an additional temperature sensor, as described in Hack #37.

Monitor Memory Split

Whether hardcoded or dynamically allocated, the `vcgencmd get_mem` command returns the value for either the ARM CPU or the video GPU.

To see the amount of memory currently split off for the ARM CPU, run:

```
$ su -c 'vcgencmd get_mem arm'
arm=448M
```

To see the amount of memory currently split to the video GPU, run:

```
$ su -c 'vcgencmd get_mem gpu'
gpu=64M
```

Check Custom Configuration Overrides

Have you forgotten what configuration changes you have made to your Raspberry Pi? Specifically, the ones that change settings in the firmware? While you could look in `/boot/config.txt`, the `vcgencmd get_config` command is here to help you.

To see all configurations with a number (integer) datatype, run:

```
$ su -c 'vcgencmd get_config int'
arm_freq=900
```

To see all configurations with a text (string) datatype, run:

```
$ su -c 'vcgencmd get_config str'
```

There are very, very few configuration options that store string values instead of integers. Don't be too surprised if the vcgencmd get_config str *command doesn't return anything.*

If you just want to check the value of a specific configuration, pass that config name instead:

```
$ su -c 'vcgencmd get_config arm_freq'
arm_freq=900
```

The vcgencmd utility is not the most user-friendly tool, but it does have a deep connection into the inner workings of the Raspberry Pi. Since this tool is open source (and the source code is available in the aforementioned Raspberry Pi GitHub firmware checkout), if you want to go very deep into the inner workings of the Raspberry Pi hardware, looking at the vcgencmd source code is a good jumping-off point.

HACK 06 Overclock Your Pi

> The Raspberry Pi is not a notably fast computer. For most projects, it is more than capable of providing enough performance to get the job done, but for other projects, you might want to overclock the hardware to get a little bit more horsepower.

The Raspberry Pi hardware is preconfigured to what the manufacturer believes is the best balance of reliability and performance. Now that we've stated that for the record, it also comes with a lot of tuning knobs, and if you are feeling brave, you can turn them up to get extra performance out of the hardware.

This is what the cool kids call *overclocking*. People have been overclocking their computers since the beginning of the PC era, but it really became common when owners realized that the only difference between the high-end and low-end model of the same Intel CPU was whether it passed speed tests. The ones that passed got labeled at the higher clock speed, while the rest got the lower clock speed. If you were lucky, you could adjust settings to get a higher clock speed.

These days, overclocking refers to changing any sort of setting to get performance above and beyond the default configuration of the hardware. As an example, some people have resorted to any number of tricks and hacks to get a performance boost, including immersing the entire system in liquid nitrogen cooled Flourinert. Some people are crazy.

This is an excellent time to warn you: trying to overclock your Raspberry Pi will almost certainly make the hardware burn out quicker, possibly immediately. It will also probably not double your performance, and if by some miracle it did, you probably wouldn't be able to run anything reliably on the overclocked Raspberry Pi.

Then again, this is a $35 PC. You live only once. (When you decide to really take that advice to heart, try Hack #40.)

Remember that the heart of the Raspberry Pi is a Broadcom system-on-chip, with an ARM CPU, a Videocore IV GPU, and 512 MB of RAM. Each of these parts have its own clock frequencies, and the GPU has adjustable clock frequencies for its subcomponents. Specifically, the GPU has a core frequency, an H264 frequency (the H264 hardware video decoder block), a 3D processor frequency, and an image sensor processor frequency.

You can tweak all of these settings by changing options in `/boot/config.txt`. This file may or may not exist; if it does not, just create a new empty file.

Increase ARM CPU Frequency

Let's start with the most obvious overclock: the ARM CPU. The frequency of the ARM CPU (`arm_freq`) defaults to 700 MHz. To speed it to 900 MHz, add this line to `/boot/config.txt`:

```
arm_freq=900
```

Then, when you reboot, the hardware will try its best to honor your request. But remember, this isn't magic. No matter how badly you want to put `30000000` as the frequency, it isn't going to work. People with a lot of experience overclocking hardware have determined that the Raspberry Pi does not usually successfully overclock beyond 900 MHz, unless you use *overvolting* (see Hack #07).

Increase SDRAM Frequency

Another simple way to overclock is to increase the frequency of the SDRAM memory. The frequency of the SDRAM memory (`sdram_freq`) defaults to 400 MHz. You can usually increase this value to 500 Mhz without issue by adding this line to `/boot/config.txt`:

```
sdram_freq=500
```

Just like with `arm_freq`, you'll need to reboot your Raspberry Pi for this to take effect.

Increase GPU Frequency

Your last major overclocking option is the GPU components, the frequencies of which are all defined by `gpu_freq` and default to 250 MHz.

`gpu_freq` is a sort of *super setting*. Setting it assigns the same value to the `core_freq` (GPU processor core frequency), `h264_freq` (hardware video block frequency), `isp_freq` (image sensor pipeline block frequency), and `v3d_freq` (3D block frequency). If you have a GPU-intensive task, you might get some extra performance by increasing the `gpu_freq` to 325. You can do this by adding this line to `/boot/config.txt`:

```
gpu_freq=325
```

That said, we don't recommend changing the `gpu_freq` value, because it will take performance away from the CPU. Instead, you might try just changing the `core_freq` value. If you do this, it is important to keep all of the GPU frequencies (listed previously) either the same or different by a factor of an integer multiplier. If you do not do this, the GPU components will receive a mixture of incompatible pulses and things will stop working very quickly.

However, because the `core_freq` value also includes the L2 cache and some of the SDRAM memory clock cycles, increasing just that value could give the ARM CPU a performance boost. Multiply the default value by 2 (the largest integer that will really work) and set the value to 500 in `/boot/config.txt` like this:

```
core_freq=500
```

Note that this might not work. Some people report success, while others report failure. If you try to mix this `core_freq` change in with the other overclocking features, it might work only when they are set low (or left at the default).

We cannot emphasize this enough: sometimes, when overclocking fails, it does so in less-than-obvious ways. Reliable programs become buggy, hardware devices stop working at random, and the system might just reboot for no good reason.

When you do overclock, you'll want to have a quantifiable test case that you can run over and over again to see what gives you the best performance for the workload that you care about on your specific Raspberry Pi. Do not simply download a canned benchmark and trust it. A benchmark designed to show GPU performance will not help you optimize your overclocked Raspberry Pi system for tasks that are CPU-bound.

Pretested Overclock Presets

Newer versions of the Raspberry Pi firmware contain the option to choose between five overclock (*turbo*) presets that try to get the most performance out of the SoC without impairing the lifetime of the Pi. This is done by monitoring the core temperature of the chip and the CPU load and dynamically adjusting clock speeds and the core voltage.

So, when there is a low demand on the CPU, or it is getting too hot, the performance is throttled down, but if the CPU has much to do, and the chip's temperature allows it, performance is temporarily increased, with clock speeds up to 1 GHz, depending on the individual board and which of the turbo settings is used. Table 1-4 details the current settings of the five overclock presets.

Table 1-4. Overclock presets

PRESET	ARM	CORE	SDRAM	OVERVOLT
None	700	250	400	0
Modest	800	250	400	0
Medium	900	250	450	2
High	950	250	450	6
Turbo	1000	500	600	6

If you are running a current version of Raspbian, you will notice that the `raspi-config` tool has support for configuring your Pi into any of these five presets. For other distributions, you will need to define the preset you want to use in `/boot/config.txt` by passing the values for each option individually. For example, to set the Medium preset, add these lines to your `/boot/config.txt`:

```
arm_freq=900
core_freq=250
sdram_freq=450
over_voltage=2
```

Also, just because the Turbo setting has been known to work with some Raspberry Pi units, that doesn't mean it will work with yours. Quite a few users have reported SD card corruption when trying to run their Raspberry Pi at that overclock preset.

HACK 07 Overvolt for Higher Performance

> Overvolting, also known as "dynamic voltage scaling to increase voltage," is a trick to get more performance out of an electrical component.

The circuits in your Raspberry Pi are made up of transistors that act as logic gates or switches. The voltage at these nodes switches between a high voltage and a low voltage during normal operation. When the switch changes, the capacitance of the transistor and the voltage applied affect how quickly the switch output changes. Configuring a circuit to use higher voltage ("overvolting") allows the circuit to react faster, which permits you to overclock the hardware further than what would normally be possible.

The Raspberry Pi firmware exposes some configurable voltages, which map up with the following values in /boot/config.txt:

- over_voltage (core)
- over_voltage_sdram_c
- over_voltage_sdram_i
- over_voltage_sdram_p

If you do overvolt your Raspberry Pi by changing any of these settings, it might permanently set a fuse in your BCM2805 system on chip. That means that the vendor will know if you overvolt the hardware, it burns out, and you try to return it as defective. We shouldn't have to say that it's not OK to return things as defective when you were responsible, but you should be aware that this is warranty-voiding behavior.

The biggest change comes from adjusting the over_voltage value, which is the core voltage for the ARM CPU and GPU in the BCM2835. The possible values for over_volt age run from -16 (0.8 V) to 8 (1.4 V), with default value at 0 (1.2 V). Each integer above (or below) 0 steps the voltage by 0.025 V. You cannot go over 6 without also setting force_turbo=1 (note that this will probably trip the "warranty voided fuse").

The over_voltage configuration setting is a *super-setting*; changing it applies the value to the over_voltage_sdram_c (SDRAM controller voltage), over_voltage_sdram_i (SDRAM I/O voltage), and over_voltage_sdram_p (SDRAM physical voltage) settings. It is possible to set those settings independently, but you are far more likely to get them wrong (or mismatched) and end up with memory corruption, so we strongly recommend that you use the over_voltate super-setting instead.

If you decide to overvolt, just set these configuration options in /boot/config.txt, and then reboot.

When you're overvolting (or overclocking as well), monitoring the voltage levels of the components you've bumped up suddenly makes more sense. These methods can nudge out a tiny bit more performance from the hardware, but you're trading that extra bit of performance for a reduction in hardware lifetime (and possibly stability as well).

HACK 08 Get More USB Ports

> The Raspberry Pi Model B has two dedicated USB connector ports, but really, that just isn't enough for an awful lot of use cases. Here's how you can hack in a few more.

Universal Standard Bus (USB) has become the de facto standard connector for computing accessories. Keyboards, mice, hard drives, joysticks, flashlights, and even foam missile launchers all connect via USB. The Raspberry Pi (Model B) comes with two dedicated USB 2.0 ports to allow you access to this wide world of peripheral goodness, but these ports get used up quickly. The normal use case of a keyboard and mouse will use up both of these connectors, and you're left with no place to put anything else!

This is not a new problem for computer users. Laptops usually come with one to three USB connectors as well, even though a single USB host controller can support many more devices running simultaneously on the same BUS (up to 127 devices, to be precise). The trick to getting more is to use a USB hub.

Once upon a time, USB hubs were expensive. That time is long past. In fact, they're regularly given away for free. But there is a catch with these USB hubs. They come in two flavors:

Bus powered

> This type of USB hub draws all its power from the host computer's USB interface and is the type you're likely to acquire as a free giveaway or in the cheap-stuff bin at the electronics store.

Externally powered

> Also known as *self-powered*, this type of USB hub has an external power supply and uses it to provide full power to each USB connector on the hub.

USB 2.0 current is allocated in units of 100 mA (called *unit loads*), up to a maximum total of 500 mA per port. This means that if you are using a bus-powered hub, in the best possible scenario (getting 500 mA from the host computer), it can power four devices. That's what the specification says, so it must be true, right? But in the real world, this isn't quite the case.

For starters, the USB hub needs some power to run, so it won't be able to take the 500 mA from the host computer and give it all to the ports. Even if we assume it is an extremely efficient device (they usually are not), that means it can provide one unit load to four devices at once. But that's not the whole story.

The USB specification is pretty loose as specifications go (partially as a result of its ubiquity), and lots and lots of devices want more than 100 mA to work properly—most notably, wireless networking USB devices and keyboards with fancy features (LCD displays, integrated USB hubs, backlights, blenders, etc.). These devices are classified as *high-power* USB devices and can use up to the maximum of five unit loads (500 mA) per port. They are rarely (if ever) labeled as such, and they look visually identical to low-power (single-unit load) devices.

On top of all that, the dedicated USB connectors on the Raspberry Pi provide only one unit load (100 mA) per port instead of the five unit loads that a "normal" computer would. This amount isn't nearly enough to power a bus-powered hub with anything else connected to it, so that won't work for you at all. The free (or extremely cheap) USB 2.0 hubs? They are *always* bus powered. Sorry. You're going to have to buy something a little nicer.

This is why if you connect a high-power USB device directly to the Raspberry Pi, it will either attempt to operate in low-power mode (sometimes these devices can do that), or the Raspberry Pi will simply power off or refuse to see the device. The majority of high-power devices will detect at low power, then try to pull additional power when put into active use (this is particularly common with wireless devices), resulting in a confusing scenario where the device appears to work, and the Linux kernel drivers load, but it doesn't actually work reliably or properly.

The solution to this problem space for the Raspberry Pi is to use an externally powered USB hub. You will want to use a good one, though, because there are plenty of awful choices here as well. It is common for the manufacturers of these USB hubs to cut corners and design the hub to run off of a low-amperage power supply. They do this because they assume that most of the devices you will connect to it are low powered and that you will not have all of the ports used at once.

It is not uncommon for inexpensive, seven-port hubs to use a 1 A power supply. If each of those seven ports is connected to a high-power (five unit loads, 500 mA) device, they would need a 3.5 A power supply. More, really, because the hub needs power too!

To be safe, you should assume the opposite from what these cost-cutting manufacturers do. Just assume that any USB device you want to connect to your Raspberry Pi is high powered and that each port in your USB hub will have a high-powered device connected to it. Then it is a simple math problem to confirm if a USB hub will be a good choice:

1. Take the number of ports on the USB hub, and add 1 (to account for the USB hub itself).
2. Multiply that number by the size of a high-power load (.5).

The result will be the number of amps that the power supply for your USB hub should be providing (at a minimum).

Even if you do use an externally powered USB hub, you might still run into issues using it with the Raspberry Pi. Some hubs will send power across the USB interconnect cable (the cable connecting the USB hub to the Raspberry Pi). This is called *backpower*.

The standard says that hubs aren't supposed to do this, but plenty of them do. Backpower can result in a situation where the connected USB hub has power before the Raspberry Pi has power (across the standard micro-USB power connector), which would cause the Raspberry Pi to be in a partially powered-on state. While partially powered on, your Raspberry Pi might start to make unwanted writes to the SD card.

To avoid this, you can plug the USB hub's power supply and the power supply for your Raspberry Pi into the same power strip, then use the switch on the power strip to power them on simultaneously.

The Pi Hut sells a *seven-port USB hub* (*http://thepihut.com/products/7-port-usb-hub-for-the-raspberry-pi*) designed specifically to be ideal for the Raspberry Pi. It avoids the need for careful power-on ordering, because it will never feed any power back over the interconnect cable. Sadly, however, it has only a 2 A power supply, which means you can have high-power devices (using five unit loads) on only three ports at once, with the leftover power going to the hub. Still, this unit is designed not to backpower, so you'll never have to worry about that.

There is also a *four-port hub* (*https://www.modmypi.com/shop/raspberry-pi-accessories/New-Link-4-Port-USB-Hub-%28USB-2.0-with-Mains-Adaptor%29*) that is known to not have backpower issues. Even though it also has a 2 A power supply, you're arguably less likely to exceed that on a four-port USB hub than you would be on a seven-port USB hub.

The best hub for the Raspberry Pi that we've seen so far is the *PIHUB* (*http://shop.pimoroni.com/products/pihub*). It is a four-port externally powered hub with a 3 A power supply, and it is in the shape of the Raspberry Pi logo. They don't have a U.S. version at the time of this writing, but they say it is coming soon!

HACK 09 Troubleshoot Power Problems

> The Pi doesn't need a lot of power, but that also means that it needs what it's asking for, and you can run into trouble when it gets too much or too little.

The Raspberry Pi runs off a 5 V (DC) power source, pulled either from a dedicated Micro USB Type B port (labeled as Power on the board) or via the GPIO expansion (labeled as P1 on the board) pins, specifically the 5 V pins at P1-02 and P1-04.

If you have a charger for most Android phones, you have the Pi's power cable (sorry, iPhone fans). It is possible (but not the best scenario and might not work at all) to plug the other end into the USB port of your computer rather than the wall. And for other projects, you'll want to get power through the GPIO. That said…

Think Twice Before Using the GPIO to Power the Pi

Before you rush to input 5 V over the GPIO pin, remember that when you do this you're bypassing the hardware's input fuse. That fuse is there to protect your hardware in case of malice or stupidity.

For example, imagine that you think you're passing 5 V, but you're actually passing more than that into the Raspberry Pi via the GPIO. That might be because you weren't entirely clear on what you were doing, or it could just be an accident. Either way, out comes magic smoke! And by "magic," we mean, "that project just disappeared like a bunny in a hat!"

Plenty of power supplies aren't perfectly "clean," meaning it might *say* "5 V," but what it means is "more or less 5 Vish." Even if it just spikes above 5 V, you're bypassing the transient-voltage-suppression (TVS) diode!

That diode is what would normally protect the Raspberry Pi from those unexpected voltage spikes (by shunting away the excess current when it exceeds the avalanche breakdown potential), but you're just going right around it. And then out comes the magic smoke.

Last, but not least, you have to put *regulated* 5 V into the GPIO, and most power adapters do not output regulated voltage. This means you need to have a voltage regulator circuit between the GPIO pin and the power adapter.

For all of these reasons, we highly recommend you just feed power into the Micro USB Type B port, unless you have a truly excellent reason not to.

Do Not Backpower the Pi over USB

Hack #08 explains how some USB hubs will backpower over the interconnect cable, which can actually partially power the Raspberry Pi. Do not do this.

USB hubs are not supposed to backpower. This is not regulated or reliable power in any real sense. It can (and likely will) result in unpredictable behavior including (but not limited to) unexpected program failures, kernel panics, and SD card corruption.

I Still Want to Backpower the Pi!

OK, fine. There is a reasonably reliable way to do this. Some industrious hackers in Australia had a custom USB 3.0 hub produced with the explicit purpose of providing backpower for a Raspberry Pi.

Specifically, the interconnect port on their hub will send over the 1000 mA (1 A) that the Raspberry Pi needs for normal operation. This will power the Pi entirely off the connection to the USB hub (no separate power source is necessary). You can check it out here:

http://www.buyraspberrypi.com.au/shop/4-port-usb-3-0-powered-usb-hub/

The only downside to using this hub is that it has only a 2 A power supply, and 1 A is going to the Raspberry Pi, leaving a little less than 1 A (some of that needs to go to the hub itself) for the connected devices. That doesn't leave a lot of room for too many high-power devices (.5 A at maximum five-unit load).

Get Power Through GPIO Safely

Note that there is a big difference between using the Raspberry Pi GPIO pins to power an attached device and pushing 5 V into the GPIO to power the Raspberry Pi. Lots of the hacks in this book need to draw some current from the GPIO pins, and this is safe to do.

There are 3.3 V pins (P1-01 and P1-17), in addition to the 5 V pins (P1-02 and P1-04). Maximum permitted current draw from the 3.3 V pins is 50 mA. Maximum permitted current draw from the 5 V pins varies between the Raspberry Pi Model A and Model B hardware. The value for the maximum permitted current draw from the 5 V pins is calculated by starting with the USB input current (nominally 1 A), then subtracting the current draw from the rest of the board.

On the Model A, the board has a current draw of 500 mA, so the max current draw off the 5 V pin is 500 mA. On the Model B, because it has a higher current draw on the board of 700 mA, the max current draw off the 5 V pin is 300 mA.

Remember, be very, very careful with those 5 V pins! If you short 5 V to any of the other GPIO P1 pins, you're likely to fry the entire Raspberry Pi. While deep-fried raspberry pie sounds like a delightful carnival snack, a fried Raspberry Pi circuit board is neither tasty or desirable.

Solve Power Problems

Now that you've reviewed your power options, you have to figure out what to do when things go awry.

When the power is too low (or the current is too low), the Raspberry Pi starts to act... well, the technical term is "weird." USB devices might not show up, or they might blink in and out randomly. Software might not run reliably. Cats and dogs living together, mass hysteria!

If things are just being "weird," there's a good chance insufficient power is to blame. There are two main reasons why this can happen, even when you think you've done everything right: a subpar power supply or a faulty Micro USB cable.

Get a better power supply

It's the opposite of that power spiking problem mentioned in "Think Twice Before Using the GPIO to Power the Pi" on page 25. It *says* "5 V," but what it means is, "I might consider delivering 5 V on my best day when all the stars are aligned and you perfectly hum the *Doctor Who* theme song backward to appease my cranky nature." But they couldn't fit all those words on the plug, so they just put "5 V." (Or at least that's our theory.)

Sadly, this is a common scenario. A lot of cheap Micro USB cell phone chargers are cheap for a good reason: they don't work very well. (Did you buy it at a dollar store? That could be a clue it's a cheap one.)

When it's for your phone, it's no big deal. It just takes longer to charge your battery. But the Raspberry Pi won't take so kindly to the drop in desired power.

The best way to avoid this is to buy a proven reliable power supply. For example, Adafruit sells an excellent *5 V 1A power supply* (*http://www.adafruit.com/products/501*) that actually outputs 5.25, which makes up for any voltage drop across the resistance of the USB cable between the power supply and the Raspberry Pi.

Get a better micro USB cable

Your Micro USB cable is less likely to be subpar in quality than the power supply, but it does happen. Cables have conductors in them that provide some resistance, but that's usually irrelevant.

For example, at 5 ohms and 50 mA of current, the voltage drop across the cable might be about 250 mV. Most devices are OK with that, because the USB specifications require that they be tolerant of voltage drops of that amount. However, some devices, like the Raspberry Pi, want more power (especially if you have some hungry USB devices plugged directly into the Raspberry Pi's USB ports).

As mentioned previously in this hack, the Model B draws a peak current of 700 mA, so if your USB cable has 5 ohms of resistance, it would result in a 3.5 V voltage drop. As far as the Pi is concerned, that's huge.

The good news is that most USB cables don't have 5 ohms of resistance, and the really good ones will be very close to 0. We haven't really had problems with cables that came with modern phones, which seems to be most people's source of such cables.

If you need to purchase a USB Micro B cable, Mediabridge's "USB charging cables" test with a low resistance and are available on Amazon. Adafruit's USB Micro B cables also work fine in peak-current draw on the Model B.

Why Do USB Devices Cause My Pi to Reboot?

Hotplugging (plugging in a USB device when the Pi is already running) will often cause the Pi to reboot. Plugging in the device causes a power spike, which means a drop in power to the Pi, which leads to the reboot.

The Rev 1 board had two 140 mA polyfuses on the USB ports that prevented this but caused other problems, so Rev 2 boards do not. If you do anticipate the need to hotplug a device, do it through a powered USB hub.

Test Your Cable's Resistance

If you have a cheap power supply, you can almost guarantee that's your problem. But if you think you have a problem with your cable and want to test its resistance, you can either take the cable apart or you can use an accessible Micro USB Type B device (something that has ground pins on it).

The USB Type A connector is big enough that you can get to the ground pin directly. (It's Pin 4, the first pin on the left if you're looking down the cable with the hollow space at the top of the connector.) Measure resistance with a calibrated multimeter set to the lowest ohm setting from ground on the Micro USB-B connected device to ground on the USB Type A connector to get a good idea of the cable's resistance.

You can also get a little hardware tool to simplify this. Bitwizard B.V. makes a *USB prodder* (*http://www.bitwizard.nl/catalog/product_info.php?products_id=134*) just for this purpose.

Some people have even made their own cables by soldering low-resistance wires to a power supply and a Micro USB Type B connector. This is a neat hack if you just want to try making cables, but it's not really necessary.

Most modern USB cables do not seem to have serious resistance issues. If it will charge a Micro USB Type B cell phone quickly and reliably, it is probably good enough for the Raspberry Pi. If it won't, a new one is generally easy and cheap to come by.

HACK 10 Unbreak Your Raspberry Pi

> The Raspberry Pi hardware is pretty rugged for its size, but it does have one notable weak point that you might discover. Here's how to find it and how to hack it back to life if it breaks.

The Raspberry Pi comes with a built-in self-destruct button that many people have accidentally triggered the first time they plugged it in. OK, that's not *precisely* true. But the placement of one of the Pi's fragile components makes it really easy to destroy your new toy before you've gotten to play with it. Here's what to do in case you broke it before you got around to reading this hack.

Just behind the power connection on the board is a small silver cylinder (see Figure 1-4). It's called *capacitor C6*, and it's a 220 µF, 16-volt, surface-mount electrolytic capacitor that smooths out the voltage going to the Pi. It also seems like a really good spot to grip when you're plugging in or unplugging your micro USB cable. It's not. Don't touch it. It's not a *critical* component, and your Pi *could* still work without it, but it also might not.

Figure 1-4.
C6 is the black and silver cylinder beside the power connector

The relative fragility of this piece's connection is one of several good reasons to make or buy a good case for your Raspberry Pi. Meanwhile, if you need to carry it around, use the original static bag and box it came in.

Test Your Power Supply

If you do happen to break off the capacitor, and your Pi stops working, take consolation in the knowledge that you're not the only one, and though it's not covered under warranty, you have a few options. First, a new and better power supply might fix the problem. With a stable power supply, you shouldn't have any problems.

If you don't know whether your power supply is doing what it should (beyond the obvious evidence of "it works" or "it doesn't work"), you can test it. The first sign that you're not getting consistent or strong enough power is not an *unworking* Pi, but rather an *unreliable* one.

When things start acting up mid-stream—all was fine at first, then maybe when you get into the GUI, the peripherals stop working—that's when it's time to check your voltage. The Pi has test points labeled TP1 and TP2 to help you. TP1 is just under the Raspberry Pi logo, and TP2 is between the GPIO and the RCA out.

Set your multimeter to 20V in the DC range and touch the leads to TP1 and TP2. The reading should be near 5 volts and certainly no more than 0.25 volts away in either direction.

Replace the C6 Capacitor

If your Pi is still not working or if you just want the capacitor back on there, you can solder a new one on.

Soldering on a new capacitor might *make your Raspberry Pi as good as new*. It definitely *will void your Raspberry Pi warranty*.

When you solder it back on, note that the capacitor is polarized, and thus it is critical to have the black stripe facing the edge of the board. For some basic soldering tips, check out "Soldering Reminders" on page 42.

`HACK 11` Go Headless

> Even though the Raspberry Pi supports 1080p HDMI video out, there are lots of projects where it is not cost effective or practical to connect it to a video display. Here's how to go without a monitor.

The Raspberry Pi is often touted as an inexpensive computer, but if you don't have a monitor and other assorted peripherals already available, the cost soars quickly. Also, since one of the most appealing features of the Raspberry Pi for creative projects is its diminutive size, you're likely to discover that you need to run in "headless" mode: no monitor, no keyboard, and no mouse. Just a Pi flying solo (perhaps literally if you're building Hack #44!). That's when it's time to run headless.

Change Your Root Password

Don't forget to change your root password early on. It's a good practice in general, but it's particularly important in headless mode. Most Raspberry Pi distros have well-known default root passwords.

In general, your eventually headless Pi projects will begin life connected to a monitor and input devices just to get everything ready. If nothing else, it seems like the easiest way to get the IP address, which is the first step to being able to SSH to the Raspberry Pi. However, if you use Pidora, you can go headless from the beginning, thanks to a configuration option that bypasses the first boot process and is meant specifically for going headless.

Once you've installed Pidora on your SD card (you can download the latest version from *http://www.pidora.ca*), create a file called `headless` in the partition named `boot`.

For a static IP address, list it along with the netmask and gateway in the `headless` file:

```
IPADDR=192.168.1.123
NETMASK=255.255.255.0
GATEWAY=192.168.1.1
```

You can also use this file to initiate `rootfs-resize` by adding:

```
RESIZE
```

If you would like to set the swap amount, add it here as well:

```
SWAP=512
```

If your Pi should obtain its IP address dynamically (DHCP), `headless` should stay empty. But then how do you find out what the IP address is? This is where Pidora's headless mode comes through for you!

Once you boot the Raspberry Pi with this headless file, the IP address will first flash through the speakers two minutes after powering on. Thirty seconds later, it will flash the IP address through the green OK/ACT LED. These functions are provided through ip-info, a package that contains the aptly named ip-read and ip-flash. The flashes indicate numbers in the following way:

- Digits 1–9 are indicated with short flashes (e.g., three short flashes is a 3).
- 0 is indicated with 10 short flashes.
- Digits are separated by a pause.
- Dot (.) is indicated with a long flash.

You can read more about the ip-info package and download it at *https://github.com/ctyler/ip-info/*.

As mentioned earlier, Pidora would usually run through the first boot process and have you set up a root password and another user. But that script will run only if input devices are found. Otherwise, the system configures the ethernet interface via IPv4 DHCP and assumes you'll set up any other preferences you would have made at first boot on your own.

HACK 12 Connect with SSH

For any headless project, as well as a matter of convenience when you're away from your project or just too lazy to walk across the room, you'll need to know how to SSH to your Raspberry Pi.

OpenSSH, the open source set of tools for secure communcation created by the OpenBSD project, is likely available in any distro you choose.

If you're going a little retro, note that "Squeeze," the version of Raspbian before "Wheezy," didn't have SSH running by default.

If you aren't certain, all you have to do is attempt to SSH to your Pi, and you'll find out pretty quickly. Attach a monitor and keyboard, and then run:

```
$ service sshd status

'Redirecting to /bin/systemctl status  sshd.service
sshd.service - OpenSSH server daemon
        Loaded: loaded (/usr/lib/systemd/system/sshd.service; enabled)
           Active: active (running) since Wed 2013-02-13 13:06:40 EST; 28min
ago
```

```
        Process: 273 ExecStartPre=/usr/sbin/sshd-keygen (code=exited, sta
tus=0/SUCCESS)
        Main PID: 280 (sshd)
          CGroup: name=systemd:/system/sshd.service
              └─280 /usr/sbin/sshd -D
```

If your output doesn't look similar to that, it's quick to install. Here's the command on Fedora:

```
$ su -c 'yum install openssh-server openssh-clients'
```

And here's how to install it on Debian/Ubuntu:

```
$ su -c 'apt-get install ssh'
```

Once you've determined that it is installed, set it to start the daemon automatically at each boot:

```
$ su -c 'chkconfig sshd on'
```

If you're not going headless from square one with the Pi, you can connect it to a monitor and run `ifconfig`. That's the simple way, assuming you've got a monitor and keyboard handy. Note that if you're using a newer version of Fedora or Pidora, you'll need to use `ip addr` instead.

Or check your router's default IP address, which is probably on a sticker somewhere on it or on a website if you search for your router brand. (192.168.0.1 is a common one.) You can also run `route -n` to find it. The numbers under Gateway on the line flagged UG are the default IP. Go to that address in a web browser, and you'll almost certainly find some sort of router control panel where you can see connected devices, including your Pi.

You could also use `nmap`, the network mapper tool. This is a fun way to learn a new tool if you haven't used it. That said, you should do your `nmap` learning only on your home network and not at the office, in the coffee shop, or anywhere else you're not in charge of said network. When you run `su -c nmap 192.168.1.1/24`, replacing the IP address with that of your network, you'll see a list of everything connected to that network. One of them will have a MAC address labeled Raspberry Pi Foundation, and it will list your Pi's IP address as well.

If you're going to frequently connect via SSH, you'll want to simplify things by giving your Pi a static IP address (see Hack #13*).*

And now you're ready to connect to your Pi by running `ssh username@host`, where `username` is an account you've set up on the Raspberry Pi and `host` is the IP address you found or configured. If you haven't yet set up a user, you might need to refer to the default login. On Pidora, it's `root/raspberrypi`. On Raspbian-based systems, it's `pi/raspberry`.

The first time you connect to any machine, it will store a record of that machine in `.ssh/known_hosts`. This list is checked on each connection. That means the first time you connect, you'll see a dialog that asks you:

```
The authenticity of host '192.168.1.174 (192.168.1.174)' can't be establish
ed.
RSA key fingerprint is 78:75:1d:1c:a1:79:11:18:15:e5:04:08:15:16:23:42.
Are you sure you want to continue connecting (yes/no)?
```

It sounds a little ominous, but "yes" is the right answer, despite the "warning" that follows.

Now you're ready to use the command line to transfer files to and from your Raspberry Pi and to work on it almost as if you were working directly on it. If you'd like to be able to launch GUI interfaces over SSH, use `-X` when you connect:

```
$ ssh -X ruth@192.168.1.118
```

Most (but not all) graphical applications will work with this method, known as "X forwarding."

HACK 13 Give Your Pi a Static IP Address

If you always want to be able to connect to your Pi through the same IP address without looking it up, you'll need to assign it a static IP address (as opposed to a dynamically assigned one).

Many ISPs use *dynamic IP addressing*, which means that you get a different IP address each time you connect to the Internet. If you're connecting to the Pi over SSH regularly (see Hack #12), using VoIP (see Hack #32), or have other reasons to always have the same IP address, you'll want to set up static IP addressing.

In Pidora, you can either follow the instructions in Hack #11 if you're running headless, or if you're not, edit the files in `/etc/sysconfig/network-scripts`.

If you're usually a Debian user, these files are analgous to `/etc/network/inter faces`.

You'll see the available network interfaces configurations listed as `ifcfg-<interface-name>`. Choose the one you'll be using for the connection and edit it in your favorite text editor, for example:

```
$ vi ifcfg-eth0
```

You'll see something like this:

```
DEVICE=eth0
BOOTPROTO=dhcp
ONBOOT=yes
NM_CONTROLLED=yes
```

You need to change the BOOTPROTO line from dhcp to static. Also make sure ONBOOT is set to yes. Then add IPADDR, NETMASK, BROADCAST, and NETWORK information like you would have in the headless file. Remember not to choose an IP address already in use elsewhere in your network. NETMASK is always 255.255.255.0. GATEWAY is your router's IP address:

```
IPADDR=192.168.1.123
NETMASK=255.255.255.0
BROADCAST=192.168.1.255
GATEWAY=192.168.1.1
```

Finally, restart the network service to apply your new settings:

```
$ systemctl restart network.service
```

If you're using a Raspbian-based distro, you'll follow similar steps, just in a different place. Rather than looking for separate files, open /etc/network/interfaces (as root):

```
$ su -c 'vi /etc/network/interfaces'
```

Then look for the line:

```
iface eth0 inet dhcp
```

Change dhcp to static, and add your static IP address, gateway, broadcast, and netmask:

```
iface eth0 inet static
address 192.168.1.123
gateway 192.168.1.1
broadcast 192.168.1.1
netmask 255.255.255.0
network 192.168.1.0
```

If you need a little help gathering these, you can find the current IP address, netmask, and broadcast by running ifconfig and noting the inet addr, mask, and bcast, respectively, while route -n will give you the gateway and network, which it calls Destination. (Again, on newer Fedora and Pidora versions, use ip addr instead of ifconfig.)

Choosing a Unique Static IP Address

You should be sure to pick an IP address that is not already in use by any other devices on your network. Otherwise, your network connection will not work properly. When DHCP is in use, duplication is prevented, but it is possible to accidentally do it when setting the IP statically.

Additionally, you will need to manually specify a DNS server when setting a static IP address. DHCP configurations usually configure the DNS server for you, but there is no way for a static IP configuration to know what the DNS server is. To set the DNS server, edit /etc/resolv.conf (as root), and add the following line:

```
nameserver 11.23.58.13
```

Replace 11.23.58.13 with the IP address of your DNS server. If you have multiple DNS servers, you can have multiple nameserver $IP lines in this file.

After saving your changes, restart networking for the new settings to take effect:

```
$ su -c '/etc/init.d/networking restart'
```

You now have a static IP address that won't change each time you access the Internet.

HACK 14 Learn to Speak GPIO

> GPIO stands for General-Purpose Input/Output, and its presence on your Raspberry Pi makes many hacks in this book possible. This hack helps dymystify it.

The Raspberry Pi contains standard connectors that you are probably familiar with (Ethernet, HDMI, audio, and USB), but it also includes 26 pins (in two rows of 13) that are intended to connect directly to lower level devices. These pins are called the GPIO (general-purpose input/output) pins, because they are programmable input/output pins intended for a wide range of purposes.

Practically, this means we can use the GPIO pins to connect almost *anything* to a Raspberry Pi. The header of these pins is labeled on the Raspberry Pi as P1, as shown in Figure 1-5.

Figure 1-5.
Raspberry Pi Model B with the GPIO header in the upper-left corner

Simple enough, right? Well, here's where it gets a little more confusing. There are two ways of numbering the GPIO pins on the Raspberry Pi.

Pin-Number Labeling

The first way to label the GPIO pins is to refer to the pin numbers on the P1 header on the Raspberry Pi board. If you look at the pins in Figure 1-5, Pin 1 is the first pin to the left in the bottom row, Pin 2 is the first pin to the left in the bottom row, and they continue to alternate in values to the right. In table form, the board pin numbers look like Table 1-5.

Table 1-5. Board pin numbers

2	4	6	8	10	12	14	16	18	20	22	24	26
1	3	5	7	9	11	13	15	17	19	21	23	25

This method of labeling the Raspberry Pi GPIO pins by their board numbers is simple to understand by looking at the hardware. If you use this numbering scheme, you should prefix the pin numbers with the board label, "P1-".

BCM Labeling

But another labeling system for the Raspberry Pi GPIO pins uses the channel numbers on the Broadcom SOC. This system is referred to as the *BCM system*. It is the most common system in use, especially because the GPIO pins are not completely inter-changeable and they are wired differently between the various models and revisions of the Raspberry Pi.

Table 1-6 shows the mappings of the BCM pin labels to the pins as shown in Figure 1-5 (for the Raspberry Pi Model B Revision 2, the current revision as of this writing).

Table 1-6. BCM pin labels (Raspberry Pi Model B revision 2)

5 V	5 V	GND	14 (TXD)	15 (RXD)	18	GND	23	24	GND	25	8	7
3.3 V	2 (SDA)	3 (SCL)	4		GND	17	27	22	3.3V	10 (MOSI)	9 (MISO)	11 (SCKL)	GND

Let's dig a little deeper. As you can see from the labeling, some of the pins are pre-configured for special purposes. The pins marked as 3.3 V and 5 V are power pins, with the voltage as labeled. The GND pins provide ground for wiring up circuits. BCM Pins 2 (P1-03) and 3 (P1-05) are pre-setup to provide I2C bus 1. BCM Pins 14 (P1-08) and 15 (P1-10) are configured to provide a serial console. BCM pin 18 (P1-12) supports Pulse-Width Modulation (PWM).

For these reasons (and also because it is the most common Raspberry Pi GPIO labeling scheme used on the Internet), this book uses the BCM pin labels.

We realize this might be confusing when you are wiring up devices to your Pi, but see the next section for a clever way to help you remember what is what.

Label Your Own GPIO Pins

GPIO should be simple, but the common labeling scheme (BCM) is so confusing and easy to forget. Here's a simple hack to make sure you always remember which pin goes where.

Dr. Simon Monk had a problem: he wanted to wire all sorts of temporary connections to his Raspberry Pi GPIO pins, but every time he wanted to do so, he had to go online and look up the BCM pin labels. Then there was the task of counting down the pins to find the right one, and while this sounds easy, trust us, you'll likely get this wrong just as he did.

To solve this problem, he created something called the Raspberry Leaf (shown in Figure 1-6). The Raspberry Leaf is a perfectly sized and scaled diagram of the Raspberry Pi GPIO pins, with the BCM labels next to them.

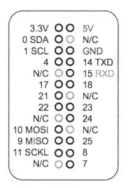

Figure 1-6.
Raspberry Leaf, created by Simon Monk

You can photocopy and use this image for reference, but it's probably easier to download from this book's Git repository or the *original PDF from Dr. Monk's website* (*http://www.doctormonk.com/2013/02/raspberry-pi-and-breadboard-raspberry.html*).

HACK 15   Connect GPIO Pins to a Breadboard

A solderless breadboard is a helpful friend when building electronics hacks, especially when you are prototyping or just testing out a device. Let's hack a simple connector to our Raspberry Pi.

While you can simply connect your Raspberry Pi GPIO pins to devices via common jumper wires, or solder wires directly between your add-on device and the GPIO pins, it is almost always helpful to have a little more space to work. Enter our old reliable friend, the solderless breadboard, shown in Figure 1-7. Even if you've never done an electronics project before, you may have seen this fellow with rows and columns of little holes in a rectangle of white plastic.

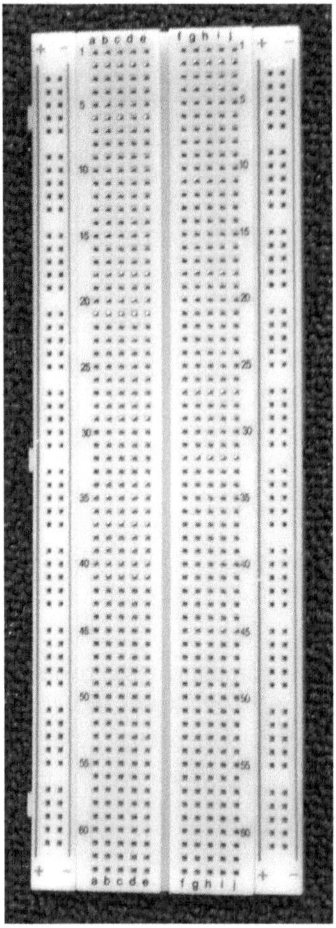

Figure 1-7.
A breadboard

A breadboard works by providing horizontal rows of connector holes (often separated by a gap) that are wired together. When you want to connect two wires together, you can simply insert them into holes along the same horizontal row. Need more holes? Just jump a wire from one row to another.

Additionally, most breadboards have vertical "rails" down each side, marked with red and black. These rails are intended to be used for power and ground connections, to simplify wiring circuits.

Our friends at Adafruit built a handy kit called the Pi Cobbler, which allows you to connect a standard 26 pin ribbon cable (just like you'd use on a PC motherboard) to a labeled printed circuit board (PCB) with a cable connector and individual pin break-outs. That PCB breakout board has pins that allow it to push right into your breadboard. Then, connect the cable to the Raspberry Pi GPIO pins and to the Cobbler PCB breakout board, and you can start connecting devices directly through your breadboard.

The instructions in this hack are also inspired by Limor "Ladyada" Fried's excellent assembly tutorial (http://learn.adafruit.com/downloads/pdf/adafruit-pi-cobbler-kit.pdf).

Adafruit sells the Pi Cobbler in a couple variants:

Compact version (https://www.adafruit.com/products/914)

Comes preassembled, so you can use it as soon as it arrives in the mail. (They used to sell this as an unassembled kit, but it doesn't look like they do anymore.)

T-Cobbler version (http://www.adafruit.com/products/1105)

Slightly larger, but covers less of the pins on the breadboard due to its "T" layout. At the time of this writing, the T-Cobbler is sold only as part of a kit (not preassembled).

If you end up with an unassembled kit for either of these versions, do not fret. It is easy to assemble it yourself. Here's everything you need:

- A soldering iron
- Some solder
- A breadboard
- Your Pi Cobbler kit, containing a blue PCB, a 26-pin ribbon cable, a black connector, and some male header pins (this might be in a single stick or in two smaller sticks)

If your male header pins (these are the metal pins with black plastic header in the middle, splitting the pins into one short and one long end) are in a single long stick, gently break off two pieces of 13 pins each. You can do this with your fingers or pliers. These correspond to the two pairs of 13 holes on the long edges of the Pi Cobbler PCB.

Also, go ahead and plug in your soldering iron and set it on a stand (see "Soldering Reminders" on page 42 if you need some help or if it's been a while). Give it 5–10 minutes to come up to full temperature. If you have a fancy soldering iron with a temperature setting, Adafruit recommends you set it to 700 degrees Fahrenheit.

Place the Pi Cobbler PCB in front of you so that the pin labels (e.g., GND) are legible and oriented normally. On the T-Cobbler kit, the board is aligned like a T. On the original kit, the board's longer sides should be parallel to you.

The PCB is labeled with a box, indicating where the black header connector should be placed. Gently press the header into the box, making sure to align the notch in the header with the notch indicated in the box. On the original Cobbler PCB, the notch must be right next to the "21/27" label; on the T-Cobbler PCB, the notch must be between the two large round holes at the T junction point. You need to get this right, because if you get the notch backward, this will cause the pins to be reversed when the cable is connected between the Cobbler and the GPIO pins, and the labels on the Cobbler will all be wrong.

Soldering Reminders

Soldering might seem scary at first, but it really isn't very difficult if you're careful and respectful of the iron. Keep a few things in mind:

- Solder, when heated, releases mildly toxic smoke. You should always solder in a well-ventilated area.

- The soldering iron gets hot. Very hot. (The actual temperature varies on the type, quality, and condition of your soldering iron.) It will burn you if you touch the tip of the iron, so always hold it by the handle, and don't lean in too close.

- Always assume a plugged-in soldering iron is hot and treat it that way. Heck, we usually assume unplugged soldering irons are hot, too.

- Every soldering iron should come with a stand. Use it. This keeps you from accidentally burning holes in your workstation, project, hand, leg...

- Keep a small, moist sponge handy, and as needed, use it to wipe off excess solder from the tip of the hot iron. If the tip of the iron becomes coated in solder, it will no longer work effectively.

- You don't need to put a giant blob of solder down to make a good connection. When heated, solder quickly becomes a liquid and will flow into heated connections. Just a tiny bit will do. Practice will help you realize how much to apply.

Flip over the PCB, with header connector still in place, so that it is now sitting on the header. You should see little bits of the 26 connector pins poking out from 26 metal rings on the PCB. Press the tip of your soldering iron simultaneously against a pair of the rings and pins. Hold it there for a few seconds to heat up the metal, and then touch some solder against the tip of the iron. The solder will melt instantly, liquify, and flow between the pin and the ring, making a complete connection.

You want to use enough solder so that you cannot see air between the pin and the ring, but not so much that you make a connection between neighboring pins. Really, it doesn't take much, just a tiny bit. This solder will be completing the electrical connection, but it will also be providing a mechanical bond that holds the device together. Repeat this process for all 26 pins, until the header connector is neatly soldered to the PCB, and then put your soldering iron back on its stand (you'll use it again in a moment).

Get your breadboard and place it in front of you. Place the two sets of male header pins into the breadboard, with the long ends into the breadboard, until the middle header plastic on each pin is resting against the breadboard.

You want to do this so that they are in the same spacing and alignment as they appear on the PCB Cobbler. For the original Cobbler, this is about five breadboard rows apart; for the T-Cobbler, this is only three rows apart.

Flip the PCB back over and set it into the short ends of the male header pins. The breadboard is acting as a stand for us now. Push the PCB gently down until all of the pins are poking through the labeled rings, and the PCB is resting up against the plastic header middles. Pick your soldering iron up again, and solder each of these 26 rings and pins.

When you're finished, clean off the tip of your soldering iron with a moist sponge and unplug it. Put it back on the stand to cool off. You can now connect the ribbon cable between the completed Pi Cobbler and the Raspberry Pi GPIO pins. You'll notice that the cable will only go into the Pi Cobbler one way, because of the notch on the connector. However, be careful, because the Raspberry Pi GPIO pins do not have any connector, and the cable can connect two possible ways. The ribbon cable included in your kit will have two indicators to help you align it properly:

- The ribbon cable has one wire of a different color. This uniquely colored wire should be on the edge closest to the SD card slot on the Raspberry Pi.
- Both ends of the ribbon cable have a notched connector. The notch on the connector going to the Pi should be pointed *toward* the Raspberry Pi logo on the board, as shown in Figure 1-8, never away from it.

The finished and connected Pi Cobbler will look something like Figure 1-9 (this is an original Pi Cobbler).

Figure 1-8.
Close-up of a properly connected Cobbler ribbon cable

Figure 1-9.
Completed and connected Pi Cobbler

It might not seem like much, but trust us, when you are wiring up multiple devices to the Raspberry Pi GPIO pins, being able to easily use a breadboard (and see the GPIO labels at a glance) will make you happy that you completed this hack.

GPIO Quick Reference

If you turn your Pi so that the GPIO pins are in the upper right, the pins are numbered from top to bottom, with odd numbers on the left and even on the right (thus, the first row is 1 and 2, second row is 3 and 4, etc.). Note that these do not correspond to GPIO numbers; for example, GPIO 22 is on pin 15. Table 1-7 explains the purposes of the pins of a Version 2 board.

Table 1-7. GPIO pin purposes for Version 2 board

PIN NUMBER	PURPOSE
1	3.3 V power
2	5 V power
3	GPIO 2 (SDA)
4	5 V power
5	GPIO 3 (SCL)
6	Ground
7	GPIO 4 (GPCLK0)
8	GPIO 14 (TXD)
9	Ground
10	GPIO 15 (RXD)
11	GPIO 17
12	GPIO 18 (PCM_CLK)
13	GPIO 27
14	Ground
15	GPIO 22
16	GPIO 23
17	3.3 V power
18	GPIO 24
19	GPIO 10 (MOSI)
20	Ground
21	GPIO 9 (MISO)
22	GPIO 25

PIN NUMBER	PURPOSE
23	GPIO 11 (SCLK)
24	GPIO 8 (CE0)
25	Ground
26	GPIO 7 (CE1)

The pins are meant for input no higher than 3.3 V, and there is no overvoltage protection.

Inter-Integrated Circuit (I2C)

The I2C interface (SDA and SCL), which you can access through pins 3 and 5, is a connection for low-speed peripherals or sensors. You can have multiple devices connected through the same pins.

Pulse-Width Modulation (PWM)

Pin 12 offers control for motors similar to analog control through pulse-width modulation (labeled PCM_CLK). For some purposes, you can achieve the same effect through software, which may be useful since the Pi has only one PWM pin.

Universal Asynchronous Receiver/Transmitter (UART)

The UART pins (14/TXD and 15/RXD) are used for serial console access. If you don't need that, you can switch them to GPIO for an extra two GPIO pins. This is also true of the I2C and SPI pins, but you're least likely to want to use the UART pins.

Serial Peripheral Interface Bus (SPI)

The SPI pins are the pins you'll use for some types of sensors or attaching other devices. SPI operates in master/slave fashion:

- 19 - Master Out, Slave In (MOSI)
- 21 - Master In, Slave Out (MISO)
- 23 - Serial Clock (SCLK)
- 24 - CE0 (chip select)
- 26 - CE1 (chip select)

The two chip select pins mean you can control two SPI devices.

For those who would like to better understand GPIO and to effectively use this feature of the Raspberry Pi, we recommend looking through *this page* (*http://wiringpi.com*), which provides an access library for the Pi's GPIO. It will be particularly useful if you are already familiar with Arduino wiring.

`HACK 16` Add a USB Serial Console

> Arguably the most common way to access embedded devices like the Raspberry Pi is via the built-in serial device. This easy hack gives you a USB serial console from your Raspberry Pi.

Almost all of the common embedded computers and microcontrollers available today have built-in Universally Asynchronous Receiver/Transmitters (UARTs). The UART provides a mechanism for receiving and transmitting serial data, one bit at a time. This method of serial communication is sometimes referred to as transistor-transistor logic (TTL) serial. The data rate varies by device, but it is measured in bits per second. The Raspberry Pi has a built-in UART connected to BCM Pins 14 (TXD) and 15 (RXD), with a data rate of 115200bps (or baud).

Hey, That's Not Really Baud!

OK, from a semantic point of view, yes, baud is the unit of symbol rate, which is not always identical to gross bit rate (bps). Wikipedia says that baud is "the number of distinct symbol changes (signaling events) made to the transmission medium per second in a digitally modulated signal or a line code." Then it goes on for several more pages of mathematical distinction about baud, which may be fascinating to you or may put you to sleep.

The key takeaway is this: the computer and electronics industry has been widely misusing the term baud for about 40 years now. As a result, lots of software and hardware uses bps and baud interchangeably. In the specific case of the USB serial console on the Raspberry Pi, the data rate in bps and the baud rate are the same. The units here don't matter to us as much as making sure you have a functional serial console, and for that, you need to know that the data rate is 115200. Bits, baud, giant hamsters of doom, pick your units as you will, but 115200 is the magic number for the Raspberry Pi UART serial device.

If you've been using computers for a few years, you probably remember when almost every computer came with an RS-232 serial port, but in the last few years, these ports have been disappearing, and most laptops no longer include them (or they only have them on the optional laptop dock). Believe it or not, for connecting to the Raspberry Pi UART serial port, this is actually a good thing. The Broadcom chip that the Raspberry Pi depends on uses 0 and 3.3 V logic levels, not the +/- 3 to 15 V range used by PC RS-232 serial ports. This means even if you have one of those RS-232 serial ports on your computer, you'd need a board or adapter to convert the signal levels before it would work.

RS-232 or Bust!

Here's a pretty good tutorial on how to build a 3.3 V to RS-232 level converter (http://bit.ly/1eWGDyA).

The good news is that there is a better way to connect the Raspberry Pi UART serial port to your computer: USB! Adafruit sells a wonderful *USB-to-TTL Serial Cable* (*http://www.adafruit.com/products/954*), which connects directly to the GPIO pins on the Raspberry Pi and provides a USB serial device on the other end. This cable has four female jumper connectors on one end (the end that doesn't have a USB connector). These jumpers have color-coded wires: red for 5 V power, black for ground (GND), green for receiving data into the Raspberry Pi (RXD), and white for transmitting data from the Raspberry Pi (TXD). You might also notice that the USB connector end is larger than normal, because it also has a USB-to-Serial conversion chip inside it.

To make the physical connection, you simply need to connect three of the female jumper connectors directly to the appropriate pins on the Raspberry Pi GPIO. The white transmitting wire goes into the TXD port (BCM Pin 14 (P1-08)), and the green receiving wire goes into the RXD port (BCM Pin 15 (P1-10)). The black ground wire can go into any of the GND pins, but for simplicity, we recommend you put it in the GND pin immediately to the left of the TXD port (P1-06). You can confirm your wiring by comparing it to Figure 1-10.

A Hack for the Red Wire

You may note that we did not ask you to connect the red power wire. This is because the USB serial device will power itself with 5 V at 500 mA directly from the USB port. You may also note that we said that the Raspberry Pi UART uses 3.3 V logic levels, not 5 V, and this is true, but the receiving and transmitting wires are already converted to 3.3 V. It all works fine, stop noting and move on.

There is, however, a cool mini hack you can do with that red power wire. Because 5 V is going across that red wire, you can use it to power the Rasp-

---

berry Pi, instead of doing so via the normal mini-B USB connector. Just connect the red wire to the 5 V pin (P1-04), then without any other power source connected, plug the USB-to-TTL Serial cable into your laptop. The Raspberry Pi will boot up!

This is really just a parlor trick, because the power coming off that red wire is not the ideal way to power the Raspberry Pi for a number of reasons, as discussed in "Think Twice Before Using the GPIO to Power the Pi" on page 25.

Figure 1-10.
A properly wired USB to TTL serial cable

Now, go ahead and connect the USB connector to your computer.

To connect to the UART serial device, you first need to know its device name. The kernel assigns it a device name when the USB serial driver successfully loads (which it should have already done when you inserted the USB end of the cable), so you just need to look through the output from dmesg.

Specifically, we know that the device name will be ttyUSB#, where # is a number. It's probably ttyUSB0, but let's look to be sure. If you have multiple USB serial devices present on your system (you naughty super hacker, you), you're looking for the one with the pl2303 converter type. If you have more than one pl2303 converter type USB serial device present, pick one at a time and try until you find the right one. Anyway, here's how you can check:

```
$ dmesg | grep -B2 ttyUSB
[23882.896558] usbserial: USB Serial support registered for pl2303
[23882.896578] pl2303 1-1.5.1:1.0: pl2303 converter detected
[23882.898285] usb 1-1.5.1: pl2303 converter now attached to ttyUSB0
```

Sure enough, our device is ttyUSB0. This means that the full device node name is /dev/ttyUSB0. Unprivileged users do not normally have access to /dev/ttyUSB# devices; you need to be in a special group. If you look at the file permissions on the device node name, you will see that it is owned by `root` and access is granted to users in the `dialout` group:

```
$ ls -l /dev/ttyUSB0
crw-rw----T 1 root dialout 188, 0 Aug 22 19:11 /dev/ttyUSB0
```

You can either connect to the `/dev/ttyUSB0` device using the root account (via `su` or `sudo`), or you can add your normal user to the `dialout` group. To add your user to the dialout group, run:

```
$ su -c 'usermod -a -G dialout $USER'
```

This will not take effect in your terminal sessions until they are restarted. Either log out and log in again, or reboot your Linux system.

Not Using Linux to Connect to the Serial Port?

You can imagine the face the authors are making right now. It is a disapproving face. ಠ_ಠ However, we can give you a few tips anyway.

Windows and Mac OS X systems will need to install PL2303HXA drivers, which you can download for *Windows XP/Vista/7* (*http://www.prolific.com.tw/US/ShowProduct.aspx?p_id=225&pcid=41*) and *Mac OS X* (*http://sourceforge.net/projects/osx-pl2303*).

According to the vendor, Windows 8 is *not* supported for this device. Maybe if you're a Windows 8 user, this is a good time to consider dual booting to Linux?

As far as terminal software goes, if you are using Windows XP or older, it comes with a program called Hyperterminal that can connect to a serial console. If you are using a newer version of Windows, you'll need to download a third-party terminal program. We recommend *PuTTY* (*http://www.chiark.greenend.org.uk/~sgtatham/putty/download.html*). For Mac OS X, you can either use screen in the same way that we've described for Linux, or you can try *ZOC* (*http://www.emtec.com/zoc/*).

Now it's time to connect to the Raspberry Pi UART serial device. You'll need to use a client that supports a serial connection; there are lots and lots out there, but the two common ones are minicom and screen.

Minicom

Minicom was written to look like Telix, a popular MS-DOS terminal program that was probably written before you were born. We now feel old(er). It has that MS-DOS look and feel to it—namely, it is old, crufty, and confusing—but it does work. To install it on Fedora:

```
$ su -c 'yum install minicom -y'
```

or on Debian/Ubuntu:

```
$ su -c 'apt-get install minicom'
```

Once installed, to use minicom to connect to the Raspberry Pi UART serial device, run:

```
$ minicom -b 115200 -o -D /dev/ttyUSB0
```

To test it, reboot the Raspberry Pi while it is connected; you should see Linux kernel messages scroll down the screen, and it will look similar to Figure 1-11.

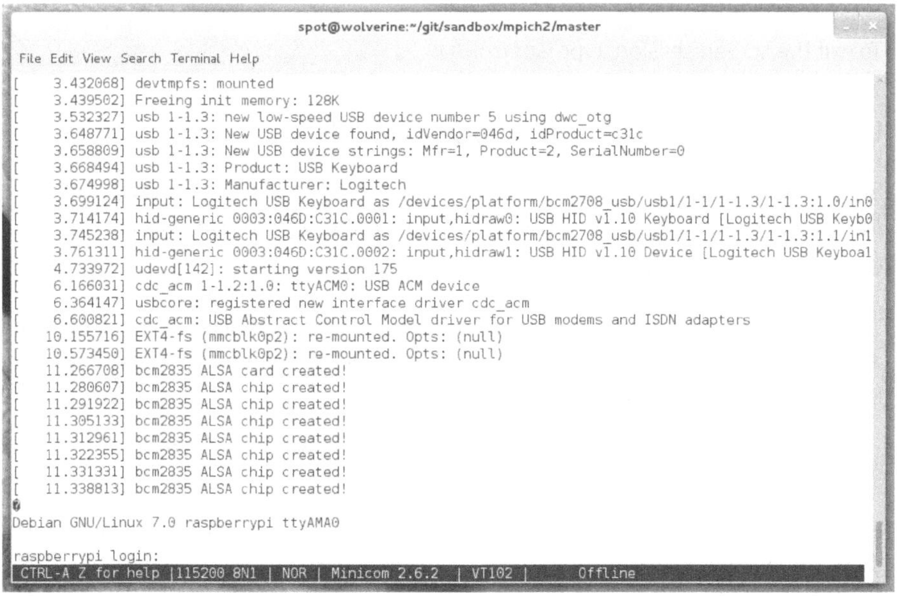

Figure 1-11.
minicom interfacing with the Raspberry Pi UART serial device

You can exit minicom with Control-A X, or get into its somewhat helpful help menu with Control-A Z. If you end up manually configuring minicom, just leave the Parity/Bits at 8N1, and disable the Software Flow Control. You don't need to go in there though. There are bats in there.

Screen

Screen is a powerful utility, normally used to multiplex multiple virtual consoles. If this were *Linux in a Nutshell*, we'd have a whole chapter about using screen. Since this is a different book, we'll just focus on using it as a serial terminal client.

To install it on Fedora, run:

```
$ su -c 'yum install screen -y'
```

or on Debian/Ubuntu:

```
$ su -c 'apt-get install screen'
```

Once installed, to use screen to connect to the Raspberry Pi UART serial device, run:

```
$ screen /dev/ttyUSB0 115200
```

To exit the screen session, type Control-A K.

Using the Serial Device as a Login Console

Raspbian preconfigures the UART serial device as a login-capable console, but Pidora does not. To enable the UART serial device as a login console session, run:

```
$ su -c 'systemctl start serial-getty@ttyAMA0.service'
```

This will turn it on immediately. If you have a serial cable connected, you should see a login prompt appear. To make this login session permanent (and automatically loaded on boot), simply run:

```
$ su -c 'ln -snf /usr/lib/systemd/system/serial-getty@.service \
    /etc/systemd/system/getty.target.wants/serial-getty@ttyAMA0.service'
```

By making that symbolic link in the systemd directory tree, you are telling systemd to start the ttyAMA0 device as a "getty" or login console.

Fun Serial Console Trivia

The name "getty" comes from the term "get teletype." A teletype was originally a device with a typewriter for input and a printer for output for use as telegraph machines, but as computers evolved, these devices found a use as a method of inputting data to a computer. The teletype was also widely used in a "receive only" format in newsrooms in the 1940s and 1950s. The "clickety clack" sound effect of news coming in "over the wire" is that of a teletype. Eventually, these devices became proper serial consoles, and they are the reason why we call console devices in Linux "TTYs".

Both Pidora and Raspbian come with the UART serial device preconfigured as a console for kernel messages. You can see this in the `/boot/cmdline.txt` file:

```
dwc_otg.lpm_enable=0 console=ttyAMA0,115200 kgdboc=ttyAMA0,115200 con
sole=tty1 root=/dev/mmcblk0p2 ro rootfstype=ext4 rootwait quiet
```

The `console` value tells the Linux kernel where to output messages at boot time, and the `kgdboc` value enables kernel debugging over that console.

If you are working on a project that wants dedicated access to the UART serial device, you will probably want to remove the `console=ttyAMA0,115200` and `kgdboc=ttyA MA0,115200` entries from `/boot/cmdline.txt` and reboot your Raspberry Pi. If you do not, you will get unexpected line noise across the serial line from the Linux kernel that your program/project is probably not ready to deal with.

If you have enabled the serial devices as a login console, you will also want to disable that. To disable it on Raspbian, comment out the following lines in `/etc/inittab` (by changing the line to start with a `#`):

```
T0:23:respawn:/sbin/getty -L ttyAMA0 115200 vt100
```

On Pidora, you simply need to remove the systemd getty service symlink for the `ttyAMA0` device, by running:

```
$ su -c 'rm -f /etc/systemd/system/getty.target.wants/serial-
getty@ttyAMA0.service'
```

On either Linux distribution, after making these changes, reboot for them to take effect.

Weird Noise (or Missing Signal) on the Serial Connection?

Both Ubuntu and Fedora include a piece of software called `ModemManager`, which handles setting up all sorts of modem devices, from old dial-up modems to more modern 3G/4G devices. Unfortunately, quite a few current modems just have the same generic converter chip that our USB serial connector cable uses (the pl2303) stuck in front of the modem.

As a result, `ModemManager` will try to access it (and keep trying, and keep trying ...), because it has no way of knowing that the device behind `/dev/ttyUSB0` is a modem, or a Braille terminal, or in our case, a Raspberry Pi. This might prevent you from being able to open `/dev/ttyUSB0`, or it might simply cause noise to appear across the console.

Since we know what that USB device is connecting to, we can tell `ModemManager` to leave it alone and explicitly blacklist our connector device with udev rules.

As root, edit the `/lib/udev/rules.d/77-mm-usb-device-blacklist.rules` file, and add these lines before the `LABEL="mm_usb_device_blacklist_end"` line at the bottom:

```
# Adafruit USB to TTL Serial Cable (PL2303HXA)
ATTRS{idVendor}=="067b", ATTRS{idProduct}=="2303", ENV{ID_MM_DEVICE_IG
NORE}="1"
```

If you use a different USB serial cable from the Adafruit cable, and you're trying to fix this problem, you should be able to run the `lsusb` application (from the `usbutils` package) to determine the `idVendor` and `idProduct` string (they will show up in the output in the syntax XXXX:YYYY where XXXX is the `idVendor` and YYYY is the `idProduct`).

For example, the `lsusb` value for the Adafruit USB serial cable looks like this:

```
Bus 003 Device 002: ID 067b:2303 Prolific Technology, Inc. PL2303 Serial
Port
```

`Udev` automatically detects changes to rules files, so changes take effect immediately without requiring udev to be restarted. That said, sometimes you need to reboot the Linux system for `udev` to reread its rules. Either way, whenever `udev` reads in its new rules, the USB serial converter device should now be blacklisted, and `ModemManager` should ignore it from then on out.

HACK 17   Add a Reset Button

Perhaps you've noticed your Pi lacks something pretty common among electronics: a power switch. The Model B revision 2 boards come with a small fix.

It's somewhere between vaguely uncomfortable and outright inconvenient to remove the power supply from your computer as an on/off switch, but that's what you do on the Raspberry Pi. One easy fix, regardless of what board you have, is to plug it into a power strip with an on/off switch and use that. But with the Model B revision 2 boards, you have another option.

One of the added features on these boards is labeled P6. It's easy to miss. P6 is just two small holes on the opposite side of the board from the GPIO, near the HDMI port (see Figure 1-12).

Figure 1-12.
P6 holes

If you solder a pair of header pins into these two holes (see "Soldering Reminders" on page 42 if you're new to soldering), you have a reset switch, as shown in Figure 1-13. Just use a metal object to connect the two pins and short them.

Figure 1-13.
Reset pins in place

This short will also reset the CPU from shutdown, causing the Pi to start.

HACK 18 Get Power to the Pi on the Move

> Power doesn't have to mean a plug in the wall. You have a few more options to increase portability.

To get power to your Pi, you need five stable volts at 700 mA through a Type B Micro USB plug. As mentioned elsewhere, it's not a bad idea to get a power adapter specifically intended for the Raspberry Pi, though your phone charger or other similar adapter will likely work.

Less-than-Recommended Power Options

Much like trying to substitute anything for eggs in a recipe, there are options that aren't particularly recommended but work out for some people. For example, powering your Pi through your laptop's USB port. It doesn't *officially* work and isn't recommended, but we've seen it work. Trying to push power through the GPIO isn't a great idea either. See "Get Power Through GPIO Safely" on page 26 for more on power and the GPIO pins.

We've also heard of success with power over Ethernet and even intentionally backpowering through USB to power the Pi. Again, not the recommended

---

method, but hacks are about trying something new. As long as you conduct your electrical experimentation safely, the worst you'll end up with is the loss of a $35 board but the gain of a good story, possibly featuring smoke, which enhances any story.

But if you want portability, what you need is a battery pack. You might think of these devices as emergency power for your cell phone. They come in assorted strengths, shapes, sizes, and colors, but in the end, they're two things: power and a USB port, which are the two things that you need to power the Pi.

Look for one that has 5V regulated output. We use the New Trent iCarrier (IMP120D), a 12,000 mAh pattery pack with two USB ports and an on/off button. Depending on activity on the Pi, that's enough power to last 14– 16 hours or more.

This portable power is critical to some of the hacks in this book, most notably Hack #44. It's an enhancement for others. And worst case, it's spare juice for your phone.

HACK 19 Test Your Might (in Volts)

If you aren't already friends with a multimeter, you will be soon. Pi projects all need power, and the Pi provides a way for you to check the voltage of the board on the board.

Assuming you don't have a few power supplies around to swap out, or if you're determined to get a particular and unusual power source working, you're going to want to check the voltage on the Raspberry Pi.

There are two test points on your Raspberry Pi for just such a need, as shown in Figure 1-14. TP1 is the 5 V point and TP2 is ground.

They're in slightly different but nearby places on the Model A board, but they're still labeled TP1 and TP2 in that tiny white PCB label text.

Figure 1-14.
Test point locations (a.k.a. "electronics vision test")

To test the voltage:

1. Plug in all the peripherals you expect to use, and power on the Pi (and the peripherals).
2. Set your multimeter range to 20 V.
3. Touch the red lead of your multimeter to TP1 and the black lead to TP2 (as shown in Figure 1-15).

Figure 1-15.
Testing the voltage

The Pi needs a good 5 V supply but has a tolerance of +/-0.25 V or so. That means that, at a minimum, you should be seeing 4.75 V, preferably more like 4.8 V or more. Below that, and either your peripherals will start acting up or the Pi might not even boot at all. It might also reboot spontaneously.

You can also try unplugging various peripherals, using different monitors, removing Ethernet, etc. Test again to see how the result changes.

It's Electric!

It's entirely possible that the Raspberry Pi is the first place you've gotten this close to the electricity part of your electronics. If that's the case, it's worth some light reading about how all this power stuff works. But at the most basic level, you'll want to understand these three terms and the relationship among them:

Voltage

>   The difference in charge between two points

Current

>   The rate at which charge is flowing

Resistance

>   A material's tendency to resist the flow of charge (current)

If you know two of them, you can figure out the third, thanks to Ohm's law, which says that V=I*R, or the voltage (volts) is equal to the current (amps) times the resistance (ohms). Those who are mathematically disinclined can get an assist from the handy tool at the online *Ohm's Law Calculator* (*http://ohmslawcalculator.com/*).

Keep this in mind when things act funny and you're not sure why: it might be worth a quick power check.

You can also use the Pi's test points to test its polyfuse. A *polyfuse* is a type of fuse that can repair itself after it has been blown. The Raspberry Pi has at least one of these, labeled F3 on the bottom of the board, as shown in Figure 1-16.

Figure 1-16.
F3 polyfuse beneath SD card slot

>   *Earlier Pis also had two on the USB ports, which have since been replaced by 0 Ohm resistors. They were known as F1 and F2.*

You'll find F3 to the left of the SD card slot if you turn the Pi over and hold the SD slot toward you.

How long it takes for it to "heal" is variable, as much as a few days, and they can be permently damaged. They are replaceable, though. To test whether you're having a problem with the F3 polyfuse:

1. Remove the SD card and all of the peripherals, unlike testing the voltage, but leave it plugged in.

2. Turn the board upside down.

3. With the same settings (range 20 V), touch one lead to the back side of TP2 (since the board is upside down) and the other to the metallic part of F3 facing the SD card slot. This will tell you the voltage coming from the fuse.

4. Next, touch one lead to the back side of TP2 and the other to the metallic part of F3 facing the outside of the board. Check the voltage. This will tell you the voltage coming in.

It's normal for the reading on F3 to be 0.2 V lower than the power coming in, but any more than that indicates a problem with the polyfuse.

HACK 20   Add Additional Memory with Swap

> Need a little more memory on your Raspberry Pi? Swap will let you trade disk space for memory.

Linux has long inclued the concept of *swap*, where the kernel is capable of moving memory pages between RAM and disk. In practical application, this provides more usable memory to the OS (at the cost of disk space). Because the Raspberry Pi Model B only has 512 MB of memory, the idea of adding swap files (or partitions) to increase the usable memory is compelling.

Swap Hazards

Before we begin, you should be aware of a downside to this approach. Swap is only as fast as the speed of the storage device that it is written to. It also is a highly write-intensive operation. From a practical perspective, this means that if you add swap to your SD card in your Raspberry Pi, it will cause the overall disk performance to drop significantly and notably shorten the life of the SD card.

Because the entire OS on the Raspberry Pi runs off the SD card, we strongly recommend that you not place swap files or partitions on the SD card. These downsides also apply to a USB flash drive connected to the Raspberry Pi. Because they are also flash-based storage devices, adding swap files from USB flash drives will cause the same overall performance slowdowns and

> shortening of life span. If you really want to add swap, the best possible case is over an actual external hard drive connected via a SATA-to-USB converter.

Raspbian comes preconfigured with a 100 MB swap file enabled, via `dphys-swapfile`. You can change the settings of this swapfile by editing `/etc/dphys-swapfile`. It has only one option: `CONF_SWAPSIZE`. If you want to increase the size of the swapfile, change the value from `100` to a larger value (depending on the free space on your SD card). Alternatively, you can disable this option by changing the value to ++0.

Any changes to this value will not take effect until you run the following commands:

```
$ /etc/init.d/dphys-swapfile stop
$ /etc/init.d/dphys-swapfile start
```

Pidora configures 512 MB of swap by default at firstboot (unless the user specifies otherwise). This is placed in the file `/swap0` and configured in `/etc/fstab` by the rootfs-resize service.

For other Linux distributions (or to place a swapfile on a different location), you will need to manually create the swapfile:

```
$ sudo dd if=/dev/zero of=/path/to/swapfile bs=1M count=1024
$ sudo mkswap /path/to/swapfile
$ sudo swapon /path/to/swapfile
```

These commands will generate a 1 GB swap file (1024 x 1 M = 1 GB) at `/path/to/swapfile`, which you should change to the location of your swapfile. To make the swap file automatically enabled on boot, add a new line to your `/etc/fstab` file:

```
/path/to/swapfile none swap defaults 0 0
```

You will see the additional memory (as swap) in the output of the `free` command:

```
$ free
total used free shared buffers cached
Mem: 448688 436960 11728 0 6776 395392
-/+ buffers/cache: 34792 413896
Swap: 1048572 0 1048572
```

2

Hacking Linux for the Raspberry Pi

While there are many available operating systems for the Raspberry Pi, the most supported one is Linux. The Raspberry Pi Foundation maintains a Linux kernel source tree with support for the Raspberry Pi hardware.

Linux is famous for its flexibility and support for a large number of devices. Whether you are just interested in learning Linux, or if you need to make some modifications in order to enable an awesome hack, this chapter will help you through the process.

HACK 21 Build a Cross-Compiler Toolchain

> The Raspberry Pi is well-suited for many things, but compile speed is not one of them. To build anything of consequence from source in a reasonable amount of time, you'll need to to use a cross-compiler running on a faster computer.

A *cross-compiler* is a compiler (and dependent libraries) built to run on one architecture but that generates binaries for a different architecture, usually an incompatible one. In this case, you need a cross-compiler that will allow you to build binaries optimized for the Raspberry Pi Linux environment.

Like most tasks in Linux, you can generate a cross-compiler in a few ways, but to ensure that you end up with a toolchain optimized for the best performance on the Raspberry Pi, we suggest not installing prepackaged cross-compilers that come with your Linux distribution. Instead, the following sections will walk you through the process of using `crosstool-ng` to build it from scratch.

Install crosstool-ng

`crosstool-ng` is designed to assist you in the complicated task of generating a compiler toolchain. It provides a powerful frontend and build scripts that let you choose what you need your toolchain to do, then automate the build, while keeping you from needing to understand exactly how the numerous pieces of the toolchain hook together. Compared to building cross-compilers manually, this is a lifesaver.

> `crosstool-ng` *is built using the same configuration frontend technology as the Linux kernel source, so the menu structure that it uses will likely be familiar to you. Just like the Linux kernel, many options might not make sense to you or might seem confusingly similar. Never fear, brave hackers! You'll need to change only a few of these options from their defaults.*

You can put your Raspberry Pi aside; you won't need it. Instead, start with an x86-based system running your preferred Linux distribution. Any distribution you are comfortable working with that includes a working compiler will be fine. As far as the system goes, the bigger, the better. More CPU cores and more memory will result in faster builds, and x86_64 is always preferred. Also, you'll want to have a healthy amount of available disk space (10 GB should be more than sufficient).

To build the cross-compiler toolchain, you first need to make sure you have some development components. Specifically, you'll need a native compiler (in this case,GCC with support for C & C), `libstdc` (standard C++ libraries, both shared and static), libtool and make (for the build infrastructure), GNU MP (for fast precision mathematics), gperf (a perfect hash function generator), bison (a C grammar parser), flex (a lexical pattern recognition engine), ncurses (a terminal graphics library), sed (a stream editor), subversion (client tooling for accessing SVN code repositories), and texinfo (a documentation generation and parsing tool).

Don't worry too much about these pieces: you do not need to know how they work (or even why you need them), just know that you do. Really, all you need to do is install them, and you accomplish that by running the following commands.

On Fedora, enter:

```
$ su -c 'yum install gcc gcc-c++ bison make ncurses-devel texinfo flex
gperf \
    libtool sed subversion gmp-devel libstdc++-devel libstdc++-static'
```

For Ubuntu, enter:

```
$ su -c 'apt-get install gcc g++ bison make ncurses-dev texinfo flex
gperf \
    libtool sed subversion libgmp-dev libstdc++-dev'
```

Next, download a copy of the `crosstool-ng` *source code* (*http://crosstool-ng.org*). At the time of this writing, the latest version is 1.18.0.

Unpack the `crosstool-ng` source tarball into your home directory:

```
$ tar xvfj crosstool-ng-1.18.0.tar.bz2
```

Fix for PPL Bug

The version of the Parma Polyhedra Library (PPL) that `crosstool-ng` uses (0.11.2) has a bug in it. Specifically, it is not compatible with newer versions of the GNU Multiple Precision Arithmetic Library (GMP). We have provided a fix for this, to allow PPL to compile properly against more recent versions of GMP. There is a patch file named **101-gmp-build-fix.patch** in our *GitHub repository (https://github.com/spotrh/rpihacks)*. First, clone a local copy of our GitHub tree into your home directory, then copy the patch file into the `crosstool-ng` source directory:

```
$ cd ~
$ git clone https://github.com/spotrh/rpihacks
Cloning into 'rpihacks'...
remote: Counting objects: 247, done.
remote: Compressing objects: 100% (190/190), done.
remote: Total 247 (delta 75), reused 206 (delta 37)
Receiving objects: 100% (247/247), 251.84 KiB | 0 bytes/s, done.
Resolving deltas: 100% (75/75), done.
$ cp -a rpihacks/101-gmp-build-fix.patch ~/crosstool-ng-1.18.0/patch
es/ppl/0.11.2/
```

By placing this patch file in the **crosstool-ng-1.18.0/patches/ppl/ 0.11.2/** directory, it allows `crosstool-ng` to apply this fix to PPL 0.11.2 before it builds it.

On systems with older GMP versions, this patch may not be necessary, but applying it will not cause any problems. We strongly recommend that you copy this patch into the `crosstool-ng` patches tree before proceeding.

Configure crosstool-ng

Go into the `crosstool-ng-1.18.0` source directory and run `configure`. The only option you will need to pass to it is a prefix value for where you want to install `crosstool-ng`. We strongly recommend that you use /opt/crosstool-ng-1.18.0, just to give it a space that is guaranteed to be far, far away from the rest of your Linux system:

```
$ ./configure --prefix=/opt/crosstool-ng-1.18.0
```

This `configure` script, like virtually every `configure` script ever created, will check your Linux system to ensure that all of `crosstool-ng`'s dependencies are present and accounted for. If it fails, simply use your Linux distribution tools (`yum` or `apt-get`, as appropriate) to install the missing packages. Once this completes successfully, it will create a Makefile. To build the `crosstool-ng` code, run:

```
$ make
```

This should result in success, because `crosstool-ng` isn't difficult to build. Once it finishes, you just need to make install it into its new home (`/opt/crosstool-ng-1.18.0`). Don't forget to run this as root:

```
$ su -c 'make install'
```

Add crosstool-ng to Your PATH

Now that you have the `crosstool-ng` software installed and configured, add it to your PATH. This will allow you to run commands specifically for `crosstool-ng` without needing to type a long command string.

The easiest way to accomplish this varies by Linux distribution and shell choice. On Fedora, using the default bash shell, you need to make a change to the `~/.bash_profile`. On Ubuntu, edit `~/.profile`. What you're looking for is a configuration (or *dot*) file that lives in your home directory and sets the PATH. Usually, this file will contain a line that explicitly exports the PATH variable, like this:

```
export PATH
```

Just above that line, add this line:

```
PATH=$PATH:/opt/crosstool-ng-1.18.0/bin
```

This will append `/opt/crosstool-ng-1.18.0/bin` to the end of the existing value of PATH (`$PATH`). Save the file, and then you can either open a new shell instance or source the modified file. Since we're brave hackers, we'll just source the new file like this:

```
$ source ~/.bash_profile
```

These directions will vary if you're using a shell other than bash, but if you have made that choice, most of the previous section is common sense to you, and you should be able to add a directory to your PATH in the shell of your choice.

Configure the Cross-Compiler

Now it is time to actually build the Raspberry Pi cross-compiler. In the process of doing so, `crosstool-ng` will download quite a lot of source files from the Internet. To keep things clean, you should make a temporary home (a *sandbox*) and work in that directory:

```
$ mkdir ~/cross-sandbox
$ cd ~/cross-sandbox
```

Now you can safely launch the `crosstool-ng` configuration utility by running:

```
$ ct-ng menuconfig
```

`crosstool-ng` supports a wide variety of different toolchains and subvariants of toolchains. For the best optimization, we recommend using the Linaro variant of the GCC compiler. Linaro is a nonprofit organization that specializes in optimizing and improving open source technologies for the ARM platform, and they tend to make the nicest ARM Linux compilers.

On that recommendation, next you're going to build a Linaro GCC cross-compiler specifically optimized for the hardware inside the Raspberry Pi.

In GCC language, this is an `arm-bcm2708hardfp-linux-gnueabi` *toolchain. The* `bcm2708` *describes the specific CPU type (Broadcom 2708),* `hardfp` *means that it is using a hardware floating point unit (specifically, it means that values are being passed to functions in the floating-point registers),* `linux` *is the OS, and* `gnueabi` *means that it supports the GNU Embedded Application Binary Interface (EABI). The EABI allows for different compilers to generate compatible code.*

While most of the `crosstool-ng` settings are fine at their default values, you will need to double-check some of them. When you launch `ct-ng menuconfig`, it will open a Text User Interface (or TUI for short) in your terminal window. It will present you with a series of menus that you can navigate using the arrow keys, the Enter key (to select an item or menu), and the spacebar (to enable or disable specific items). Items which are enabled have either an asterisk or a set value next to them.

The top menu looks like Figure 2-1.

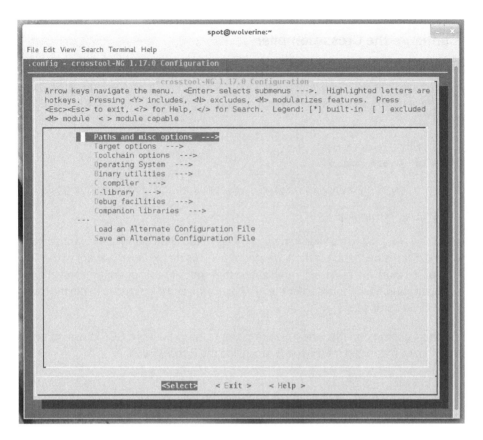

Figure 2-1.
Main configuration menu

The following sections describe the changes you'll need to make, grouped by menu sections from the top down.

Paths and Misc Options

In this section of the crosstool-ng menu (shown in Figure 2-2), make the following changes:

- Enable "Try features marked as EXPERIMENTAL".
- Set "Prefix directory" to the location where you want your cross-compiler toolchain to be installed. We suggest putting this either in its own subdirectory in /opt or your home directory to ensure you don't get your cross-compiler toolchain confused with your system native toolchain. We leave this at the default value of ${HOME}/x-tools/${CT_TARGET}, which evaluates to ~/x-tools/arm-rpi-linux-gnueabi/.

- Set "Number of parallel jobs". This value will be passed to `make` to accelerate the build time for the cross-compiler toolchain. Setting this value too low will make the build take longer than it needs to, but setting it too high will result in the CPU resources being spread too thin (and will also make the build take longer than it needs to). The magic value seems to be the number of CPU cores in your system multiplied by 1.5. On our 8 core laptop, this is `12`. If you're not sure how many CPU cores your system has, run:

```
$ cat /proc/cpuinfo |grep processor
```

Count the number of lines, as each CPU core will appear to Linux as a unique processor.

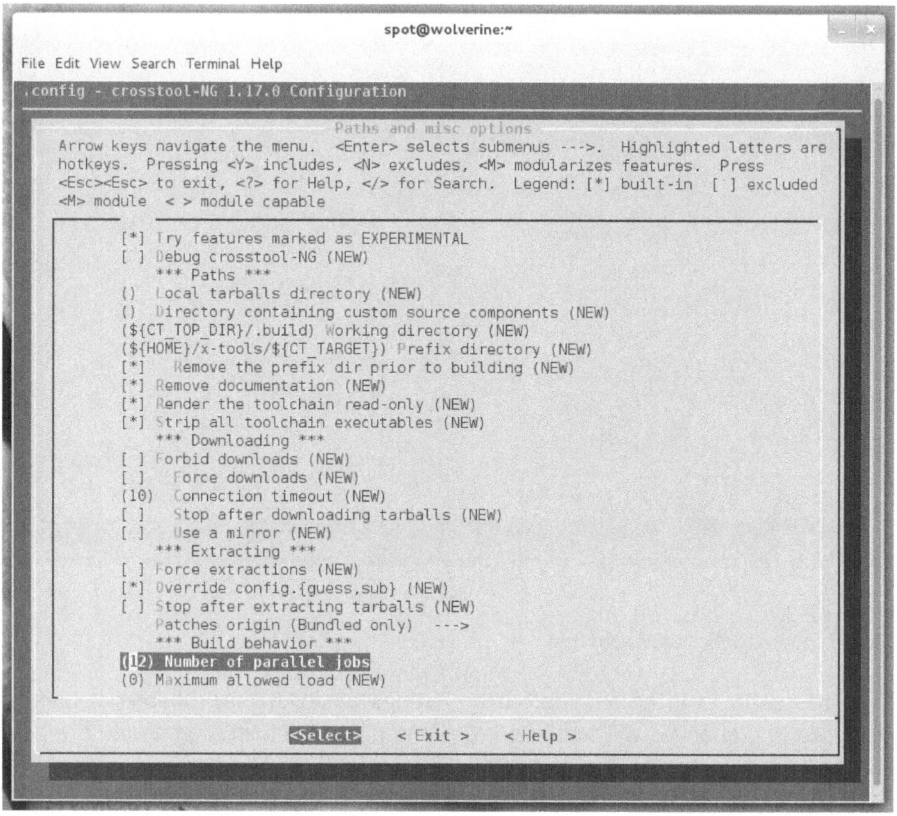

Figure 2-2.
Paths and misc options configuration submenu

Target Options

In this menu (shown in Figure 2-3), make sure the following settings are set:

- Set "Target architecture" to arm.
- Set "Endianness" to Little endian.
- Set "Bitness" to 32-bit.

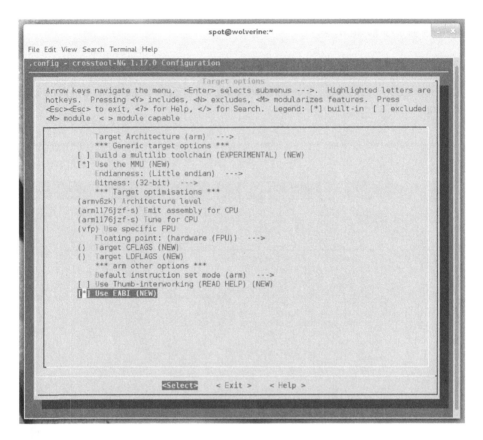

Figure 2-3.
Target options configuration submenu

All of these should be the defaults, but the settings that follow are probably not. Making the following changes will tune the cross-compiler toolchain to generate the best possible binaries for the Raspberry Pi:

- Set "Architecture level" to armv6zk. This is the specific ARM architecture revision of the Raspberry Pi ARM CPU.
- Set "Emit assembly for CPU" to arm1176jzf-s.
- Set "Tune for CPU" to arm1176jzf-s.
- Set "Use specific FPU" to vfp.
- Set "Floating point" to hardware (FPU).

- Set "Default instruction set mode" to `arm`.
- Enable "Use EABI".

Toolchain Options

Make the following change to the Toolchain options (shown in Figure 2-4):

- Set "Tuple's vendor string" to `rpi`. Really, we could put anything we wanted in here. We strongly recommend doing this to ensure that you know you're using the Raspberry Pi cross-compiler toolchain.

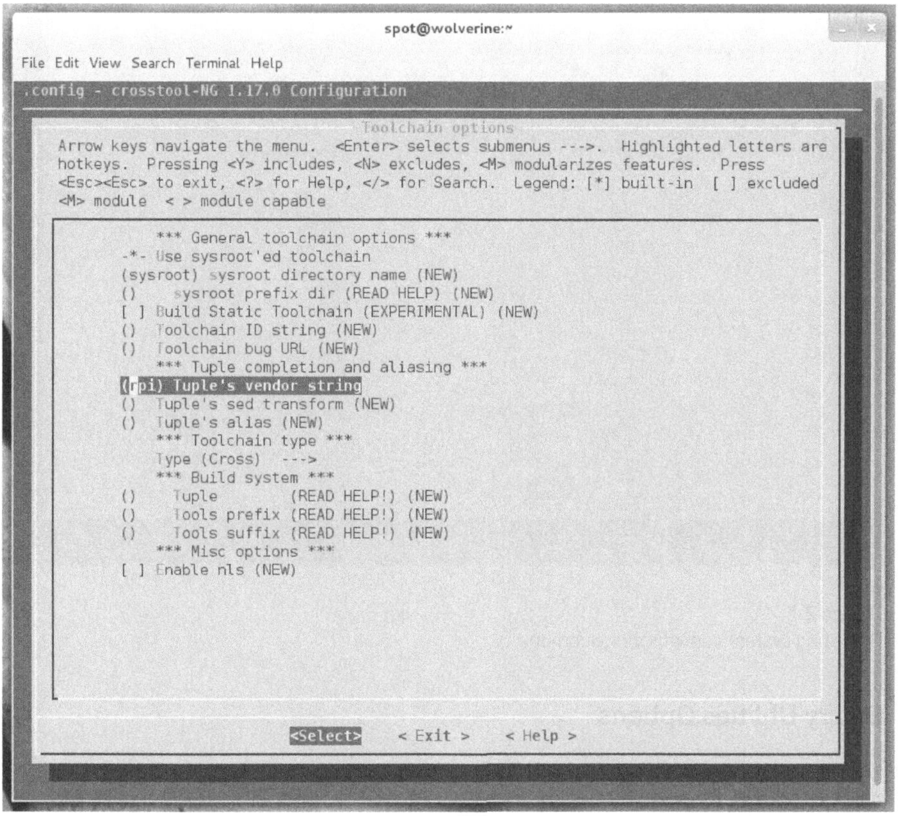

Figure 2-4.
Toolchain options configuration submenu

Operating System Options

Make the following changes to the Operating Systems Options (shown in Figure 2-5):

- Set "Target OS" to linux.

- Set "Linux kernel version" to 3.6.11. (Your Raspberry Pi might not be running the 3.6.11 kernel yet, but this is a safe value.)

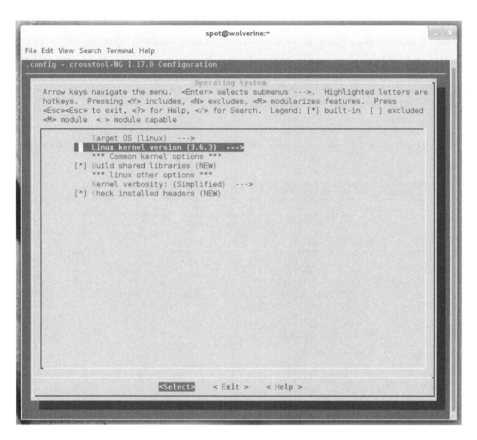

Figure 2-5.
Operating system configuration submenu

Binary Utilities Options

Make the following changes to the Binary Utilities (shown in Figure 2-6):

- Set "Binary format" to ELF.

- Set "binutils version" to 2.22

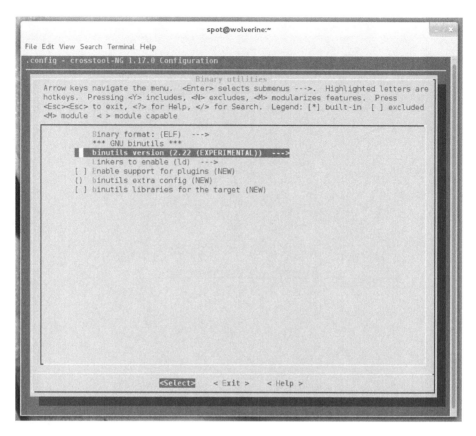

Figure 2-6.
Binary utilities configuration submenu

C Compiler Options

Make the following changes to the C Compiler options (shown in Figure 2-7):

- Enable "Show linaro versions".
- Set "gcc version" to linaro-4.7-2013.01. (Feel free to try newer ones if they are available when you are reading this.)
- Enable "C++".
- Set "gcc extra config" to --with-float=hard.
- Enable "Link libstdc++ statically into gcc binary".

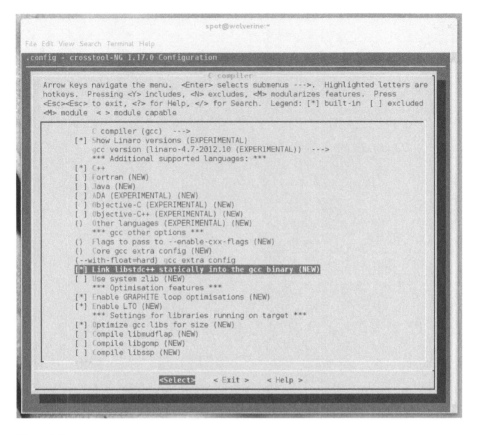

Figure 2-7.
C compiler configuration submenu

C-library Options

Make the following changes to the C-library options (shown in Figure 2-8):

- Set "C library" to "eglibc".
- Set "eglibc version" to "2_13".

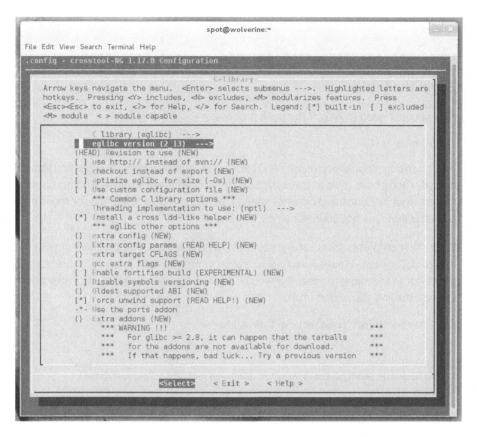

Figure 2-8.
C-library configuration submenu

That completes the configuration portion. Go to the main screen, exit, and save the configuration file when prompted.

Disable CT_WANTS_STATIC_LINK

On some systems, `crosstool-ng` sets the CT_WANTS_STATIC_LINK value to Y, even though you didn't select that. This will cause it to fail early in the build process, but you can use **sed** to ensure it is disabled. Run this command:

```
$ sed -i 's|CT_WANTS_STATIC_LINK=y|# CT_WANTS_STATIC_LINK is not set|
g' .config
```

This command might look complicated, but all it is doing is disabling the CT_WANTS_STATIC_LINK feature in the `crosstool-ng` configuration file by searching for the string that exactly matches the CT_WANTS_STATIC_LINK

Begin the Build

Now you just need to kickoff the build process:

```
$ ct-ng build
```

It will then download everything it needs and build your Raspberry-Pi-optimized cross-compiler toolchain. This is the longest part. The time will vary depending on your system specifications and Internet speeds, but 45 minutes to an hour or more on a powerful laptop is not unreasonable.

When this completes successfully, you will now have a cross-compiler toolchain in the `~/x-tools/arm-rpi-linux-gnueabi/bin` directory. You will want to add this directory to your PATH, in the same manner that you added the `crosstool-ng` directory previously. Change the line you added from:

```
PATH=$PATH:/opt/crosstool-ng-1.18.0/bin
```

to:

```
PATH=$PATH:$HOME/x-tools/arm-rpi-linux-gnueabi/bin:/opt/crosstool-
ng-1.18.0/bin
```

Save the file, and then source it again to update the PATH value. Now you can test your toolchain by running:

```
$ arm-rpi-linux-gnueabi-gcc -v
```

It will return a lot of information on how gcc is configured and optimized, along with printing the compiler version. If you see that, your Raspberry Pi cross-compiler toolchain is ready to go.

HACK 22 Build a Custom Kernel

For many hacks, the standard prebuilt Linux kernel images are sufficient, but some require options or drivers that are not enabled. This hack turns on some additional options that will be useful for other hacks in this book.

The Linux kernel is a fantastic operating system core for a number of reasons, starting with its versatility, its native support for a large number of architectures and devices, and its open source code base. The Raspberry Pi Foundation provides prebuilt Linux kernel images customized to support the Raspberry Pi hardware, as well as the corresponding source code tree, so that you can build a custom kernel image of your own that will work on the Raspberry Pi. This is necessary, because not all of the code needed for the Linux kernel to work on the Raspberry Pi is yet merged into the official Linux kernel source tree.

The first step to building your own kernel is to decide whether you want to do so natively from within the Linux instance running on the Raspberry Pi or to build it on an x86 Linux system with a properly configured cross-compiler toolchain. We strongly recommend the latter approach, because it will go much much faster (several hours faster) and it is not that much more complicated.

We'll assume that you're building your new kernel with a cross-compiler toolchain—specifically, the one described in Hack #21. You will also need to have the `make` and `ncurses-dev` (or `ncurses-devel`) packages installed on your x86 Linux system.

If you really prefer to build the kernel natively on the Raspberry Pi, make sure that you have the `gcc`, `make`, and `libncurses-dev` (or `ncurses-devel`) packages installed. Then, simply omit the `ARCH=arm CROSS_COMPILE=arm-rpi-linux-gnueabi-` flags from each command-line invocation. You will also need to have a copy of the Raspberry Pi Linux kernel source tree present in the running Linux filesystem.

Download the Kernel Source Tree

First you'll need to download a copy of the Raspberry Pi Linux kernel source tree. There are currently several branches under development:

`rpi-3.2.27`

This was the original kernel source that the first Raspberry Pi Linux distributions were using, but it is rather out of date at this point.

`rpi-3.6.y`

This is the *active development* kernel source tree, based on the kernel indicated (3.6.11 as of this writing).

`rpi-3.8.y`, `rpi-3.9.y`, `rpi-3.10.y`, *and* `rpi-3.11.y`

These branches were created to track the various newer kernels. If you need something specific with a newer branch, these might help you out.

The instructions in this hack will work for any kernel branch, but we strongly recommend that you start with the `rpi-3.6.y` source tree, because it is still getting new functionality and has the added advantage of several additional upstream releases' worth of bug fixes and features.

Either way, you need to check out the Raspberry Pi Linux kernel source tree from Git. We recommend you put this checkout in your `~/raspi` working directory on your Linux laptop (which you created in Hack #04), but if it doesn't exist, just run `mkdir ~/raspi`):

```
$ cd ~/raspi
$ git clone git://github.com/raspberrypi/linux.git
```

This currently defaults to a 3.6.y checkout, but you can always confirm that by trying to manually switch to the `rpi-3.6.y` branch:

```
$ cd ~/raspi/linux
$ git checkout rpi-3.6.y
```

If you want to use a different version of the source tree (e.g., 3.2.27-based), manually switch to the `rpi-$VERSION` branch using the same method, but substitute `rpi-$VERSION` for the Git checkout.

Alternatively, you can download a tarball from the GitHub website, which contains a current copy of the code tree:

- `rpi-3.2.27`: *https://github.com/raspberrypi/linux/archive/rpi-3.2.27.tar.gz*
- `rpi-3.6.y`: *https://github.com/raspberrypi/linux/archive/rpi-3.6.y.tar.gz*

These links should never go stale, because GitHub generates these tarballs each time you request them. This method has the advantage of being slightly faster, but we usually prefer to checkout the full Git source tree, because we can then use the Git tools to apply the latest changes from the upstream repository without needing to download a new Linux kernel source tree again.

If you download these tarballs (into `~/raspi`), simply unpack them using the following `tar` command:

```
$ cd ~/raspi
$ tar xvfz rpi-3.6.y.tar.gz
```

This will create a `linux-rpi-3.6.y/` (or `linux-rpi-$VERSION`) directory in `~/raspi` (the Git checkout will create a `linux/` directory instead).

Next, you need to make sure you have a clean working kernel source tree. Change into your Raspberry Pi Linux kernel source directory and run:

```
$ make mrproper
```

Linux Kernel Trivia

The Linux kernel contains a `make clean` target as well as the `make mrproper` target. The `make mrproper` target is a sort of "super clean," as it does everything that the `clean` target does, but a whole lot more (the `clean` target leaves generated artifacts behind, while `mrproper` brings the kernel source tree back to a pristine state).

> But why is it called `mrproper`? It's named after Mr. Proper, the internationally used name of a well-recognized mascot for cleaning products. In the United States, he is known as Mr. Clean.

Configure the Linux Kernel

Now you're ready to start configuring the Linux kernel. This can be a daunting task if you have never done it before, but that doesn't mean you shouldn't give it a shot! (That's the whole reason you bought a book called *Hacks*, right?)

The key to success is to start with a good default configuration that is known to work properly on the Raspberry Pi. A base default configuration file is included in the Linux kernel source checkout. This config file has the options enabled to support the hardware embedded within the Raspberry Pi. Just copy it to the top-level Raspberry Pi Linux kernel source directory (as `.config`):

```
$ cp arch/arm/configs/bcmrpi_defconfig .config
```

We recommend this approach, because it will minimize the number of questions that you have to answer later.

Other Sources for Kernel Config Files

There are other places to get kernel config files. If you have an active Raspberry Pi Linux instance that you just want to make minor kernel changes to, you can get a copy of the configuration file that corresponds to that running kernel image. To do this, type the following from within the Raspberry Pi Linux instance:

```
$ zcat /proc/config.gz > ~/.config
```

Then, copy `~/.config` from the Raspberry Pi Linux instance onto your Linux laptop and place that copy in your Raspberry Pi Linux kernel source directory (as `.config`).

You should be aware that if you take this `.config` file from a kernel that is of a different version than the source tree you are working on, this `.config` file will not match up with the same configuration options that those kernels have. It will still work, but you will end up having to answer a lot of questions about these missing options in a later step.

We've also placed a copy of our Raspberry Pi kernel configuration file here into the GitHub repository for this book. You should be able to use it as a starting point if nothing else works. To download it, simply clone our repository:

```
$ git clone https://github.com/spotrh/rpihacks
```

In the new `rpihacks` directory, you will see a file named **kernel-book.config**. Copy this file into your top-level Raspberry Pi Linux kernel source directory (as `.config`).

From here onward, you will need to specify the ARCH=arm CROSS_COMPILE=arm-rpi-linux-gnueabi- *options to all of the make invocations. This tells the Linux kernel code that you are building for a non-native architecture (ARM) and with a specific cross-compiler toolchain. The "-" at the end of the* arm-rpi-linux-gnueabi- *string is important, because the Makefiles will append the necessary binary commands (e.g.,* gcc, ar, ld) *to the end.*

Now you need to make sure that this base configuration file is brought up to date:

```
$ make ARCH=arm CROSS_COMPILE=arm-rpi-linux-gnueabi- oldconfig
```

This command will ask you to provide answers to any values that are not defined in the `config` file, and you're likely to have more than a few blanks to fill in. For the vast majority, you should simply hit Enter to accept the default, but there are a few that we recommend you set if prompted:

`Cross-compiler tool prefix (CROSS_COMPILE) [] (NEW)`

Set this to `arm-rpi-linux-gnueabi-`. This is not entirely necessary, but it is better to be safe than sorry here.

`Local version - append to kernel release (LOCALVERSION) [] (NEW)`

Set this to something unique. This will help you differentiate your custom kernel from the prebuilt kernel images. We suggest using something that you will identify easily as it relates to your project, or something containing the build date.

Those two settings will come early on (usually as the first two you see). After they're set, you just need to hit Enter several hundred times over the span of about 10 minutes. Don't worry too much about reading or changing these other options, as there is a better way to find and make configuration changes in the next step. Just keep hitting Enter until it says:

```
#
# configuration written to .config
#
```

Once that has happened, you should be back at a shell prompt. Now you can use the better, more intuitive menuconfig option to make specific configuration changes:

```
$ make ARCH=arm CROSS_COMPILE=arm-rpi-linux-gnueabi- menuconfig
```

This will present you with an ncurses-based Text User Interface (TUI) menu configuration system, as shown in Figure 2-9.

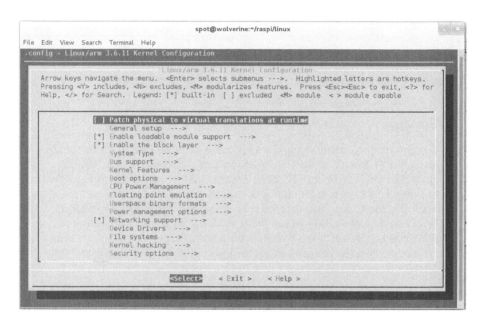

Figure 2-9.
TUI menu configuration system

You can navigate through this system with the arrow keys and the Enter button.

Here you can make all sorts of configuration changes. Generally, if you're doing this, you're enabling drivers or specific kernel features that you need for a hack. While we can't possibly list every option in the Linux kernel configuration universe (that would be an entirely different book), we do point out options that need to be enabled in several hacks in this book.

If you aren't sure about an option, the TUI will let you see more information about any specific configuration option by using the right arrow to move to Help (when an option is highlighted) and then pressing Enter. The following screen presents a short summary of the option (usually in English, although sometimes in kernel-hacker dialect) beneath the Kconfig syntax name for the option.

There are usually two ways to enable an option:

Compiled-in

> If you opt to compile in a feature or driver, it will appear in the TUI with an asterisk. You can select to compile in an item by hitting the spacebar when it is highlighted. The upside to compiling things into the Linux kernel is that the feature/driver will always be active. The downside is that the kernel becomes bigger and will use more memory.

Modular

> To enable a feature or driver as a module, just hit the *M* key when the item is highlighted. Not everything can be built as a module, but most things can.

PinMux

One advantage to modularizing drivers is that it simplifies PinMux control on the Raspberry Pi. PinMux is short for Pin-Multiplexing. The Broadcom BCM2835 system-on-chip used in the Raspberry Pi uses PinMux to select which signals will be present on the pins of the chip. The multiplexing is necessary because the number of available signals exceeds the number of available pins. Or, to put it simply, some of the GPIO pins can be connected to different things within the BCM2835 at different times. If your drivers which affect the GPIO pins or devices are built as modules, you can switch the PinMux by simply loading/unloading the module.

You should also be aware that some items, when enabled in the TUI, will expose additional items (or even new submenus).

Quite a few of the hacks in our book connect to the Raspberry Pi across the I2C bus, so you will definitely want to enable "I2C Support" (`CONFIG_I2C`). This option is under the Device Drivers menu, and you will want to compile it into your kernel.

Additionally, you will need to go into the I2C Support submenu, and enable compiled-in support for the "I2C device interface" (`CONFIG_I2C_CHARDEV`) and "Autoselect pertinent helper modules" (`CONFIG_I2C_HELPER_AUTO`). Figure 2-10 shows the menu with these options properly enabled.

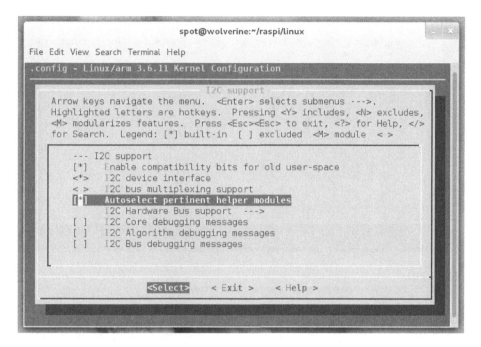

Figure 2-10.
I2C support options properly enabled

Then, in the "I2C Hardware Bus support" submenu, enable the BCM2708 BSC (`CONFIG_I2C_BCM2708`) driver (again, as compiled-in, not as a module). This is the hardware driver for the Raspberry Pi's I2C bus controller. The BCM2708 I2C baud rate defaults to 100000, and that is fine. It should look like Figure 2-11.

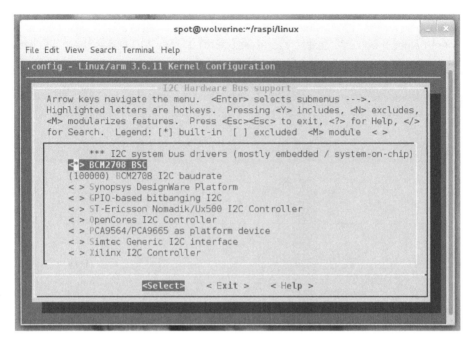

Figure 2-11.
BCM2708 BSC driver enabled to be compiled-in to the kernel

It is almost never risky to enable something as a module ("M"), unless it is marked as EXPERIMENTAL or DANGEROUS. However, it is rather risky to disable something that is enabled in the default configuration. Unless you know what you are doing, you are probably better off leaving all of the default settings alone.

That said, do not be overwhelmed by the sheer volume of configuration choices. Feel free to explore by navigating through menus and reading the help entries. You just might find something interesting.

When you're done configuring your kernel, return to the top-level menu and select Exit. The TUI will prompt you to save your new configuration. It will exit and leave you at a shell prompt, at which point you're ready to build the kernel image.

Build the Kernel Image

To speed up the build, you can parallelize the compilation by passing the `-j` flag to `make`. You'll need to know how many CPU cores are present on your build system to determine the ideal value.

Hack #21 provides a longer explanation of this concept, but the basic formula we recommend trying is the number of CPU cores you have multiplied by 1.5. For example, on an eight-core laptop, it would be 12. Using that example with this flag, the command to kickoff the build is:

```
$ make ARCH=arm CROSS_COMPILE=arm-rpi-linux-gnueabi- -j12
```

If you do not want to run a parallel compilation, simply omit the -j## flag from the command (note, however, that this will cause the build to take significantly longer).

At this point, your laptop is cross-compiling the core Linux kernel image. Depending on the options you have selected, this might take a while, but if all goes well, it will finish compiling without errors. Next, you'll need to build the matching kernel modules.

To keep the size of the core Linux kernel image small, many of the drivers for devices, filesystems, and optional functionality are normally configured to be built as Linux kernel modules. These make up a large tree of files, where each file is an individually loadable device driver.

Most Linux distributions (including Pidora and Raspbian) contain support for auto-loading appropriate kernel modules as they are needed, but you might find some situations in which you'll want to load a kernel module manually. This model also helps with memory management and boot object size. The default configuration we provide with this book modularizes as much as possible.

To start the Linux kernel modules build, run:

```
$ make ARCH=arm CROSS_COMPILE=arm-rpi-linux-gnueabi- modules -j12
```

This will also take some time, but it should finish without errors. If a module fails to build, you might need to disable it in the kernel configuration file and restart the whole process, but this is unlikely. Now, you just need to install your new kernel.

Install a New Kernel

The core Linux kernel image for the Raspberry Pi is a specially formatted copy of the zImage binary, compiled as an ARM boot executable. This image contains the primary functions of the Linux kernel, and it contains all the necessary code for booting into the Linux operating system.

This is the file that is booted by the Raspberry Pi GPU firmware. It is not usually a large file (slightly less than 3 MB). If you've built a custom Linux kernel from source as described in the previous sections, you can find a copy of the core Linux kernel image at arch/arm/boot/Image within that kernel source tree.

To install a new kernel, you will need to copy files onto the SD card containing your Raspberry Pi Linux distribution. If you have not already mounted your SD card on your Linux laptop, go ahead and do so by following the directions in Hack #02. Make sure that both the root and boot partitions are mounted, because you will need to copy files to both partitions.

Go ahead and copy the new core Linux kernel image into the mounted boot partition on the SD card:

```
$ su -c 'cp -a arch/arm/boot/Image /mnt/raspi-boot/new-kernel.img'
```

By default, the Raspberry Pi GPU firmware attempts to boot kernel.img from the boot partition. Since you are installing a new kernel, you probably want to override this behavior.

If you want it to boot a different filename, you can specify that by adding a line to config.txt (also found on the boot partition). If for some reason config.txt is not present on the boot partition (it is not necessary for the Raspberry Pi to boot Linux), simply create a new file with that filename.

To boot a specific file, edit /mnt/raspi-boot/config.txt and add a line like this:

```
kernel=new-kernel.img
```

In this example, the Raspberry Pi GPU will now look for new-kernel.img on the boot partition of the SD card and try to execute it at boot time. Conveniently, this is the name we used when we copied over the new kernel image. We used a new name here to avoid conflicts with the stock Linux kernel image file kernel.img that came with your Raspberry Pi Linux distribution. From here on, we will assume that the Raspberry Pi Linux distribution is configured to boot your new kernel image file (as specified by kernel=).

The second set of files that you need to copy over are the prebuilt Linux kernel modules that match the new kernel image file. If you built a new Linux kernel from source, you'll need to install your new modules into a temporary directory. To do this, simply run these commands from the top level of your kernel source code tree:

```
$ mkdir ~/modules
$ make ARCH=arm CROSS_COMPILE=arm-rpi-linux-gnueabi- \
    INSTALL_MOD_PATH=~/modules modules_install
```

Unlike the core Linux kernel image (which has to be on the boot partition), the kernel modules live in the root partition—specifically, in the /lib/modules directory. All you need to do to install them is to copy the whole versioned directory (or directories) into /lib/modules on the mounted root SD card partition. For your custom-built kernel, these commands will copy over the proper modules:

```
$ cd ~/modules
$ su -c 'cp -a lib/modules/* /mnt/raspi-root/lib/modules/'
```

Post-Installation Tasks

When the last of these modules finishes copying onto the root partition, make sure you have `config.txt` on the mounted boot SD card partition configured to boot the new kernel image (or unconfigured, so that `kernel.img` is booted). Then run the `sync` command a few times to ensure the data has all arrived onto the SD card:

```
$ sync;sync;sync
```

Now it should be safe to unmount the SD card partition(s) and eject the SD card. You can unmount these partitions either from the GUI interface of your Linux laptop, or you can manually unmount them from the terminal by running these commands:

```
$ cd ~
$ su -c 'umount /mnt/raspi-boot'
$ su -c 'umount /mnt/raspi-root'
```

Make sure to change into a directory that is not in either of the mounted partitions before attempting to run the umount command, or that command will not succeed.

Next, put your SD card into your Raspberry Pi and plug it in. You should see it boot into the Linux kernel successfully. Once you've logged in, you can now run:

```
$ uname -a
Linux myrpi 3.6.11+ #24 PREEMPT Sun Aug 19 21:28:36 BST 2013 armv6l GNU/
Linux
```

This will print out a list of system information, but the most important one is the version of the running Linux kernel. It should match the version of the modules directory (or directories) that you just copied over. You can also confirm that the build date printed out for the running kernel matches the date that you built your new kernel.

HACK 23   Update to the Latest Prebuilt Kernel

Want the latest Linux kernel features for your Raspberry Pi? Of course you do, and there is a way to get them without having to build it from source.

The nice folks at the Raspberry Pi Foundation are regularly hard at work adding new features to their Linux kernel source tree. They also go one step beyond and regularly update a copy of a prebuilt Linux kernel image. This kernel is configured with a set of options and modules intended specifically for the Raspberry Pi. Using this kernel means that you can be sure that all of the hardware built into the Raspberry Pi will be properly enabled, along with any Raspberry-Pi-specific functionality.

Distribution specific features

Some Linux distributions may assume the presence of features which are not enabled or supported in the Raspberry Pi Foundation prebuilt kernel images. Examples include SELinux, some extended filesystem attributes, and some typos of cryptography. This is one of the reasons we recommend that you keep a backup copy of the distribution provided kernel image around, just in case.

The Raspberry Pi Foundation offers prebuilt binary kernel images in the same Git repository that they use for firmware. To get a copy of this Git tree, see the instructions in Hack #04.

Remember that this Git tree has two branches: `master`, which is targeted for the Raspberry Pi Linux kernel 3.2-based source tree, and `next`, which is targeted for the Raspberry Pi Linux kernel 3.6-based source tree. You need to make sure that your kernel and firmware revision versions match; otherwise, your kernel might not boot (or features might not work the way that you expect). The file locations for the prebuilt kernel files are identical for both branches of the Git repository.

The Raspberry Pi Foundation's prebuilt Linux kernel is handy, having been designed for use with the Pi, and it contains a wide range of common device driver modules. However, it is missing some modules that you might need when connecting peripherals. If this is the case, you will want to build a custom Linux kernel from source, as covered in Hack #22.

Get the Prebuilt Linux Kernel

The prebuilt Linux kernel images come in two parts:

- The core Linux kernel image (`firmware/boot/kernel.img`)
- The prebuilt Linux kernel modules that correspond to that image (`firmware/modules`)

You can view the history of builds for the core Linux kernel image via the *GitHub website* (*https://github.com/raspberrypi/firmware/commits/master/boot/kernel.img*). If you want to see the history for the `next` branch, just change the branch via the drop-down on the website, or replace `master` with `next` in the URL.

Alternative Prebuilt Kernel Variants

The Raspberry Pi foundation also provides two alternative variants of this prebuilt kernel:

`kernel_cutdown.img`

> This is the smallest possible Linux kernel that can be booted on the Raspberry Pi. It contains minimal peripheral support outside of what is absolutely needed to use the embedded devices on the Raspberry Pi. It comes with a much smaller set of kernel modules than the standard kernel image.

`kernel_emergency.img`

> This is a Linux kernel image that contains a wide range of support compiled directly into the Linux kernel. Because so much support is compiled directly into this kernel, it can be treated as a "safe mode" kernel, and it should boot properly even if the Raspberry Pi Linux userspace has problems. The downside to this kernel image is that it is large in comparison (9.2 M) and thus will have a performance impact. Also, it does not come with any kernel modules, as all of the device drivers are compiled into the kernel image!

> Both of these alternative kernel images are built from the same source tree as the normal kernel image and are present in the Git checkout (`firmware/boot`). You can copy these to the boot partition using the same methods described for the usual image. Simply change directory into the mounted boot partition, rename any existing copies of these files to serve as backups, and then copy the new files from the Git checkout into the mounted boot partition.

> Remember, if you want to boot into one of these kernels (or one of your backup kernel images), just add an appropriate `kernel=` line to `config.txt`. You might want to add multiple lines to correspond to different kernel images, but be sure to comment out any entries that you are not using by prepending a `\#` character to the beginning of the line.

Now you can safely copy the new core Linux kernel image from your Git checkout onto the boot partition (as root). You'll want to rename this file from `kernel.img` when you do this (or rename the existing `kernel.img` in the SD card boot partition).

Install the Prebuilt Kernel Modules

Next, it is time to install the matching prebuilt kernel modules. You can find these modules under the `firmware/modules` directory from your Git checkout. There will be at least two directories here, and each will contain a version that corresponds to the version of the Linux kernel used to build these images (and modules). At the time of this writing, this version was 3.6.10, which shows as:

```
$ ls -l
total 8
    drwxrwxr-x 3 spot spot 4096 Dec 12 21:57 3.6.10+
    drwxrwxr-x 3 spot spot 4096 Dec 12 21:57 3.6.10-cutdown+
```

What's Up with That +?

You might have noticed that the versioned directories here have a \+ appended to them. This is a custom identifier that the Raspberry Pi Foundation uses for their kernel builds, mostly to prevent conflicts with custom kernel builds (which by default, do not contain a custom identifier).

The prebuilt core Linux kernel images will be looking for their modules in these exact directory names (including the +), so do not rename them. If there is an existing directory with the same name, it is reasonably safe to overwrite it (assuming that you have also copied the matching kernel image file from the same firmware checkout), but you can always rename the directory to act as a backup.

Just be aware that even if you boot the older kernel image via kernel= in config.txt, it will not know how to look in the renamed modules directory and will try to load its modules from the original versioned directory.

The 3.6.10+ directory contains the modules that are built for kernel.img, while the 33.6.10-cutdown+ directory contains the modules that are built for kernel_cut down.img. Makes sense, right? If you have copied kernel_cutdown.img into the boot partition of your SD card, you will want the corresponding modules, but if you have copied only kernel.img, you can leave them alone. It will not hurt anything to also copy the cutdown kernel modules, but it will eat up about 15 MB more on your SD card.

For the prebuilt kernel, this will copy the proper modules:

```
$ cd ~/raspi/firmware/modules
    $ su -c 'cp -a 3.6.10+ /mnt/raspi-root/lib/modules/'
```

From here on out, you will need to complete the same post-installation tasks that you would do for a kernel installed from source, as described in "Post-Installation Tasks" on page 87.

Merging Raspberry Pi Changes into Upstream Linux Kernel Source

At some point, ideally, the Raspberry Pi Foundation will be able to merge all of its Raspberry Pi (and BCM2835 system-on-chip) changes into the upstream Linux kernel source. This will mean that it is no longer necessary to have a separate Raspberry-Pi-specific Linux kernel source tree, and it is possible that the Raspberry Pi Foundation will stop providing new prebuilt kernel images as a result.

This is just speculation, though, because while the Raspberry Pi Foundation has indicated a desire for merging its patches into the upstream Linux kernel tree, and there are various kernel hackers working toward this goal, it has not yet happened. To date, the Foundation has not given any indication that it will stop making prebuilt kernel images. This should not be too big of a problem if it does happen, because the Linux distributions will easily be able to produce prebuilt Raspberry-Pi-specific Linux kernel images that they maintain from the upstream "Linus" source tree.

We point this out only so that if you are reading this book at a future time when this has indeed occurred and you are not seeing recently updated prebuilt kernel images in their GitHub firmware repository, you might have an idea why.

HACK 24 Split Memory Between the GPU and Linux Userspace

The performance that you get from your Raspberry Pi is tightly coupled to the amount of memory that you allocate to its core components. Because this isn't a system you can just drop more RAM into, you should consider the needs of your project and the best way to split the available memory.

In the embedded hardware universe, memory is almost always a precious and scant commodity. The performance of the system is usually tightly coupled to the amount of present (and accessible) memory. Additionally, most embedded systems do not have any user-serviceable method to increase the amount of physical memory, and the Raspberry Pi is no different.

When the Raspberry Pi Model B was first released, it came with 256 MiB of memory (either Hynix MobileDDR2 or Samsung Mobile DRAM, depending on when it was produced). The memory rests physically on top of the Broadcom media processor in the BCM2835 system-on-chip. This is known as *package on package* (PoP). PoP allows for an embedded system to combine multiple ball grid array (BGA) packages in a vertical stack.

The Raspberry Pi system-on-chip uses a mixed logic-memory stack, which is useful to save space and allows the hardware vendor to choose from a wide range of compatible options (and helps them to keep costs down). This design decision allowed them to easily upgrade the amount of on-board memory on the Model B from 256 MiB to 512 MiB (all Model B units sold after October 15, 2012 have the larger amount).

How to Tell Which Pi You Have

If you have a Pi that's been sitting around for a while, and you're not sure which one it is, you can use `cat /proc/cpuinfo` to find out. The results look like this:

```
Processor      : ARMv6-compatible processor rev 7 (v6l)
BogoMIPS       : 795.44
Features       : swp half thumb fastmult vfp edsp java tls
CPU implementer : 0x41
CPU architecture: 7
CPU variant    : 0x0
CPU part       : 0xb76
CPU revision   : 7

Hardware       : BCM2708
Revision       : 000e
Serial         : 0000000011185abc
```

The part after `Revision` tells you which board you have. Refer to this table:

Revision code	Model	Rev number	RAM (MB)
0002	B	1.0	256
0003	B	1	256
0004	B	2	256
0005	B	2	256
0006	B	2	256
0007	A	2	256
0008	A	2	256
0009	A	2	256
000d	B	2	512
000e	B	2	512
000f	B	2	512

This significantly improved the performance of the Raspberry Pi. Unfortunately, making a change to the amount of memory is a decision that can really be made only at fabrication time, and it's not one that a user can easily hack. Stacking these tiny BGA units is best done by robots, not clumsy human hands.

Even with the newer 512 MiB of memory, it's a precious resource. Because of how the BCM2835 system-on-chip works, some of this memory must go to the GPU. You might have seen this sort of behavior on lower-end GPU cards for x86 computers, which do not include dedicated on-GPU memory and dedicate some system memory for GPU usage. The Raspberry Pi firmware allows for you to customize the amount of memory that is allocated to the GPU.

Before the 512 MiB Raspberry Pi Model B units existed, customizing memory allocation was accomplished by choosing a `start.elf` file corresponding to the splits shown in Table 2-1.

Table 2-1. Memory allocation on 256 MiB Raspberry Pi Model B

ARM CPU	VIDEOCORE GPU	FILENAME
128 MiB	128 MiB	`arm128_start.elf`
192 MiB	64 MiB	`arm192_start.elf`
224 MiB	32 MiB	`arm224_start.elf`
240 MiB	16 MiB	`arm240_start.elf`

This worked well when the Raspberry Pi Model B firmware had only one possible memory size (256 MiB) to support, but when they started producing the 512 MiB Model B units, this approach no longer made sense. Among other reasons this didn't work, the most obvious is that twice as many splits are possible on the 512 MiB units (even if some of them are pretty ludicrous). They also wanted the firmware to be able to support both units, and the split-out `start.elf` model was very much hardcoded to the 256 MiB size.

Allocate Memory with config.txt

The current firmware (necessary for the 512 MiB units) abandons the separate `start.elf` file approach and adds support for `start.elf` to read in a variable (`gpu_mem`) from `config.txt` that specifies exactly the amount the user wants to allocate to the GPU in chunks of 16 MiB, with 16 MiB as the minimum and 448 MiB as the maximum.

To set this, open `config.txt` (on the boot partition of the SD card containing the Raspberry Pi Linux image) in the editor of your choice and use the following syntax (where `value` is an integer representing the total MiB to dedicate to the GPU, in chunks of 16 MiB, 16 to 128 MiB):

```
gpu_mem=(value)
```

The Raspberry Pi firmware sets `gpu_mem=64` as the default. But just how much memory *should* you allocate to the GPU? The answer depends on what your Raspberry Pi will be used for.

If you're using it in a headless mode (see Hack #11), you can set `gpu_mem` to the minimum value of `16`. If you do this, you will need to be sure that `start_cd.elf` and `fix up_cd.elf` are present, because they will be used instead. Be careful with this, because video will not work at all at this minimal setting, but on the upside, it will leave 496 MiB for the ARM CPU (this gets used by Linux userspace).

For an only slightly video-friendly option, at `gpu_mem=32`, the Linux kernel can drive the framebuffer at 1080p, but 3D and video processing will not work properly. At `gpu_mem=128`, you will get excellent 3D and video decoding performance, but you will leave the Linux userspace with only 384 MiB.

In the middle of the road with a 256 MiB/256 MiB split, you will give the GPU enough memory to handle big textures, but the Linux userspace will really struggle. It is possible to increase this value up to 448 MiB, but we don't recommend exceeding 128 MiB unless you have an exceptionally GPU-intensive use case.

While the core Linux kernel is capable of running in memory-starved environments, most userspace applications (especially graphical ones) rely on the availability of tens of MiB of memory to run properly. The Raspberry Pi contains less memory than most popular smartphones (for example, the Galaxy Nexus and iPhone 5 have 1 GiB, and the Nexus 4 has 2 GiB).

Also keep in mind that Linux aggressively pre-caches available memory that is not currently being used by applications to improve system performance. This means that the more memory you can allocate to the ARM CPU, the better performance you'll get from Linux.

Make a config.txt Compatible with 256 or 512 MiB Models

It is possible to make a `config.txt` that works on both 256 MiB and 512 MiB Raspberry Pi Model B units. To set the GPU memory to be compatible with both units, you need to use the `gpu_mem_256` and `gpu_mem_512` parameters. The `gpu_mem_256` parameter is used on the 256 MiB Raspberry Pi Model B, overrides any value set in `gpu_mem=`, and is ignored entirely on the 512 MiB Raspberry Pi Model B.

The same is true of the `gpu_mem_512` setting, except that it is used on the 512 MiB unit and ignored on the 256 MiB unit. `gpu_mem_256` has a max value of 192, and `gpu_mem_512` has a max value of 448.

On Raspbian, it is also possible to configure an explicit memory split by using the `raspi-config` utility. Launch `raspi-config` as root, and select the Memory Split option.

For most of the hacks and projects in this book, `gpu_mem=128` should be a good place to start. It's the setting that has given us the best possible overall performance in most of our tinkering. Feel free to experiment, though, as the only real damage you can do is to the Raspberry Pi's performance, and you can always change it back.

Automatically Share Memory

While you might be able to guess how much memory you want to split between the CPU (OS) and the GPU (graphics), there are a lot of situations where you probably will not know for sure. In cases like this, you really want to be able to configure your Raspberry Pi to split the memory on the fly, allocating it between the CPU and the GPU as needed.

As of the post-November 2012 firmware and 3.6 Linux kernel updates, there is a better way to manage the GPU/CPU memory split. Called the Contiguous Memory Allocator (CMA), it enables a dynamically managed memory split between the GPU and the ARM CPU by setting low- and high-water marks for the GPU.

The `config.txt` parameter for the GPU low-water mark is `cma_lwm`, and `cma_hwm` is the parameter for the GPU high-water mark. In order to use these parameters, you also must pass some options to the Linux kernel at boot time. You can do this by adding these options to `cmdline.txt` (on the boot partition of the SD card):

```
coherent_pool=6M smsc95xx.turbo_mode=N
```

> *This change to* `cmdline.txt` *also has the side-effect of disabling the* turbo mode *for the built-in ethernet controller on the Raspberry Pi, but you might not mind too much unless you have a network-intensive use case. Disabling* turbo mode *also sometimes improves wireless network performance (and eliminates a lot of DE-BUG noise in the system logs in some cases).*

In this configuration, you will also need to set the following values in `config.txt`:

```
gpu_mem_256=112
gpu_mem_512=368
cma_lwm=16
cma_hwm=32
cma_offline_start=16
```

Once you have rebooted the Raspberry Pi with these settings in place, it will result in 466 MiB memory free (212 MiB on the 256 MiB Model B unit) for the Linux userspace by default, with more allocated to the GPU as needed (within the watermarks).

While this CMA support is comparatively new, we highly recommend trying it instead of hardcoding the split for most common use cases. It will improve things like web browser performance while still allowing for high GPU memory utilization cases on-demand.

Update the Firmware and Prebuilt Binary Kernel the Easy Way

Everything's easier when there's a tool for it, and fortunately, Liam McLoughlin (a.k.a. "Hexxeh") has created one for updating your Raspberry Pi firmware and kernel.

`rpi-update` is a shell script that automates the process of updating the firmware, prebuilt binary kernel, and prebuilt VideoCore SDK files on an SD card containing a Raspberry Pi Linux distribution image.

First, make sure that you have the `readelf` and `git` binaries installed in your chosen Raspberry Pi Linux distribution. You will need these commands for successful use of the rpi-update script. On most Linux distributions, `readelf` is in the `binutils` package and `git` is in the `git` package.

To install it, run the following (as root) on Pidora:

```
$ su -c 'yum install binutils git'
```

or Raspbian:

```
$ su -c 'apt-get install binutils git-core'
```

To use this script, download it from within your running Raspberry Pi Linux Distribution image with the following command:

```
$ wget https://raw.github.com/Hexxeh/rpi-update/master/rpi-update
```

You will need to put it in your $PATH and set it executable. The simplest way to do this is to run the following commands (as root):

```
$ su -c 'cp rpi-update /usr/bin/'
$ su -c 'chmod +x /usr/bin/rpi-update'
```

Then, to update the firmware, prebuilt binary kernel, and VideoCore SDK libraries all at once, simply run (as root):

```
$ su -c 'rpi-update'
```

There are, however, a few caveats to using this shortcut tool:

- It does require you to run the script from within the running Linux environment. Make sure that the time is set properly within the environment, or you might get script failures relating to clock drift.

- The script does not let you perform fine-grained update operations (e.g., just update the firmware). It is an all-or-nothing experience.

- The script assumes that the VideoCore files are located under /opt/vc. Some Raspberry Pi Linux distributions (such as Pidora) place the VideoCore files in a different location or include them in the system library directories, so this script will not work well for them.

The rpi-update script does not use the official GitHub repository for prebuilt files because of the size of that repository. Instead, Hexxeh keeps a copy of those files in a separate GitHub repository with a different filesystem layout.

While this separate repository seems to be manually synced with the official repository on a regular basis, keep in mind that it is possible that you will not be getting the absolute latest available revisions of these files. Sometimes, that's how it goes when you try to take shortcuts.

HACK 26 Emulate the Pi

> Whether you're travelling without your Pi, need to test something in a hurry, or your kids have taken over the Pi while you weren't looking, it can sometimes be convenient to emulate it on another machine. QEMU can help.

QEMU (short for *Quick EMUlator*) is an open source, hosted hypervisor. That means that you can use it to run a Linux distro that was made for your Raspberry Pi (which uses ARM hardware) on your usual computer (an x86 laptop, for example).

It has two modes. The first is user-mode emulation, which lets you run single programs that weren't compiled for your machine. But this hack focuses on QEMU's full-system emulation, which lets you emulate an entire computer—in this case, a Raspberry Pi.

First install QEMU, by running this command on Fedora:

```
$ su -c 'yum install qemu'
```

Or, you can run this on Debian/Ubuntu:

```
$ su -c 'apt-get qemu-system-arm'
```

Download kernel-qemu from *http://xecdesign.com/downloads/linux-qemu/kernel-qemu*. You can also *compile your own kernel* (*http://xecdesign.com/compiling-a-kernel/*).

Why Is This Kernel Special?

*You might have noticed that we have not pointed you to the hack in this book (*Hack #22*) that covers building a custom kernel for booting on the Raspberry Pi. This is intentional, because that kernel will not work on* qemu_*.* Qemu *emulates a wide range of hardware environments, but the exact hardware found in the Raspberry Pi is not yet one of them.*

The kernel-qemu *file uses the closest match available in* qemu *and provides the same level of ARM optimization and runtime support. This allows you to use almost everything in your Raspberry Pi Linux distribution userspace as is. The most notable exception is the videocore libraries (and any applications which use them). Because* qemu *has no BCM2835 system-on-chip hardware emulation, these applications will fail to operate properly in* qemu *emulation.*

Create a directory to work in, and put a copy of your distro's image and kernel-qemu in it. The rest of this example will use the Pidora 18 image (pidora-18-r1c.img) and qemu as that directory, though you can replicate these instructions for other distros and of course name your directories whatever you like.

Run file on the image:

```
$ file pidora-18-r1c.img

pidora-18-r1c.img: x86 boot sector; partition 1: ID=0xc, active, starthead
32, startsector 2048, 102400 sectors; partition 2: ID=0x83, starthead 32,
startsector 104448, 3389858 sectors, code offset 0xb8
```

Take the startsector number from partition 2 (bold in the previous output) and multiply it by 512 to use as the offset number when you mount the image:

```
$ sudo mount qemu/pidora-18-r1c.img -o offset=53477376 /mnt/pidora
```

Now open /mnt/pidora/etc/ld.so.preload in a text editor and comment out the one line you find there by adding a # in front of it and saving the file. You can now unmount:

```
$ sudo umount /mnt/pidora
```

And you're ready to start Pidora in QEMU:

```
$ qemu-system-arm -kernel kernel-qemu -cpu arm1176 -m 256 -M versatilepb -
serial stdio -append "root=/dev/sda2 panic=1" -hda pidora-18-r1c.img
```

These are the options you're setting:

-kernel

You're telling it to use the kernel-qemu kernel file you downloaded. If you created your own, specify its name+/path+ here instead.

`-cpu`

> The Raspberry Pi contains an ARM1176 core, which you specify here. To see the complete list of options QEMU offers, use the command `qemu-system-arm -cpu help`.

> *If you have an older QEMU installation or acquire it from a package that hasn't been updated, you might encounter a problem with the -cpu option, because older versions didn't support ARM1176. You might be able to make this work by substituting arm1136-r2, but it would be better to update your version of QEMU.*

`-m`

> This sets the virtual RAM in megabytes. It is unlikely to work with more than 256.

`-M`

> This sets the emulated machine type. (We're specifying the Versatile PB platform here.)

`-serial`

> This redirects the virtual serial port. The default is vc in graphical mode and stdio in non-graphical mode.

`-append`

> This option gives the kernel command-line arguments.

`-hda`

> This is the location of the image of the distro you're emulating.

You can read further documentation of QEMU's options at *http://qemu.org*.

This will take you to the first boot screen, and you can go through that process just like you would on an actual Pi. It will reboot at the end, but QEMU will close, and you'll have to start it again. Just press the up arrow once to get to the previous qemu-system-arm command and run it again.

This time you'll boot through to the login screen and can use it as if you were on an actual Raspberry Pi.

HACK 27 Try Occidentalis: The Raspberry Pi Distro for (Advanced) Education

If you're interested in using the Pi for hardware-hacking education (or learning!), Adafruit's Raspberry Pi Educational Linux Distro (a.k.a. Occidentalis), is a great place to start.

Raspbian was one of the first Linux distributions designed specifically for the Raspberry Pi, and it was based on Debian 7.0, nicknamed "Wheezy." Thus the Raspberry Pi version was named with the portmanteau "Raspbian Wheezy." But online electronics shop Adafruit (http://adafruit.com) found that Raspbian Wheezy didn't have some of the features it most wanted for hacking through the Raspberry Pi's breakout pins, so it decided to create its own. It's called Occidentalis and is based on Raspbian Wheezy with hardware SPI, I2C, and WiFi support built in, among other things.

Occidentalis is recommended for those with Linux experience who are interested in taking full advantage of the hardware. Despite the "for education" aspect, it's not meant for beginners. That doesn't mean it's useless for kids; rather, it means that this is a do-it-together sort of project.

Occidentalis is worth mentioning in this book, because it is intended for use with electronics. This means that it comes preconfigured in kernel and userspace to access and control some commonly available sensors and components. This is especially true if they come from Adafruit. Using Occidentalis will save you some time if you're attempting Hack #37.

As of this writing, the current version of Occidentalis is v0.2, based on Raspbian Wheezy from August 16, 2012. Version 0.1 includes:

- Firmware updating: Liam McLoughlin ("Hexxeh") created a tool called `rpi-updater` to update the Raspberry Pi's firmware. We talk about it in more detail in Hack #25.
- I2C and hardware SPI supported and initialized at boot.
- Ready-to-go sshd at first boot: At boot, the ssh keys are generated with a username and password of pi/raspberry on raspberrypi.local.
- Support for WiFi through the Realtek RTL8188CUS USB module, a tiny 802.11b/g/n WLAN controller, which you can purchase from Adafruit and other vendors for about $12.
- One-wire support on GPIO 4. See *this GitHub page (http://github.com/Frank-Buss/linux-1/commit/71871509238d3e7bce4a74cdf616c3f12542acaa)*.

Version 0.2 includes those features as well as:

- Removed persistent wlan0 entry
- RTC, lm-sensors
- Kernel modules DS1307, AD626 I2C digipots, HMC6352, BMP085, and ADS1015, which support common sensors, like weather sensors
- Custom PWM/Servo kernel module

Occidentalis and Hynix

If your CPU says "Hynix" in a handwriting-style font on it, that indicates that you have Hynix RAM. It will not work with Occidentalis as of version 0.2. The next version is expected to be compatible.

Download the most recent version of Occidentalis at *http://learn.adafruit.com/*. It is only a 99 MB download, which decompresses to a 2.6 GB image, so you only need a 4 GB card, unless you want extra room for storage. As of v0.2, you should see the `raspi-config` tool at boot. If not, or if you'd like to return to it later, enter:

```
$ sudo raspi-config
```

What's with the Crazy Name?

For starters, it's a lot quicker to type "Occidentalis" than "Adafruit Raspberry Pi Educational Linux Distro." But if you go to http://learn.adafruit.com, you'll notice that the Occidentalis logo looks a lot like the Raspberry Pi logo, but a bit darker.

Rubus occidentalis is a particular species in the rose family more commonly known as "black raspberry," hence the name and the logo.

Your options in `raspi-config` should look familiar if you've used Raspbian, upon which Occidentalis is based. Here are the ones you'll most likely want to use or change up front:

expand_rootfs
Clicking this will give you no further options; it will simply expand the root partition to fill the available space on the SD card, which will be available after the next reboot.

change_pass
Since the `pi` user's password is publicly known, it's a good idea to change it at first boot.

boot_behaviour
Tell it whether you want to boot to the command line or to the GUI desktop.

update
Update to the latest packages.

Of course, for `update`, you're going to need to be online, which is easy if you plugged into a wired connection. But if you're using a WiFi dongle, you'll have to set up the wireless connection first. Though Raspbian offers a GUI tool on the desktop to do so, Occidentalis does not. Open the network interfaces file in a text editor:

```
$ sudo vi /etc/network/interfaces
```

Edit the last two lines for your network configuration:

```
auto lo

iface lo inet loopback
iface eth0 inet dhcp

allow-hotplug wlan0
auto wlan0


iface wlan0 inet dhcp
        wpa-ssid "Change this to your network SSID"
        wpa-psk "Change this to your network password"
```

Remember to leave the quotation marks intact. Reboot, and your wireless connection should be working.

It's also worth noting, particularly if you're using the Raspberry Pi with your kids, that Occidentalis (and generally anything on the Pi) is not going to be up to the speed they expect. In fact, it's almost certain that at some point you're going to assume that something's not working when really it's just taking much, much longer than you expect—even "simple" things, like opening a Midori browser window or going to a web page. Patience is the key with the Pi.

HACK 28   Monitor the Pi's IP Address

> Sure, you can ifconfig every time you need to know your Pi's IP address. Or you could see it at a glance any time.

This hack is all about knowing the IP address on your Pi. Unless you keep your Pi connected to a monitor and a keyboard all of the time, or have its IP statically assigned, you might not be able to easily determine its IP address. With a little bit of hardware and a little bit of software, you'll be able to answer that question whenever you want to, simply by taking a look at your Pi, as shown in Figure 2-12.

Figure 2-12.
Raspberry Pi showing the eth0 IP

How do we perform this magical feat? Well, the trick is in another Adafruit project kit: the *LCD Pi Plate* (*http://www.adafruit.com/products/1115*). The lovely and talented folks over at Adafruit have designed a simple way to stack an 16 x 2 LCD and a simple keypad right on top of a Raspberry Pi. It comes as an unassembled kit, but putting it together is simple.

Build the LCD Pi Plate

To assemble the LCD Pi Plate, you will need:

- A soldering iron (and solder)
- A LCD Pi Plate Kit (it includes a 16x2 Blue LCD, but Adafruit sells other colors)
- Fine wire cutters
- A narrow-tipped Phillips screwdriver
- Tall *stacking header* (*http://www.adafruit.com/products/1112*) (optional)

There are many different ways to connect an LCD to a Raspberry Pi, but the LCD Pi Plate has some notable advantages for this hack. The LCDs that Adafruit uses require a lot of digital pinouts (six to nine, depending on the functionality of the LCD device). If you attached this device directly to your Raspberry Pi, you'd take up a lot of GPIO pins simply to add an LCD.

But the LCD Pi Plate provides a stackable way to add an LCD (think Arduino shield) that uses only two pins, the I2C pins. Also, because of how the I2C bus works, you can attach additional devices to those pins and they will appear on the I2C bus (as long as they do not have conflicting addresses). On top of that, you get five push buttons that you can use to interact with the LCD.

Adafruit has a *fantastic tutorial* (*http://learn.adafruit.com/adafruit-16x2-character-lcd-plus-keypad-for-raspberry-pi/*) that walks you through the process of assembling the LCD Pi plate. But if you're unable to view it for some reason, the kit is very straight-forward.

Basically, you solder in the two 220 ohm resistors (labeled Red, Red, Brown, Gold) in the slots labeled RED and BLUE, and the 1 remaining resistor (330 ohm, labeled Orange, Orange, Brown, Gold) goes in the slot labeled GREEN. Trim the excess leads away after soldering. Then, insert all of the push buttons in the marked button slots (all the way flush with the board) and solder them in.

Next, solder in the potentiometer (it has three "legs") in the slot marked Contrast, and the MCP23017 i2c port expander chip gets soldered into the slot marked (MCP23017). Just make sure you align the notch in the chip with the notch in the silkscreened outline, or it will not work.

At this point, we recommend deviating from the Adafruit kit a bit. It comes with a normal height header connector (looks like a black plastic rectangle with holes and pins on the other side), which will work fine, but if you want to be able to connect other devices through the LCD Pi Plate (specifically, the Pi Cobbler), you should buy one of the extra-tall stacking headers. Either way, put the header in the underside of the board so that the pins stick up through the top. The header is where it will connect to the Raspberry Pi GPIO pins. Solder it in (on the top).

Then, stick the rubber bumper to the underside of the board, right above where you soldered in the buttons, sitting flat, as close as you can get it to the buttons and the left edge without overlapping or going off the board.

Break off a 16 pin length of the header pins (or 18, if you bought a different LCD that requires more), and insert it into the top of the LCD Pi Plate with the long pins sticking up. Put the LCD into position, setting into to the long header pins. Solder each of the header pins on the underside of the board and on the top of the LCD.

At this point, it should be completely assembled (and sturdy). You can push it onto your Raspberry Pi, inserting the GPIO pins into the connector so that it lines up neatly on top of the Raspberry Pi.

Again, if any of these steps are unclear, the Adafruit online tutorial is excellent, so you should refer to it if you get confused along the way.

Install Software to Control the LCD Pi Plate

Adafruit is also worthy of respect because it writes open source software to drive the hardware that it sells. The LCD Pi Plate has a Python library written for it that you can use to access and program the LCD and buttons. You can get a copy from their *GitHub repository* (*https://github.com/adafruit/Adafruit-Raspberry-Pi-Python-Code*), but we have also included a copy in the *GitHub repository for this book* (*https://github.com/spotrh/rpihacks*) (along with some additional code that we wrote to monitor the IP address on the Pi).

Go ahead and clone our GitHub repository on your Raspberry Pi (if you haven't done it already):

```
$ git clone https://github.com/spotrh/rpihacks
```

In order for any of this software to work, you need to enable the I2C support in the Linux kernel. If you're using a custom kernel (on any Linux flavor), configured as described in Hack #22, you don't need to do anything here. If you're running Pidora or Occidentalis without a custom kernel, you also have everything you need need preconfigured.

But if you're running a Raspbian instance running your kernel, you will need some additional configuration to enable I2C support. Specifically, you need to run the following command:

```
$ su -c 'modprobe i2c-bcm2708'
```

To make that persistent, you will also want to edit /etc/modules and add these lines to the end of the file:

```
i2c-bcm2708
i2c-dev
```

On any distro, you'll need to install some software to add a Python module for System Management Bus (SMBus) support (you can think of SMBus as a stricter version of I2C), the python-rpi, the I2C utilities, and the python-netifaces module (this is how you will get the IP address information).

Pidora doesn't have a packaged version of python-smbus in release 18 (the current release as of this writing), so we've included a RPM package for you in the book's GitHub repository.

On Pidora, run:

```
$ su -c 'yum install i2c-tools python-rpi.gpio python-netifaces -y'
$ su -c 'yum install rpihacks/i2c-tools-python-3.1.0-5.fc18.armv6hl.rpm --nogpgcheck'
```

On Raspbian/Occidentalis, run:

```
$ su -c 'apt-get install python-dev python-rpi.gpio python-smbus i2c-tools python-netifaces'
```

Run the Code

With this software installed, you can scan the I2C bus (bus 1) for the LCD Pi Plate:

```
$ su -c 'i2cdetect -y 1'
     0  1  2  3  4  5  6  7  8  9  a  b  c  d  e  f
```

```
00:             -- -- -- -- -- -- -- -- -- -- -- --
10: -- -- -- -- -- -- -- -- -- -- -- -- -- --
20: 20 -- -- -- -- -- -- -- -- -- -- -- -- --
30: -- -- -- -- -- -- -- -- -- -- -- -- -- --
40: -- -- -- -- -- -- -- -- -- -- -- -- -- --
50: -- -- -- -- -- -- -- -- -- -- -- -- -- --
60: -- -- -- -- -- -- -- -- -- -- -- -- -- --
70: -- -- -- -- -- -- -- --
```

Sure enough, you can see the Adafruit LCD Pi Plate on the I2C bus, as device number 20.

Now, go ahead and change into the `Adafruit_CharLCDPlate/` directory within your checkout of our GitHub repository:

```
$ cd rpihacks/Adafruit_CharLCDPlate
```

In that directory, you will see a few Python files. Most of these provide the library of functions necessary to access the LCD Pi Plate. If you just want to test proper operation of your wiring and soldering work, you can run the Adafruit test script:

```
$ su -c 'python ./LCDtest.py'
```

This will cycle through the background colors and print text strings to the LCD when you press the buttons on the Pi Plate. If you are using the Blue 16x2 LCD that normally comes with this kit, it does not support different background colors, so this program will seem to dim the background depending on which button you press. Don't get scared if this happens.

If no visible text appears, but you can see the LCD blinking, you probably just need to adjust the contrast. Use your fine-tipped Phillips screwdriver to turn the potentiometer (it's the round knob next to the buttons with a Phillips-shaped slot in it) until text appears.

When you're satisfied with the test script, it's time to get to the good stuff. We've written a different Python script that, when executed, will run a simple program that displays the IP addresses for eth0 and wlan0. It also has a crude menu structure, so that you can push the Up and Down button on the LCD Pi Plate to switch between displaying the IP address for eth0 and wlan0, respectively. The other buttons will return you to the menu screen.

To run that program, simply run:

```
$ su -c 'python ./LCD-pi-plate-demo.py'
```

If you want that program to run in the background, just add a & after `./LCD-pi-plate-demo.py` (but within the ' ' marks for the `su -c` invocation).

You should see this on the LCD panel:

```
Pi IP Addrs
UP:eth0 DN:wlan0
```

If you press the Up button on the LCD Pi Plate, it will try to display the address for eth0 (if any).

If you press the Down button on the LCD Pi Plate, it will try to display the address for wlan0 (if any).

While we know that the Raspberry Pi does not have built-in wireless networking support, it is common for people to add that support by connecting a USB wireless device.

While eth0 and wlan0 devices are hardcoded in our script, you can easily change them if you'd prefer to display other networking devices. This code is simple: if you have a basic understanding of Python, you should be able to figure out how it works. Feel free to take what we've made and improve upon it!

HACK 29 Run Android on the Raspberry Pi

> Read through this chapter and got tired of all the Linux? Or maybe you just love Android. Either way, it's not impossible to run Android rather than a Linux distribution on your Raspberry Pi, but this is a project for the dedicated hackers.

The good news is that there is a community based around running Android on the Raspberry Pi, which means if you've decided to give it a shot, there are people to whom you can turn. They gather information on a wiki at *http://androidpi.wikia.com/wiki/ Android_Pi_Wiki*. For a quick status check, log into their IRC channel, #razdroid, on Freenode.

The bad news is that this isn't one of the faster moving communities you'll find. This isn't a reflection on the community at all. Rather, the Raspberry Pi was simply not designed for Android. In July 2012, Eben Moglen posted on the Raspberry Pi blog about the progress on a *port of Android 4.0 (Ice Cream Sandwich) for the Pi (http:// www.raspberrypi.org/archives/1700)*. Unfortunately, that was well over a year ago as of this writing, and it is also the last update on the subject. The Razdroid wiki now states "Very doubtful that any Android that will be usable will ever be released."

But even a nonfunctional system is an opportunity for learning, and learning is what the Raspberry Pi was designed for. So if Android and Raspberry Pi both interest you, there's no harm in giving it a shot. The worst outcome is that you say, "Well, that didn't work," which you expected from the beginning anyway. The best outcome is that you learn something about the Android, the Pi, or both in the process.

Since that official Android built by Broadcom hasn't appeared yet, the working builds are based on CyanogenMod, a popular replacement firmware for Android-based phones and tablets. CyanogenMod isn't the only such replacement, but it is one of the most popular ones.

```
┌─────────────────────────────────────────────────────────────┐
│                    Another Odd Name                           │
│                                                               │
│  "Cyanogen" was the screen name of developer Steve Kondik,    │
│  whose re-placement firmware for the HTC Dream was built on   │
│  one by a developer who stopped work on his popular mod and   │
│  directed its users to Cyanogen's.                            │
└─────────────────────────────────────────────────────────────┘
```

The short way to go about this is to download one of the images that others have built and install it to your SD card. CyanogenMod 9 (based on Android 4.0)is so useless as to be considered unusable. Thus the available images are built on CyanogenMod 7.2 (based on Android 2.3).

If you're an Android phone or tablet user who enjoys CyanogenMod, you recognize that the current version is well past either of these.

The wiki describes this version as "Boots, very slow, barely usable." However, there are more than a few blog posts from people who enjoy it for some purpose or another, so don't let that deter you.

The bottom of the *main page of the Android Pi wiki* (*http://androidpi.wikia.com/wiki/Android_Pi_Wiki*) includes several download links. The first has notes that state it may or may not work only on Model A Raspberry Pis. We used `cm7_img_24-7-2012.tar.gz`, the image for CyanogenMod 7.2.

Download the ZIP file and extract the image using `dd`, replacing `/dev/mmcblk0` with the location of your SD card and the img filename with the correct one if you're using a different image:

```
$ dd bs=4M if=cm7_img_24-7-2012.img of=/dev/mmcblk0
```

Then put your SD card in the Pi, power it on, and you've got Android on Pi, as shown in Figure 2-13.

If you have never built Android (or Cyanogenmod, or perhaps anything else) before, you will need to install quite a few packages. You should also follow the steps in Hack #21 before proceeding.

Figure 2-13.
Android running on the Raspberry Pi

The *Android Pi wiki* (*http://androidpi.wikia.com/wiki/Android_Pi_Wiki*) offers a set of instructions for compiling CyanogenMod to run on your Raspberry Pi. We have run them several times on multiple systems with varied results—mostly of the negative sort. It's a learning exercise if this is unfamiliar territory for you, and that is always a worthwhile venture. We offer this information largely as fair warning to those who might get excited about the possibility but disappointed with the result.

Note that if you do want to compile CyanogenMod yourself for the Raspberry Pi on Fedora, you'll need a slightly different set of packages installed from the instructions on the wiki:

```
$ su -c 'yum install make curl gnupg git bison unzip zip flex gperf gcc-c++
libstdc++-devel glibc-devel.i686 zlib-devel.i686 ncurses-devel.i686 libX11-
devel.i686 mesa-libGL-devel.i686 readline-devel.i686'
```

Other than that, the build instructions are the same. Ideally you will end up with usable files you can flash to your SD card. Don't be too frustrated if it doesn't successfully finish—you're certainly not alone, and this is a complicated problem. Take what you've learned from the experience, and then if you still want to try Android on the Pi, simply use the image offered on the wiki.

3

Raspberry Pi Around the House

Your Raspberry Pi has one handy feature when it comes to household projects: its size. You can easily hide it in a wall or behind a piece of furniture or put it inside larger build projects like robots and costumes.

This chapter will give you ideas for using your Raspberry Pi for assorted projects around the house, from the practical (like Hack #31, printing from all your computers to one printer) to the simply fun (like Hack #35, using your Pi in your next Halloween costume).

HACK 30 Share Files with Samba

> We accept that there's a possibility not all of the computers in your house run Linux. Some might even use Windows (like that one used for PlayOn in Hack #54). In that case, this hack should help your systems communicate.

Samba is an open source suite of tools for SMB/CIFS clients. In plainspeak, it lets a Linux computer (like your Raspberry Pi) talk to a Windows machine as if it were a Windows file or print server.

SMB (Server Message Block) is a protocol for sharing files, printers, and assorted communications. CIFS (Common Internet File System) is the modern form of SMB. SMB was designed to run on the NetBIOS API and runs by default on versions of Windows since Windows 2000. Samba started as a project to reverse engineer SMB to allow users on Microsoft systems to access files on Sun systems.

Samba works by creating a network share for directories and subdirectories you choose on your Raspberry Pi. From your Windows machine, you can mount the share with smbmount, and they will look like networked Windows folders. There is also an smbclient utility that will feel like using an FTP program, if you're more comfortable with that method.

Samba requires two daemons, smbd for the sharing services and nmbd for the NetBIOS name requests, which are controlled by the smb service. (You can use a third daemon, winbindd, to help the Linux machine understand the Windows user and group information on Windows NT 2000 and Windows Server 2003 systems.)

Let's Samba!

Samba is also a Brazilian dance style popularized by Carmen Miranda, or as you may know her, "the person who inspired the Bugs Bunny cartoons in which he wears a hat made of fruit." Despite thorough experimentation on the authors' part, there is no evidence that dancing the samba with your Raspberry Pi will do anything but make you look silly.

The name was borrowed for the software we're discussing here by grepping a UNIX system's dictionary for words that had the letters S, M, and B. You can try this yourself by running `grep -i ^s.*m.*b /usr/share/dict/words`, although as of a *1998 message about the history of Samba* (*http://www.rxn.com/services/faq/smb/samba.history.txt*), creator Andrew Trigdell notes, "Strangely enough, when I repeat that now I notice that Samba isn't in /usr/dict/words on my system anymore!" We're just glad he didn't go with "Sulphmethemoglobin."

We'll assume you're using a USB external hard drive with your Raspberry Pi for this project (and it's likely you'll want to if you're bothering with Samba). If you're starting from scratch, consider formatting it as either FAT32 or NTFS (if you're borrowing it from a Windows machine, it probably already is). It's not really necessary, but it will be handy later if you decide to no longer use it with the Raspberry Pi and want to use that drive with the Windows machine.

Locate said drive (or USB flash drive or just the SD card—whatever you're intending to share):

```
$ fdisk -l
```

The output will look something like this:

```
Disk /dev/mmcblk0: 7822 MB, 7822376960 bytes
4 heads, 16 sectors/track, 238720 cylinders, total 15278080 sectors
Units = sectors of 1 * 512 = 512 bytes
Sector size (logical/physical): 512 bytes / 512 bytes
I/O size (minimum/optimal): 512 bytes / 512 bytes
Disk identifier: 0x000d4f0f

Device Boot Start End Blocks Id System
/dev/mmcblk0p1 4096 147455 71680 c W95 FAT32 (LBA)
```

```
/dev/mmcblk0p2 151552 15278079 7563264 83 Linux

Disk /dev/sda: 1037 MB, 1037041664 bytes
2 heads, 63 sectors/track, 16075 cylinders, total 2025472 sectors
Units = sectors of 1 * 512 = 512 bytes
Sector size (logical/physical): 512 bytes / 512 bytes
I/O size (minimum/optimal): 512 bytes / 512 bytes
Disk identifier: 0x0101bc87


Device Boot Start End Blocks Id System
/dev/sda1 * 32 2025471 1012720 6 FAT16
```

The first disk, /dev/mmcblk0, is the SD card in the Raspberry Pi. The second, /dev/
sda/, is a USB flash drive we put in one of the Pi's USB connections to use as the
example shared storage. Create a mount directory for the drive:

```
$ mkdir /mnt/PiShare
```

To see whether you were successful, run ls /mnt, and you should see PiSamba listed.

Open /etc/fstab in your favorite text editor, so you can tell it to connect to PiSamba
at boot:

```
$ sudo vi /etc/fstab
```

The contents of the file will look something like this:

```
#
# /etc/fstab
# Created by anaconda
#
# Accessible filesystems, by reference, are maintained under '/dev/disk'
# See man pages fstab(5), findfs(8), mount(8) and/or blkid(8) for more info
#
LABEL="rootfs"               /                         ext4    defaults,noa
time                1 1
LABEL="boot"                 /boot                     vfat    noauto,comment=sys
temd.automount 1 2
/swap0                       swap    swap
```

Add the following line at the bottom:

```
/dev/sda1 /mnt/PiShare vfat defaults 0 0
```

For the first part, use the device name you saw listed when you ran fdisk (in this
example, /dev/sda/). Be sure to change PiSamba if you used a different name for your
mount, and make ntfs-3g whatever type of hard drive format you used. Save the file,
exit, and mount the share:

```
$ mount -a
```

If you run `ls /mnt/`, you should see your files. If you don't, check your disk type in the line you added in `/etc/fstab`.

Samba is included with many Linux distributions and is set to start automatically. It is not, however, necessarily included with your Raspberry Pi Linux distribution. But that's easy to fix.

To install Samba on Pidora, run the following command:

```
$ sudo yum install samba
```

For Raspbian, run this one:

```
$ sudo apt-get install samba samba-common-bin
```

Once it's installed, the service will start automatically. The Samba configuration file lives in `/etc/samba/smb.conf`. Open it in your editor to get it set up for your particular needs.

If you're nervous about editing config files, create a backup first by running `cp /etc/samba/smb.conf /etc/samba/smb.conf.backup`*.*

It's also a well-commented file, so feel free to read it all to get a better feel for what you're doing:

```
$ sudo vi /etc/samba/smb.conf
```

At the bottom of the first large chunk of comments, you'll see this:

```
[global]
workgroup = WORKGROUP
#usershare allow guests = yes
#security=share
security=user
follow symlinks = yes
wide links = no
unix extensions = no
lock directory = /var/cache/samba

[pi]
browsable = yes
read only = no
#guest ok = yes
valid users = pi
path = /home/pi
```

```
#force user = pi (no longer needed)

[devices]
browsable = yes
read only = no
#guest ok = yes
valid users = pi
path = /media
force user = root
```

Add this to the bottom of the file:

```
[PiShare]
browsable = yes
read only = no
path = /mnt/PiShare
create mask = 0660
directory mask = 0771
```

Save the file, exit, and restart Samba. On Pidora, reboot the Samba service with:

```
$ su -c '/sbin/service smb restart'
```

On Raspbian, use:

```
$ su -c '/etc/init.d/samba restart'
```

Configure Samba Without the Command Line

If you're using Pidora, a package available for the GUI Samba Server Configuration Tool can modify the /etc/samba/ files for you. To install this tool, run:

```
$ su -c 'yum install system-config-samba'
```

You can start it from the command line by typing system-config-samba.

Now connect to your share from another machine. From Fedora, for example, use the Connect to Server dialog (similar dialogs exist in any Linux distribution or on OS X or Windows). The share address is smb:// followed by the IP address, a slash, and the name of your share, as shown in Figure 3-1.

Figure 3-1.
Fedora Connect to Server dialog

Finally, you'll be asked to log in. Use the information you set in /etc/samba/smb.conf, as shown in Figure 3-2.

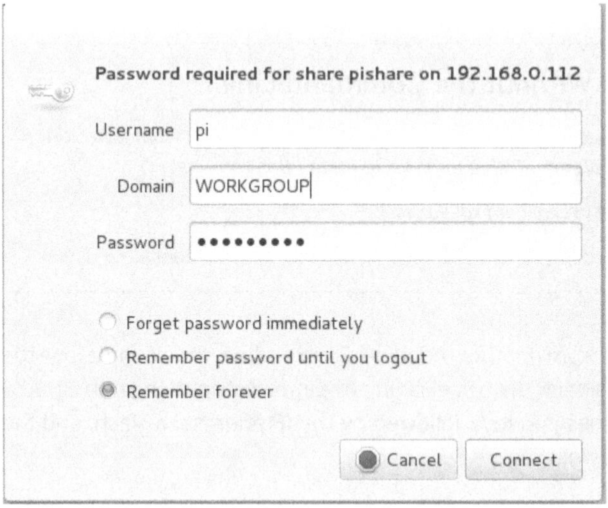

Figure 3-2.
Log into shared drive

Your drive is now shared and accessible from beyond your Pi.

HACK 31 Use Your Raspberry Pi as a Remote Print Server

You're never on the computer with the bulky, unsightly printer when you want to print something. The Raspberry Pi is small enough that you can hide your printer just about anywhere and let the Pi do the work of being a print server.

You might think it would be nice to hide the bulky printer out of sight, but you'll need to connect to it to actually print something. If you connect the printer to a discreet Pi running as a print server, you can connect to it from your primary computer remotely. You might even be able to find ways to mount the Pi on the back of the printer, or just tuck it away nearby. Either way, physically connect the printer cable to your Raspberry Pi, and let's get started!

The easiest and most logical way to turn your Raspberry Pi into a print server is to set up CUPS (the Common UNIX Printing System). It's another one of those things that's often included in a Linux distribution, but probably not with your Raspberry Pi distribution. That's what packages are for.

Install it on Pidora with the following command:

```
$ su -c 'yum install cups'
```

Or install it on Raspbian:

```
$ su -c 'apt-get install cups'
```

When you install CUPS, it creates a group called lpadmin whose members CUPS will authenticate:

```
$ su -c 'usermod -aG lpadmin user'
```

Replace user with the username that will be responsible for the printers. (Create one first if you prefer.)

Then you need to make a few changes to the CUPS configuration file in /etc/cups/cupsd.conf. It never hurts to make a backup before you go editing such things:

```
$ cp /etc/cups/cupsd.conf /etc/cups/cupsd.conf.backup
```

Open the configuration file in a text editor and comment out the line under "Only listen for connections from the local machine" that says Listen localhost:631. Then add the following line under it:

```
Listen 192.168.0.122:631
```

Change the first part to your Pi's IP address with :631 appended. (631 is the port that CUPS listens on.)

Under "Restrict access to the server...", add the following lines in bold, replacing the subnet with your own:

```
<Location />
Order allow,deny
Allow 192.168.0.
Allow Localhost
<Location>
```

Under "Restrict access to the admin pages...", add the following lines in bold, replacing the subnet with your own:

```
<Location /admin>
Order allow,deny
Allow 192.168.0.
Allow Localhost
<Location>
```

Under "Restrict access to configuration files...", add the following lines in bold, replacing the subnet with your own:

```
<Location /admin/conf>
AuthType Default
Require user @SYSTEM
Order allow,deny
Allow 192.168.0.
Allow Localhost
<Location>
```

Firewalling

Some Linux distributions come preconfigured with a iptables firewall for security. They do not usually have the CUPS ports (631 for TCP and UDP) open in the default configuration. Since you want to permit traffic to access the CUPS server through the firewall, you'll need to punch a hole. For Pidora and Raspbian, you can add these lines into /etc/sysconfig/iptables:

```
-A INPUT -i eth0 -p tcp -m tcp --dport 631 -j ACCEPT
-A INPUT -i eth0 -p udp -m udp --dport 631 -j ACCEPT
```

You can also edit the configuration file from within a web interface (see Figure 3-3) by opening a browser on the Pi (Midori is usually the included web browswer), going to *http://localhost:631/admin*, and selecting "Edit Configuration File" in the right column under Server.

RASPBERRY PI HACKS

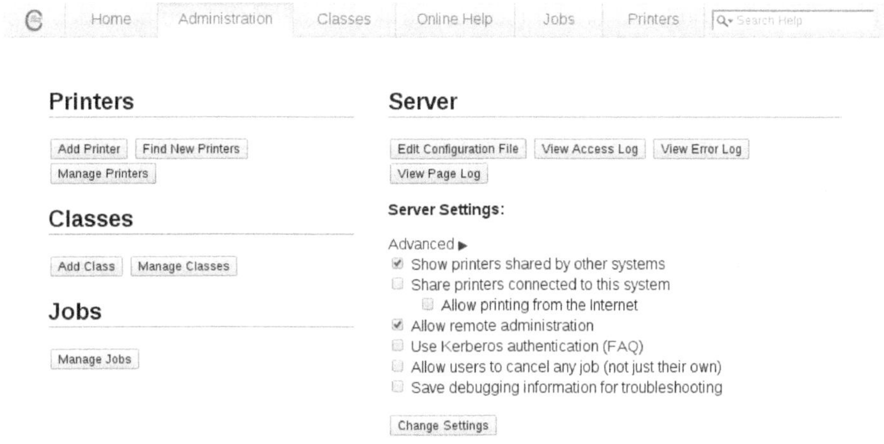

Printers

| Add Printer | Find New Printers |

| Manage Printers |

Classes

| Add Class | Manage Classes |

Jobs

| Manage Jobs |

Server

| Edit Configuration File | View Access Log | View Error Log |

| View Page Log |

Server Settings:

Advanced ▶
- ☑ Show printers shared by other systems
- ☐ Share printers connected to this system
    - ☐ Allow printing from the Internet
- ☑ Allow remote administration
- ☐ Use Kerberos authentication (FAQ)
- ☐ Allow users to cancel any job (not just their own)
- ☐ Save debugging information for troubleshooting

| Change Settings |

Figure 3-3.
The CUPS administration web portal

Once you've made those edits, restart CUPS:

```
$ su -c 'service cups restart'
```

Then use a web browser to go to *http://192.168.0.122:631*, replacing the first part with your Pi's IP address. (This can be on the Pi, your laptop, or any machine within the subnet.) Choose the Administration tab, and select Add Printer.

When you're asked for a username and password, enter the information for the user you added to the `lpadmin` group. On the Add Printer page (Figure 3-4), choose your printer from the list under Local Printers.

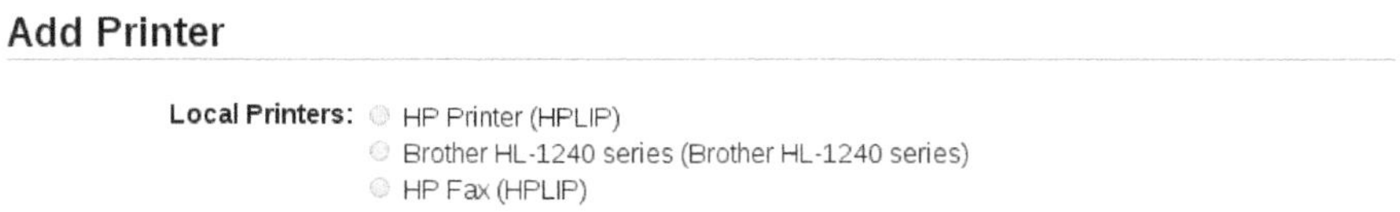

Add Printer

Local Printers: ○ HP Printer (HPLIP)
○ Brother HL-1240 series (Brother HL-1240 series)
○ HP Fax (HPLIP)

Figure 3-4.
The Add Printer configuration page

> In the list shown in Figure 3-4, you see three printers. The two HPLIP devices are actually just printer drivers from the HP Linux Imaging and Printing (http://hpli-popensource.com/hplip-web/index.html) project.

You'll be asked to add or edit the name, description, and location of the printer. If you would like to, enable Share This Printer.

In the next step, you'll be asked to choose the printer driver. You can scroll through the list until you find your printer (several are likely marked as "recommended"), or you can browse to a PPD file that you have from your printer's manufacturer for the driver.

Finally, you're offered the chance to set some generic print settings, like page size and source. When you're finished setting your preferences, click Set Default Options, and you'll be back to the main administration page for that printer.

If you haven't already, move to another machine on the network and get it ready to print. Use that particular computer's printer settings system (see Figure 3-5 for Fedora) to add a printer and select the one that you've just set up.

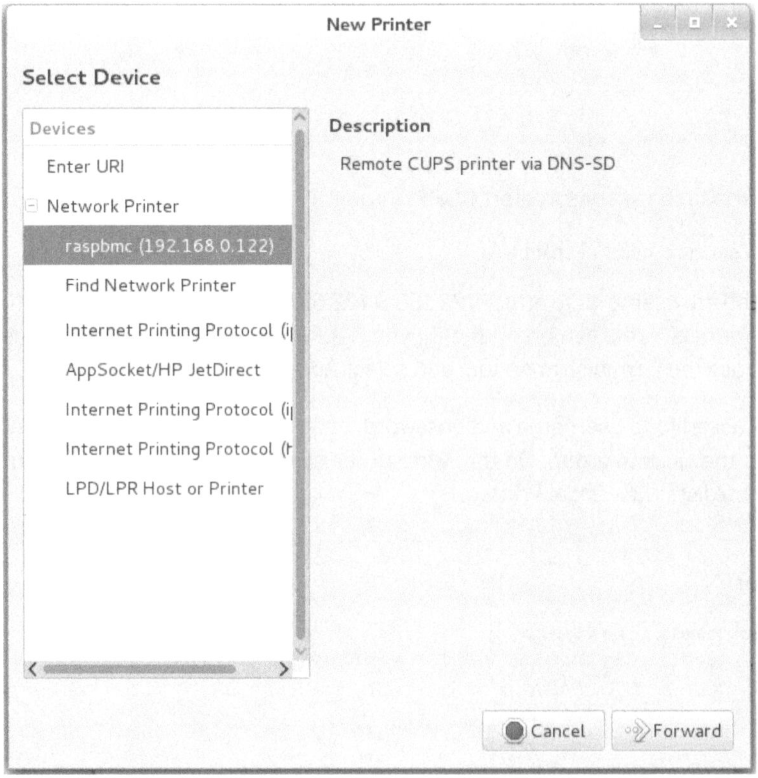

Figure 3-5.
Fedora New Printer setup dialog

Print a test page, and you're finished!

Make Calls with a Raspberry Pi Asterisk Telephone System

Asterisk is a telephone system in software. It is typically used to bridge callers together, or offer up features such as voicemail or call queues. Because it's built totally in software, you can run it on your Raspberry Pi.

Because the Raspberry Pi doesn't have any sort of analog telephone connections, setting up Asterisk means using a technology called *voice over IP* (VoIP) to communicate on the Raspberry Pi. You'll use a computer program called a *softphone*, together with a microphone and speakers, to emulate a telephone. The softphone will then communicate across the network to Asterisk running on the Raspberry Pi.

For more information on Asterisk, check out the Asterisk website (http:// www.asterisk.org) or Asterisk: The Definitive Guide *from O'Reilly Media.*

Installing Asterisk

Installing Asterisk is fairly simple, as most modern Linux distributions have packages rebuilt for Asterisk. On Pidora, just run the following command:

```
$ su -c 'yum install asterisk asterisk-voicemail-plain asterisk-sounds-core-
en-gsm'
```

Here's the command to run on Raspbian:

```
$ su -c 'aptitude install asterisk asterisk-config asterisk-core-sounds-en-
gsm'
```

This will install Asterisk with a basic configuration, common features such as voicemail, as well as some sound prompts. Feel free to search your distribution's package list for additional Asterisk modules.

This hack uses a VoIP protocol called SIP to communicate between one or more softphones and Asterisk. Getting SIP working through a firewall (especially a NAT firewall) is difficult and beyond the scope of this hack. In order for your connections to work, you'll need to turn off the firewall, so that it doesn't block connection attempts.

Don't leave your Raspberry Pi connected to the Internet with the firewall disabled, because someone will likely attempt to try to break into your Raspberry Pi. This is especially imporant if you haven't changed the password on your Raspberry Pi from the defaults. We suggest you turn off the firewall on your Raspberry Pi only long enough to test out things, and then turn it back on.

Starting Asterisk

Once Asterisk has been installed, you'll need to start the Asterisk process. You can start it with the `initscripts`, or simply type (as root):

```
$ asterisk
```

This should start Asterisk running in the background. After Asterisk is running in the background, you can connect to the running Asterisk system with the following command:

```
$ asterisk -r
```

If for some reason Asterisk isn't starting on your system, you can start it in console mode:

```
$ asterisk -c
```

Be aware that running it in console mode is recommended only for debugging purposes, because as soon as you exit out of the console, Asterisk stops running.

You can also increase the verbosity level of the Asterisk command prompt by supplying one or more -v arguments to Asterisk, like this:

```
$ asterisk -vvvr
```

This example sets the verbosity level to three, if it wasn't already three or higher. At verbosity level three, Asterisk tells you about every step it executes in its dialing plan, so it's a nice level to use when you're learning Asterisk.

When you successfully connected to the Asterisk process, you should be greeted with a prompt that looks something like this:

```
Asterisk 1.8.23.1, Copyright (C) 1999 - 2013 Digium, Inc. and others.
Created by Mark Spencer <markster@digium.com>
Asterisk comes with ABSOLUTELY NO WARRANTY; type 'core show warranty' for
details.
This is free software, with components licensed under the GNU General Public
License version 2 and other licenses; you are welcome to redistribute it un
der
certain conditions. Type 'core show license' for details.
=========================================================================
Connected to Asterisk 1.8.23.1 currently running on hockey (pid = 23801)
Verbosity was 0 and is now 3
hockey*CLI>
```

In this example, we're running Asterisk version 1.8.23.1 on a computer named "hockey."

Did you notice the last line ends in *CLI>? This is the prompt for the Asterisk command-line interface (CLI), and it is the primary tool for interacting with the Asterisk system and debugging within Asterisk. Before going any futher, here are a few commands to help you feel comfortable.

To see how long Asterisk has been running, type:

```
*CLI> core show uptime

hockey*CLI> core show uptime
System uptime: 55 seconds
Last reload: 55 seconds
```

Most commands in the Asterisk CLI follow the "subsection-verb-details" model, where the first word of the command tells which part of the system you want to interact with (core in this case, which is a verb to tell Asterisk what you'd like to do: show), and then any other details the system needs to know in order to perform the action.

To stop Asterisk immediately, type:

```
*CLI> core stop now
```

You can also use core stop when convenient to have Asterisk stop the next time there are no active calls on the system, or core stop gracefully to reject any new calls, and then shut down the system when the call volume reaches zero. Don't shut down Asterisk just yet (unless you'd like to practice stopping it and starting it again just to get a feel for it).

The Asterisk CLI also has built-in help (type help at the CLI) and tab-completion. For an example, type help and then press the TAB key twice before - -, and you'll see that the Asterisk CLI shows you all the possibile commands that begin with "help."

Setting Up a Softphone

There are three steps to setting up a softphone with Asterisk. The first is to configure an account within Asterisk for the phone to connect to. Second, you'll need to configure the softphone itself to connect to Asterisk. And finally, you'll need to set up a list of instructions (called a *dialing plan* or *dialplan*) that Asterisk should follow when a particular extension is dialed.

Configure an SIP account

To set up an account for the softphone, you'll first need to find the configuration file for the type of connection you'll be using. Asterisk speaks a number of different voice over IP protocols, but the most popular one is SIP, so that's what this example will use.

To add an account for your SIP softphone, add the following lines to the very bottom of /etc/asterisk/sip.conf:

```
[one]
type=friend
host=dynamic
secret=cHaNgEmEpLeAsE!
context=raspi-demo
```

The first line (in square brackets) is the name of the account. The type line tells it what kind of a device you're talking to. This example uses the friend type, because that means that the softphone can call Asterisk and that Asterisk can also call the softphone.

The host line says that the IP address assigned to the softphone isn't known (or might change at any moment), so instead of hardcoding an IP address, the softphone will periodically tell Asterisk where it is. This is called *registration* (covered in more detail in the next section).

The secret setting is the password on this account. Pick a different password, and make it long and difficult to guess. Last, the context setting tells the system which part of the dialplan to execute when a call comes from the softphone.

Once you've added these lines to the sip.conf configuration file, you'll need to tell Asterisk to reload that configuration file. From the Asterisk CLI, type:

```
$*CLI> sip reload
```

You can then use the sip show peers command to see which SIP accounts you have configured:

```
hockey*CLI> sip show peers
Name/username            Host                               Dyn
Forcerport ACL Port      Status
one                       (Unspecified)                      D
N            0           Unmonitored
1 sip peers [Monitored: 0 online, 0 offline Unmonitored: 0 online, 1 off
line]
```

Did you notice that the host says (Unspecified)? This means that the softphone hasn't registered with Asterisk yet, so we don't know where to find the softphone to send messages to it. We'll rectify that shortly.

Register your SIP client

Next, you'll need to use a SIP softphone to be able to connect to Asterisk for testing. There are a number of free SIP softphones available. I prefer Blink for Mac and Windows, Twinkle on Linux, and CSipSimple on Android.

While configuring each of these softphones is beyond the scope of this hack, the basics are the same. Simply configure the softphone with one as the username (and auth username, if it's required by your softphone), cHaNgEmEpLeAsE! as the password (or the new password you entered in the secret setting in sip.conf), and the IP address of your Raspberry Pi for the SIP server, registrar, domain, proxy, and/or outbound proxy settings.

Once your softphone has registered, you should be able to run sip show peers from the Asterisk CLI again and see that the Host field now shows an IP address, like this:

```
hockey*CLI> sip show peers
Name/username         Host                              Dyn
Forcerport ACL Port    Status
one/one                192.168.55.187                    D
N          7060        Unmonitored
1 sip peers [Monitored: 0 online, 0 offline Unmonitored: 1 online, 0 off
line]
```

If you're having problems getting your softphone to register, double-check that you've (temporarily) disabled the firewall on the Raspberry Pi. For simplicity's sake, you should use a softphone within the same network as your Raspberry Pi, as the SIP protocol is notoriously difficult to use when it has to pass through a firewall or router.

You can also watch the Asterisk CLI closely when the softphone attempts to register, as it will often give you useful information (such as telling you that the password provided by the softphone doesn't match the password in the sip.conf configuration file).

Set up an extension in the dialplan

The final step is to set up one or more extensions in the dialplan to execute when that extension is dialed by the softphone. If you were to dial extension 100 on the softphone at this point, you would likely get back a 404: Extension not found error. The Asterisk CLI would report something like this:

```
NOTICE[24237]: chan_sip.c:23437 handle_request_invite: Call from 'one'
(192.168.55.187:7060) to extension '100' rejected because extension not
found in context 'raspi-demo'.
```

In order to make extension 100 do something a bit more useful, you need to add a new section to the /etc/asterisk/extensions.conf configuration file. This section name needs to match the context setting from our account in the sip.conf configuration file. In this case, call it [raspi-demo].

Add the following lines to the end of /etc/asterisk/extensions.conf:

```
[raspi-demo]
exten => 100,1,Answer()
```

```
exten => 100,2,Playback(hello-world)
exten => 100,3,Playback(tt-weasels)
exten => 100,4,Hangup()
```

Let's walk through each line quickly, and then try it out. The first line (in square brackets) is the name of the context, which is an independent section of the dialplan. Extension 100 in the [raspi-demo] context is independent from extension 100 in another context, such as [not-my-demo]. Contexts are often used to keep different clients isolated from parts of the dialplan, or to provide different features to different clients.

The second line defines an extension (100, in this case) and a priority (or step number, which is 1 in this case) and says that the first thing extension 100 should do is to call the Answer() application. This application, as its name implies, answers the call.

Note that the priority numbers must be in numerical order, and should not skip any numbers. For example, if Asterisk executes priority number three and can't find a priority number four, it will simply hang up the call for security reasons.

The next line (priority 2), calls the Playback() application, which plays a prerecorded sound file in which you'll hear a female voice say "Hello, World." The next line (priority 3) also plays a sound file, which tells you that "Weasels have eaten our phone system." The last line calls the Hangup() application, which ends the call.

The parameter to the Playback() application is the name of the sound file to play, without the extension. Asterisk is smart enough to choose the best sound prompt format to play if there are multiple files with the same name but in different formats. It chooses the format that requires the least amount of CPU power to transcode (or convert) to the current audio format of the call.

Once you've added those five lines to the end of your extensions.conf configuration file, you'll need to tell Asterisk to reload the dialplan. To do this, go to the Asterisk CLI and type dialplan reload.

To test that your new [raspi-demo] context has been successfully read and parsed, type:

```
hockey*CLI> dialplan show raspi-demo
[ Context 'raspi-demo' created by 'pbx_config' ]
   '100' =>          1. Answer()
[pbx_config]
                     2. Playback(hello-world)
[pbx_config]
                     3. Playback(tt-weasels)
```

```
[pbx_config]
                    4. Hangup()
[pbx_config]


-= 1 extension (4 priorities) in 1 context. =-
```

Now's the time for the big test! From your softphone, dial 100, and listen for Asterisk to play the sound prompts.

We're only scratching the surface with the most basic of applications here. For a full list of the dialplan applications you can use in your dialplan, type `core show applications` *at the Asterisk CLI.*

Of course, there's much more that you can do with Asterisk on your Raspberry Pi, including implementing call menus, voicemail, allowing clients to call each other, and so forth. Now that you've learned the basics, you can dive into all the wonderful things that Asterisk can do. And don't forget to turn your firewall back on when you're done!

—Jared Smith

HACK 33   Build Your Own Web Server

From kids with creative urges to grown-ups with pet projects, wanting your own website is a common desire. Having a Raspberry Pi makes it easy to set up your own web server, whether it's for your blog or a web interface for interacting with a larger Pi project.

There are as many reasons to want a web server as there are websites. We'll cover two options: first, how to set up your own blog on a Raspberry Pi; second, getting started with a development environment called Coder that helps you learn the basic building blocks of the web: HTML, JavaScript, Cascading Style Sheets (CSS), and Node.JS.

Set Up a Basic Blog Server

There are hundreds of millions of blogs out there. Why not let your Pi add a voice to the chorus? The easiest way to get your Pi online and yourself blogging is by setting up the LAMP stack: Linux, Apache (web server), MySQL (database), and PHP. Together they give you a base on which you can run WordPress, one of the most popular blogging platforms.

By setting up a distro on your Pi, you already have the L down, so let's move to the A. Here's how to install Apache on Pidora:

```
$ su -c 'yum install httpd mod_ssl'
```

And here's the command for Raspbian:

```
$ su -c 'apt-get install apache2'
```

The detail of possibilities for using and configuring Apache are well beyond the scope of this book, but also well documented elsewhere. We recommend starting with the online documentation (http://httpd.apache.org/docs). If you're interested in a book, try Apache Cookbook *(O'Reilly), or for a broader introduction to web development,* Beginning PHP5, Apache, and MySQL Web Development *(O'Reilly).*

Next you'll need to install MySQL, PHP, and the PHP gd module (required by Word-Press). Here's the command for Pidora:

```
$ su -c 'yum install mysql mysql-server'
$ su -c 'yum install php php-mysql php-gd'
```

And here's the command for Raspbian:

```
$ su -c 'apt-get install mysql-server'
$ su -c 'apt-get install php php-mysql php-gd'
```

Start the MySQL daemon and Apache, on Pidora:

```
$ su -c 'systemctl start mysqld.service'
$ su -c 'systemctl start httpd'
```

or on Raspbian:

```
$ su -c 'service start mysqld'
```

Then ensure that they will both start on their own in the future, on Pidora:

```
$ su -c 'chkconfig mysqld on'
$ su -c 'chkconfig httpd on'
```

or on Raspbian:

```
$ su -c 'update-rc.d mysqld enable'
$ su -c 'update-rc.d httpd enable'
```

Then set up the installation:

```
$ su -c '/usr/bin/mysql_secure_installation'
```

You'll be asked to set a root password and several other settings, which are well described by the script along with recommended choices. If all goes well, at the end you'll see:

```
Cleaning up...
```

All done! If you've completed all of these steps, your MySQL installation should now be secure:

```
Thanks for using MySQL!
```

For WordPress, you'll need a database and a user. Log in to MySQL using the root password you just set up:

```
$ mysql -u root -p
```

Then create your database and user. Replace piblogger with whatever you'd like your database to be named and ian with the user who will be in charge of it (and it should go without saying that mypassword is a terrible password choice that you should change):

```
mysql> CREATE DATABASE piblogger;
Query OK, 1 row affected (0.00 sec)

mysql> CREATE USER 'ian'@'localhost' IDENTIFIED BY 'mypassword';
Query OK, 0 rows affected (0.00 sec)

mysql> GRANT ALL PRIVILEGES ON * . * to 'ian'@'localhost';
Query OK, 0 rows affected (0.00 sec)

mysql> FLUSH PRIVILEGES;
Query OK, 0 rows affected (0.00 sec)

mysql> EXIT
```

Download the latest WordPress tarball from *https://wordpress.org/latest.tar.gz* or:

```
$ wget https://wordpress.org/latest.tar.gz
```

Extract the tarball into the public HTML folder:

```
$ sudo tar -xvzf latest.tar.gz -C /var/www/html
```

This will create a directory called wordpress in /var/www/html. Next you need to set up the config file:

```
$ vi /var/www/html/wordpress/wp-config-sample.php
```

The things you need to configure are at the top of the file, and the parts you need to fill in are in all caps:

```
// ** MySQL settings - You can get this info from your web host ** //
/** The name of the database for WordPress */
define('DB_NAME', 'piblogger');

/** MySQL database username */
```

```
define('DB_USER', 'ian');

/** MySQL database password */
define('DB_PASSWORD', 'mypassword');

/** MySQL hostname */
define('DB_HOST', 'localhost');

/** Database Charset to use in creating database tables. */
define('DB_CHARSET', 'utf8');

/** The Database Collate type. Don't change this if in doubt. */
define('DB_COLLATE', '');
```

Finally, change the name of the sample config to config.php. We like to save a copy of the sample until everything's running properly, so for now:

```
$ cp /var/www/html/wordpress/wp-config-sample.php var/www/html/wordpress/wp-
config.php
```

When your site is running as you would like, delete wp-config-sample.php.

Now, when you go to the site in a browser (by default it's at /wordpress after a domain if you've registered one, or your IP address if you haven't). It's only a one-page setup (see Figure 3-6), after which you can add one more voice to the blogosphere.

Figure 3-6.
The one-page WordPress web-based setup

You can now log into your WordPress dashboard and start configuring its themes and posting. Learn more about how to use all of its features at *http://codex.wordpress.org*.

Use Coder for Your Website

Coder (http://goo.gl/coder) is a tool created by Jason Striegel in the Google Creative Lab as a way to teach kids basic web programming using the Raspberry Pi. It doesn't have that kid-program feel, though, so if you're an adult who's never tried learning HTML, CSS, or JavaScript, it's handy for you as well.

On the Coder website, you'll find a ZIP file with an installer for Mac users and instructions for using it with Windows. However, there are not any instructions for using it with Linux. To do so, download the Coder ZIP file, which contains a folder (at the time of this writing, `coder_v0.4`) within which you'll find two files: `CoderSetup.app` and `raspi.img`. The latter is all you need. Extract it and then use a tool like Fedora-arm-installer or `dd` from the command line to flash the image to your SD card:

```
$ sudo dd bs=4M if=raspi.img of=/dev/mmcblk0
```

> ## Fedora ARM Installer
>
> The Fedora ARM Installer is a convenient tool for flashing your SD card images if you're less-than-comfortable with the command line. You don't have to use it for Fedora or Pidora images; it will work with any image you want to flash to the Pi. If you're on Fedora, you can install it with `yum install fedora-arm-installer`. For other systems, you can download it at *http://fedoraproject.org/wiki/Fedora_ARM_Installer*.

Boot the Pi with your newly flashed SD card, and you'll see the Raspbian raspi-config screen. You don't need to change anything, although you probably want to resize the partition (option 1, `expand_rootfs`). Then select `Finish` and reboot.

Now move back to your Linux machine and open Chrome or Chromium and go to *https://coder.local* in the browser. You'll be welcomed to Coder, and all you have to do for setup is choose a password (Figure 3-7).

Figure 3-7.
Coder setup screen

One of the first blocks you see is "Hello Coder," which helps you explore how Coder works. The edit button is represented by the `</>` symbol at the upper right of the page. If you click it in Hello Coder, you find pages that give you a brief introduction to HTML, CSS, JavaScript, and Node.JS through tabs across the top of the screen.

Coder also offers two prebuilt apps, Space Rocks! and Eyeball, whose code you can explore and edit to see how they were built (which is perhaps the best way to learn how code works). You see their blocks on the home page when you start as well.

Once you enter one of these, you have two choices in the upper-right menu. You can click HACK to quickly edit a few settings to see how they affect the app (see Figure 3-8). You can also click the Coder edit button (`</>`) to edit all of the code behind them. In either case, you see the code on the left and the results on the right each time you click the Save button.

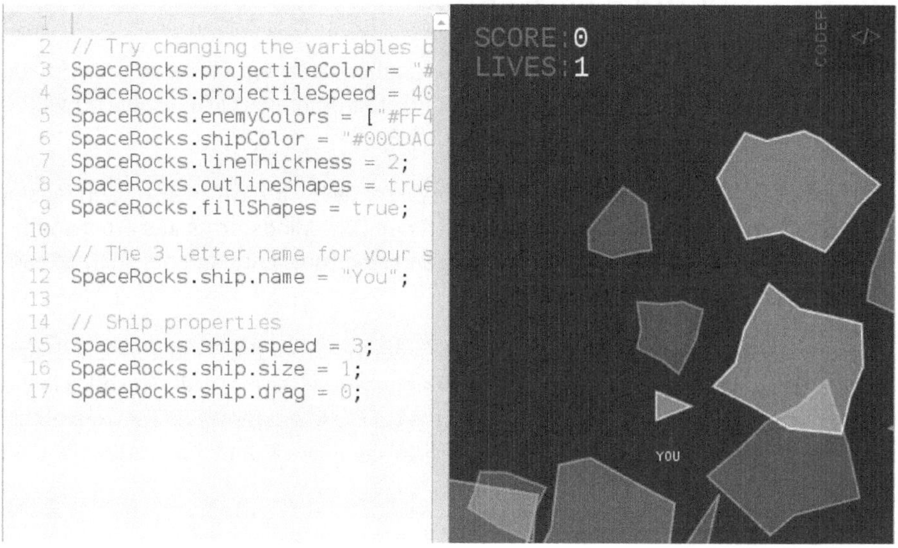

```
 1  |
 2  // Try changing the variables b
 3  SpaceRocks.projectileColor = "#
 4  SpaceRocks.projectileSpeed = 40
 5  SpaceRocks.enemyColors = ["#FF4
 6  SpaceRocks.shipColor = "#00CDAC
 7  SpaceRocks.lineThickness = 2;
 8  SpaceRocks.outlineShapes = true
 9  SpaceRocks.fillShapes = true;
10
11  // The 3 letter name for your s
12  SpaceRocks.ship.name = "You";
13
14  // Ship properties
15  SpaceRocks.ship.speed = 3;
16  SpaceRocks.ship.size = 1;
17  SpaceRocks.ship.drag = 0;
```

SCORE:0
LIVES:1

YOU

Figure 3-8.
The Space Rocks! HACK screen

Finally, when you're ready to go on your own, you click the green rectangle on the Coder homepage with a + sign in the middle and start creating your own app by naming it and giving it a color for its block on your Coder homepage. Once you've created it, at first all you'll see is a basic web page. Click the Coder edit button (</>) in the upper right to start creating from scratch (Figure 3-9).

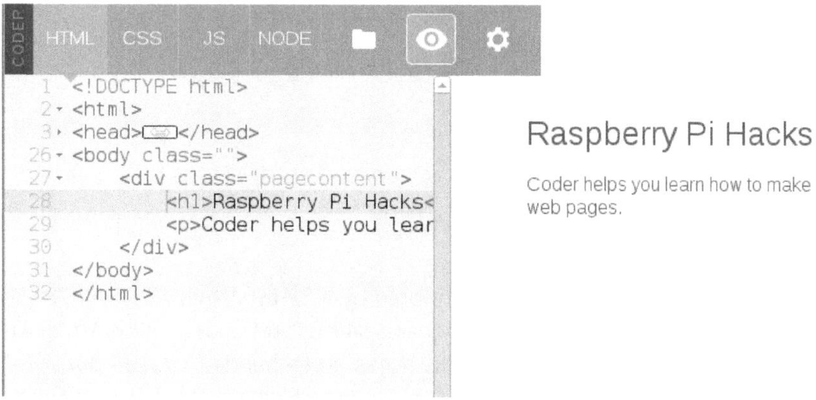

```
HTML    CSS    JS    NODE

 1  <!DOCTYPE html>
 2  <html>
 3  <head>▭</head>
26  <body class="">
27      <div class="pagecontent">
28          <h1>Raspberry Pi Hacks<
29          <p>Coder helps you lear
30      </div>
31  </body>
32  </html>
```

Raspberry Pi Hacks

Coder helps you learn how to make web pages.

Figure 3-9.
Creating your own web page and apps in Coder

You can click the small, vertical word CODER at the top of any screen to return to the home page and edit or create more apps.

Control a LEGO Robot

What could be cooler than a functioning, programmable robot made from LEGO bricks? A functioning, programmable LEGO robot connected to and controlled by a Raspberry Pi.

We love LEGO. Possibly more than our kids do (or ever will). We've also been fans of the LEGO Mindstorms kits for a long time. The LEGO Mindstorms kits are a combination of LEGO (and Technic-style) bricks and electronic components such as sensors, motors, and a programmable brick.

The brick is especially notable because it is the "brain" of the Mindstorms set, and you can program it directly to control the peripheral devices in the kit. The brick in the most recent version of the LEGO Mindstorms (LEGO Mindstorms NXT 2.0, as of this writing) is, unsurprisingly, called the NXT Intelligent Brick, and it's pretty cool (see Figure 3-10).

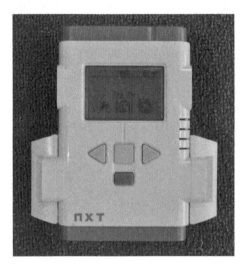

Figure 3-10.
NXT Intelligent Brick

At its core, the NXT Intelligent Brick is powered by a 32-bit Atmel AT91SAM7S256 microcontroller (with 256 KB flash memory and 64 KB RAM) and an 8-bit Atmel ATmega48 microcontroller running at 4 MHz. It has an embedded 100x64 pixel LCD screen (controlled by push buttons below it) with support for four input devices (ports 1–4) and three output devices (ports A–C).

It also supports both Bluetooth and USB connections, which is important because, while you can program the brick itself to operate the attached devices for the robot (with simple programs), you can also control the brick directly via USB, and that is exactly how you'll do it in this hack.

The LEGO Mindstorms NXT 2.0 kit comes with a lot of Windows software to control and program the brick, and there are some official (and unofficial) bindings for a wide array of languages. The official Windows software will obviously not run on a Raspberry Pi, but there is a software suite that does: ROS.

Installing ROS and Dependencies

ROS (short for *robot operating system*) is an open source suite of software that provides libraries and tools to help software developers create robot-related applications, including hardware abstraction, device drivers, libraries, visualizers, message-passing, and package management. It was originally developed by the Stanford Artificial Intelligence Laboratory, but that work has spun off into a company called Willow Garage, a robotics research institute and incubator. The goal is to provide a level of open source standardization on the application programming interface (API) for robotics so that a consistent set of software can be used on any type of robotic component with minimal new software necessary and the common functionality shared.

This is a thriving effort with an active community that regularly puts out major, named releases. We'll start by installing the current stable release, as of the time of this writing: Groovy Galapagos (*Groovy*, for short).

NXT Intelligent Brick Firmware

The ROS nxt *component software requires the NXT Intelligent Brick to be running a recent version of the default LEGO firmware (v1.28 or newer). To do this, you'll need to have a Windows (or OS X) system with the LEGO Mindstorms software installed and the NXT Intelligent Brick connected. Run the software, and go into the Tools → Update NXT Firmware menu option. You might need to download the NXT firmware files (http://mindstorms.lego.com/en-us/support/files/firmware.aspx) manually.*

There is also a way to flash the NXT firmware from Linux. Download and install libnxt *(http://code.google.com/p/libnxt) and use the* fwflash *executable.*

Start with a clean installation of Raspbian.

There are two ways to install ROS: from prebuilt binary packages or from source. While it is certainly possible to install ROS from source on a Raspberry Pi, it takes far too long. Instead, using a community repository of ROS packages optimized for the Raspberry Pi will significantly speed up the time it takes to install ROS. To enable this APT repository of packages (called ROSpbian), run:

```
$ sudo echo "deb http://64.91.227.57/repos/rospbian wheezy main" > /etc/apt/
sources.list.d/rospbian.list
```

Then add the package signing key (for package verification) and reload the `apt` package data:

```
$ wget http://64.91.227.57/repos/rospbian.key -O - | sudo apt-key add -
--2013-08-27 19:31:41--  http://64.91.227.57/repos/rospbian.key
Connecting to 64.91.227.57:80... connected.
HTTP request sent, awaiting response... 200 OK
Length: 1739 (1.7K) [application/pgp-keys]
Saving to: `STDOUT'

100%
[===========================================================================
=================================>] 1,739        --.-K/s   in 0s

2013-08-27 19:31:41 (20.2 MB/s) - written to stdout [1739/1739]

OK
$ sudo apt-get update
```

Now you can install ROS packages from the ROSpbian repository. The `ros_comm` components are a good starter package, because they will pull in all of the core ROS components and tools as dependencies and install everything in one pass:

```
$ sudo apt-get install ros-groovy-ros-comm ros-groovy-rosbuild
```

It will take a little while to complete. When it finishes, you'll need to configure your user account to enable the ROS environment by default. ROS includes a bash script containing a number of environment variables (and amendments to $PATH) so that you can run ROS commands. Make sure your account sources this file (in bash, `source` is roughly analogous to using `#include` in a C program).

To source the ROM environment every time you log in (or instantiate a bash shell), you need to add it to the `.bashrc` file in that user's home directory:

```
$ echo "source /opt/ros/groovy/setup.bash" >> ~/.bashrc
```

You also want root to be aware of the ROS environment, so do the same for the root user. Use `sudo` and `su` - together to switch to a root user session, then run the command again to source `/opt/ros/groovy/setup.bash` during `.bashrc`:

```
$ sudo su -
$ echo "source /opt/ros/groovy/setup.bash" >> /root/.bashrc
$ exit
```

Now you're ready to download and prepare the ROS components for the NXT Mindstorms. As mentioned before, the ROS software provides a framework of standardized components, but each specific robotic device needs a module (or modules) to support its specific quirks. NXT Mindstorms requires the `nxt` family of modules. Max Sieber forked off a copy of the `nxt` codebase to add support for the Groovy ROS and the Raspberry Pi, but it needed some additional patches to build properly. We've forked a copy of his work and added fixes. Clone a copy of our GitHub repository to work with:

```
$ sudo apt-get install git
$ git clone https://github.com/spotrh/nxt
```

ROS is very, very picky about where its files live on the filesystem, so you need to move your `nxt` checkout to the proper location:

```
$ sudo mv nxt /opt/ros/groovy/share/
```

If you do not move the `nxt` "stack" into that ROS directory, none of the ROS tools will find it.

You'll need to set up Raspbian to give permission for the `pi` user to communicate with the NXT Intelligent Brick as a normal user (rather than using root). To do this, start by adding the `lego` group:

```
$ sudo groupadd lego
```

Then add yourself to that group:

```
$ sudo usermod -a -G lego <username>
```

The value for `<username>` is either the default `pi` username in Raspbian or a custom user, if you have created one.

Next, set up `udev` rules to allow any users in the `lego` group to have read/write access to the NXT Intelligent Brick. The `nxt/70-lego.rules` file contains prewritten rules, so you just need to copy it into the udev rules directory:

```
$ sudo cp -a nxt/70-lego.rules /etc/udev/rules.d/70-lego.rules
```

Then restart `udev` to make the new rules take effect:

```
$ sudo service udev restart
```

Locale Handling in Raspbian

Raspbian defaults to a locale setting of en_GB.UTF-8. You might encounter weird errors if you're actually trying to communicate from en_US.UTF-8 (or any other UTF-8 locale that isn't en_GB). ROS does this sometimes. Specifically, this sort of thing:

```
terminate called after throwing an instance of 'std::runtime_error'
  what():  locale::facet::_S_create_c_locale name not valid
Aborted
```

This error is caused because the en_US.UTF-8 (or other requested) locale does not exist. The easiest way to fix this is by running `dpkg-reconfigure`:

```
$ sudo dpkg-reconfigure locales
```

This loads a text interface to configure additional locales on Raspbian. Either select "All locales" (this will eat up some disk space), or scroll down with the arrow keys and select `en_US.UTF-8 UTF-8` (or any other locales relevant to you). On the next screen, set the proper default language/locale for you. It will regenerate the locale files, reset the `LC_*` environment variables, and resolve this issue.

Normally, you'd build your ROS stack here, but it is worth noting that ROS is migrating away from stacks. The ROS NXT code is still configured to use stacks, as opposed to using `catkin`, which is the tool that most of the Groovy ROS prefers. As a result, you'll need to install some additional `nxt` dependencies manually (it doesn't help that the ROSpbian repository is missing a lot of `catkinized` components, too):

```
$ sudo apt-get install ros-groovy-geometry-msgs ros-groovy-nav-msgs ros-
groovy-sensor-msgs \
   ros-groovy-visualization-msgs ros-groovy-tf ros-groovy-image-transport
ros-groovy-laser-geometry \
   ros-groovy-python-qt-binding ros-groovy-urdfdom ros-groovy-rosconsole-
bridge ros-groovy-image-geometry \
   libcurl4-openssl-dev libxml2-dev ros-groovy-geometric-shapes libassimp-
dev ros-groovy-orocos-kdl \
   libogre-dev libyaml-cpp-dev python-wxgtk2.8 wx2.8-headers libwxgtk2.8-dev
ros-groovy-tf-conversions \
   python-usb ros-groovy-python-orocos-kdl
```

This will take a few minutes to complete.

Next, you'll need to build `collada-dom` from source. The COLLADA Document Object Model (DOM) is an API that provides a C++ object representation of a COLLADA XML instance document. The COLLADA format is used for interactive 3D applications, and ROS uses it.

Download and unpack a copy of the `collada-dom` *source tarball from SourceForge* (*http://sourceforge.net/projects/collada-dom/files/latest/download*):

```
$ sudo mkdir /opt/ros/collada
$ cd /opt/ros/collada
$ sudo wget http://downloads.sourceforge.net/project/collada-dom/Collada
%20DOM/Collada%20DOM%202.4/collada-dom-2.4.0.tgz
$ sudo tar xf collada-dom-2.4.0.tgz
```

Make a `build` directory within the source directory and build and install the `collada-dom` code:

```
$ cd collada-dom-2.4.0
$ sudo mkdir build
$ cd build
$ sudo cmake ..
$ sudo make
$ sudo make install
```

That will take several hours to build on the Raspberry Pi. Once it has finished, you need to build a newer version of `assimp`.

Assimp is the library short name for the Open Asset Import Library, which provides support for a variety of 3D file formats. You might have noticed that you installed `libassimp-dev` as a dependency, but the version packaged in Raspbian does not work properly with the `collada` code in ROS. Never fear, you just need to build a newer version from source code to replace it (you still want to install the `libassimp-dev` package, to keep all the `dpkg` dependencies are happy):

```
$ cd ~
$ git clone https://github.com/assimp/assimp
Cloning into 'assimp'...
remote: Counting objects: 17035, done.
remote: Compressing objects: 100% (4368/4368), done.
remote: Total 17035 (delta 12579), reused 16717 (delta 12293)
Receiving objects: 100% (17035/17035), 60.56 MiB | 594 KiB/s, done.
Resolving deltas: 100% (12579/12579), done.
Checking out files: 100% (1646/1646), done.
```

Once you have the `assimp` source code handy, you just need to build it and install it (into the system paths, not /usr/local). You also need to explicitly delete the packaged `assimp` libraries before installing the newer `assimp` version:

```
$ sudo rm -rf /usr/lib/libassimp*
$ mkdir build
$ cd build
$ cmake -DCMAKE_INSTALL_PREFIX:PATH=/usr ..
$ make
$ sudo make install
```

This will completely overwrite the `assimp` files from the Raspbian package with the newer ones that work with the ROS `collada` code.

If Raspbian updates libassimp3 *and does not have the fix for* ROS collada *(https://
github.com/assimp/assimp/commit/
fca079d61457f574f6a8fad3c081ae20fee814dd), you might undo this work by applying that update.*

At this point, you should have collada-dom and a working assimp installed. Now, manually build the catkinized ROS components that are not yet in ROSpbian. To build
catkinized ROS components, create a catkin workspace to use:

```
$ mkdir -p ~/catkin_ws/src
$ cd ~/catkin_ws/src
$ catkin_init_workspace
```

Download the urdf component source into the catkin workspace (it is part of the
robot_model component) with a git checkout into catkin_ws/src/:

```
$ git clone https://github.com/ros/robot_model.git
Cloning into 'robot_model'...
remote: Counting objects: 4176, done.
remote: Compressing objects: 100% (1715/1715), done.
remote: Total 4176 (delta 2257), reused 4141 (delta 2232)
Receiving objects: 100% (4176/4176), 2.16 MiB | 418 KiB/s, done.
Resolving deltas: 100% (2257/2257), done.
```

GitHub repositories for fast-moving projects like ROS often support multiple branches
at once, so it is important to make sure you have the correct branch for the version of
ROS you are using. In this case, you are using groovy, so you need to change your
robot_model checkout to reflect the groovy-devel code branch:

```
$ cd robot_model
$ git checkout groovy-devel
Branch groovy-devel set up to track remote branch groovy-devel from origin.
Switched to a new branch 'groovy-devel'
$ cd ..
```

Manually download the map_msgs component in the same method and directory (cat
kin_ws/src) as for urdf:

```
$ git clone https://github.com/ethz-asl/map_msgs
Cloning into 'map_msgs'...
remote: Counting objects: 43, done.
remote: Compressing objects: 100% (27/27), done.
remote: Total 43 (delta 12), reused 43 (delta 12)
Unpacking objects: 100% (43/43), done.
```

Download the next component (`cmake_modules`), needed to build ROS COLLADA support:

```
$ git clone https://github.com/ros/cmake_modules
Cloning into 'cmake_modules'...
remote: Counting objects: 125, done.
remote: Compressing objects: 100% (61/61), done.
remote: Total 125 (delta 60), reused 119 (delta 58)
Receiving objects: 100% (125/125), 17.46 KiB, done.
Resolving deltas: 100% (60/60), done.
```

Download the `interactive_markers` component:

```
$ git clone https://github.com/ros-visualization/interactive_markers
Cloning into 'interactive_markers'...
remote: Counting objects: 10659, done.
remote: Compressing objects: 100% (5209/5209), done.
remote: Total 10659 (delta 5297), reused 10484 (delta 5138)
Receiving objects: 100% (10659/10659), 7.90 MiB | 976 KiB/s, done.
Resolving deltas: 100% (5297/5297), done.
$ cd interactive_markers
$ git checkout groovy-devel
Branch groovy-devel set up to track remote branch groovy-devel from origin.
Switched to a new branch 'groovy-devel'
$ cd ..
```

While a package for this exists in ROSpbian, it is not current enough. Be sure to switch this to the `groovy-devel` branch as well (it may or may not already be on this branch when you check it out).

Last, but not least, download the source tree for the `rviz` component and switch the code checkout to use the `groovy-devel` branch:

```
$ git clone https://github.com/ros-visualization/rviz
Cloning into 'rviz'...
remote: Counting objects: 14175, done.
remote: Compressing objects: 100% (6144/6144), done.
remote: Total 14175 (delta 8853), reused 13288 (delta 7980)
Receiving objects: 100% (14175/14175), 11.31 MiB | 820 KiB/s, done.
Resolving deltas: 100% (8853/8853), done.
$ cd rviz
$ git checkout groovy-devel
Branch groovy-devel set up to track remote branch groovy-devel from origin.
Switched to a new branch 'groovy-devel'
$ cd ..
```

Go back to the top-level directory of your `catkin` workspace and run `catkin_make`:

```
$ cd ~/catkin_ws
$ catkin_make -DCMAKE_INSTALL_PREFIX=/opt/ros/groovy
```

The catkin_make command is a sort of "super cmake": it orders all of the components in the catkin workspace, then iterates through them, configuring each of them in order and then building them in order.

The -DCMAKE_INSTALL_PREFIX flag tells catkin_make that you want to install your files into /opt/ros/groovy. You will start to see output from catkin_make immediately, but it will take a long time to successfully complete. The output provides a percentage progress indicator to let you know how far along the build process is:

```
[ 26%] Building CXX object rviz/src/rviz/CMakeFiles/rviz.dir/tool_manag
er.cpp.o
[ 26%] Building CXX object rviz/src/rviz/CMakeFiles/rviz.dir/
uniform_string_stream.cpp.o
[ 27%] Building CXX object rviz/src/rviz/CMakeFiles/rviz.dir/view_control
ler.cpp.o
```

This is going to take a few hours to complete (we just left it building overnight and came back to it in the morning). When it finishes, it should look something like this (ignore the warnings; like Earth, they're mostly harmless):

```
{standard input}:10893: Warning: swp{b} use is deprecated for this architec
ture
[100%] Meta target for rviz_sip Python bindings...
[100%] Built target librviz_sip
```

You also need to use catkin_make to install these files into the /opt/ros/groovy ROS structure, but because you need to run this as root, you have to take a few extra steps (you can't just use sudo). Just switch to a root session with sudo and su -, then change back into your catkin workspace directory (/home/pi/catkin_ws). Once there, run cat kin_make install, with the CMAKE_INSTALL_PREFIX definition set to /opt/ros/groovy:

```
$ sudo su -
$ cd /home/pi/catkin_ws
$ sudo catkin_make install -DCMAKE_INSTALL_PREFIX=/opt/ros/groovy
$ exit
```

That should not take long to complete, but now you have all of your catkinized ROS components ready and installed. Now you build the legacy ROS stacks (including the NXT stack that you need to use):

```
$ cd ~
$ rosmake -i nxt
```

The -i flag tells `rosmake` to mark components hatbuild successfully with the `ROS_NO BUILD` flag, which keeps `rosmake` from building things over and over later without any good reason.

The `rosmake` build process generates a lot of output, but most of it isn't terribly useful. It will attempt to build all the components in the `nxt` stack, along with the dependencies you've downloaded. You can see that `rosmake` is iterating through all the `catkinized` components and looking for its build files (and not finding them), which is where most of the noisy output comes from. It should finish with output that looks something like this:

```
[ rosmake ] Results:
[ rosmake ] Built 66 packages with 0 failures.
[ rosmake ] Summary output to directory
[ rosmake ] /home/pi/.ros/rosmake/rosmake_output-20130909-141408
```

At this point, you should have an installation on your Raspberry Pi that contains the core ROS stack and the additional ROS components necessary to support the NXT Mindstorms brick and sensors. If you've made it this far, you should be proud. While ROS is an awesome toolkit, installing it for the Raspberry Pi is no easy task at the moment.

Testing the ROS Connection to the NXT Brick

It's time to make sure that ROS can see the NXT Intelligent Brick. Make sure your brick has fresh batteries (or an AC adapter plugged in), and power it on (the orange button in the center is the power button). Connect the USB cable from the NXT Brick to the Raspberry Pi. (Feel free to put a powered USB hub in the middle.)

Get out one of the touch sensors from the NXT Mindstorms kit. This sensor is used by the kit to indicate when your robot runs into something (and thus "touches" it). It has an orange button on its tip that you can easily press in with your finger. Connect the touch sensor to Port 1 (lower left of the NXT brick).

Then open two sessions to the Raspberry Pi (either terminals if you are running locally, or SSH sessions if not—see Hack #12 for help). In the first session, you're going to start `roscore`, the heart of ROS. It provides support for the nodes that allow the ROS infrastructure to function. You can start it manually to test your connection by running `roscore`, which should result in output that looks like the following:

```
$ roscore
... logging to /home/pi/.ros/log/bffc809a-1957-11e3-b0b1-b827eb545e36/
roslaunch-raspberrypi-12155.log
Checking log directory for disk usage. This may take awhile.
Press Ctrl-C to interrupt
Done checking log file disk usage. Usage is <1GB.
```

```
started roslaunch server http://raspberrypi:44402/
ros_comm version 1.9.41


SUMMARY
========

PARAMETERS
 * /rosdistro
 * /rosversion

NODES

auto-starting new master
process[master]: started with pid [12174]
ROS_MASTER_URI=http://raspberrypi:11311/

setting /run_id to bffc809a-1957-11e3-b0b1-b827eb545e36
process[rosout-1]: started with pid [12187]
started core service [/rosout]
```

At this point, the session will stop (although roscore is still running), and ROS will be ready to run tasks. Switch to your second session or terminal.

In this session, you need to be root to access the USB device, so go ahead and use sudo and su - to switch to a root session. Then you can use the rosrun command to run a ROS Python script to check the touch sensor. This script is simple; it polls the sensor and prints True or False for the state of the touch sensor. "True" means it is touching something; "False" means it is not.

It will time out after a few seconds, so have the sensor handy, and then run:

```
$ sudo su -
$ rosrun nxt_python touch_sensor_test.py
```

As you press the sensor, your screen should scroll messages indicating the sensor state, like this:

```
TOUCH: False
TOUCH: True
```

For good measure, let's test the color sensor as well (using color_sensor_test.py from the nxt_python component). The color sensor can emit a range of colors from its LED and can also detect the color and intensity of objects in front of it. Plug it into Port 1 (unplug the touch sensor) and run (as root):

```
$ rosrun nxt_python color_sensor_test.py
```

This will flash the LED on the front of the color sensor to red, blue, green, white, and then off. Next, it will take intensity readings for the amount of "blue" light (try covering the sensor completely to watch it drop to zero). Finally, it will detect the color in front of the sensor and return a decimal value corresponding to the color codes in Table 3-1.

Table 3-1. NXT RGB color sensor detected values

NUMBER	COLOR
1	Black
2	Blue
3	Green
4	Yellow
5	Red
6	White

Pretty nifty, huh? Go ahead and disconnect the color sensor, as it might be left on after the test script completes, and you don't want to burn it out.

Now that you know that the ROS environment is working with the NXT Intelligent Brick, you can build a test robot model. There are a few different ways to do this, but the simplest is to create a new ROS package and modify it.

First, use the roscmd tool to change into the nxt component directory, and then create a new ROS package called my_nxt_robot with the aptly named roscreate-pkg command (you do not need to be root):

```
$ roscd nxt
$ roscreate-pkg my_nxt_robot rospy nxt_ros
Created package directory /opt/ros/groovy/share/nxt/my_nxt_robot
Created python source directory /opt/ros/groovy/share/nxt/my_nxt_robot/src
Created package file /opt/ros/groovy/share/nxt/my_nxt_robot/Makefile
Created package file /opt/ros/groovy/share/nxt/my_nxt_robot/manifest.xml
Created package file /opt/ros/groovy/share/nxt/my_nxt_robot/CMakeLists.txt
Created package file /opt/ros/groovy/share/nxt/my_nxt_robot/mainpage.dox

Please edit my_nxt_robot/manifest.xml and mainpage.dox to finish creating
your package
```

This command also tells roscreate_pkg that your new my_nxt_robot ROS package will depend on rospy and nxt_ros.

Now, prepare the new my_nxt_robot ROS package with rosmake and change into the directory:

```
$ rosmake
$ cd my_nxt_robot
```

You need to write out a configuration file, which will tell the NXT ROS bindings what you have connected to the NXT Intelligent Brick. Open a file editor and save out the following as robot.yaml:

```
nxt_robot:
  - type: touch
    frame_id: touch_frame
    name: my_touch_sensor
    port: PORT_1
    desired_frequency: 20.0
```

This configuration says that you have a touch sensor connected on Port 1 (named my_touch_sensor) that you wish to check the status of 20 times per second (or 20 Hz). The NXT brick is not capable of handling high check frequencies, so you probably don't want to set this value any larger (smaller is fine, though). Go ahead and reconnect the touch sensor to Port 1 (and make sure your NXT brick is powered on).

Each device connected to the brick should be specified in this file, starting with a - before the type definition. For this example, we're keeping it simple, but when you want to build a more complicated robot, you'll need more than one item in this file.

To get ROS to run the robot, you need to create a ROS launch file named ro bot.launch. Using a text editor, create a new file with that name and add the following inside it:

```
<launch>

  <node pkg="nxt_ros" type="nxt_ros.py" name="nxt_ros" output="screen" re
spawn="true">
    <rosparam command="load" file="$(find my_nxt_robot)/robot.yaml" />
  </node>

</launch>
```

Now you can test your simple, one-sensor robot. You must be root, so switch to a root session first, change back into the my_nxt_robot package directory, and then use ro slaunch to launch the ROS robot:

```
$ sudo su -
$ roscd my_nxt_robot
$ roslaunch robot.launch
... logging to /root/.ros/log/bffc809a-1957-11e3-b0b1-b827eb545e36/
roslaunch-raspberrypi-20985.log
Checking log directory for disk usage. This may take awhile.
```

```
Press Ctrl-C to interrupt
Done checking log file disk usage. Usage is <1GB.

started roslaunch server http://raspberrypi:43572/

SUMMARY
========

PARAMETERS
 * /nxt_ros/nxt_robot
 * /rosdistro
 * /rosversion

NODES
 /
    nxt_ros (nxt_ros/nxt_ros.py)

ROS_MASTER_URI=http://localhost:11311

core service [/rosout] found
process[nxt_ros-1]: started with pid [21027]
[INFO] [WallTime: 1378757674.921416] Creating touch with name my_touch_sen
sor on PORT_1
```

You should see output similar to these messages, which indicate that ROS is running your robot. It will not return you to a shell prompt and will run in that session until you kill it (Ctrl+C will do the trick). Go ahead and open a second session to your Raspberry Pi.

This robot configuration defines one sensor: my_touch_sensor. You can confirm that this touch sensor is active by running the rostopic list command:

```
$ rostopic list
/my_touch_sensor
/rosout
/rosout_agg
```

You can see the raw output from the touch sensor by running rostopic echo my_touch_sensor. This will stream a running status to your terminal as the headers come in from the touch sensor. Press and hold the touch sensor and note that the contact field changes from False to True:

```
header:
  seq: 2088
  stamp:
    secs: 1378758120
```

```
      nsecs: 589009046
    frame_id: touch_frame
  contact: True
```

If you want to add a servo motor (connected to output Port A), you could add a section like this to your `robot.yaml`:

```
- type: motor
  name: l_motor_joint
  port: PORT_A
  desired_frequency: 10.0
```

In this example, we've defined a motor as a "joint," which makes sense in the context of a LEGO Mindstorms robot. The motor turns, and it makes the robot flex at that point. Because we've added a joint, we also need to tell ROS to aggregate the joint states in our `robot.launch` file. Edit that file so that it now looks like this:

```
<launch>

  <node pkg="nxt_ros" type="nxt_ros.py" name="nxt_ros" output="screen" re
spawn="true">
    <rosparam command="load" file="$(find my_nxt_robot)/robot.yaml" />
  </node>

  <node pkg="nxt_ros" type="joint_states_aggregator.py"
name="joint_state_publisher" output="screen" />

</launch>
```

By adding sensors and output motors, you have the building blocks of an ROS robot. The ROS framework is incredibly powerful, but also very complicated.

Unfortunately, going into details on building more complicated robots in ROS would be a whole book unto itself! In fact, there has been *at least one published* (*http:// www.lulu.com/shop/r-patrick-goebel/ros-by-example-volume-1/ebook/ product-20953517.html;jsessionid=6F5B3E774DC2D36F2DF01C34597A9CCE*)   so far. There is a lot of *documentation on how to use ROS* (*http://wiki.ros.org/ROS/Tuto-rials*), and the ROS community is generally very helpful to newcomers, which will help you get to the next step of the robot of your imagination.

Just Python, Please

ROS is very cool, but if you just want to build a simple Mindstorms robot, you can use a set of NXT Python bindings without the complexity of ROS.

Raspbian has a `python-nxt` package that you can install via `apt-get`:

```
$ sudo apt-get install python-nxt
```

This code is similar to the ROS `nxt_python` component, but it is much newer and does not depend on ROS. The `python-nxt` component includes a simple sensors test case. Connect a touch sensor to Port 1, a sound sensor to Port 2, a light sensor to Port 3, and an ultrasonic sensor to Port 4. Then run the test code (as root):

```
$ sudo python /usr/share/doc/python-nxt/examples/test_sensors.py
Touch: False
Sound: 0
Light: 0
Ultrasonic: 22
```

If ROS is still running, this might give you an error about not being able to access the NXT Intelligent Brick (only one application at a time can talk to the NXT Brick). Kill any running ROS processes and try again.

Obviously, your own readings will vary from these examples. Another example in /usr/ share/doc/python-nxt/examples/spin.py shows how you can trigger motors attached to the NXT Intelligent Brick output ports. This code is short, so we will walk through it here:

```
#!/usr/bin/env python

import nxt.locator
from nxt.motor import *
```

The first line tells the shell that this is a Python program and needs to be run through the Python interpreter when executed directly. The next two lines import the specific functions from the `python-nxt` library that the script is using, the `nxt.locator` function that finds and connects to the NXT brick, and all of the `nxt.motor` functions.

This section defines the `spin_around` function:

```
def spin_around(b):
    m_left = Motor(b, PORT_B)
    m_left.turn(100, 360)
    m_right = Motor(b, PORT_C)
    m_right.turn(-100, 360)
```

It creates the `m_left` variable, which is mapped to the motor connected to the brick's output Port B, and the `m_right` variable, which is mapped to the motor connected to output Port C. It then tells `m_left` to do a 360° turn with 100 power units (the possible range is from -127 to 128, and the `python-nxt` code recommends that you have an absolute value greater than 64). Next, it tells `m_right` to do a 360° turn at -100 power. In other words, this function does exactly what it says: it uses the motors to spin the robot around.

This last part of the code finds the NXT Intelligent Brick and assigns it to the b variable, then tells that brick to spin_around:

```
b = nxt.locator.find_one_brick()
spin_around(b)
```

Try not to get too dizzy.

There are other good examples of using python-nxt in /usr/share/doc/python-nxt/ examples/, as well as on the python-nxt website (*http://code.google.com/p/nxt-python/*).

HACK 35 (Appear to) Survive a Gaping Chest Wound

The Raspberry Pi isn't bulletproof. It won't actually save you from looking like an extra on a crime show. But you can take your video-game armor costume to the next level with a Pi, its camera, and a small screen.

Cosplay (short for *costume play*), has boomed in the last few years. Even if you haven't considered costuming much since your mom dressed you as a pumpkin for the second-grade Halloween play, you've probably seen some of these amazing works online from events like the Comic Con and Dragon Con fan conventions or on shows like SyFy's Heroes of Cosplay.

Build the Costume

One area in particular that has taken off is armor building. It sounds like something you'd need welding skills for, but you might be surprised what the best way to pull of a realistic, inexpensive armor costume is: foam. Simple sheets of foam.

This could mean a couple of different things, starting with the thin craft foam you find at your local craft supply store, usually in 12" x 18" sheets alongside buckets of adhesive foam cutout shapes for kids to make cheesy craft projects at summer camp. This type of foam is great for areas that need to look or be thin, like finger pieces, or for detail work.

At the other end of the spectrum, you can purchase pieces of EVA foam up to an inch thick or more. The easiest way to obtain this is to go to a hardware supply store (we find it at Harbor Freight Tools, which has locations all over the United States) and look for interlocking foam floor mats. The ones Harbor Freight sells come in a pack of four (and are often on sale!) with a smooth side and a textured side that looks great for certain types of armor.

Other Materials for Armor Building

Foam isn't the only way to go. When you're ready to graduate to the next level, it's time to learn how to build with fiberglass. Before fiberglass, there were thermoplastics. If you bought craft store plastic in the '80s, heated it up in a pot of water, and molded it into strange shapes and earrings, that's what we're talking about (products like Friendly Plastic and Wonderflex). The currently popular version is called Worbla. It's easy to cut, takes paint well, and you can use all the scraps by heating it up and balling it up like clay. Creative costumers have even used plastic garbage cans. Or if you're just not ready for the investment, there's always the pile of cardboard boxes in your garage. Don't scoff. The Dragon Con 2013 Masquerade winner was a pretty great cardboard RoboCop.

The fabric store doesn't sell armor patterns alongside the sewing patterns, though, so you're going to have to look elsewhere. Pepakura to your rescue! *Pepakura* is the Japanese word for "papercraft," as well as the name of a piece of software for creating 3D paper models. If you expand one of those models to be human-sized, you have a pattern for making your armor. Unfortunately, the software is Windows-only, but it's worth it to get your armor made.

You can create your own 3D models in software like *Blender* (*http://www.blender.org*), but if you want to make a costume of a fairly well-known character like Iron Man or Commander Shepard from *Mass Effect*, you can find patterns freely available online from someone else who did it first. Just search for "pepakura [costume name]." There is also a *handy Instructables tutorial* (*http://www.instructables.com/id/What-is-Pepakura-and-how-to-start/*) to get you started.

Resources for Costume Building

If you're interested in general costume building, the first place you should go is the forums on *The Replica Prop Forum* (*http://therpf.com*). Other groups exist for specific interest groups, such as the *405th Infantry Division* (*http://www.405th.com*) for *Halo* and the *501st Legion* (*http://www. 501st.com/*) for people interested in joining others with *Star Wars* costumes for the Imperial side. (Those on the "good guy" side should check out the *Rebel Legion* (*http://www.rebellegion.com/*).)

Once you get involved with all of this, you'll find that unless you've done a particularly spectacular job or something incredibly creative, your costume armor is just another in a sea of the same character. For example, more than 60 people showed up to the *Mass Effect* photo shoot at Dragon Con in 2013. That's a lot of Sheps, and that's just the ones who showed up for the shoot!

Even if you create an original design, it'll look like Just More Armor to all the people who think it looks cool but would totally believe you if you told them Big Daddy was this guy in the *Brotherhood of Steel* from *Half-Life*, which was this really dark spinoff of *Super Mario Brothers*. (You should play it!) What you need is something just a little bit different.

Add the Battle Wound

Enter your battle wound. The goal is to hide the tiny camera in one side of your armor with the screen in the opposite side, flush with the armor. With an image of what's behind you showing in front on the screen, the effect is that someone can see through you. You might remember some news stories from around the time the third *Harry Potter* film was released about a "real invisibility cloak." This is a far, far cruder version of the camera-and-screen technique used to make that cloak.

Resolution, Parallax, Details, Details...

Understand that this is not a perfect effect. Though it's going to look awesome in a still photo in the right pose, someone standing close to you will clearly see that this is a screen. A tiny TFT LCD has pretty good resolution, but few screens (especially any you can afford to embed in a costume) have lifelike resolution. On top of that, there's the matter of parallax*. Imagine a hole in a wall. (OK, we often call those "windows," but we're talking armor here, so imagine you just blasted a hole in the wall with your massive fictional weapon that goes "pew pew pew.") As you walk past the window or stand and sit in front of it, what you see changes. What a viewer sees through your chest screen will change only when you or the background move.*

For this project, you'll need a TFT like the one in Hack #57 (or other small screen), a Raspberry Pi camera, and your armor-building (a.k.a. foam-destroying) tools. If you get this far in the project, you'll have discovered that it's a lot easier to cut the foam, particularly the thick kind, with a hot knife. You can get kits that include a hot blade, such as a woodburning or leatherworking kit. Most appropriate to the projects in this book is a soldering iron/hot knife combination (such as the X-Acto X73780), so if you're embarking on this project and don't have a soldering iron yet, that's the way to go.

The first step is to choose a location for your faux wound. You don't have to make this look like a chest wound, despite the hack title. (Although if you're going to be severely injured and freakishly survive, why not?) Just choose the best location that suits your character and story. The technological factor that may influence your choice is the shape and size of your armor pieces and where you can (a) hide the Pi and camera and (b) have cables long enough to reach both such that the camera is roughly opposite the screen.

Lay out your armor and estimate the locations of each component so that you can figure out how long your cables will need to be. Consider various possibilities regarding where you can hide the three pieces and their wiring. Remember, you'll also need to power the Pi with a portable battery pack (see Hack #18).

The Pi camera comes with a 150 mm (~6") cable, which isn't very long, and the cable itself is a bit fragile. Likewise, the TFT screen comes with a short cable, and its ribbon connection to its board is also fragile. When you finalize a place for all of these components, be sure to secure them well and make sure they're not going to snag on other parts of your costume when you're moving around or taking it on and off.

A longer cable to the camera is a possibility, although it will introduce more noise, which is a problem since we're hoping for a reasonably realistic look (at least from a distance). Several vendors sell kits to extend (or 1:1 replace) the camera's 15-core, 1 mm pitch ribbon cable:

- BitWizard B.V. says that it has successfully extended the cable to 4 meters (~13 feet) with an *extension kit* (*http://www.bitwizard.nl/catalog/product_info.php? products_id=146*) that contains both straight and right-angle connectors, which also could be useful depending on the way you need to place parts in your costume. The ribbon cable does not come with the kit, but the company sells it separately for €0.15/10 cm.

- *ModMyPi* (*http://www.modmypi.com*) and *Toby Electronics* (*http://www.toby.co.uk/*) sell direct replacement mm cables (15-way flat flex cables). The ModMyPi one is 150 mm; the Toby one (type number FFC1-15-B-150-10-5-160MM) is 160 mm.

- The *Pi Hut* (*http://thepihut.com/*) sells replacement ribbon cables from 50–300 mm, but only through its eBay storefront (the_pi_hut), not through its usual website.

To replace the ribbon cable, pull the black connector out of the camera module by the corners, but just a bit—not all the way off. Then you can slide the flat ribbon out.

A Simple Script

The software to power the camera is the `raspivid` utility, provided as part of Raspbian (or downloaded and installed along with the latest firmware in the *Raspberry Pi Foundation firmware repository* (*https://github.com/raspberrypi/firmware/*)).

We recommend this specific invocation of `raspivid`:

```
raspivid -w 320 -h 240 -t 0 -b 5000000 -o -
```

This will run the camera in video mode, at a resolution of 320 x 240, with a bitrate of 5 MBits/s, forever. It won't ever save the result to a file; if you want to change that, replace the `-o -` syntax with `-o /path/to/filename`, but be careful, since you'll overwrite that file every time this command is run. You should test this command with the hardware connected to make sure that it works well for you (you might want to change the resolution or bitrate, if you are using a different screen).

When you are happy with the `raspivid` command line, you'll want to put it into a script. This is a very simple script, so just open up your favorite text editor (as root) and write out these lines:

```
#!/bin/bash

# script to run raspivid at 320x240, 5MB/s, forever
raspivid -w 320 -h 240 -t 0 -b 5000000 -o -
```

Write out the file to `/usr/bin/camloop.sh`. You'll need to make it executable, too, which can be accomplished by running:

```
$ sudo chmod +x /usr/bin/camloop.sh
```

You can execute this script and confirm that indeed, it displays the camera on the TFT screen at the desired resolution and bitrate in a never-ending loop. To end it, just hit `Control-C` and the script will die.

We recommend that you configure this script to run automatically on boot, since you're not likely to have a keyboard connected to your costume when you're showing this off. The procedure to do this varies by distribution.

For Raspbian, you simply need to invoke this script from `/etc/rc.local`. Open that file with a text editor (as root), and add this line directly *above* the line that says `exit 0`:

```
/usr/bin/camloop.sh &
```

The use of the & command at the end of the line tells the Python script to run in the background. This is important, because otherwise, `rc.local` would wait for it to finish before proceeding. Since this script runs in an infinite video loop, it would never proceed, and your boot process would sit there waiting.

Pidora uses a different boot software (`systemd`), which does not use the `rc.local` concept. As a result, you will need to create a new `systemd` service file for the Python script. Copy this file (also in the book's GitHub repository) to `/usr/lib/systemd/system/camloop.service` (as root):

```
[Unit]
Description=Camera Loop
```

```
[Service]
Type=simple
ExecStart=/usr/bin/camloop.sh

[Install]
WantedBy=multi-user.target
```

Then, you can start it immediately by running:

```
$ su -c 'systemctl start camloop.service'
```

To make this service start on each boot, run:

```
$ su -c 'systemctl enable camloop.service'
```

Finish the Costume

Once you've figured out part locations and cable lengths and tested your script, you're ready for the real work—carving up your hard work. Unless you're already particularly adept at foam cutting, we suggest doing this a few times with scraps before you go slicing up your hard work on the real thing. You have a few aims in this shape that are probably a bit different from the sculpting you did on the rest of your armor:

- You probably want to cut a round hole smaller than the square screen, since even the worst shot from a Stormtrooper doesn't blast a square hole.
- The visible side of the hole should be as flush with the screen as possible.
- The back side should then be sturdy enough to support the screen and its fragile cable.

To accomplish this, lay the screen on the back side of the foam and outline it with a marker. You want an accurate outline to ensure a snug fit.

First cut the round hole, cutting all the way through the foam. Then carefully make cuts following the outline shape going nearly all the way through but not piercing the front of the foam. (This is why you practice on scraps.)

Working from the hole out to those edges, slice parallel to the foam, cutting out a rectangle for the screen to sit in, as shown in Figure 3-11. It doesn't have to be perfectly smooth. The goal is just to get it as close to the surface of the foam as possible.

Figure 3-11.
Hole to set screen into foam, viewed from back side

You might need to cut a notch on one side for the ribbon connector. Remember, that's a fragile connector, and if you tear it, about all you can do is wipe your tears and buy a new screen set.

Once the hole is sized properly, you can set the screen into the hole, as shown in Figure 3-12. Turn it over and admire your work!

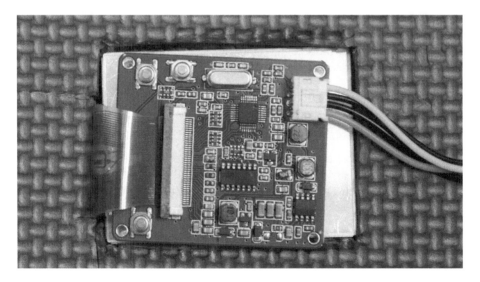

Figure 3-12.
Screen set into finished hole, view from back side

Once you get all that taken care of, it's time to add some realism. You're going to want the hole to look a bit burnt. Conveniently, you have a burning device in your hands—your hot knife. Use the metal extension between the knife and the handle, which also gets hot, to melt the edges of the hole. They'll both get smoother and blackened.

You can also paint some scorch marks around the edges and in various other spots for added realism. If you accidentally tapped some other part of your foam with the hot knife while you were working, that's a great place to create more "battle damage" so it doesn't look like your shiny, fresh armor got shot through the second you stepped out of the pod/ship/space station.

Put It All Together

Finally, put it all together. Mount the screen in the hole and secure the Raspberry Pi, power supply, and cables in the places you've found to hide them. If you're using the TFT display we use here (see Hack #57 for further instructions on connecting it), remember also that its ribbon connector is rather fragile and should be secure and protected.

Turn everything on, run your script (or let it autostart), and you're ready to be a walking war wound, as shown in Figure 3-13. We recommend some nice zombie makeup to complete the look.

Figure 3-13.
Screen running in hole window

You can take this hack in other directions as well. Embed a larger screen in the chest of a robot to show its "controls," or have music videos playing on a dancing robot. Build a Fallout Pip-Boy. Put the camera and screen together in front and create a steampunk "explorer" character whose rig displays a first-person account of what he finds. Dream up all sorts of other possibilities and get to costuming!

`HACK 36` Look for Aliens

> Your Raspberry Pi can be a part of the world's largest distributed computing project. You might not actually find signs of alien life, but then, wouldn't it be fun if you did? And your Pi does all the work.

For more than a decade, the Search for Extraterrestrial Intelligence (SETI) project has used distributed computing through SETI@Home to help with the massive task of sifting through the data from radio telescopes for signs of intelligence beyond Earth. These telescopes receive more noise than anything else, and every bit more data that can be processed means a wider range of frequencies that can be examined. This was originally done using supercomputers until David Gedye organized the SETI@Home project to enable anyone, anywhere to help process all of the data they were acquiring. You can conduct your own piece of the ET hunt with your Raspberry Pi (or several of them!).

You may remember the SETI@Home Classic project as a screensaver that launched in May 1999, which was used by millions. This version, known as SETI@Home Classic, was retired in December 2005 when funding ran out. In those six years, 5,436,301 users from 226 countries provided the equivalent of 2,433,979.781 years of CPU time. While the project didn't find signs of extraterrestrial life, it did make its mark as the largest computation in history. From then on through today, the project continued through the Berkeley Open Infrastructure for Network Computing (BOINC) open source platform for volunteer grid computing.

BOINC was originally created for SETI@Home in the Space Sciences Laboratory at the University of California, Berkeley and now receives funding from the National Science Foundation. In addition to SETI@Home, it now runs more than 40 other projects, from Enigma@home, which is attempting to decode the remaining three unbroken Enigma messages from World War II, to QMC@Home, which calculates molecular geometry for the field of quantum chemistry.

If you've followed the work at CERN's Large Hadron Collider (LHC), you can use your BOINC installation to participate in the LHC@home project. Once you've installed it, you can also connect to those other projects that process data for research in nearly every area of math and science. Data processed by more than 8 million hosts using BOINC, the world's largest distributed computing project, has led to breakthroughs in AIDS research, found new celestial objects, and even helped find a stolen laptop. The most popular projects running on BOINC as of this writing are:

SETI@Home
    The subject of this section

Einstein@Home
>   Searches for gravitational signals from pulsars and has discovered nearly 50 new pulsars

World Community Grid
>   An IBM-sponsored humanitarian project that has partnered with hundreds of other organizations on research from cancer to clean energy

BOINC can run continuously, taking advantage of unused processor time as it's available. Some people wholly devote older equipment to personal "SETI farms." Devoting a Raspberry Pi to always looking for ET could be your way of contributing to the project. You could even build a "Raspberry Pi farm," though it would unfortunately not grow pie. But maybe that credit-card-sized computer will be the one that finds definitive signs of life beyond Earth.

> Read more about the early history of *SETI@Home* at *http://setia thome.berkeley.edu/classic.php*

Begin by installing the BOINC manager and client:

```
$ su -c 'yum install boinc-manager boinc-client'
```

or:

```
$ sudo apt-get install boinc-client boinc-manager
```

To ensure that the BOINC client starts every time you boot the system, enter:

```
$ sudo systemctl enable boinc-client.service
```

Then reboot. If you would prefer to start the BOINC client manually, you can do so any time with the following command:

```
$ systemctl start boinc-client.service
```

If your alien-hunting Pi will be devoted to the cause and not needing a monitor, you have the option of installing only the client and starting it at boot. In this case, enter only:

```
$ su -c yum install boinc-client
```

or:

```
$ sudo apt-get install boinc-client
```

Setting Up BOINC

The following instructions assume that you are using the BOINC Manager, which you can find under System in the Applications Menu if you're using Fedora or start from the command line by typing `boincmgr`. It might take a moment before anything appears in the BOINC Manager window the first time. When it does start, you'll see the error "Unable to connect to the core client."

Open a terminal and first check that the BOINC Client is running:

```
$ sudo systemctl status boinc-client.service
```

You should see something similar to the following:

```
boinc-client.service - Berkeley Open Infrastructure Network Computing Client
        Loaded: loaded (/usr/lib/systemd/system/boinc-client.service; enabled)
        Active: active (running) since Wed, 2013-04-17 14:37:22 EST; 1min ago
       Process: 19413 ExecStartPre=/usr/bin/chown boinc:boinc /var/log/
boinc.log /var/log/boincerr.log (code=exited, status=0/SUCCESS)
       Process: 19410 ExecStartPre=/usr/bin/touch /var/log/boinc.log /var/log/
boincerr.log (code=exited, status=0/SUCCESS)
       Process: 19406 ExecStartPre=/bin/sleep 1 (code=exited, status=0/
SUCCESS)
      Main PID: 19416 (boinc)
        CGroup: name=systemd:/system/boinc-client.service
                ├ 19416 /bin/bash /usr/bin/boinc --dir /var/lib/boinc
                ├ 19417 /usr/bin/boinc_client --allow_multiple_clients --
dir /var/lib/boinc
                ├ 19422 ../../projects/setiathome.berkeley.edu/
setiathome_6.03_i686-pc-linux-gnu
                ├ 19423 ../../projects/setiathome.berkeley.edu/
setiathome-5.28.x86_64-pc-linux-gnu
                ├ 19424 ../../projects/setiathome.berkeley.edu/
setiathome-5.28.x86_64-pc-linux-gnu
                └ 19425 ../../projects/setiathome.berkeley.edu/
setiathome-5.28.x86_64-pc-linux-gnu

Apr 17 14:37:21 localhost.localdomain systemd[1]: Starting Berkeley Open In
frastructure Network Computing Client...
Apr 17 14:37:22 localhost.localdomain systemd[1]: Started Berkeley Open In
frastructure Network Computing Client.
```

You can also see if the client is running by looking for it in the list of currently running processes:

```
$ ps aux | grep boinc
```

You should see several boinc processes, including `boinc_client` in a list similar to the following:

```
root      16818  0.0  0.0 196284   2656 pts/0    S    Apr17   0:00 su boinc
boinc     16819  0.0  0.0 114084   1760 pts/0    S+   Apr17   0:00 bash
jnettles  18734  0.0  0.0 111848   1264 ?        S    10:27   0:00 /bin/
bash /usr/bin/boincmgr
jnettles  18741  0.1  0.7 706868  28800 ?        Sl   10:27   0:16 boinc_gui
boinc     20117  0.0  0.0 113948   1328 ?        SNs  14:41   0:00 /bin/
bash /usr/bin/boinc --dir /var/lib/boinc
boinc     20118  0.1  0.1 306116   5716 ?        SN   14:41   0:00 /usr/bin/
boinc_client --allow_multiple_clients --dir /var/lib/boinc
boinc     20123 93.4  0.9  36920  35768 ?        RNl  14:41   0:58 ../../
projects/setiathome.berkeley.edu/setiathome_6.03_i686-pc-linux-gnu
boinc     20124 90.5  1.1  58124  45052 ?        SNl  14:41   0:57 ../../
projects/setiathome.berkeley.edu/setiathome-5.28.x86_64-pc-linux-gnu
boinc     20125 91.7  1.1  57616  44536 ?        SNl  14:41   0:57 ../../
projects/setiathome.berkeley.edu/setiathome-5.28.x86_64-pc-linux-gnu
boinc     20126 92.0  1.1  56964  43892 ?        SNl  14:41   0:58 ../../
projects/setiathome.berkeley.edu/setiathome-5.28.x86_64-pc-linux-gnu
root      20144  0.0  0.0 109180    880 pts/1    S+   14:42   0:00 grep --
color=auto boinc
```

If you do not, try starting the service by entering +systemctl start boinc-client.service+.

Once you've confirmed that the client is running, it's time to configure the BOINC Manager:

```
$ sudo vi /var/lib/boinc/gui_rpc_auth.cfg
```

This file contains a long string of characters that is your BOINC password. Copy it (Shift+Ctrl+V), then exit (:q!).

Flush the IP tables:

```
$ sudo iptables -F
```

Now go to the BOINC Manager window. Go to View → Advanced View (or use Shift+Ctrl +A to switch). Under Advanced → Select Computer, enter `127.0.0.1` for the hostname (using `localhost` may or may not work) and paste the password you copied from `gui_rpc_auth.cfg`.

For security reasons, BOINC Manager requires this password each time you start it. At this point, unless you intend to walk away from it and never use the manager again, you should change some permissions to save yourself from having to copy and paste the password each time.

As you saw when you listed the BOINC processes, installing it created a `boinc` user as well. That user is currently the owner of everything under `/var/lib/boinc/`. By adding yourself to the boinc group, you can create permissions that let your BOINC Manager connect to the client without looking up that password each time:

```
$ su
[Enter password]
$ /usr/sbin/usermod -G boinc -a  YOURNAME
$ chmod g+rw /var/lib/boinc
$ chmod g+rw /var/lib/boinc/*.*
$ ln -s /var/lib/boinc/gui_rpc_auth.cfg /home/YOURNAME/gui_rpc_auth.cfg
```

After you have logged out and back in, you will be added to the boinc group and should no longer have to repeat the password steps when using the BOINC Manager.

BOINC Account Managers

There are several BOINC account managers (which in a sense means BOINC Manager is really just middle management). They manage your BOINC accounts if you're participating in multiple projects or have BOINC running on multiple systems.

Even if you're running it only on this one Raspberry Pi, using an account manager will make things easier, and BOINC Manager will prompt you to set one up. The website for BAM!, one of the account managers, explains some of the *differences between using an account manager and not using one* (*http://boincstats.com/en/bam/*).

BOINC Account Manager (BAM!)

Despite its name, BOINC Account Manager (BAM!) is not run by the same team as BOINC. It was created by the group that runs *BOINCstats* (*http://www.boinc-stats.com*), which, as the name implies, provides statistics related to the various projects running on BOINC.

As you're setting up the BOINC Manager for the first time, you'll be asked to select an account manager. If you choose BAM!, you will be directed to set up a BAM account at *http://bam.boincstats.com*, where can create and access your accounts for SETI@Home and other projects.

You can use the same account on multiple Raspberry Pis (or other computers), but make sure that you consistently use the same email address when joining projects and teams. If, after creating an account, you don't get the BAM! verification email, check your spam folder, or add boincstats.com to the accepted domains filter.

1. Sign in.

2. Select Tools → Add projects. You'll notice the long list of other distributed computing projects from a wide variety of math and science purposes that you can contribute to using BOINC. You can choose multiple projects—that's what the BOINC Manager is for.

3. Select SETI@Home. You'll be asked to either create a login or to give ones you already use. If you create an account, you'll then be directed to the SETI@Home website, where you'll finish the registration process.

4. Optionally, find a team to join or create one. If you search for "raspberry pi" in the keywords section, you'll find the *Raspberry Pi Team* (*http://setiathome.berkeley.edu/team_display.php?teamid=144455*), created specifically for people using the Pi to run BOINC. Those who simply like the Raspberry Pi but are running BOINC from another system are welcome, too, so don't take the team's statistics as being purely from Pis. You can view this team's statistics at *http://boinc stats.com/en/stats/-1/team/detail/51ef74e7931bf4eaaf10fe521d6b9df0*.

GridRepublic

GridRepublic (*http://www.gridrepublic.org/*) is an account manager built on the BOINC manager code. It is created by the GridRepublic nonprofit organization that was formed shortly after BOINC to establish the manager concept—a place from which to the control the projects.

To use the GridRepublic manager, you must *create an account with them* (*http://www.gridrepublic.org/index.php?param=signin&sparam=regs1*), using the same name as your World Community Grid account if you have one. You then "attach" it to your BOINC installation. You can learn more on *the Grid Republic site* (*http://www.gridrepublic.org/joomla/components/com_mambowiki/index.php/GridRepublic_Desktop_and_BOINC_client_software*).

AndroBOINC

If you use an Android smartphone, you can remotely control your BOINC client(s) from your phone. Search in Google Play for "boinc." There are several unofficial apps, but we recommend AndroBOINC (Figure 3-14). If you don't have an unlimited data plan, be careful how you set the autorefresh rate when not on WiFi, lest you be sad when next month's bill comes.

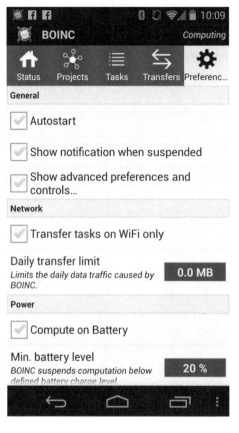

Figure 3-14.
AndroBOINC client

> There is also an official BOINC Android app (http://boinc.berkeley.edu/dev/
> forum_thread.php?id=8203) available for alpha testing. Read the instructions
> there carefully if you're interested in joining the testing.

AndroBOINC offers basic control and status of your BOINC client. Think of it as the
BOINC Manager, but on your phone. (You don't want to run the client on your phone
unless you really hate having battery left to do anything else.)

4

Hacking the Outdoors

Electronics outside, you say? Isn't that a bad idea? We do have a couple of water-resistant suggestions (Hack #39 and Hack #40). But we also have ideas for how to put your Pi to use on your outdoor projects, from monitoring your garden (Hack #38) to controlling your holiday lights (Hack #45).

HACK 37 Tell the Temperature Outside (Without Going Out There)

The outside temperature is not a constant value; it fluctuates, and we know you like to know what it is. Whether you're helping plants stay healthy or just want to know how many layers of clothes to wear, this hack can help!

Hack #05 shows that the Raspberry Pi measures the temperature of its BCM2835 system-on-chip, but this is different. In order to read the temperature near the Raspberry Pi (or even nowhere near it), you'll need to connect a temperature sensor. While Linux supports some USB thermometers, it is just as simple (and arguably more fun), to wire up a simple temperature sensor to the GPIO on the Raspberry Pi.

This hack uses the Texas Instruments TMP102 I2C temperature sensor for the following reasons:

- It is very small. Smaller than a quarter. See Figure 4-1 for proof.
- It is a digital sensor (this makes the wiring much easier and the results much more accurate).
- Sparkfun sells it already *connected to a breakout board* (*https://www.spark-fun.com/products/9418*).
- It is cheap (less than $6 USD at the time of this writing).
- It is accurate over a range of temperatures from -25°C and +85°C. (That's -13° to 185°F.)

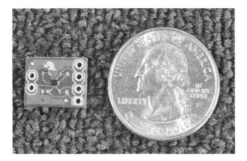

Figure 4-1.
TMP102 and a shiny quarter

Depending on which Linux distribution you are using, you might not have all the drivers necessary to use the TMP102. Both Raspbian and Pidora are missing the driver for the TMP102. You can enable the support for this driver if you build a custom kernel from source, as covered in Hack #22. Be sure that you have enabled (compiled in) `CONFIG_I2C`, `CONFIG_I2C_CHARDEV`, and `CONFIG_I2C_BCM2708`.

Because you will be using the `lm_sensors` userspace component to get readings from the TMP102, you will need to be sure to enable "Hardware Monitoring support" (`CONFIG_HWMON`) under Device Drivers. You also need to have `CONFIG_SENSORS_TMP102` enabled as a module. We will assume that the TMP102 support is present as a module going forward. Figure 4-2 shows an example of what this option looks like.

Alternatively, Occidentalis supports the I2C and TMP102 sensor support out of the box, so you could just use that (and avoid the need for a custom kernel for this hack). For more information about Occidentalis, see Hack #27.

What is I2C?

I2C (Inter-Integrated Circuit) is a protocol for connecting low-speed devices with two wires. It is common in embedded systems, especially for sensors. The Raspberry Pi has two dedicated GPIO pins (2 and 3 on the current Raspberry Pi Model B) preconfigured for I2C.

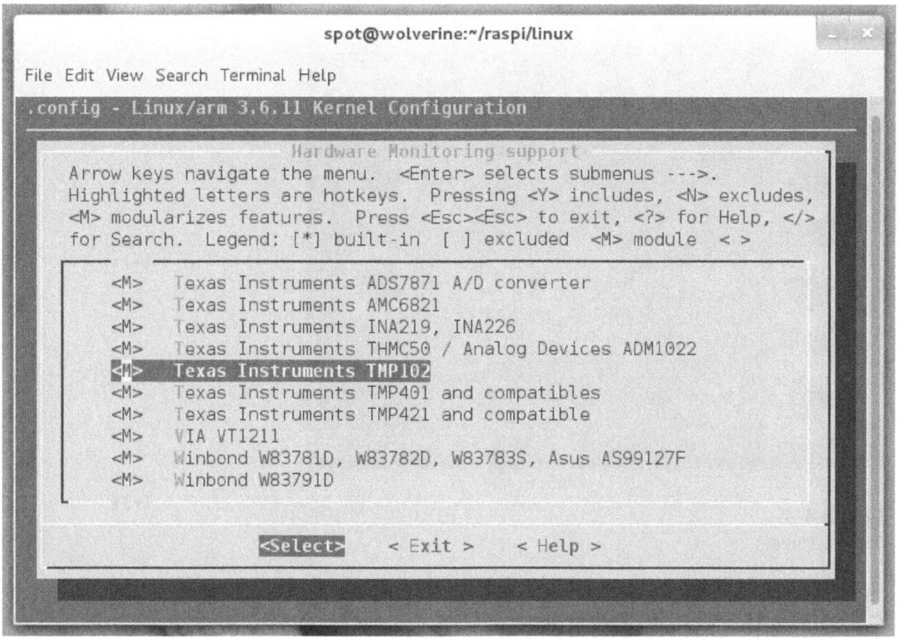

```
                    spot@wolverine:~/raspi/linux

 File  Edit  View  Search  Terminal  Help
 .config - Linux/arm 3.6.11 Kernel Configuration
                        Hardware Monitoring support
   Arrow keys navigate the menu.  <Enter> selects submenus --->.
   Highlighted letters are hotkeys.  Pressing <Y> includes, <N> excludes,
   <M> modularizes features.  Press <Esc><Esc> to exit, <?> for Help, </>
   for Search.  Legend: [*] built-in  [ ] excluded  <M> module  < >

         <M>   Texas Instruments ADS7871 A/D converter
         <M>   Texas Instruments AMC6821
         <M>   Texas Instruments INA219, INA226
         <M>   Texas Instruments THMC50 / Analog Devices ADM1022
         <M>   Texas Instruments TMP102
         <M>   Texas Instruments TMP401 and compatibles
         <M>   Texas Instruments TMP421 and compatible
         <M>   VIA VT1211
         <M>   Winbond W83781D, W83782D, W83783S, Asus AS99127F
         <M>   Winbond W83791D


                  <Select>    < Exit >    < Help >
```

Figure 4-2.
Texas Instruments TMP102 sensor support enabled as a module

Sparkfun's breakout board makes connecting it to the Raspberry Pi simple. There are six *pins* (or *leads*) coming off of the breakout. These pins are labeled on the back of the breakout board, and the ones you care about are on the left side.

The first pin is Ground (GND), the second pin is the Serial Clock (SCL), the third pin is the Serial Data Line (SDA), and the fourth pin is 5 V (V+). The SCL and SDA pins are how the sensor sends/receives data across the I2C bus.

You should not need to use the pins labeled ALT or ADD0 (they're on the right side of the breakout board), unless you already have a conflicting device on the same I2C bus and need to change the device number. Because this is the only device on the Raspberry Pi GPIO I2C bus for this hack, you can just leave those pins alone. You can see these labels on the TMP102 device, as shown in Figure 4-3.

Figure 4-3.
TMP102 labels

But the Datasheet Says...

If you happen to look at the datasheet provided by Sparkfun (https://www.spark-fun.com/datasheets/Sensors/Temperature/tmp102.pdf), you might notice that its numbering is different from what we've provided. It numbers the pins as they come off the TMP102 sensor itself, not as they appear on the breakout board. The TMP102 sensor is that tiny black chip in the middle of the breakout board. If you look closely (possibly with a magnifying glass), you'll see the leads coming off the TMP102 to the breakout pins. The ordering is different, but the breakout board labels make a lot more sense to use, so we use those instead.

The mapping of the TMP102 breakout pins to the Raspberry Pi GPIO is fairly obvious, as shown in Table 4-1.

Table 4-1. TMP pin mapping

TMP102 BREAKOUT PIN LABEL	RASPBERRY PI BCM GPIO PIN
GND	GND
SCL	3 (SCL)
SDA	2 (SDA)
V+	5 V

Remember, the mapping in Table 4-1 referes to the BCM GPIO pin labels. See Hack #14 if this doesn't make sense to you.

To connect this device to the Raspberry Pi, you'll first need to solder wires to the TMP102 breakout pins that you are using (GND, SCL, SDA, and V+).

See "Soldering Reminders" on page 42 for some basic soldering tips.

If you are lazy, you can use male jumper wires and bend them tightly to make the connection, but this is really sloppy and hackish, even for a *Hacks* book. Either way, once you have wires coming off the TMP102 breakout, you need to connect them to the Raspberry Pi. You can either use jumper wires to connect directly to the appropriate GPIO pins, or you can use a Pi Cobbler and a breadboard for the simplest wiring (see Hack #15 for more about the Pi Cobbler).

To use your TMP102 sensor (and make sure it is working on the Raspberry Pi I2C Bus), you need to install some software. To install `i2ctools` and `lm-sensors`, run the following command on Pidora:

```
$ su -c 'yum install i2c-tools lm_sensors -y'
```

On Raspbian, run:

```
$ su -c 'apt-get install i2c-tools lm-sensors'
```

Now, let's try to find your device on the Raspberry Pi's I2C Bus. To look for the device, you need to run `i2cdetect` on bus 1. On the original Raspberry Pi Model B units, this was bus 0, but with the current hardware, it is bus 1. Bus 0 actually exists on the current Raspberry Pi Model B, but you have to connect to it via the camera connector. Here's the `i2cdetect` command line you want to run:

```
$ su -c 'i2cdetect -y 1'
```

You should see output like this:

```
     0  1  2  3  4  5  6  7  8  9  a  b  c  d  e  f
00:          -- -- -- -- -- -- -- -- -- -- -- -- --
10: -- -- -- -- -- -- -- -- -- -- -- -- -- -- -- --
20: -- -- -- -- -- -- -- -- -- -- -- -- -- -- -- --
30: -- -- -- -- -- -- -- -- -- -- -- -- -- -- -- --
40: -- -- -- -- -- -- -- -- 48 -- -- -- -- -- -- --
50: -- -- -- -- -- -- -- -- -- -- -- -- -- -- -- --
60: -- -- -- -- -- -- -- -- -- -- -- -- -- -- -- --
70: -- -- -- -- -- -- -- --
```

This is a graphical way of telling you that there is a device on I2C bus 1, with the numeric identifier 48. This is your TMP102 sensor.

Hey, That Didn't Work!

If you try the command to install i2ctools and lm-sensors on a default install of Raspbian, it will look like this:

```
$ su -c 'i2cdetect -y 1'
Error: Could not open file `/dev/i2c-1' or `/dev/i2c/1': No such file
or directory
```

Why? Raspbian's kernel has CONFIG_I2C_CHARDEV and CONFIG_I2C_BCM2708 enabled as modules, instead of built in to the kernel like Pidora does (and like we recommend). If you got this error, it means you didn't build a custom kernel, as recommended in Hack #22. Go back and do that now. If you do not and you just load these modules, you'll run into trouble trying to access the TMP102, because that driver isn't built at all in Raspbian.

If you did build a custom kernel, but left CONFIG_I2C_BCM2708 as a module for some reason, you can manually load the i2c-dev module with this command:

```
$ su -c 'modprobe i2c-bcm2708'
```

That will make /dev/i2c-1 appear, and your i2cdetect invocation will succeed.

You now know that our TMP102 device is device number 48 on I2C bus 1, but you need to tell the Linux kernel that it exists:

```
$ su -c 'echo tmp102 0x48 > /sys/class/i2c-adapter/i2c-1/new_device'
```

At this point, you are ready to start reading temperature data from your TMP102 sensor. The standard tool for doing this in Linux (lm_sensors) comes with a library (lib sensors) that lots of tools support, but as a beginning point, you are going to use the included sensors command:

```
$ sensors
bcm2835_thermal-virtual-0
Adapter: Virtual device
temp1:        +42.8°C

tmp102-i2c-1-48
Adapter: bcm2708_i2c.1
temp1:        +24.8°C  (high = +160.0°C, hyst = +150.0°C)
```

In this output, you can see two readings:

`bcm2835_thermal-virtual-0`

> This is the temperature sensor inside the Broadcom BCM2835 system on chip at the heart of the Raspberry Pi. It is also the same reading you can get from `vcgencmd`, as described in "Measure Temperature" on page 16.

`tmp102-i2c-1-48`

> This is your TMP102 sensor, reporting for duty.

From this output, you can see that your TMP102 sensor is reporting a lovely temperature of 24.8°C. The `high` value is the value at which the TMP102 shuts down due to extreme overheating (160.0°C qualifies).

It also has a `hyst` value, which refers to "temperature hysteresis limit" (sadly, not Def Leppard's legendary 1987 album *Hysteria*). The hysteresis limit value is the value at which the sensor reading no longer fluctuates, as it approaches the shutdown temperature.

If you just want to see the TMP102 reading, you just need to pass the `lm_sensors` "chip name" for that device as an option. As configured, the TMP102 is `tmp102-i2c-1-48` (`$sensortype-$bustype-$busnumber-$devicenumber`). If you want to see the values in Fahrenheit, just pass `-f`:

```
$ sensors -f tmp102-i2c-1-48
tmp102-i2c-1-48
Adapter: bcm2708_i2c.1
temp1:        +76.5°F  (high = +320.0°F, hyst = +302.0°F)
```

If you want to parse the sensor values directly, you can either use the aforementioned `libsensors` library, or you can access the values directly via `/sys`. `/sys/class/i2c-dev/i2c-1/device/1-0048/` is the device node where you can find the values stored in special `/sys` files. These files represent the values reported from the device driver, and are updated constantly. If you want to get an updated value, just reopen one of these files:

```
$ cd /sys/class/i2c-dev/i2c-1/device/1-0048/
$ ls
driver  modalias  power      temp1_input  temp1_max_hyst
hwmon   name      subsystem  temp1_max    uevent
$ cat temp1_input
23312
```

To convert that value to Celsius, just divide it by 1,000. If you need to convert it to other temperature units, refer to "Fun with Math and Science" on page 16.

Check on Your Plants

> Plants are an important part of the ecosystem of life on our planet. Or
> maybe you just want tasty toppings on your burger. Either way, you can
> use your Raspberry Pi to help them grow big and healthy.

Gardening is tricky stuff. Plants can't talk, so they can't tell us what they need. Gardeners are like hackers in a lot of ways: they learn a lot by doing, getting experience in how to grow plants, where to keep them, how much to feed them, and what songs they like to listen to (hey, I heard they love music). At the heart of this, whether they realize this or not, is data gathering. By adding a dedicated temperature and humidity sensor to a Raspberry Pi, we can gather useful data about the state of the garden.

Most plants need a few things to grow properly:

Soil

> This supports the plant and gives it an anchor for the roots to grow in. The roots draw in the water and minerals that the plant needs. You want to use a healthy, well-nourished soil with the right sort of minerals and ingredients for your plant. Potting soil is usually a good start, but there are much larger books about getting the perfect soil for your plant.

Sunlight

> Plants perform *photosynthesis*, which is the process of converting sunlight into the chemical fuels to "power" the plants biological processes. All green plants need light, but the amount varies by plant. Some plants prefer a lot of of light, and some plants prefer much less.

Air

> Specifically, carbon dioxide. If the air near your plant is too polluted, your plant will not grow well.

Water

> Everything alive (that we know of) needs water. Plants are no different, but the amount of water that a plant requires varies by the type of plant. If this is confusing to you, think about a cactus in the desert and then compare it to a palm tree next to an oasis. Both are plants, both need water, but the cactus needs far less to survive (and wouldn't really be able to use more than a little anyway).

Space

> Plants need space to grow, usually up, but sometimes outward.

Optimum temperature

> Again, this is specific to the type of plants, but all plants have a range of temperatures that they prefer. The U.S. Department of Agriculture calls this "plant hardiness" and maps it out into zones across the United States. Each zone is indi-

cated by the range of temperatures it experiences, and each zone is given an identifier code. For example, Tom's plant hardiness zone is 5b, and Ruth's is 7a. See *http://planthardiness.ars.usda.gov* for a map of all the U.S. zones (and to discover your zone). Also, some plants tolerate frost and freezing better than others, so depending on your plants, temperatures dropping below 0°C could result in plant death.

Measuring the space, soil, and air is not simple to do, but we can measure the amount of water in the air and the temperature of the garden. You can also measure the intensity of light near the plants using the light sensor in Hack #42, but this hack will focus on monitoring temperature and water (humidity).

Serious Gardeners

If you're a hardcore gardener, you might point out that while humidity is interesting, it is less interesting than rainfall measurement (assuming your garden is not in a water-controlled greenhouse). To get that, you need to wire up a rain gauge sensor.

There are several different rain gauge sensors on the market, but connecting them to a Raspberry Pi and getting the data is a bit more complicated. There are some 1-Wire rain gauge units, but the Raspberry Pi does not have a 1-Wire connector. You can get around that by building a circuit to connect it to GPIO (either via the w1-gpio driver or the I2C bus), or you can buy a 1-Wire-to-USB converter (like the Maxim Integrated DS9490R#).

From a software side, you can use OWFS (http://owfs.org/) to read the data from the 1-Wire device. This can get complicated quickly, so we'll leave this as an exercise for the motivated and serious gardener. For the rest of us, we'll start with humidity and work our way up.

While it is technically true that your plants are growing in real time, they are doing it so slowly that you have to watch them over long periods of time to see the growth. (Search YouTube for "time lapse of plants"; it is rather freaky and cool.) As a result, we do not need to have real-time measurements of temperature and humidity, so using a sensor like a TMP102 (as in Hack #37) is overkill. Instead, we can use an "all-in-one" temperature and humidity sensor. Adafruit has an excellent one from Adsong, the *AM2302* (*http://www.adafruit.com/products/393*).

Here are the main reasons the AM2302 sensor is a good one for this hack:

- It is sealed up in a plastic body, which will help it be resistant to Mother Nature's wrath. It also has a mounting hole, so you can attach it (either by hanging or screwing) in a secure location in your garden.
- It is a digital sensor, so it is accurate and simple to wire.
- It reads in new data every two seconds, which is nowhere near real time, but is more than sufficient for monitoring plants in a garden.

- It uses three wires, and only one wire for communication! This means that only three GPIO pins on your Raspberry Pi will be used (and only one general-purpose pin needs to be reserved).

In fact, the only real downside to using the AM2302 is that it does not (as of the time of this writing) have a native Linux kernel driver for it. This means that we cannot easily plug it into the lm_sensors infrastructure, as described in Hack #37.

Adding the AM2302 to the Linux Kernel

The AM2302 has a DHT22 temperature-humidity sensor at its core. It should be rather simple for someone with a basic understanding of C and the Linux kernel to add a hwmon driver for the DHT22. If you're looking for a good starter Linux kernel development project, this might be it! We hope that one day this note will become obsolete once someone writes this code, and then this hack becomes much simpler for everyone!

Again, Adafruit comes to the rescue. They provide an open source C program for reading the temperature and humidity values off the AD2302. We'll get to that in a moment, but first, you'll want to wire it to your Raspberry Pi. The AD2302 has three wires coming out of the plastic case:

Red
    For 3.3 V power

Black
    For Ground (GND)

Yellow
    Where the data comes out

Technically, you can connect any of the generic I/O pins on the GPIO header and it will work, but we know you're going to ask us to tell you which pin to use ... so just go ahead and connect the yellow data wire to BCM Pin 4 (P1-07). Why? Well, it is the first generic I/O pin underneath the 3.3 V (the two pins above it are I2C pins).

Connect the red wire to the 3.3V power pin (P1-01) and the black wire to a Ground (GND) pin. If you aren't sure what all of these GPIO terms mean, check out Hack #14. The simplest way to wire these pins to the Raspberry Pi is with a solderless breadboard and a Pi Cobbler (Hack #15). The wires coming from the AD2302 are a little too thin to insert into the breadboard, so you'll probably want to connect them directly to some thicker wire first. There are a number of ways to do this:

- Solder the wire to a thicker wire.

- Twist the ends of the two wires together, then seal them with electrical tape (or hot glue).
- Crimp the wires together using a crimping tool.

No matter which method you use, you'll probably need to strip off some of the insulated connector covering the wires. You really should use a wire stripper for this, and not try to use a pair of scissors (or the cutting part of a pair of pliers), because you run the risk of cutting off part of the wire itself.

Once you have these three wires connected and properly inserted into your breadboard (with a Pi Cobbler connecting it to your Raspberry Pi GPIO ports), you can install the software to test it out.

On your Raspberry Pi, clone a copy of the Adafruit Git Raspberry Pi repository:

```
$ git clone git://github.com/adafruit/Adafruit-Raspberry-Pi-Python-Code.git
$ cd Adafruit-Raspberry-Pi-Python-Code/Adafruit_DHT_Driver
```

Even though the name of this repository is `Adafruit-Raspberry-Pi-Python-Code`, you will notice that the code in this directory is in C. Adafruit had to use C code to talk to the AM2302 sensor since it requires extremely fast timing to read, and Python would not be able to easily accomplish this task.

Adafruit includes a precompiled binary that should work on any distribution of Linux for the Raspberry Pi, but if you do not trust their binary (or it doesn't work for some reason), you can rebuild it. Just have `gcc` and `make` installed, and run:

```
$ rm -f Adafruit_DHT
$ make Adafruit_DHT
```

Either way, you need to run the `Adafruit_DHT` binary. To talk to the AM2302 sensor on BCM Pin 4, run:

```
$ su -c './Adafruit_DHT 2302 4'
Using pin #4
Data (40): 0x2 0x16 0x0 0xe6 0xfe
Temp =  23.0 *C, Hum = 53.4 %
```

The first option passed is the sensor type (this code also supports interfacing with a raw DHT11 (11) and DHT22 (22) in addition to the AM2302 (2302)). The second option is the GPIO pin that it is connected to. You can see that it is reporting a temperature of 23.0°C and a humidity of 53.4%.

You now have a reliable way of measuring the data from the AM2302. Adafruit has also included a Python script (`Adafruit_DHT_googledocs.ex.py`), which will run the `Adafruit_DHT` binary every 30 seconds, and upload the humidity and temperature readings into a Google Docs spreadsheet.

To use it, you will need to configure the script with your own Google Docs account details. Open `Adafruit_DHT_googledocs.ex.py` with your favorite text editor and then look for this section of code:

```
# Account details for google docs
email      = 'you@somewhere.com'
password   = '$hhh!'
spreadsheet = 'SpreadsheetName'
```

Change the values for the `email`, `password`, and `spreadsheet`, making sure to keep the actual values wrapped in single quotes, and save out the file. To run the script, simply execute it from a terminal:

```
$ ./Adafruit_DHT_googledocs.ex.py
```

You might want to run this in a `screen` session, so that you do not need to keep that terminal open. To do that, simply execute the `screen` command before running the `Adafruit_DHT_googledocs.ex.py` script, and then press Control-A-D to disconnect from the `screen` session. You can reconnect to that `screen` session later by running `screen -r`.

You can now go to your Google Docs account in a web browser and watch the humidity and temperature data for your plants get uploaded over time.

This is a simple monitoring setup, but it is possible to make more complicated setups using this model:

- You could write a wrapper script to check for alert conditions (temperature approaching freezing) and have it send you notification emails (or tweets).
- You could use the AM2302 as a data source for automating your garden (think automated watering).
- Or if you really don't like plants, it could be part of a homemade weather station. Monitoring home-brewed beer or your wine cellar?

Really, anything that doesn't handle temperature or moisture well is ideal for this hack.

HACK 39   Make Your Pi Water-Resistant (with a Case)

> If you want to run your Raspberry Pi outdoors, you're going to need to put it in a water-resistant case. Here's one way to do it.

If you are working on a project that involves readings from the great outdoors, the best place for your Raspberry Pi is inside, but that isn't always practical or possible. Whether you are trying to monitor plants in a garden, or automating your mailbox, you'll need to protect your Raspberry Pi from:

Water

This includes, but is not limited to, rain, snow, sleet, hail, dew, sprinkler, and animal ... fluids.

Nature

Dirt doesn't hurt children, but it is no friend to electronics. Lots of animals like warmth, and the Raspberry Pi is an oasis of heat in a cold night. Also, the combination of nature and water means mold and mildew, neither of which is good for your Pi. Oh, and insects, we can't forget them.

Weather

We're not too worried about a tornado or a hurricane here. If that happens, you've got bigger problems than a broken or missing $35 Linux PC. That said, we don't want it to fly away or break in normal weather conditions.

Here's how to build a water-resistant, outdoor-friendly case for your Raspberry Pi. Start with a water-tight plastic container and lid (or, if you want to really up your game, get an ammo box with a rubber O-ring seal from an Army-Navy surplus store instead). We recommend getting a large one, as opposed to the smallest one the Raspberry Pi will fit completely into.

The plastic container will serve as a general protection from most of the main concerns highlighted earlier. Using a larger container will allow you to weight it down from the inside as needed and also gives it a bit more of an air pocket for the heat generated by the Raspberry Pi to dissipate outward.

You'll probably want to connect cables to the Raspberry Pi, so you'll need to make some holes in the container. Try to make these as small and as few as possible, but don't just make one big hole and run all of your cables through it.

The trick is to make a hole, run a cable through it, and then use common silicon sealant (available at any large hardware store) to permanently seal the cable into the hole and restore the watertight seal for the plastic container. The trouble with this arrangement with multiple cables in the same hole is that it can be tricky to completely seal the gaps that occur between the cables. Also, if you opted for the metal ammunition box, you'll need to get specialized sealant for metal (and a pretty good drill setup to make the holes).

Using a large container also gives you the opportunity to connect the USB power plug directly to a weatherized extension cord *inside* the container. Then, you can seal the extension cord through the hole, and the USB power plug is not exposed to the elements at all.

Since this arrangement is good, but not perfect (and it will condense some), go ahead and toss in several silica gel packets. This can be purchased rather cheaply from a variety of sources (including Amazon). The silica will dry out the air inside the container even further, and it is nontoxic.

Silica gel packets usually contain the warning not to eat them because of silica's extreme dessicant nature and the fact that it is commonly doped with other chemicals that allow it to visually alter its color as it takes on moisture. Those chemicals are usually carcinogenic.

Also, depending on how waterproof (or animal-proof) you want the case to be, you can take the extra step of sealing the container lid into place "permanently" when you've finished.

We recommend that you consider wiring a temperature sensor (and possibly a humidity sensor) inside of this container case in addition to any external sensors or input/outputs (see Hacks Hack #37 and Hack #38 for details).

And as a bonus idea, you could also use this hack as the basis for a more elaborate Raspberry Pi-powered interactive geocache (as described in Hack #41).

HACK 40   Make Your Pi Water-Resistant (Without a Case)

Have you ever wanted to run your Raspberry Pi underwater without a case? This hack can make that happen (at least for a while).

Normally, electronics of any sort coming into contact with water results in the release of the magic smoke and one dead electronic component. Electronics used in the same environment as water are carefully sealed in watertight components (think about underwater cameras for example), but the Raspberry Pi is just a bare electronics board.

You could make it water resistant with a case (as described in Hack #39), but that can get expensive, and at the time of this writing, there were not many water-resistant cases for the Raspberry Pi out there. You could seal the entire Raspberry Pi in transparent resin, but that isn't something most people have immediately available.

Safety Warning and Disclaimer

This hack is not for the faint of heart. It could very well result in a dead Raspberry Pi and some serious pain. It goes without saying that the Raspberry Pi is not designed or intended for use in water. By mixing electricity and water, you expose yourself to a very real risk of electrocution. Unless you are really prepared to undertake this hack safely, you might consider skipping it and moving on to something else. We don't want you to hurt yourself. No hack is worth injury.

Enter NeverWet. NeverWet is a spray-on paint-type product from Rustoleum that, when applied to a surface, makes it extremely hydrophobic (as the name implies). The NeverWet paint applies a coating that causes water to form nearly perfect spheres, which roll off the surface, keeping items dry and clean. In the United States, you can find it in home improvement stores for $20. It comes in a box with two spray cans. The first is a primer, and the second applies the super-hydrophobic layer.

What Rustoleum Thinks About This Hack

We feel at this point we should tell you what Rustoleum thinks about using Never-Wet on electronics. From their FAQ page (http://www.rustoleum.com/homeowner/faqs/neverwet-faqs/):

Q: Can NeverWet be used on electronics? A: No, NeverWet should not be used on electronics.

OK, you've read that, right? Rustoleum isn't interested in hearing about how this hack didn't work for you or how you destroyed a $35 mini-computer. (For the record, we aren't interested in hearing about it either.) All righty then, let us continue. Regardless of what the FAQ says, we know this works (at least for a while). We've done it.

There is an aesthetic downside to this hack. The NeverWet paint is not transparent, not even a little bit. When it dries, it looks like someone has applied a chalky white film over the surface of the Raspberry Pi. (Because you actually did by spraying it repeatedly with NeverWet paint.) It looks weird, to say the least.

Here's what you'll need for this hack:

- A Raspberry Pi that you have no sentimental attachment to. You're never getting that $35 back.
- An SD card that you never plan on using again. We recommend a full-sized SD card, not a mini card in a converter, since that just adds another crevice for water to try to get in.
- Cables that you never want to use again. We used a USB power cable and a USB to TTL serial console cable, as the bare minimum to access the Pi, but you might want to add an Ethernet and HDMI cable into the mix or a WiFi dongle.
- One package of NeverWet spray paint.

Go to a dry, cool, still, well-ventilated place with your supplies. (We went with "the backyard on a nice fall day.") You should already have your SD card configured with a Linux image. If you're using a console over the UART serial device, have that properly configured as described in Hack #16.

Firmly and completely insert your SD card and the cables you want to use. Make sure the system works right now, then leave all the cables connected to the Raspberry Pi, but disconnect the other ends from everything (like electricity!).

Now get out the NeverWet paint. The paint comes with instructions, but here's the basic workflow:

1. Prep your Raspberry Pi and cables for painting. We hung the Raspberry Pi in mid-air using the attached cables, but you might want to set it down on a table. Generally, dangling electronics from their cables is a bad idea, but in the name of a solid coat, we'll let it slide this time.

2. Shake can #1 (the primer) for a few minutes.

3. Holding the can 6–12 inches away from the Raspberry Pi, apply a quick (but complete) coat of the NeverWet primer to ALL exposed surfaces, including a few inches on each cable, as shown in Figure 4-4. Spray inside every possible nook and cranny you can, including connectors you are not using and all around each connector you are using. Don't forget to spray the edges and the GPIO pins.

4. Let the primer dry for 30–60 minutes.

5. Shake can #2 (super-hydrophic paint) for a few minutes.

6. Repeat the process you used with the printer for can #2. Be thorough, but don't waste paint. You want a solid coating on every possible surface that might contact water, but you don't want to end up with a drippy mess. You want to be making smooth passes with the spray paint.

7. Let it dry for five minutes, and then apply another layer of the paint in can #2. You want to repeat this cycle 3–4 times.

8. When you've put on all the layers, let the Raspberry Pi dry for 12–24 hours.

Figure 4-4.
Spraying the primer on the Raspberry Pi

After the last drying period, your Raspberry Pi is ready to use again. Power it up to make sure that the act of painting it with NeverWet didn't kill it before it ever hits the water.

If you are planning to to immerse your Raspberry Pi in water, you should not hold it with your bare hands (for what we hope are obvious safety reasons). You should be able to gently insert it by holding the cable and lower it into a small container of water (either powered on or off). If you insert it into the water before powering it on, you might want to be a good distance away before sending power over to the Raspberry Pi. Having the Pi plugged in via a USB power cable run to a power strip (that is switched off) might be a good idea, since you can turn on the power strip from a distance. Additionally, whenever there is a risk of water, you should consider having a Ground Fault Circuit Interruptor (GFCI) in use. You can get this built into your power strip, or as an adaptor for the plug.

This is not a magic spell. It might not work at all. If you didn't do a thorough paint job, it might immediately go "zap" and die. Heck, it might do that even if you do the best paint job known to mankind.

That said, even if you do manage to make a Raspberry Pi water-resistant using this method, you shouldn't assume you can put it in a fish tank on your desk and use it forever. The coating isn't permanent; it will fade with time and friction. Rustoleum notes that NeverWet relies on a layer of air to form the super-hydrophobic coating on the surface of the object. This means if you submerge a treated object over time, the coating will dissipate.

If you are putting a Pi in a space where humidity is a real possibility, this might be a good insurance against occasional humidity ending your project in heartbreak. However, we admit that in most cases, this is just a fun hack that allows you to say that you've run Linux in a computer completely underwater with no case.

HACK 41 Find Geocaches from Your Car

> Geocaching is a great way to be geeky *and* get outdoors. Why not convert a Raspberry Pi into a Cacheberry Pi?

Geocaching taps into the thrill of finding something hidden, of going on a treasure hunt. If you've never heard of geocaching before, the idea is simple. People hide a storage container somewhere publicly accessible (although not necessarily *easily* accessible) and upload the GPS positioning coordinates for that container to the Internet.

The size of the container varies from the very small (just large enough to hold a miniature pencil with a tiny sheet of paper rolled around it), to small (35 mm film canister or Altoids tin), all the way up to large containers such as metal ammunition boxes.

These are then hidden in plain sight, such as attached under park benches, hanging from trees, or in the crevices between rocks. One particularly memorable geocache is secured inside a large hollow tree by a tension pulley system. You reach inside the tree, pull a ring, and the geocache would drop down. Pull the ring again, and the cache goes back up inside the tree.

The ideas behind geocaching are not new by any means; people were doing real-world treasure hunts in the form of letterboxing for years beforehand. But when GPS was made available to the public in 1991, followed by the ubiquity of highly accurate GPS systems and the explosion of the Internet, geocaching-type treasure hunting was able to flourish.

At the time of this writing, *http://geocaching.com* (the primary website for logging and adding geocaches) is tracking more than two million active geocaches and more than six million registered geocachers. It is a game that can be played by people of all ages and abilities, with nothing more than a smartphone and tenacity. The rules of the game are simple: find as many as you can, be discreet when finding caches, leave the cache better than you found it, and log your finds (or failure to finds) so that the cache's activity can be tracked.

There are other complexities:

Exchange items

Goodies, trinkets, toys, and "treasures" are left by geocachers in caches of supportable sizes. The rule of thumb is that if you take one, you also leave one behind.

Travel bugs and geocoins

Tracked objects that move via geocachers from cache to cache.

Travel bug hotels

Geocaches specifically set up to facilitate the drop-off and retrieval of travel bugs. These are usually found near transportation hubs, such as airports, so that geocachers can help travel bugs move around the world.

Puzzle caches

Geocaches where the GPS coordinates must be decoded from a puzzle.

Multi-stage caches

Sequences of caches where only the first set of GPS coordinates are provided, and each cache provides another set of GPS coordinates until they lead you to the final cache (usually a much larger cache with tradable goodies).

While there are any number of smartphone applications (or add-ons for in-car GPS systems) to help you find geocaches near you, Jeff Clement created the Cacheberry Pi (Figure 4-5) to be embedded in a car. This Raspberry Pi-based project is primarily intended to show you what the next nearby geocache is in a big, obvious way (as opposed to staring at little icons on a general-purpose GPS). It empowers you to not have to do as much prep before setting out to go geocaching by letting you simply get in your car, pick a direction, and drive.

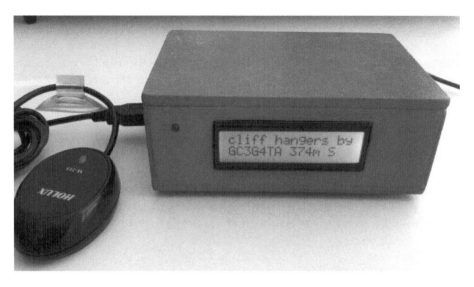

Figure 4-5.
Cacheberry Pi (photo by Jeff Clement, *http://cacheberrypi.jclement.ca*)

This hack is also smart about how it presents geocaches to you. When still, it presents the nearest cache in a 3 km radius. When the Cacheberry Pi detects that you are traveling at highway speeds, it will instead focus its search in front of you and show you only the nearest geocache in the direction that you are traveling. It has the ability to maintain a database of 20,000+ geocaches and to track a log of which caches you have visited (and allow you to transfer that log via USB storage device). It displays the nearest geocache to you, the distance to that cache, and the compass bearing to the geocache.

Gathering Hardware

To build the Cacheberry Pi, you will need some hardware in addition to the Raspberry Pi unit.

GPS receiver

The Cacheberry Pi project assumes that you are using a USB-powered GPS receiver (GPSr) and recommends the *Holux M-215* (*http://dx.com/p/genuine-holux-usb-gps-receiver-black-106778?item=8*), but any other standards-compliant GPS should work properly.

You can also use the *Adafruit Ultimate GPS Module* (*http://www.adafruit.com/products/746*), but if you do that, you will need to disable the serial console so that the GPS can use it (as covered in Hack #16). If you choose this hardware, you will also need to reconfigure gpsd within the Cacheberry Pi Linux OS to point to the serial GPSr by running:

```
$ sudo dpkg-reconfigure gpsd
```

This step is not necessary if you use a supported USB-powered GPSr.

LCD screen

The LCD screen is where the Cacheberry Pi will present geocache information to you while you're on the hunt. The Cacheberry Pi project recommends the *IIC/I2C/TWI SPI Serial LCD 1602 Module Electronic building block for Arduino* (*http://dx.com/p/arduino-iic-i2c-twi-spi-serial-lcd-1602-module-electronic-building-block-136922?item=4*).

You can also use the *Sainsmart 1602 ICD LCD unit* (*http://www.amazon.com/gp/product/B0085J9996/*), but you will then have to modify the driver in the Cacheberry Pi codebase. Steve Whitcher has documented *how he was able to get it working* (*http://www.neighborgeek.net/2013/02/using-16x2-lcd-with-i2c-on-raspberry-pi.html*).

It might also be possible to use other 16 x 2 LCD units (such as the one on the Adafruit LCD Pi Plate, covered in Hack #28), but we have not tested them.

Power cord

Because the Cacheberry Pi is designed to be used in an automobile, you can plug it into an available 12 V power (cigarette lighter) receptacle. Hack #55 covers this sort of power arrangement in detail.

Since the only device normally plugged into the Cacheberry Pi USB bus is the GPSr (and a USB flash drive when updating the geocache database), you should not need to use an externally powered USB hub.

Serial console

This is optional (and not available if you are using the Adafruit Ultimate GPS Module), but the Cacheberry Pi is configured by default to support a serial console over the Raspberry Pi GPIO pins.

If you want to add a serial console, just follow the instructions in Hack #16, and make a hole in the project box for the wire to come out.

Indicator LED

You can optionally connect an indicator LED. It will flash when a geocache is nearby, but you don't really need this unless geocaches are few and far between in your part of the world (or you only have a few in the Cacheberry Pi database).

Project box

Admittedly, this is purely an aesthetic component, but you can get a standard plastic project box, cut a hole for the LCD to mount, then place the Raspberry Pi inside of the box as well. Holes for the power cable and both USB ports will finish off the box, then you can attach your finished Cacheberry Pi (in a box) to the dash of your car.

Preparing the Software Image

The Cacheberry Pi project offers a prebuilt image (based on Raspbian). Put a fresh SD card into your Linux computer, and then download and uncompress a copy of the Cacheberry Pi image:

```
$ wget http://cdn.jclement.ca/cacheberrypi/cacheberrypi.img.20120921.bz2
$ tar xf cacheberrypi.img.20120921.bz2
```

By the time you read this, there might be a newer image than the 2012-09-21 image. You can confirm on the Cacheberry Pi project website (http://cacheberrypi.jcle-ment.ca).

After it downloads sucessfully, use the dd command to write the Cacheberry Pi image onto the SD card. Be extra careful that you know which device is your inserted SD card (Hack #02 explains how to figure that out). In Fedora, this is almost always /dev/mmcblk0, but on other distributions it is a /dev/sd* device. You do not want to use dd to overwrite your laptop's hard drive with the Cacheberry Pi image!

Once you're sure you know the SD card device name, run the dd command as root, changing the of= value as needed:

```
$ sudo dd bs=4M if=cacheberrypi.img.20120921 of=/dev/mmcblk0
```

When that finishes, run the sync command a few times to ensure the image was properly written onto the SD card (and not just into the memory buffers):

```
$ sync;sync;sync
```

Finally, remove the SD card from your laptop and insert it into your Raspberry Pi.

Wiring the Cacheberry Pi

This hack assumes you are using the components recommended by the Cacheberry Pi project. If you differ from them, you will need to adjust accordingly.

Plug the USB GPSr directly into a USB port on the Raspberry Pi. The LCD screen has four pins, labeled SCL, SDA, VCC, and GND. You will need to connect these pins to the appropriate pins on the Raspberry Pi GPIO using female-to-female jumper wires. Table 4-2 shows the pin mapping.

Table 4-2. Cacheberry LCD pin mapping

CACHEBERRY LCD PIN LABEL	RASPBERRY PI BCM GPIO PIN
GND	GND
SCL	3 (SCL)
SDA	2 (SDA)
VCC	5 V

If you want to connect an indicator LED, wire it into BCM Pin 25 (P1-22), with an appropriate resistor between the BCM 25 pin and the positive leg of the LED. The type of resistor will depend on the specifications of the LED being used. For example, if you use a Red LED with a voltage of 2 V and a current of 15 mA, the 5 V circuit will require a 220 ohm resistor. You can calculate the resistor value for your LED with this website: *http://led.linear1.org/1led.wiz* The negative leg of the LED should wire to an available GPIO ground (GND) pin.

Connect the Raspberry Pi to the mini-USB power cable (fed from the 12 V cigarette lighter receptacle), and the OS image should boot up.

Loading Cache Data

Because the Cacheberry Pi is not networked, you need to load geocaches via a USB flash drive. It is configured to always listen for a USB drive to be inserted, and when one is inserted with the proper filesystem layout, it will automatically import the geocache database off of the USB drive. It will also copy the track history from the Cacheberry Pi to the USB flash drive.

To set up a USB flash drive, insert it into your Linux computer and make sure it is mounted. Most Linux distributions will automount USB storage devices when they are inserted. Check the output of the `mount` command for a `/dev/sdb` or `/dev/sdc` device (`/dev/sda` is usually the laptop hard drive), and then change into the directory where the USB drive is mounted.

Download and decompress the "sample" ZIP file for the Cacheberry USB filesystem layout. Then copy the files into the mounted USB drive (in this example, we assume it is mounted at /mnt/usbdrive):

```
$ cd ~
$ wget http://cdn.jclement.ca/cacheberrypi/cacheberrypi_usbstick_sample.zip
$ unzip cacheberrypi_usbstick_sample.zip
$ cp -a cacheberrypi_usbstick_sample/* /mnt/usbdrive
```

The USB drive is now prepared for use, but you'll want to add some cache entries. The Cacheberry Pi will look for a file named nav.csv in the cacheberrypi/ directory. This comma-separated values (CSV) file contains the list of geocaches in what is commonly referred to as "Microsoft Streets and Trips" format.

The simplest way to generate this CSV file is to run *GSAK* (*http://www.gsak.net*) on Windows or *Open Cache Manager* (*http://opencachemanage.sourceforge.net*) on Linux/OSX. You can also generate a CSV file directly on *http://geocaching.com* if you have a premium account and set up a "pocket query."

Save the nav.csv file to the USB flash drive, unmount it, and insert it into the running Cacheberry Pi. It should detect the USB flash drive, and the LCD screen will show a progress indicator as it copies over the updated geocache database (Figure 4-6).

Figure 4-6.
Cacheberry Pi (photo by Jeff Clement, *http://cacheberrypi.jclement.ca*)

Detecting the presence (and intensity) of light can help you to automate all sorts of tasks, from the garden to home automation and beyond. Hack your Raspberry Pi and it will see the light!

Few things are constant in our world, but the rising and setting of the sun is close enough that you can count it as one, at least for the next five billion years or so. By monitoring the presence and intensity of light, you can tell whether it is day or night, whether it is sunny or cloudy, or if someone has turned on a lamp in a room. But to do that, you need a luminosity sensor.

There are lots of different luminosity sensors out there, but because you want to wire it to our trusty friend, the Raspberry Pi, you want to pick something that you can add to that device easily. Because the Raspberry Pi does not support analog inputs (without going through a converter first), you need a digital luminosity sensor, with bonus points for one that the Linux kernel supports natively. Adafruit has just the thing: the *Taos TSL2561* (*http://www.adafruit.com/products/439*) digital luminosity/lux/light sensor.

What is Lux?

Lux (abbreviated *lx*), is the SI unit for measuring illuminance, described in terms of one lumen per square meter. It can be measured with a device logically called a "lux meter." The full moon is about 1 lux, while direct sunlight is measured in the range of tens of thousands to >100,000 lux.

Why is this sensor ideal? A few reasons:

- It is a digital sensor, so you can connect it directly to the Raspberry Pi GPIO pins without any complicated wiring.
- It is precise and can be configured to detect light ranges from 0.1 to 40,000+ lux.
- It contains both infrared and full-spectrum diodes. Most luminosity sensors have only one type of detection diode, but the TSL2561 can separately measure infrared, full-spectrum, or human-visible light.
- It supports I2C (for an explanation of I2C, see What is I2C?). This means you can connect it to the Raspberry Pi GPIO with just four pins.
- It is a low-power component, about 0.5 mA when actively sensing and less than 15 uA when in powerdown mode.
- It is also small, about the size of a U.S. quarter (see Figure 4-7).

Figure 4-7.
The tiny TSL2561

When you purchase the TSL2561 sensor kit, it comes with the light sensor already attached to a six-pin breakout board (and a six-pin header strip). Plug the header strip into a breadboard, with the long end of the header pins down, and then place the light sensor breakout board onto the header pins (the shorter ends). Solder the pins permanently to the breakout board (if you need a refresher on soldering, see "Soldering Reminders" on page 42).

Then, you'll need to connect four of the six pins on the TSL2561 breakout board to the Raspberry Pi GPIO ports (see Table 4-3).

Table 4-3. TSL2561 Breakout Mapping Table

TSL2561 BREAKOUT PIN LABEL	RASPBERRY PI BCM GPIO PIN
GND	GND
SCL	3 (SCL)
SDA	2 (SDA)
VCC	3.3 V

The TS2561 is a 3.3 V-powered device, so be sure you do not accidentally connect it to the 5 V power pin on the Raspberry Pi GPIO, or it will go off to electronics heaven. The Pi Cobbler makes this wiring notably simpler (see Hack #15), but as long as you have wires connecting the TSL2561 breakout to the right pins on the Raspberry Pi GPIO, you will be fine.

As usual, the instructions in this hack refer to the BCM GPIO pin labels here (see Hack #14 for details).

Once the TSL2561 breakout board is wired up to the Raspberry Pi, you can use the I2C utilities within the Linux distribution environment to confirm it is properly connected to the I2C bus on the GPIO, assuming your kernel has I2C support properly configured. If you have built a custom kernel as described in Hack #22, you will have I2C preconfigured properly. If not, you might need to load the following modules before you can access I2C devices:

```
$ su -c 'modprobe i2c-bcm2708'
$ su -c 'modprobe i2c-dev'
```

Further, you will need to enable these additional options:

Industrial IO Support (`CONFIG_IIO`)

This option can also be found in the Device Drivers menu. The industrial I/O subsystem provides a unified framework for drivers for many different types of embedded sensors using a variety of different physical interfaces. You can also go into that menu and build support for any of the devices that you find within it that you might want to use in projects. Be sure that you compile in the top-level IIO support, as shown in Figure 4-8 (you can modularize the sensors below it if you wish). You will also want to be sure to enable (and compile in) the "Enable buffer support within IIO" (`CONFIG_IIO_BUFFER`), "Industrial I/O buffering based on kfifo" (`CONFIG_IIO_KFIFO_BUF`), and "Enable triggered sampling support" (`CONFIG_IIO_TRIGGER`) options inside the Industrial IO Support menu.

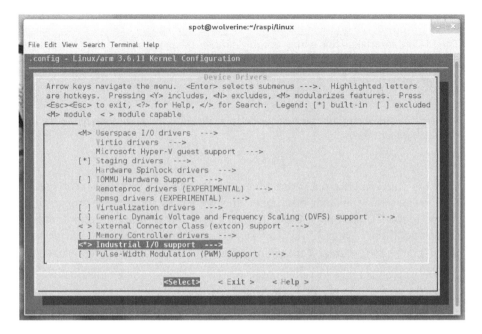

Figure 4-8.
Enabling Industrial IO Support (CONFIG_IIO)

TAOS light sensors (CONFIG_SENSORS_TSL2563)

This driver is currently in the staging level of the Linux kernel device drivers, which is reserved for drivers that are new or less tested than other drivers. To enable it, navigate into the Device Drivers menu and then the Staging drivers menu (you will need to enable it first). From there, go into the IIO staging drivers submenu and then into Light sensors. CONFIG_SENSORS_TSL2563 is labeled in that menu as "TAOS TSL2560, TSL2561, TSL2562 and TSL2563 ambient light sensors." Enable it as a module, as shown in Figure 4-9. You will also need to enable "Hwmon driver that uses channels specified via iio maps" (CONFIG_IIO_ST_HWMON) to allow IIO devices to provide basic hwmon functionality. This entry is in the Device Drivers → Staging drivers → IIO staging drivers menu. You should compile this driver into the Linux kernel so that you automatically get this feature when you use IIO devices.

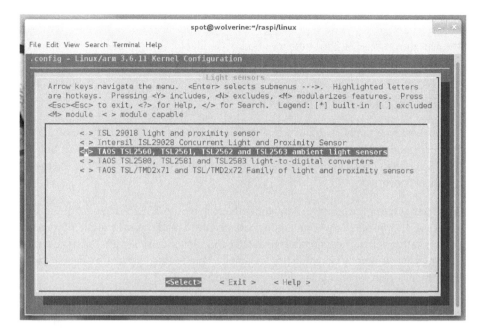

Figure 4-9.
TAOS TSL2561 light sensor support enabled as a module

To install the necessary userspace software (i2c-tools) on Pidora, run:

```
$ su -c 'yum install i2c-tools -y'
```

To install i2c-tools on Raspbian, run:

```
$ su -c 'apt-get install i2c-tools'
```

To look for the device, you need to run i2cdetect on bus 1 (as root). Here's the i2cde tect command line you want to run:

```
$ su -c 'i2cdetect -y 1'
```

If all of your wiring is correct, you will see output like this:

```
     0  1  2  3  4  5  6  7  8  9  a  b  c  d  e  f
00:          -- -- -- -- -- -- -- -- -- -- -- -- --
10: -- -- -- -- -- -- -- -- -- -- -- -- -- -- -- --
20: -- -- -- -- -- -- -- -- -- -- -- -- -- -- -- --
30: -- -- -- -- -- -- -- -- 39 -- -- -- -- --- --
40: -- -- -- -- -- -- -- -- -- -- -- -- -- -- -- --
50: -- -- -- -- -- -- -- -- -- -- -- -- -- -- -- --
60: -- -- -- -- -- -- -- -- -- -- -- -- -- -- -- --
70: -- -- -- -- -- -- -- --
```

The TSL2561 sensor reports as device address 0x39 on the I2C bus, and sure enough, `i2cdetect` sees it. If you want to change the device address, you can connect a wire to the `ADDR` pin on the TSL2561 breakout board. Connect it to a ground (GND) pin to set the address to 0x29, or connect it to a 3.3 V power pin to set the address to 0x49.

Accessing the Sensor via Python

The easiest way to get readings from the TSL2561 sensor is to use the Adafruit I2C Python module. The simplest value to understand from the TSL2561 is lux, but the TSL2561 doesn't read in those units directly; you have to write code to do the mathematical conversion.

As a further complication, you can adjust the gain on the TSL2561 sensor. If the gain is set low (1), the sensor will calculate more accurate readings in bright light to avoid sensor saturation. If the gain is set high (16), the sensor will calculate more accurate readings in low light by boosting the sensitivity. You can also generate a reading with "automatic" gain, which cycles between low and high gain.

You will need to install the `python-smbus` and `Adafruit_I2C` libraries. The `python-smbus` library is included in the Pidora and Raspbian package repositories, so you can install it normally. Here's the command for Pidora:

```
$ su -c 'yum install python-smbus'
```

And here's how to install it on Raspbian:

```
$ su -c 'apt-get install python-smbus'
```

The `Adafruit_I2C` code is in the Adafruit Raspberry Pi Python Code GitHub repository. Check out a copy of it, and change into the `Adafruit_I2C` directory:

```
$ git clone https://github.com/adafruit/Adafruit-Raspberry-Pi-Python-Code
$ cd Adafruit-Raspberry-Pi-Python-Code/Adafruit_I2C
```

From this directory, you can run a Python script to calculate the lux value measured by the TSL2561. This script was written by *Ty Brown* (*http://medicforlife.blogspot.com*) and is included here with his permission:

```
#!/usr/bin/python

import sys
import smbus
import time
from Adafruit_I2C import Adafruit_I2C

### Written for Python 2 <-!!!
### Big thanks to bryand, who wrote the code that I borrowed heavily from/
was inspired by
```

More thanks pandring who kind of kickstarted my work on the TSL2561 sen
sor
A great big huge thanks to driverblock and the Adafruit team (Congrats
on your many succeses
Ladyada). Without you folks I would just be a guy sitting somewhere
thinking about cool stuff
Now I'm a guy building cool stuff.
If any of this code proves useful, drop me a line at medicforlife.blog
spot.com


```python
class Luxmeter:
    i2c = None

    def __init__(self, address=0x39, debug=0, pause=0.8):
        self.i2c = Adafruit_I2C(address)
        self.address = address
        self.pause = pause
        self.debug = debug
        self.gain = 0 # no gain preselected
        self.i2c.write8(0x80, 0x03)     # enable the device


    def setGain(self,gain=1):
        """ Set the gain """
        if (gain != self.gain):
            if (gain==1):
                self.i2c.write8(0x81, 0x02)      # set gain = 1X and timing
= 402 mSec
                if (self.debug):
                    print "Setting low gain"
            else:
                self.i2c.write8(0x81, 0x12)      # set gain = 16X and timing
= 402 mSec
                if (self.debug):
                    print "Setting high gain"
            self.gain=gain;                      # safe gain for calculation
            time.sleep(self.pause)               # pause for integration
(self.pause must be bigger than integration time)


    def readWord(self, reg):
        """Reads a word from the I2C device"""
        try:
```

```python
            wordval = self.i2c.readU16(reg)
            newval = self.i2c.reverseByteOrder(wordval)
            if (self.debug):
                print("I2C: Device 0x%02X returned 0x%04X from reg 0x%02X"
% (self.address, wordval & 0xFFFF, reg))
            return newval
        except IOError:
            print("Error accessing 0x%02X: Check your I2C address" % self.ad
dress)
            return -1


    def readFull(self, reg=0x8C):
        """Reads visible+IR diode from the I2C device"""
        return self.readWord(reg);

    def readIR(self, reg=0x8E):
        """Reads IR only diode from the I2C device"""
        return self.readWord(reg);

    def getLux(self, gain = 0):
        """Grabs a lux reading either with autoranging (gain=0) or with a
specified gain (1, 16)"""
        if (gain == 1 or gain == 16):
            self.setGain(gain) # low/highGain
            ambient = self.readFull()
            IR = self.readIR()
        elif (gain==0): # auto gain
            self.setGain(16) # first try highGain
            ambient = self.readFull()
            if (ambient < 65535):
                IR = self.readIR()
            if (ambient >= 65535 or IR >= 65535): # value(s) exeed(s) data
range
                self.setGain(1) # set lowGain
                ambient = self.readFull()
                IR = self.readIR()

        if (self.gain==1):
            ambient *= 16     # scale 1x to 16x
            IR *= 16          # scale 1x to 16x

        ratio = (IR / float(ambient)) # changed to make it run under python
2
```

```
        if (self.debug):
            print "IR Result", IR
            print "Ambient Result", ambient

        if ((ratio >= 0) & (ratio <= 0.52)):
            lux = (0.0315 * ambient) - (0.0593 * ambient * (ratio**1.4))
        elif (ratio <= 0.65):
            lux = (0.0229 * ambient) - (0.0291 * IR)
        elif (ratio <= 0.80):
            lux = (0.0157 * ambient) - (0.018 * IR)
        elif (ratio <= 1.3):
            lux = (0.00338 * ambient) - (0.0026 * IR)
        elif (ratio > 1.3):
            lux = 0

        return lux


oLuxmeter=Luxmeter()

print "LUX HIGH GAIN ", oLuxmeter.getLux(16)
print "LUX LOW GAIN ", oLuxmeter.getLux(1)
print "LUX AUTO GAIN ", oLuxmeter.getLux()
```

A copy of this script is also available in *the GitHub repository for this book* (*https://github.com/spotrh/rpihacks*). Be sure you put this file in the `Adafruit_I2C` directory. To read the lux values, run:

```
$ chmod +x tsl2561-lux.py
$ su -c './tsl2561-lux.py'
```

This script does all of the hard work for you. It reads in the values from the sensor at the different gain settings and then does the math necessary to convert those values into lux units.

Accessing the Sensor Directly from the Kernel

It is also possible to interface directly to the TSL2561 sensor via the I2C bus at the kernel level, assuming you have enabled that support in a custom kernel (as described in Hack #22). First, you need to tell the kernel (as root) to attach the TSL2561 driver to the I2C device at 0x39 (or 0x29/0x49 if you changed the address with the `ADDR` pin):

```
$ su -
$ echo tsl2563 0x39 > /sys/class/i2c-adapter/i2c-1/new_device
```

When you do this, it will output a message like this to `dmesg`:

```
[  522.400407] tsl2563 1-0039: model 5, rev. 0
[  522.402650] i2c i2c-1: new_device: Instantiated device tsl2563 at 0x39
```

There is a new device node (1-0039) in `/sys/class/i2c-adapter/i2c-1/`. Inside that node is a `iio:device0` mapping, and inside *that* mapping directory are several devices that allow you to get readings:

```
$ ls -l /sys/class/i2c-adapter/i2c-1/1-0039/iio\:device0/
...
-rw-r--r-- 1 root root 4096 Sep 16 20:37 in_illuminance0_input
-rw-r--r-- 1 root root 4096 Sep 16 20:37 in_intensity_both_calibscale
-rw-r--r-- 1 root root 4096 Sep 16 20:37 in_intensity_both_raw
-rw-r--r-- 1 root root 4096 Sep 16 20:37 in_intensity_ir_calibscale
-rw-r--r-- 1 root root 4096 Sep 16 20:37 in_intensity_ir_raw
...
```

These files contain the current raw sensor values for the calibration scale and the infrared and combined luminosity readings. To do anything with them, you'll have to convert them using the math in the *TSL2561 datasheet* (*http://www.adafruit.com/datasheets/TSL2561.pdf*).

HACK 43 Listen to Aircraft Transponders

Every day, thousands and thousands of airplanes are flying the friendly skies. Some might be flying over you right now! With a USB TV tuner and a Raspberry Pi, you can listen to the aircraft transponders and find out which planes are up there.

An aircraft transponder is the device on board a plane that responds to radio frequencies and helps identify the plane for various systems, including radar. They generally send a few pieces of information, including altitutde, location, and what's called a "squawk" code that further identifies the flights. If you want to listen to aircraft transponders, it will help if you're within five miles of a local airport, but the occasional commercial plane passing by will be sufficient—you'll just have more infrequent results.

Here's what you'll need:

- Raspbian
- *NooElec R820T* (*http://www.nooelec.com/store/computer-peripherals/usb-ota-receivers/dvb-t-receivers.html*): these devices are easily found on eBay as well, but be sure you have the E4000 chipset variant. Look for "E4000" in the description to make sure your purchase will work with this project or refer to the *list of supported hardware* (*http://sdr.osmocom.org/trac/wiki/rtl-*

sdr#SupportedHardware). This device is also called an RTL-SDR, or RealTek Software Defined Radio, because of the vendor of the analog-to-digital chip it uses. It looks like a flash drive (see Figure 4-10), but it is so much more.

• Dump1090: open source code for tuning the RTL-SDR hardware and decoding the data.

Figure 4-10.
NooElec R820T

Extend Your Antenna

The antenna supplied with the NooElec R820T devices is pretty short. You can run a longer antenna over a window ledge, or to craft a more optimal antenna, see the tutorial at http://www.balarad.net. For most purposes, however, the NooElec's included antenna will suffice.

Set Up the Code

To get started, update Raspbian and install the dependencies needed for building Dump1090:

```
$ sudo apt-get update
$ sudo apt-get upgrade
$ sudo apt-get install  git-core git make cmake libusb-1.0-0-dev  build-
essential pkg-config
```

Once finished, check out a copy of the source code of the drivers for the RTL-SDR device, and then build and install them on your Raspberry Pi:

```
cd /opt/
git clone git://git.osmocom.org/rtl-sdr.git
cd rtl-sdr
```

```
sudo mkdir build
cd build
sudo cmake ../ -DINSTALL_UDEV_RULES=ON
sudo make
sudo make install
sudo ldconfig
```

Be aware that the build process that occurs during these steps will take several minutes on the Pi. The build script will update your status as it progresses.

When the install is complete, you need to copy a set of device rules for the RTL-SDR into the udev configuration directory:

```
$ cd /opt/rtl-sdr/
$ sudo cp rtl-sdr.rules /etc/udev/rules.d/
```

These rules will ensure that your RTL-SDR device is properly configured when it is inserted into your Raspberry Pi.

If you haven't already done so, go ahead and plug in your RTL-SDR device. Then, reboot the Raspberry Pi to ensure that the system cleanly and correctly loads the drivers on startup:

```
$ sudo reboot
```

Now, you should run a test script to make sure Raspbian is using the driver and can receive data from the RTL-SDR device:

```
$ rtl_test  -t
```

If all is well, happy messages will appear and test the modes of the RTL-SDR device:

```
$ rtl_test  -t

Found 1 device(s):
  0:  Generic RTL2832U (e.g. hama nano)

Using device 0: Generic RTL2832U (e.g. hama nano)
Found Elonics E4000 tuner
Supported gain values (18): -1.0 1.5 4.0 6.5 9.0 11.5 14.0 16.5 19.0 21.5
24.0 29.0 34.0 42.0 43.0 45.0 47.0 49.0
Benchmarking E4000 PLL...
[E4K] PLL not locked for 51000000 Hz!
[E4K] PLL not locked for 2204000000 Hz!
[E4K] PLL not locked for 1102000000 Hz!
[E4K] PLL not locked for 1241000000 Hz!
E4K range: 52 to 2203 MHz
E4K L-band gap: 1102 to 1241 MHz
```

Let this run and finish if you like, or stop the test program with Ctrl+C.

Move back to the **/opt/** directory to prepare Dump1090, our signal decoding script:

```
$ cd /opt/
```

Then create the **/dump1090** directory with Git:

```
$ git clone git://github.com/MalcolmRobb/dump1090.git
Cloning into 'dump1090'...
remote: Counting objects: 687, done.
remote: Compressing objects: 100% (420/420), done.
remote: Total 687 (delta 411), reused 521 (delta 259)
Receiving objects: 100% (687/687), 712.00 KiB | 72 KiB/s, done.
Resolving deltas: 100% (411/411), done.
```

Change directories into **dump1090**:

```
$ cd dump1090
```

Type **make** and press Enter. This too will take a little time as it compiles, so mark your spot in this tutorial and take a short break if you like. (We always support eating pie while building with the Pi.)

After **make** has finished, you'll be just about ready to run the app. If you haven't noted the IP address of your Raspberry Pi yet, do so now with **ifconfig**, which results in something like this:

```
eth0      Link encap:Ethernet  HWaddr b8:27:eb:81:54:dc
          inet addr:192.168.1.17  Bcast:192.168.1.255  Mask:255.255.255.0
          UP BROADCAST MULTICAST  MTU:1500  Metric:1
          RX packets:0 errors:0 dropped:0 overruns:0 frame:0
          TX packets:0 errors:0 dropped:0 overruns:0 carrier:0
          collisions:0 txqueuelen:1000
          RX bytes:0 (0.0 B)  TX bytes:0 (0.0 B)

lo        Link encap:Local Loopback
          inet addr:127.0.0.1  Mask:255.0.0.0
          UP LOOPBACK RUNNING  MTU:16436  Metric:1
          RX packets:17 errors:0 dropped:0 overruns:0 frame:0
          TX packets:17 errors:0 dropped:0 overruns:0 carrier:0
          collisions:0 txqueuelen:0
          RX bytes:2042 (1.9 KiB)  TX bytes:2042 (1.9 KiB)
```

The address after **inet addr:** will be the IP address you will use to view the plane traffic in a web browser after starting the script, which you're ready to do!

Run the Script

Before running the script, move to the dump1090 directory:

```
$ cd /opt/dump1090
```

Then, run the script:

```
$ ./dump1090 --net  --net-http-port 8080
```

You won't see much happen, but if you see no errors, the script is likely running, and if commercial planes are nearby, you will see an occasional stream of strange hex code. It might take a few minutes, but planes will transmit data from their beacon as they pass overhead, and when they do, you'll begin to see lines in the script populate, as shown in Figure 4-11.

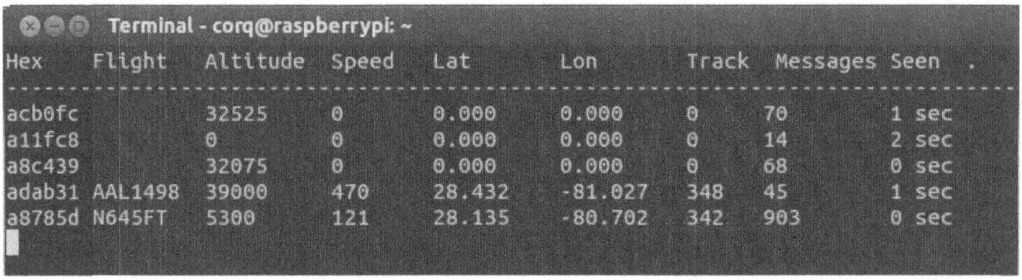

Figure 4-11.
Beacon data from passing planes

From another PC on your local network, open a web browser and enter the Pi's IP address with :8080 appended (for example, http://192.168.1.17:8080). The first time you load this page, it will seem slow, because the Pi initializes the Google Maps API for the first time.

After a moment, you will see a handy map centered somewhere in Europe that looks a lot like Figure 4-12. Just drag it to focus on your own region or double-click on your area of the map until you've zoomed into the area where you are.

RASPBERRY PI HACKS

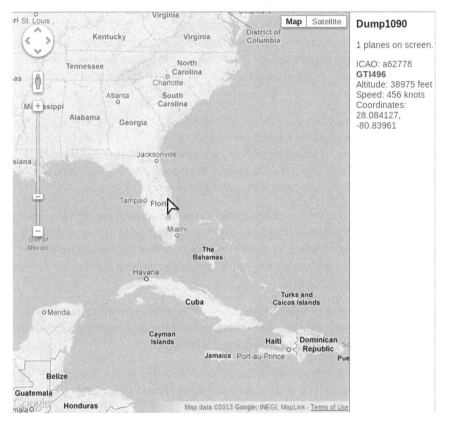

Figure 4-12.
A plane flies over Florida

You can also define your actual latitude and longitude to get your map to center in your region (instead of Europe, if that's not where you are) at startup. Visit *http://itouchmap.com/latlong.html* to pinpoint your location and note the coordinates. Use them to update script.js in /opt/dump1090/public_html/ with your actual location:

```
# find these lines below, update coordinates with the coordinates you got
from the iTouch map page, making sure the lines end with the semicolon.
var Map       = null;
var CenterLat = 28.08864;
var CenterLon = -80.609436;
```

Save the file and exit. The next time you run Dump1090, the web page will center on your region of the map.

—Lori Easterly

Control Aerial Photography

> Aerial photography, particularly from nearspace altitudes, has gained
> popularity in recent years. The Raspberry Pi makes it even easier to ach-
> ieve a low-weight payload with plenty of storage for photo, video, and
> data.

Aerial photography has been practiced since the mid-19th century when Gaspard-
Félix Tournachon photographed Paris from a balloon. For some, it's an art form. For
others, there's a distinct goal, such as when a group teamed with the Louisiana Bucket
Brigade to *map and document the Deepwater Horizon oil spill in 2010* (*http://open-
source.com/life/10/6/mapping-oil-spill-open-source-way*).

The recommendations in this hack are based on the launches by the *NC Near Space
Research group* (*http://www.ncnearspace.org/*), which started as a group entering the
Hackerspaces in Space contest, created in 2010 by Chicago hackerspace Workshop
88. They've since gone on to launch multiple balloons and found the Raspberry Pi to
be a useful tool for such projects.

The Raspberry Pi takes half an amp of currrent. Why would you want to put that in the
payload of a balloon where weight and size are critical? Because having it onboard will
give you just about everything you need and a little more:

- Small and lightweight storage in an SD card for not only the "hard drive" and
  computing, but also for the storage of all the data and photography

- GPIO that can be used for a wide range of sensors, including an accelerometer,
  magnetometer, gyroscope, and temperature sensors

- Video out, so you can drive a video transmitter directly and see the video live on
  the ground, rather than waiting until after the payload is retrieved (that is, if the
  payload is retrieved)

- The ability to send on-screen display of the project's current data while in flight,
  including its location and height

- An optional lightweight camera module designed specifically for the Raspberry
  Pi

- The ability to connect to a USB WiFi adapter for WiFi from space!

While not used on this project, the Raspberry Pi can also serve as a tracking device
for finding the payload after it lands. The sound module on the Pi can generate a
modulated APRS (Amateur Position Reporting System) data stream that can be fed
into the transmitter and broadcast to ham radio operators, allowing you to track it live.

Thus a single, credit-card-sized device provides camera, data collection, tracking, and
storage all in one incredibly cost-effective piece. When you add the prices of these

components if built otherwise, the Raspberry Pi is both the cheapest and lightest way to go, which is handy, given what else you'll have to buy.

For a near-space balloon photography project launch, you need the following major components in addition to the Raspberry Pi (which is a part of your payload):

- Balloon to lift the payload
- Parachute to bring it down safely
- The payload itself (contents described next)
- A tracking device to find it

Build the Payload

Your first step is to build your payload, because that's the only way to find out how heavy it is. Knowing that piece of information is critical to figuring out what size balloon and parachute you'll need and how much helium to lift it.

If you're launching in the United States, you should keep your payload under four pounds, which keeps you from having to do further weight/size ratio calculations for the FAA (see note on FAA Regulations). You should also contact your local FAA office (or the relevant airspace organization for your country) prior to planning a flight to make sure you follow their recommendations for the design, launch, and retrieval of the payload.

FAA Regulations

In the United States, the relevant section of the Code of Federal Regulations is Title 14: Aeronautics and Space, Part 101: Moored Balloons, Kites, Amateur Rockets And Unmanned Free Balloons. Part 101.1(4) (http://www.ecfr.gov/cgi-bin/text-idx?c=ecfr&rgn=div5&view=text&node=14:2.0.1.3.15&idno=14), which describes the size limits of the payload:

- *More than four pounds with a weight/size ratio of more than three ounces per square inch of any surface of the package (determined by dividing the total weight in ounces of the payload package by the area in square inches of its smallest surface)*
- *More than than six pounds (regardless of weight/size ratio)*
- *A payload of two or more packages that weighs more than 12 pounds*

Before launching anything, you shuld read this section of the Federal Regulations in its entirety to be sure you comply.

You should first decide what you will use for you payload container. Whatever you choose, keep it light and waterproof. A styrofoam cooler is an easy and cheap solution, because you can make modifications with nothing more than a knife. Lightweight plastic containers are also useful.

Whatever you choose needs to be large enough to house the Raspberry Pi, a battery pack, your tracking device, and your camera(s), as well as any other parts you've chosen to use as a part of the project. (You can see how space and weight can add up!) The example payload in this hack includes the Raspberry Pi connected to:

- Video out to a 144 MHz Videolinx ham radio ATV (Amateur TV) transmitter and small whip antenna Trackuino (*http://www.trackuino.org/*) which contains a GPS, and a 300 milliwat HX-1 144.39 MHz APRS transmitter, and an Arduino for decoding and modulating the GPS signal for the transmitter
- GY-80 I2C 9-Axis Magnetic Acceleration Gyroscope Module
- 5000 mAh USB cell phone backup battery
- USB WiFi adapter
- USB Y power cable to allow powering the WiFi directly from the battery and not through the Raspberry Pi's weak USB power ports
- Raspberry Pi camera module
- Nikon Coolpix camera (controlled by gphoto)

The Trackuino is an Arduino-based APRS system that includes a high-altitude GPS system and GPS antenna. The Arduino decodes the data from the GPS and then modulates it to drive a 300 mW HX-1 transmitter, which then drives an 8 W Micro Amp 3 amplifier, which is then fed into a whip antenna. The amplifier isn't necessary once your payload gets up high enough above the terrain, but it is helpful in locating the payload when it's down on the ground and away from other ham radio APRS systems.

The Trackuino and Micro Amp3 are driven by eight AA lithium cell batteries (independent of the 5000 mAh cell phone battery that powers the Raspberry Pi), which will last 5+ hours. This separate power supply is helpful in the event that the Raspberry Pi loses power before the payload is recovered.

The GPS signal of the Trackuino can also be routed to the Raspberry Pi so that it can correlate the sensor data with the time stamp, altitude, and latitude and longitude data from the GPS (you will need to disable the console port on the serial device before doing this). The GY-80 module connects to the I2C pins and ground and 3.3 V power signals from the Raspberry Pi.

For the Raspberry Pi battery, we suggest a 5,000 mAh cell phone backup battery. A pack of this size can run the Pi, record sensor data, and power the camera for more than five hours. They're lighter weight than nickel-cadmium (NiCd) batteries and can be purchased for as little as $15. Another advantage of this as a battery pack for the

Raspberry Pi is that it has two built-in USB power outputs (one for the Raspberry Pi and one for the USB WiFi Y cable), and a built-in power switch (which the Pi itself lacks).

The Raspberry Pi camera is the main camera for the payload in this hack, although it also holds a Nikon Coolpix attached through the Pi's remaining USB port and controlled by gphoto.

Gather Gas, Balloon, and Parachute

Once the payload is built, you can determine its weight, which lets you calculate the amount of lifting gas it requires. You need one cubic foot of helium per ounce of payload. Thus, for a four-pound payload, you will need about 64 cubic feet of helium.

However, that amount of helium is just enough for neutral buoyancy, so you will need an additional 1–1.5 pounds of lift to actually lift the payload. This amount of lift will give you an ascent rate of about 1,000 feet per minute. For a four-pound payload, that's 5.5 pounds of lift needed, for a total of 88 cubic feet of helium.

Manufacturers specify balloon size based on the amount of lifting gas. For this example of a four-pound payload and 88 cubic ft of helium, an 600-gram balloon will achieve altitudes of 70,000 feet or above. Smaller balloons will pop at a lower altitude, and larger balloons tend to pop at a higher altitude. However, if you choose a balloon that's too large, it might never pop, and you end up with a "drifter" that can hang around the sky for days, so it's better to choose a smaller balloon until you get experience with more launches.

Now that you know the weight of the payload, you can also calculate the size of the parachute, which you need for a slow and safe descent. Parachute companies describe parachute size based on a reasonable descent rate, typically 10–15 feet per second. We recommend *The Rocketman* (*http://www.the-rocketman.com/*), Ky Michaelson, a former Hollywood stuntman and stunt equipment designer who now runs a business selling balloon and rocket parachutes and related materials. You can read more about recovery parachutes on *his website* (*http://www.the-rocketman.com/recovery.html*).

For this size payload, a three- to four-foot parachute is appropriate. Balloon and parachute should be attached with shroud lines that are 50 pounds tensile strength or less (per FAA guidelines).

Install Software

You need to load a few things onto your Pi before you're ready to launch:

- I2C libraries (for talking to the GY-80 sensor board)
- GPSd (daemon for decoding GPS data streams)

- GPIO libraries (for controlling status LEDs and sensing switch inputs)
- gphoto (for controlling the Nikon camera—see "Geting Started with gPhoto" on page 258 for further help)
- lighthttpd web server (for displaying the web pages over ATV and WiFi)
- sqllite data base (for storing all the sensor data)
- The Python scripts (main control program, sensor libraries, startup scripts)
- The web pages (displayed over ATV and WiFi)

The main script configures the sensors, then goes into a loop that continuously polls the status of the sensors and GPS, taking photos, and storing the sensor data in a SQLite database and storing the images in a image directory.

You can stitch the images together after the mission using FFmpeg software (available as a packge `ffmpeg` in Fedora or Debian—see "How to Get ffmpeg in Fedora" sidebar) to create a video stream. For a two-hour launch, you will end up with about 3,600 pictures, which form a several-minute-long video when combined together.

How to Get ffmpeg in Fedora

FFmpeg (http://ffmpeg.org) records, converts, and streams video and audio and contains more than 100 codecs. It can encode in many formats, including MPEG4, avi, mjpeg, and Flash. Because Fedora includes only completely free software (see *http://fedoraproject.org/wiki/Objectives*), FFmpeg is not included.

The *RPM Fusion (http://rpmfusion.org/)* project provides additional package repositories for software that Fedora does not include. They offer *one-click setup from a Firefox browser (http://rpmfusion.org/Configuration)*, or you can do it from the command line:

```
$ su -c 'yum localinstall --nogpgcheck http://download1.rpmfusion.org/
free/fedora/rpmfusion-free-release-$(rpm -E %fedora).noarch.rpm
http://download1.rpmfusion.org/nonfree/fedora/rpmfusion-nonfree-
release-$(rpm -E %fedora).noarch.rpm'
```

Then you're ready to run: `su -c yum install ffmpeg`.

Download the sensor libraries, main control loop, and web pages from *this book's GitHub repo (https://github.com/spotrh/rpihacks)* into a directory on your Raspberry Pi. This is the main loop of the sensor program, `10DOFd.py`:

```
#!/usr/bin/python
```

```
#
# ==============================================================================
# 10 degree of freedom daemon for nearspace balloon telemetry
#
# Rodney Radford (AK4CH) - www.blackskytelemetry.org
#
# Interfaces to the GY-80 10DOF board, and an external GPS to log
#   the sensors into a sqllite data base
#
# ==============================================================================

#
# Standard system libraries needed
#
import os, subprocess, sys, sh, shutil, time
import RPi.GPIO as GPIO
import sqlite3 as db

#
# Custom sensor libraries created for this project
#
from GPS       import GPS        # GPS lat/long/altitude/time
from ADXL345   import ADXL345    # accelerometer
from BMP085    import BMP085     # pressure + temp
from HMC5883   import HMC5883    # magnetometer (compass) + temp
from L3G4200D  import L3G4200D   # gyroscope

#
# Camera constants
#
CAMERA_PERIOD   = 15   # Number of seconds between each photo

#
# Constants that define the GPIO pins for the LEDs and the enable switch
#
SW_enable  = 11   # if ON, take a photo and update dbase (else skip)
LED_status = 23   # RED (False/on, blinks at 0.5hz rate)
LED_gpsok  = 24   # GREEN (False/on if GPS lock valid)
LED_camera = 25   # YELLOW (False if dbase write and camera capture enabled)

#
# Simple printable timestamp of the current time
#
def timestamp():
```

```
    return time.strftime('%x %X %z')


#
# Poll each of the sensor libraries for data
#
def getSensorData():

    global GPSdata
    global timeG
    global lat
    global lon
    global altG

    # Get the GPS sensor data
    GPSdata = gps.current_value()
    if (GPSdata == None):
        print "NO FIX!!"
        timeG   = 0
        lat     = 0
        lon     = 0
        altG    = 0
    else:
        print "RETURNED: ", GPSdata
        timeG   = GPSdata.time
        lat     = GPSdata.lat
        lon     = GPSdata.lon
        altG    = GPSdata.alt

    global XYZa
    global roll
    global pitch

    # Get the accelerometer sensor data
    XYZa    = acc.readAccelerometer()
    roll    = acc.computeRoll(XYZa)
    pitch   = acc.computePitch(XYZa)

    global XYZm
    global XYZmh

    # Get the compass sensor data
    XYZm  = compass.readCompass()
    XYZmh = compass.heading(XYZm)
```

```
    global XYZr
    global tempG

    # Get the gyroscope sensor data
    XYZr  = gyro.readGyro()
    tempG = gyro.readTemperature()

    global press
    global altP
    global tempP

    # Get the pressure sensor data
    press = pressure.readPressure()
    altP  = pressure.readAltitude()
    tempP = pressure.readTemperature()


#
# Take a photo (and flash the photo status LED)
#
def takePhoto():
    GPIO.output(LED_camera, False)
    filename = time.strftime("%Y%m%d_%H%M%S.JPG")
    sh.gphoto2("--capture-image-and-download", "--keep", "--force-overwrite",
               "--filename", filename)
    if (os.path.isfile(filename)):
        sh.ln("-sf", filename, "latest.jpg")
    else:
        print "missing file:", filename
    GPIO.output(LED_camera, True)


#
# Create a brand new sqllite dbase and populate it with a dummy record
#
def createDB():
    global con

    DB_FILENAME = "../data/10DOF_data.db"
    con = db.connect(DB_FILENAME)

    with con:
        cur = con.cursor()
        cur.execute("CREATE TABLE Sensors("
```

```
                    "Lat REAL, Long REAL, AltG REAL, TimeG TEXT, "
                    "XA REAL, YA REAL, ZA REAL, ROLL REAL, PITCH REAL, "
                    "XM REAL, YM REAL, ZM REAL, XMH REAL, YMH REAL, ZMH
REAL, "
                    "XR REAL, YR REAL, ZR REAL, TempG REAL, "
                    "Pressure REAL, AltP REAL, TempP REAL)")

    data = [        # "Lat REAL, Long REAL, AltG REAL, TimeG TEXT, "
                    35.68981, -78.405353333, 84.8,
    '2013-05-02T01:53:41.001Z',

                    # XA REAL, YA REAL, ZA REAL, ROLL REAL, PITCH REAL, "
                    0.0, 0.0, 1.0, -1.0, 0.0,

                    # XM REAL, YM REAL, ZM REAL, XMH REAL, YMH REAL, ZMH
REAL, "
                    -28.0, -96.0, -216.0, -156.037511025422,
    -172.613956848733, -163.739795291688,

                    # XR REAL, YR REAL, ZR REAL, TempG REAL, "
                    0.0, -1.0, -1.0, -7.0,

                    # Pressure REAL, AltP REAL, TempP REAL)")
                    101426.0, -7.49042223835529, 16.5]

    cur.execute("INSERT INTO Sensors VALUES(?" + (",?"*21) + ")", data)


#
# Write out the current sensor data to the dbase
#
def updateDB():
    with con:
        cur = con.cursor()
        data = [lat,lon,altG,timeG,
                XYZa[0],XYZa[1],XYZa[2],roll,pitch,
                XYZm[0],XYZm[1],XYZm[2],XYZmh[0],XYZmh[1],XYZmh[2],
                XYZr[0],XYZr[1],XYZr[2],tempG,
                press,altP,tempP]
        cur.execute("INSERT INTO Sensors VALUES(?" + (",?"*21) + ")", data)


#
# Roll the dbase so we have the current and a series of older/backup dbases
```

```python
#     This allows each session to be distinct, yet protects against acciden
tal
#     erasure of all data if the payload is turned off and then back on
#
def rollDB():

    # Delete the oldest snapshot
    shutil.rmtree("../data/snapshot_09", True)

    # Rollover snapshots 01..08 into 02..09
    for version in range(8,0,-1):
        os.rename("snapshot_0" + str(version),  "snapshot_0" + str(version+1))

    # Make a new snapshot_01 directory
    os.mkdir("snapshot_01")

    # Move the existing data into the new snapshot_01
    os.system("mv *.JPG *.db *.log snapshot_01 > /dev/null 2>&1")

    # Now create the latest.jpg link in the current data set
    sh.ln("-sf", "initial.jpg", "latest.jpg")




# ----------------------------------------------------------------
# Main body of the program
# ----------------------------------------------------------------

os.environ['TZ'] = "EST"

# Add this project's bin path so we can pick up gphoto2 and then
#     change the current directory to the data directory so we
#     can deposit all the photos/data there
os.environ['PATH'] = os.environ['PATH'] + ":../bin"
os.chdir("/home/pi/balloon/data")

# Initialize the GPIO LEDs/switch
GPIO.setwarnings(False)
GPIO.setmode(GPIO.BCM)
GPIO.setup(SW_enable,  GPIO.IN)
GPIO.setup(LED_status, GPIO.OUT)
GPIO.setup(LED_gpsok,  GPIO.OUT)
GPIO.setup(LED_camera, GPIO.OUT)
```

```python
# Make sure the LEDs are off by default (will flash them later)
GPIO.output(LED_status, True)
GPIO.output(LED_gpsok,  True)
GPIO.output(LED_camera, True)

# Initialize the sensor libraries
gps      = GPS()
acc      = ADXL345()
pressure = BMP085()
compass  = HMC5883()
gyro     = L3G4200D()

# Start up the background GPS thread
gps.start()

# Roll the old dbase values and create a new one for this mission
rollDB()
createDB()

# Flash the LEDs for 2 seconds - this is a good visual indication that
#   the program is up and the LEDs all work, as well as it works as a
#   time delay to make sure the libraries are stable (background GPS task)
for loop in range(0,4):
    blink_on = ((loop & 1) == 1)
    GPIO.output(LED_status, blink_on)
    GPIO.output(LED_gpsok,  blink_on)
    GPIO.output(LED_camera, blink_on)
    time.sleep (0.5)

# Acivity boolean - toggles on each loop (controls activity LED)
activity = True

# Set up the next camera time so a photo will be taken as soon as the
#   enable switch is turned on
next_camera_time = 0

# Run forever
while True:

    # Read from each of the sensors
    getSensorData()

    # Toggle the activity LED
    activity = not activity
```

```
        GPIO.output(LED_status, activity)

        # Indicate GPS status on the green LED
        GPIO.output(LED_gpsok, (GPSdata == None))

        # If the enable switch is on, then update the dbase and take a picture
        if (GPIO.input(SW_enable)):

            # Update the dbase with the latest sensor readings
            updateDB()

            # Is it also time for a new photo?
            if (time.time() > next_camera_time):
                takePhoto()

                # Now calculate the time for the next photo
                next_camera_time = next_camera_time + CAMERA_PERIOD

        # Delay for 0.5 seconds (this controls the activity LED flash rate)
        time.sleep(0.5)
```

This is the script that generates the main station ID web page, `stationid.py`:

```
#!/usr/bin/python
# -*- coding: utf-8 -*-

import sqlite3 as db
import sys
import time

import cgitb
cgitb.enable()
import cgi


def openDB():
    global con
    DB_FILENAME = "../data/10DOF_data.db"
    con = db.connect(DB_FILENAME)

try:
    openDB()
except db.Error, e:
    print "<!DOCTYPE html><head><meta http-equiv='refresh' content='15'></
head>Error %s:</html>" % e.args[0]
```

```
        sys.exit(1)

try:
    cur = con.cursor()
    cur.execute('select * from Sensors order by TimeG desc limit 1')
    rows = cur.fetchall()

except db.Error, e:
    print "<!DOCTYPE html><head><meta http-equiv='refresh' content='15'></
head>Error %s:</html>" % e.args[0]
    sys.exit(1)

finally:
    if con:
        con.close()


template =  "<!DOCTYPE html>\n"
template += "<html><head><meta http-equiv='refresh' content='5'><ti
tle>First Library in Space</title>\n" # EDIT REFRESH TIME HERE
template += "<link href='styles.css' rel='stylesheet' type='text/css'>\n"
template += "</head><body>\n"

template += '<div id="content">\n'

# ENTER CALL SIGN HERE:
template += '<div id="page-header"><h2>First Library in Space/July 10,
2013</h2></div>'

template += '<img id="idimage" src="latest.jpg">'

template += '<div id="statbox">'

template += '<p>AK4CH</p>'
template += "<br>\n"

template += '<p>'
template += (rows[0][3])[11:19] # Chopping off date
template += "</p>\n"
template += '<p>N '
template += (str(rows[0][0]))[:7] # Truncating
template += "</p>\n"
template += '<p> W '
template += (str(abs(rows[0][1])))[:7] # Truncating
```

```
template += "</p>\n"

template += '<p>A: '
template += str(int(rows[0][2]))[:10]
template += "'</p>\n"

template += '<p>T: '
template += str(int((32 + (9*rows[0][21])/5) + 0.5))
template += "&deg; F</p>\n"

template += "</div>"

template += '</div>\n'

template += "</body></html>\n"

print template
```

If you download the complete tarball from GitHub, you'll see several directories. You can use the bin/startup.sh program to start these scripts and programs automatically. The files can live anywhere in your file structure.

Track the Payload

Some form of tracking for your payload is a must, and there are many ways to do so. One option is a SPOT Satellite GPS Messenger device. The benefit is that you don't need any sort of ham radio license to use it, but it is one of the more expensive choices since it requires a yearly license to use. It also does not provide altitude data and does not report position data above about 30,000 feet.

Another option is a ham radio Automatic Packet Reporting System (APRS) beacon, which is cheaper and requires no usage fees, but it does require a ham radio license. As an additional benefit, if you use a high-altitude GPS, APRS has the advantage of continuous telemetry data for the full flight of your payload.

Of course, an even better option is redundancy: fly both!

Prepare for Launch

Choose a launch field outside of a flight path of major airlines. You can find these maps online and find a location not in line with the runways of any nearby airports. You should also be at least 20 miles away from an airport, in an area that has good visibility in all directions, and that has no power lines or tall tress or other obstructions. Once you select a site, make sure to consult your local aviation authority to verify there are no issues with the airspace above your field or the projected path of your payload.

Once you've chosen a location and a date, you can start running simulations at *the CUSF Landing Predictor* (*http://predict.habhub.org/*) for the anticipated date and time of the launch. The CUSF pulls NOAA data from weather balloons launches twice a day at multiple sites around the United States to measure and calculate the wind speed and direction for anything free-floating.

You can plot the projected course and length of time in air of your balloon. That will let you determine whether you'd be flying into bad airspace or over large bodies of water or other bad flight/recovery areas. If the prediction doesn't look good, you have the option of moving to a different field or even trying different launch times during the day (sometimes varying launch time by just a few hours can change the predicted path direction).

At the field, you will need your helium tank, cutoff valve, hose and fill system, as well as a large tarp where you can lay out everything on the ground. Fill up the balloon, tie it to the payload, turn on all your equipment, and you are ready to go.

Depending on what you are flying in your payload, you might also have to set up a ground support system. If you are flying the WiFi USB adapter, you will need a good WiFi antenna on the ground, such as a 2' x 3' parabolic WiFi dish antenna on a mount, connected to a laptop.

For Amateur TV (ATV) reception, you will need a directional antenna (such as a Yagi) to receive the video signal. You can attach a TV and VCR (you can even get 12-volt versions meant for vehicles) for easy viewing and recording. Finally, if you're tracking with APRS, you'll want a hand-held APRS-compatible ham radio systems for tracking the signal in the field.

Mission Success

The balloon and payload described here were initially launched with the video transmitter, WiFI USB, Trackuino APRS, and a SPOT system. The video link lasted until the payload was 70,000 feet high and 20 miles down range. Unfortunately, the APRS and SPOT system failed, and the payload was never recovered. However, a new payload was put together and relaunched just a few weeks later, and more than 3,200 photos were retrieved from the Raspberry Pi camera (over 8 GB of data!), and the payload was recovered successfully. Figure 4-13 shows the type of photo results you can achieve from a successful launch.

Full details of the payload, construction techniques, as well as hints for launching and recovery and future research projects are all documented on the *Black Sky Telemetry site* (*http://www.blackskytelemetry.org*).

Figure 4-13.
The edge of the earth, as captured from a Raspberry Pi-powered payload (courtesy of Rodney Radford)

With the Raspberry Pi as the control system for the balloon payload, there are many potential areas of improvement, including adding more cameras, adding a servo-controlled camera to control where it is pointed, improving data transmission, and adding even more sensors.

—Rodney Radford

HACK 45 Have the Best Holiday Lights Display

You've probably seen a YouTube video of somebody with an animated holiday light display, putting the rest of the neighborhood to shame (and possibly torturing the people across the street). If your aspirations in life include being Clark Griswold, then this hack is for you.

The Raspberry Pi's GPIO makes controlling up to 17 changing sequences of lights easy. Your neighbors' sanity and your power bill are your only limits! Your setup consists of a Raspberry Pi connected to a relay board via a level converter, as shown in Figure 4-14.

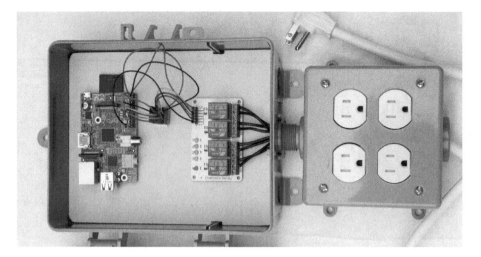

Figure 4-14.
Raspberry Pi, converter board, and relay board (on left) connected to housing with electrical outlets (on right)

The relay board connects to two pairs of power outlets just like the ones in your wall, which you'll use to plug in your light strands.

Connect the Hardware

While you could build your own separate relay controllers, plenty of vendors sell premade relay control cards with one, two, four, or eight relays on one card for less than it would cost to do it yourself. (That always hurts to say when you love to DIY, but sometimes it really is easier to just buy built.)

Then you just have to control the relays from the Pi. You'll find both 5 V and 12 V relays for sale. Avoid the 12 V ones, which will require more level shifting as well as a second power supply. With a 5 V relay, all you'll need to add is a 3.3-to-5 volt converter for the Raspberry Pi GPIO pins. Level converter boards are also readily available online from vendors like Adafruit and DX.com.

A level converter actually has several converters in one board: 5 V power, 3.3 V power, ground, and four signals going in and four signals going out. Converting the signal from 3.3 V out of the pins into the 5 V that the relay requires provides the necessary power to the relay while grounding the signal so it doesn't fry the Raspberry Pi.

Do not use the 5 V power from the Raspberry Pi to power the relays. You could burn out your Pi.

Connect four differently colored male/female jumper wires from the following GPIO to the level converter board's channels:

- Pin 23 to Channel 1
- Pin 22 to Channel 2
- Pin 27 to Channel 3
- Pin 17 to Channel 4

Next, connect the level converter to the relay board's signal pins on VCC (5 V), each of the four channels, and ground (GND). (It may also have markings for voltage (V) and ground (G).

Opto-isolated relay boards might work without the level converter board.

Now, you'll need to connect the relays to the outlets. Looking at the outlets, you will see that the screws on one side are brass, and the screws on the other side are silver. The brass side is the "hot" side that is controlled by the relay, while the silver side is the return. Start by breaking the tabs that tie the top and bottom outlets together on the brass side, so you can control the top and bottom outlets independently.

This is a potentially dangerous project! Keep the 120 V power at the relay far away from all low-voltage wiring on the Raspberry Pi. You could be seriously electrocuted by what otherwise seems like a simple short. Note that you might need to consult local/regional building codes on construction and installation of your finished project.

Next, connect a 16-gauge white copper wire to one of the silver screws (top or bottom, it does not matter) on each of the two outlets, and connect these two white wires to the white wire of a grounded power cord. You can purchase a three-wire grounded power cord at your local home improvement store—we simply pilfered one from a spare power strip.

Now it is time to run a wire to the relays. If you look carefully at the relays, you will see either two connectors per relay or three connectors per relay, depending on your specific version. If you have three wires, one is usually labeled NO (for Normally Open, which means it is off when not energized), another is labeled NC (for Normally Closed, which means it is on when not energized), and the third wire is the common.

You want to use the common wire and the Normally Open one. If you have only two connectors for each relay, you don't need to worry about this. As long as you use the common side, it really doesn't matter if you mix up the Normally Open and Normally

Closed relay output as you can either change it later, or simply reverse the relay logic by boolean inverting the GPIO.output second parameter.

Run a 16-gauge black copper wire to the common of each relay and tie them all together to the black wire of the power cord. Run another 16-gauge black copper wire from the Normally Open (or only remaining connector if only two per relay) to each of the brass screws on the outlets. You can use a metallic silver marker on the ends of each of the black wires to indicate the channel number (1–4), so it will be easy to run it to the correct outlet. Be sure to label the outlets so you later remember which one is controlled by each channel.

Run a ground wire from the ground screw on each outlet (usually green) to the ground wire of the power plug. Check your wiring to make sure it is correct with no loose or frayed wires. Once you are sure everything looks good, screw the outlet into the box and screw on the outlet box cover. If you are using this for control of outdoor lighting, you should place the setup box in an area out of the elements, such as in a garage, under a porch, or even inside the house, and then run the wires to each of the outlets.

Install the Software

First, install the GPIO control library and Python tools. Pidora includes `python-rpi.gpio` by default, but you'll need to install `python-devel` manually:

```
$ su -c 'yum install python-devel'
```

On Raspbian, you'll need to install both `python-rpi.gpio` and `python-devel`:

```
$ sudo apt-get install python-dev
$ sudo apt-get install python-rpi.gpio
```

Then add the following code (which you can also download from this book's GitHub repository) to any directory:

```
#!/usr/bin/python

import RPi.GPIO as GPIO
import time

DELAY = 1

#
# GPIO signals for the 4 relays
#
# Note that there are enough GPIO signals to control multiple
#     4-channel boards from the same RPi
#
# Name the channels and note of the colors of your wires for reference
```

```
#
CH1 = 23 # Channel 1 - Brown
CH2 = 22 # Channel 2 - Orange
CH3 = 27 # Channel 3 - Green
CH4 = 17 # Channel 4 - Yellow

#
# Set up the four channels with GPIO signals as output
#
GPIO.setmode(GPIO.BCM)
GPIO.setup(CH1, GPIO.OUT)
GPIO.setup(CH2, GPIO.OUT)
GPIO.setup(CH3, GPIO.OUT)
GPIO.setup(CH4, GPIO.OUT)

#
# The sequence for the relay controller - bit mask of each
#    of the 4 channels.  This example first turns each of the
#    channels off, then cycles through each one, one at a time,
#    and then repeats the sequence again
#
# Sequence table describes the order you want the lights to come on.
#
sequence = [0b0000,    # All off
            0b0001,    # Only channel 1 on
            0b0010,    # Only channel 2 on
            0b0100,    # Only channel 3 on
            0b1000]    # Only channel 4 on

#
# Start at the beginning of the sequence array
#
index = 0

#
# Run forever,,,
#
while True:

    #
    # Convert the integer sequence bitmask into the individual
        #    channel controls
        GPIO.output(CH1, ((sequence[index] & 1) == 1))
        GPIO.output(CH2, ((sequence[index] & 2) == 2))
```

```
GPIO.output(CH3, ((sequence[index] & 4) == 4))
GPIO.output(CH4, ((sequence[index] & 8) == 8))

#
# Delay... make this as long a you want, or make it variable
#
time.sleep(DELAY)

#
# Advance to the next pattern in the sequence
#
index = index + 1
if (index >= len(sequence)):
        index = 0
```

Move this file (as root) to /usr/bin/lightsequences.py. You can save yourself some annoyance later by also setting it to be executable:

```
$ sudo chmod +x /usr/bin/lightsequences.py
```

You probably want to make this Python script run automatically when your Raspberry Pi boots up. The way to do this is different between Pidora and Raspbian.

For Raspbian, you simply need to invoke this script from /etc/rc.local. Open that file with a text editor (as root), and add this line directly *above* the line that says exit 0:

```
python /usr/bin/lightsequences.py &
```

The use of the & command at the end of the line tells the Python script to run in the background. This is important, because otherwise, rc.local would wait for it to finish before proceeding. Since this script runs in an infinite loop, it would never proceed, and your boot process would sit there waiting.

Pidora uses a different boot software (systemd), which does not use the rc.local concept. As a result, you will need to create a new systemd service file for the Python script. Copy this file (also in the book's GitHub repository) to /usr/lib/systemd/system/lightsequences.service (as root):

```
[Unit]
Description=Christmas Light Sequence Loop

[Service]
Type=simple
ExecStart=/usr/bin/python /usr/bin/lightsequences.py

[Install]
WantedBy=multi-user.target
```

Then, you can start it immediately by running:

```
$ su -c 'systemctl start lightsequences.service'
```

To make this service start on each boot, run:

```
$ su -c 'systemctl enable lightsequences.service'
```

From here, you have many options to expand and customize your light display. Having Ethernet included means you could add a web-based interface to start and stop the lights or to control them. Thanks to the audio-out jack, you can even use it as the sound source.

You could combine this hack with Hack #49 to send the sound through a radio broadcast. With serial input coming in, you could use a MIDI sequence to control both lights and sound. With an attached camera, you could serve a picture of your changing display to the Web. And thanks to the Raspberry Pi, that's all readily available in one package. Happy holidays!

—Rodney Radford

Multimedia Hacks

One of the first things many people do with their Raspberry Pis is to set up an XMBC media center. If that's where you'd like to start as well, we've got you covered (Hack #54).

But there's a lot more you can do in the multimedia realm with this fun little device. Why limit it to being the media server when you can take it on the road and use it for in-car entertainment (Hack #55)? You can also turn it into a radio (Hack #49), play your favorite childhood video games (Hack #51), jazz up your next party with a photobooth (Hack #53), and more.

HACK 46 Play Video Files

> Want to watch a video on your Raspberry Pi? Using the right software will help you get the best performance on playback, even from HD 1080p files!

The Raspberry Pi is not quite the same as a normal computer, but one thing that it can do very well is video decoding. On your Linux laptop, when you play a video file, you are probably decoding that file entirely in software. This works fine, because your laptop CPU is fast enough to do this work in real-time. The Raspberry Pi CPU is not generally fast enough to do this, though, so to make up for it, the Broadcom 2835 system-on-chip graphics processing unit (GPU) includes dedicated hardware to decode (and encode) video files. You can access this hardware through the VideoCore libraries, but most of the video player software commonly used on Linux does not yet have support for those libraries.

Enter omxplayer, a video player specifically made to access the Raspberry PI's GPU via the VideoCore libraries. It was made by Edgar (gimli) Hucek, and while it is not fancy (it has no GUI), it just works. The maintained source code for omxplayer lives at *https://github.com/popcornmix/omxplayer*.

Omxplayer was designed for the Raspbian environment and is much more complicated to build for other platforms. If you want to build for Pidora, you should try the steps documented by Omarr Khattab (http://okhattab.wordpress.com/2012/12/08/building-omxplayer-for-raspi-fedora-remix/).

To install `omxplayer` on Raspbian, you will need to have Git installed and then clone a copy of the source tree into your home directory on the Raspberry Pi:

```
$ sudo apt-get install git
$ git clone https://github.com/popcornmix/omxplayer
Cloning into 'omxplayer'...
remote: Counting objects: 1065, done.
remote: Compressing objects: 100% (539/539), done.
remote: Total 1065 (delta 730), reused 823 (delta 523)
Receiving objects: 100% (1065/1065), 1.38 MiB | 598 KiB/s, done.
Resolving deltas: 100% (730/730), done.
```

Because you will need to build it from source, you'll need to complete some additional build dependencies and system preparations. To simplify the process on Raspbian, just run the included script (`./prepare-native-raspbian.sh`), which will prepare the OS for building `omxplayer`:

```
$ ./prepare-native-raspbian.sh
```

This will do a lot of things:

- Patch the makefiles for the Raspbian specific settings.
- Install dependent packages for building `omxplayer`.
- Install gcc 4.7, which is necessary to build `omxplayer`.
- Update the Raspberry Pi firmware.
- Install the latest prebuilt Linux kernel (and modules).
- Update to the latest videocore libraries and headers.
- Sync the changes to the SD card.
- Launch `raspi-config` to enable you to set the `memory_split`. If you have an older Raspberry Pi Model B (with only 256 MB of memory), you will need to set the `memory_split` value to 16; otherwise, the `ffmpeg` code in `omxplayer` will not compile. If you have a current Raspberry Pi Model B, the default setting (64) is acceptable as is.

Even with this process, you still have a few things left to do to get it working.

There is (at least as of the time of this writing) one minor bug in `Makefile.include` that will prevent it from building. To fix it, open `Makefile.include` with your favorite text editor and add this string to the end of the INCLUDES line (should be the last line in the file):

```
-I/opt/vc/include/interface/vmcs_host/linux/
```

Be sure there is a space between this string and any of the already present strings.

Additionally, you will need to configure gcc and g++ 4.7 to be your default compilers. Raspbian uses the alternatives mechanism to allow for multiple versions of the gcc compilers to be installed simultaneously. To switch to gcc 4.7, run:

```
$ sudo update-alternatives --install /usr/bin/gcc gcc /usr/bin/gcc-4.6 60 --
slave /usr/bin/g++ g++ /usr/bin/g++-4.6
$ sudo update-alternatives --install /usr/bin/gcc gcc /usr/bin/gcc-4.7 40 --
slave /usr/bin/g++ g++ /usr/bin/g++-4.7
$ sudo update-alternatives --config gcc
```

At the end of this, the update-alternatives command will prompt you to choose the number for the gcc version that you wish to be the default. Enter the number that corresponds to the entry for gcc 4.7.

Finally, you will need to install the dbus development headers:

```
$ sudo apt-get install libdbus-1-dev
```

When this finishes, you will need to add the dbus header include flags to Makefile.include. You can quickly determine what those are by running:

```
$ pkg-config --cflags dbus-1
```

At the time of this writing, that command returns:

```
-I/usr/include/dbus-1.0 -I/usr/lib/arm-linux-gnueabihf/dbus-1.0/include
```

Add those additional include flags to the end of the INCLUDES line (should be the last line in Makefile.include):

At this point, you will need to reboot the Pi and change back into the omxplayer source directory. From there, you will need to build ffmpeg from source (there is a version of ffmpeg in the Raspbian repositories, but it is too old):

```
$ cd ~/omxplayer
$ make ffmpeg
```

In case it was not clear from the earlier comment about allocating most of the Raspberry Pi memory to the OS (and away from the GPU), compiling ffmpeg is a resource-intensive process. It will take a while to complete, but when it does, you will be able to build the rest of omxplayer:

```
$ cd ~/omxplayer
$ make
$ make dist
```

To install `omxplayer` system-wide, go into the `omxplayer-dist` directory and copy the file tree into the top-level `usr/` directory as root:

```
$ cd omxplayer-dist
$ sudo cp -a usr/* /usr/
```

There is one last thing you will need to do to use `omxplayer`. Because `omxplayer` accesses the videocore directly on the Raspberry Pi, it uses `/dev/vchiq`. This device node is not normally accessible by non-root users, so if you want to be able to run `omxplayer` as another user, you'll need to set up a `udev` rule to allow users in the `video` group to access `/dev/vchiq`:

```
$ sudo su -
$ echo 'SUBSYSTEM=="vchiq",GROUP="video",MODE="0660"' > /etc/udev/rules.d/
10-vchiq-permissions.rules
$ usermod -aGvideo <USERNAME>
```

Substitute your username (the default user for Raspbian is `pi`) for `<USERNAME>` in the `usermod` command. Then reboot the Raspberry Pi one last time.

You are ready to watch videos with `omxplayer` now. To watch a video, simply run:

```
$ omxplayer -o hdmi myvideo.mp4
```

The `-o` flag allows you to select the output device. You are probably connected to the HDMI cable for audio and video. If so, you need to specify `hdmi` as the output device.

There's no man page for omxplayer, but the options are somewhat documented in the output of `omxplayer --help`.

To control the video during playback, use control keys. Table 5-1 shows the more common control keys for `omxplayer`.

Table 5-1. Common omxplayer control keys

KEY	FUNCTION
<	Rewind
>	Fast Forward
s	Toggle Subtitles
p / space	Pause
q	Quit
-	Volume Down

KEY	FUNCTION
+ / =	Volume Up

For the full list of control keys, see the output of `omxplayer -k`.

HACK 47 · Enable Additional Video Codecs

The Raspberry Pi hardware is capable of decoding audio and video formats directly. It ships with support for the most common formats, but you can unlock more.

One of the powerful features of the Raspberry Pi lies in the BCM2835 system-on-chip's ability to do fast hardware decoding (and encoding) of video formats. Without this, the Raspberry Pi would have to process video files with software codecs for decoding/encoding, and the Raspberry Pi is not a fast computer in this regard. As a general rule, if you can do it natively with hardware, it will run faster than it would emulated in software.

The BCM2835 system-on-chip is capable of natively decoding most video formats, but it supports only H.264/MPEG-4 video in the stock Raspberry Pi. The reason for this is simple: money. The Raspberry Pi Foundation needed to cut every possible corner to keep the per-unit costs for the Raspberry Pi as low as possible. In order to enable the BCM2835 to support a particular hardware video codec, they would have to pay a per-device license fee. As a result, they could afford only one video codec, so they picked one that they felt would be the best (and most common) codec.

While H.264/MPEG-4 is pretty common, there are a lot of video files that are encoded in MPEG-2. The Raspberry Pi Foundation looked into also enabling that codec by default, but it would have increased the cost of every Raspberry Pi by approximately 10%. They also couldn't afford a blanket license for the MPEG-2 codec, so they worked out a clever compromise. They set up a *store to sell video codec license keys* (*http://www.raspberrypi.com/license-keys/*).

For a few dollars, you can purchase a license for either the MPEG-2 or Microsoft's VC-1 codec. This license will be tied to your Raspberry Pi's unique CPU serial number. Once you purchase the license, the Raspberry Pi Foundation will send you back a numeric string. To enable the hardware video codec, you need to edit `/boot/config.txt` and pass that string as the value for the matching codec enablement option. To enable the MPEG-2 hardware codec, add a line like this to `/boot/config.txt`:

```
decode_MPG2=0x18675309
```

To enable the VC-1 hardware codec, add a line like this:

```
decode_WVC1=0x11235813
```

You can have multiple keys for multiple Raspberry Pi units (allowing you to swap out an SD card). To add additional keys, simply append them in a comma-separated list, like this:

```
decode_MPG2=0x18675309,0xdeadbeef,0x11001001
```

Feel free to try these example "license keys" out if you must, but they're not real. Sorry. You'll need to pay the license fee to get working keys for your Raspberry Pi.

```
┌─────────────────────────────────────────────────────────────────┐
```

Videocore Accelerated Video Codecs

In January, the Raspberry Pi Foundation pushed out a firmware update to add support for several free video codecs, specifically, VP6, VP8, MJPEG, and Ogg Theora. This support differs from the other codecs, because they are not handled completely in hardware, but instead, are accelerated with the videocore libraries. This means they are not as fast as they would be if the BCM2835 system-on-chip was doing all the work in hardware, but they're much much faster than they would be going through a pure software video decoder. Practically, this means that you can get pretty seamless playback for files in these formats via omxplayer (Hack #46) or XBMC (Hack #54) without having to do anything special at all.

```
└─────────────────────────────────────────────────────────────────┘
```

HACK 48 Build a Pi MusicBox

> The Pi MusicBox turns your Raspberry Pi into a controllable music player that supports Spotify, Apple Airplay, and Web Radio.

Say you have a huge library on Spotify (20+ million songs) just waiting for you to play them on your computer. Spotify is great. But how to play these songs on your audio setup? Using a headphones cable? That's not great with your laptop. Bluetooth? Unreliable.

Enter *Pi MusicBox* (*http://www.pimusicbox.com*). It turns your Pi into a music player (supporting Spotify, Apple Airplay, and Web Radio), which you can operate from your desktop computer or from your couch using a tablet, smartphone, or laptop. Connect your Raspberry Pi to an audio setup, install the software, and welcome a new way of listening to music!

It can output the sound not only through the headphones jack of the Pi, but also through HDMI and USB, and it supports playing music via WiFi, Last.fm, and from the SD card. The software will detect as much of the configuration as possible at boot, and configure the system automatically. But you have to supply the system with some information.

For this hack, you'll need a Spotify Premium account and an audio set, either head-phones or a set of USB speakers. A monitor or television is not required, but might come in handy.

Getting and Configuring the Software

Download the ready-to-go image from *http://www.pimusicbox.com*. For this guide, we used Pi MusicBox version 0.4. Newer versions should generally work the same way, though specific options could change.

After downloading the ZIP file, extract it:

```
$ unzip musicbox0.4.zip
```

Put the resulting image on your SD card (you'll need to use at least 1 GB):

```
$ su -c 'dd bs=4M if=musicbox0.4.img of=/dev/mmcblk0'
$ su -c 'sync'
```

To make it as easy as possible to configure, you can edit the settings of Pi MusicBox from any file manager, whether you're using Linux, Mac, or Windows.

In MUSICBOX, you'll see a folder called config containing a file called settings.ini, which you should open in a text editor. The file is structured like other ini files. All lines starting with a ## are comments, and some configuration lines are also commented out. If you want to use them, remove the ## at the beginning of the line.

You can also edit this file when you boot your Pi and log in (see "Getting Your Hands Dirty" on page 243). The file then is located in /boot/config/.

The most basic configuration file looks like this:

```
[MusicBox]
SPOTIFY_USERNAME = 'spotifyusername'
SPOTIFY_PASSWORD = 'spotifypassword'
```

These three settings should be enough to run Pi MusicBox:

[MusicBox]

> The section name of the configuration file. It has to be there, but you can ignore it.

spotifyusername

> The username of your Spotify Premium account (or Facebook login if you use Facebook to connect to Spotify).

spotifypassword

> Your own password, of course.

After you edit the basic settings, you can boot Pi MusicBox. You can edit many more settings, but it's good to try booting with the basic ones first, check to see that it's all working, then come back later to add the rest.

Note that the Pi MusicBox requires a network connection to operate. It will not start without one. If you use a wired network, all you have to do is plug the network cable in the Pi and it will be configured using DHCP. If you want to use a static address, you need to get into the console and configure it yourself (see "Getting Your Hands Dirty" on page 243).

Connecting through WiFi using a dongle is also supported. If you connect a supported WiFi dongle to your Pi, the MusicBox software should be able to detect and use it instead of a cable connection. Most dongles are supported, but not all. If you buy one, make sure it's supported by Raspbian, the Linux distribution on which MusicBox is based.

To make WiFi work, you have to fill in the network name (SSID) and your password in the config file. Add these lines to the basic configuration shown previously, or edit the default file supplied with MusicBox:

```
WIFI_NETWORK = 'mywifinetwork'
WIFI_PASSWORD = 'mypassword'
```

Substitute mywifinetwork and mypassword with the correct values of your own network. For now, the WiFi on Pi MusicBox supports only WPA(2) encrypted networks configured via DHCP. As with a wired network, if you want to use a static address, WEP encryption, or no encryption, you need to get into the console and configure it yourself (see "Getting Your Hands Dirty" on page 243).

Playing Music

Once you've booted the Pi MusicBox, if you have a monitor attached, you will see a message that says:

```
Now the output of Mopidy (the musicserver) appears. Nothing to worry about
(it's shown for if something's wrong), you can log in if you want (the out
put of Mopidy could continue).
```

Below that you'll see some information about your MusicBox setup, such as the active connections. You can start typing a login name (there's no prompt), but you don't need to. Pi MusicBox is designed to be operated not from the Pi itself, but from another computer, such as a laptop, desktop, tablet, or smartphone. You can use almost any device with a modern web browser (Chrome 14+, Safari 6+, Firefox 11+, or Internet Explorer 10+) to operate it.

Point your browser to the Pi at *http://musicbox.local*. Most OS X/iOS and Windows devices will find it immediately. If it doesn't work, you could try to install Apple Bonjour or iTunes in Windows to make it work. Linux should also work if Avahi or Samba/Winbind is installed. You have to add the http:// part of the address in some browsers, because otherwise, it will try to search for musicbox.local in Google.

If it doesn't work, or if you use Android (which does not support Bonjour/Avahi/Samba), you have to access MusicBox using the IP address of your Pi. This address is different on every network (e.g., *http://192.168.1.5/* or *http://10.1.100.2*). You can look it up using a network utility (see Hack #12 for more suggestions) or read it from the screen when Pi MusicBox boots.

Now that you're connected, it's time to play some music. The process varies, depending on your music source.

When you access the interface, most things are clear immediately. Your Spotify playlists will appear by default on the first tab. Select one of the playlists to show the tracks it contains. Select the track you want to play, and choose one of the play options in the pop-up menu that appears. Using this pop-up menu, you can either play the song, add it to the queue, or find more tracks from the same album or the same artist. Just play around—literally!

You can also start by searching. Use the third tab at the bottom of the screen to reach the Search functions, where you can look for artists, albums, or songs, as shown in Figure 5-1.

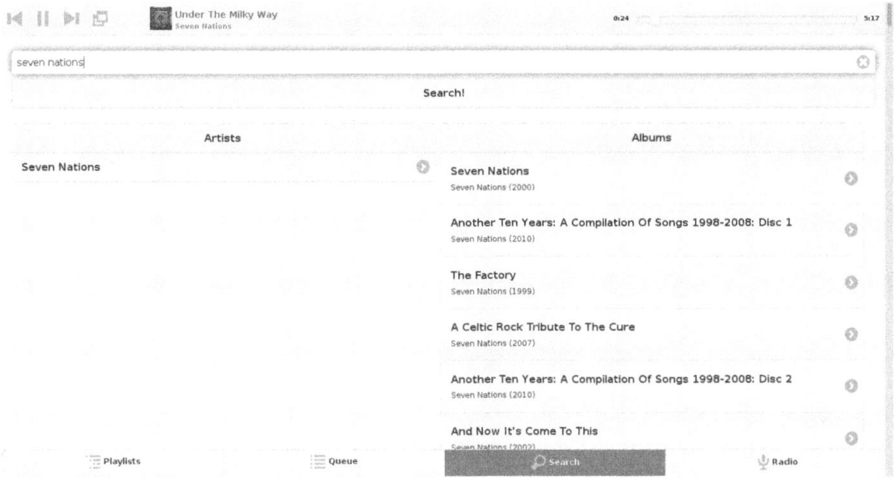

Figure 5-1.
The Pi MusicBox Search function

Once you've found a song that interests you, click it to play it or add it to your queue with the pop-up menu shown in Figure 5-2.

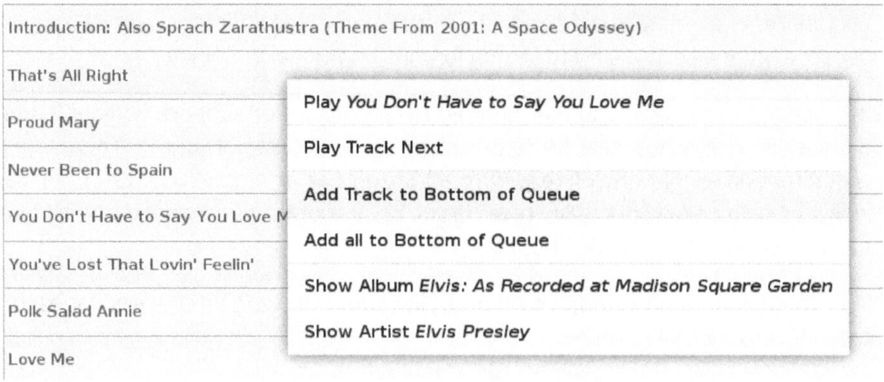

Introduction: Also Sprach Zarathustra (Theme From 2001: A Space Odyssey)
That's All Right
Proud Mary
Never Been to Spain
You Don't Have to Say You Love M
You've Lost That Lovin' Feelin'
Polk Salad Annie
Love Me

Play *You Don't Have to Say You Love Me*

Play Track Next

Add Track to Bottom of Queue

Add all to Bottom of Queue

Show Album *Elvis: As Recorded at Madison Square Garden*

Show Artist *Elvis Presley*

Figure 5-2.
Play a song immediately or add it to the queue

The second tab lists all the songs in your queue (see Figure 5-3). You can click them to get a similar menu to the one in Figure 5-2, or you can use it to remove songs from the queue.

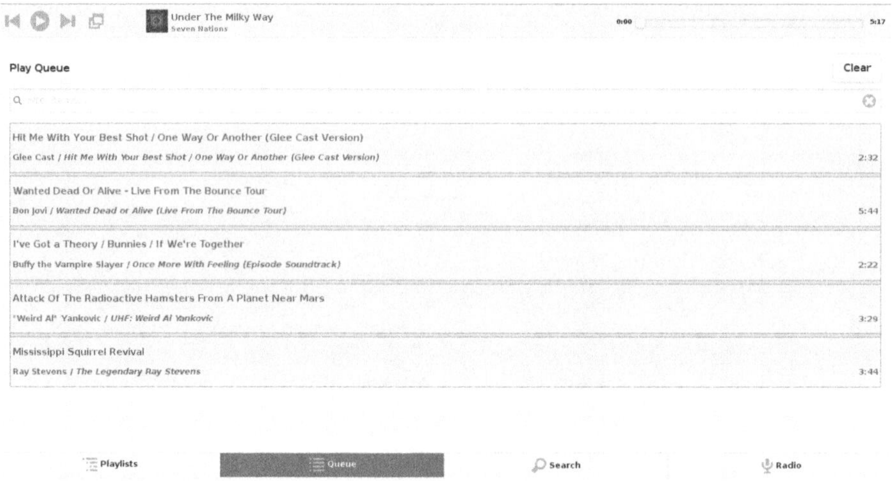

Figure 5-3.
A Pi MusicBox queue of songs for the worst (and shortest) party playlist ever

If you would rather play streams from web radio stations, you have to use a stream URL. You cannot use commonly available container files like M3U, XSPF, or PLS (yet). You have to add the real stream. This stream URL is hidden inside the M3U or PLS file. To find this URL, open the container file in a text editor. A PLS file looks like this:

```
[playlist]
numberofentries=1
```

```
File1=http://vprbbc.streamguys.net:8000/vprbbc24.mp3
Title1=BBC World Service
Length1=-1
version=2
```

The stream URL in this example is *http://vprbbc.streamguys.net:8000/ vprbbc24.mp3*. M3U and XSPF files look different, but the stream URL is always clearly visible.

As you can see in Figure 5-4, several streams are already set up when you first use Pi MusicBox.

Figure 5-4.
Ready-to-go web radio stations in Pi MusicBox

You can find radio stations (PLS and M3U) using services like *http://dir.xiph.org/*, Listenlive.eu, or Dirble.com. Add the stream URL and the name of the station and press the Play button. The last 25 stations are saved locally using a browser cookie (not on the server yet, so you need to do it on every client you use).

Pi MusicBox also supports Last.fm, which collects the tracks you play so you can discover new music. Go to *http://www.last.fm* to create an account if you don't already have one. To let Last.fm collect the tracks you play, fill in the credentials of this service:

```
LASTFM_USERNAME = 'lastfmuser'
LASTFM_PASSWORD = 'lastfmpassword'
```

Another service supported by Pi MusicBox is SoundCloud, the service that lets you "hear the world's sounds." To configure it, you need a special ID, a token that you can get from *http://www.mopidy.com/authenticate*. You have to log in with your Sound-Cloud ID to get the token. This information is not shared with the mopidy.com site.

When you log in, you'll see a token appear on the page. Add this token to the `set tings.ini` file, similar to this:

```
SOUNDCLOUD_TOKEN = '1-1111-111111'
SOUNDCLOUD_EXPLORE = 'electronic/Ambient, pop/New Wave, rock/Indie'
```

Replace the example 1-111-111111 with your token. Use the SOUNDCLOUD_EXPLORE configuration to configure the playlists you want to see in the interface.

Multi-room audio

Pi MusicBox supports multi-room audio, meaning you can have multiple Raspberry Pis on your network, even in different rooms. The devices need to have their own names to be accessible. Use this option to give your MusicBox a different name:

```
NAME = 'Kitchen'
```

The name you choose should be no than nine alphanumeric characters (no spaces, dots, etc.). After a new boot, the web interface for playing music will be accessible via a new address. Where the default would be *http://musicbox.local* from devices that support Bojour/Avahi, when you change the name, it becomes *http://newname.local*. In the previous example, it would be *http://kitchen.local/*.

It's not possible to play different music on multiple devices using the same Spotify account at the same time, unless you have multiple accounts. This is a limitation of Spotify.

Music Player Daemon (MPD)

Though the web-based interface is recommended, you can also use native software that supports the Music Player Daemon (MPD) protocol to control Pi MusicBox. Apps and applications are available for all sorts of devices and operating systems. Not all of them work great with MusicBox, though.

For Android, MPDroid is recommended. On OS X, Theremin works (without search). On Linux, you can use the excellent (and wonderfully named) console app ncmpcpp. On a Linux desktop, GMPC and Sonata work well. On iOS, try mPod and mPad. For Windows, clients either don't work well or are untested.

The Pi can play the music from Spotify in different levels of quality. The better the quality, the more data needs to be downloaded from Spotify (this is called *bitrate*). Higher quality means a higher bitrate and a bit more use of your Internet connection.

Typical broadband connections should be able to support the highest bitrate easily. If you have a good connection to the Internet, you can set the quality to high, but if your connection is slow or unstable, or if you have usage limits on your connection, you can it lower and use less data. Possible rates are 96 (low, but acceptable quality, FM-like), 160 (default), or 320 (highest quality, CD-like).

Set the bitrate to high like this in the configuration file:

```
SPOTIFY_BITRATE = 320
```

Or set the bitrate to low like this:

```
SPOTIFY_BITRATE = 96
```

You can install MPDroid from Google Play. (Or if you'd like to try others, consult the *MPD Wiki's list of clients (http://mpd.wikia.com/wiki/Clients)*.) When you first start it, you'll see the settings page. Choose "Default connection settings," which will take you to a list of options as seen in Figure 5-5.

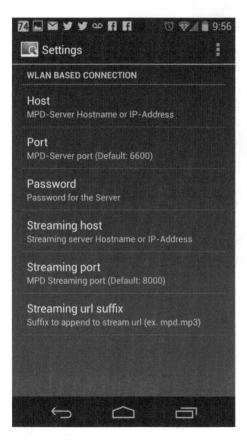

Figure 5-5.
MPDroid settings page

Select Host, and enter the IP address of your Pi MusicBox. Then return to the main menu, and you should see your playlist start playing (Figure 5-6).

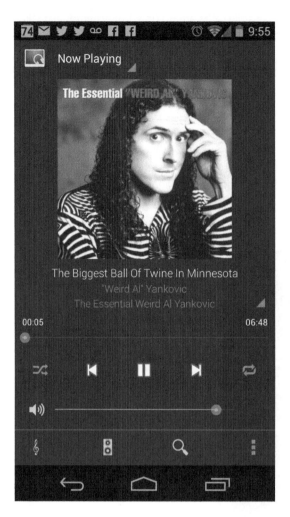

Figure 5-6.
MPDroid playing music

Remember that unless you've opened your Pi to the external Internet, you'll need to connect your phone to WiFi on the same network, or MPDroid won't work.

Networked music

If you would like to play your own music files, you can do so via a Windows network. To do so, edit the configuration file, so that MusicBox knows where your files are. This address could be a bit cryptic to a first-time user—for example:

```
NETWORK_MOUNT_ADDRESS = '//192.168.1.5/musicshare'
```

or:

```
NETWORK_MOUNT_ADDRESS = '//mynasserver/shared/music'
```

The first part (//) is the way shares in the Windows network are created. Just add it and forget it. The next part (`mynasserver` or `192.168.1.5`) is the name or IP address of the server that hosts the file. The last part (/`musicshare` or /shared/music) tells MusicBox which share to mount.

When your server is protected, you need to set the username and password for the Network share using the following configuration lines:

```
NETWORK_MOUNT_USER = 'username'
NETWORK_MOUNT_PASSWORD = 'password'
```

MusicBox will not see the files immediately. The music files needs to be scanned at boot, every time you add or remove files. This process can slow down the boot of the MusicBox, so use it with care. MusicBox will scan the files using the following configuration lines:

```
SCAN_ONCE = 'true'
```

or:

```
SCAN_ALWAYS = 'true'
```

The names speak for themselves. Using SCAN_ONCE, the music files will be scanned only once. Use this if you don't change the music files often. Use SCAN_ALWAYS if you change your music files a lot. This will enable you to change the files and reboot MusicBox. It will recognize the new files after the boot. But, again, the scanning process can slow-down the booting of MusicBox considerably.

Local music

Pi MusicBox also has an option to store music files on the SD card. This process is a bit more complicated. Since MusicBox is created for a 1 GB or larger SD card, the filesystem is also less than 1 GB. If you put MusicBox on a larger SD card, the rest of the space on the card won't be used unless you resize the filesystem.

You can do this manually using a partition manager (on Linux, try *GParted* (*http:// gparted.sourceforge.net/*)), or you can let MusicBox try to resize it automatically. If the process fails, you'll have a nonfunctional MusicBox, but since you should be doing this at the beginning, you can just start over with the installation. If you've done a lot of customization, however, you should back up the card first.

Using this line in the settings, Pi MusicBox will automatically resize the filesystem to the maximum size of the SD card:

```
RESIZE_ONCE = 'true'
```

Putting music files on the SD card is recommended only on cards larger than 1 GB. MusicBox needs the 1 GB for caching and other storage. After resizing an SD card with more storage, you can put your own music files on the Pi using either the Windows network or by mounting the root filesystem of the card on a Linux computer and copying the files. Leave at least 200 MB of free space on the device.

To use the Windows network, you have to have the workgroup name of the network set to the default name, WORKGROUP. If you want another name, you have to change it by hand in /etc/samba/smb.conf (see "Getting Your Hands Dirty" on page 243). Remember to let MusicBox scan the files at boot (see "Networked music" on page 240).

Sound Configuration

By default, Pi MusicBox will send the sound to the analog headphone output on the Pi. This sound is good enough, but due to hardware constraints, not always great. If you want to have better sound, use the HDMI to connect the Pi to an amplifier, or connect a USB sound card (also called USB Digital Audio Converter/DAC), USB speakers, or USB headphones. MusicBox supports almost all types of USB speakers, headphones, and DACs, but if you buy one, make sure it's Linux compatible. DACs with digital outputs are also available in many web stores.

When booting, Pi MusicBox will autodetect what is connected to the device and configure it accordingly. If you connect multiple devices, USB will be selected first as a sound output, HDMI after that, and lastly the analog output of the Pi itself. You can override this in the configuration file using the following line:

```
OUTPUT = 'analog'
```

If you include this, the default output will be the analog headphones jack of the Pi, even if you connected using an USB device or an HDMI cable. The options are analog, hdmi, usb.

Security

Pi MusicBox is not totally secure and is intended to run only in the cozy environment of your local network, not outside a firewall. The heart of MusicBox is not protected enough to do that. Also, your WiFi and Spotify passwords are stored in plain text on the SD card. This might be fixed in the future.

For more security, change the default password by setting this line (where mypass is your new password):

```
MUSICBOX_PASSWORD = 'mypass'
```

This will change the passwords of both the user musicbox and the user root. The password will be removed from the configuration file after it's updated.

If you want, to change the root password to something else for more security, use this line:

```
ROOT_PASSWORD = 'mypass'
```

Getting Your Hands Dirty

If you'd like to dig a bit, there are plenty more options to explore in Pi MusicBox. For the following options, you have to log into the box on the console, or via SSH (see Hack #12).

To log in remotely via SSH, you will need to enable the SSH service. Do that by adding this line to your configuration file:

```
SSH_ENABLED = 'true'
```

Reboot. After that, you can connect to MusicBox via SSH.

Mopidy

The main ingredient of MusicBox is Mopidy, an open source music server developed by people from all over the world. By default, Pi MusicBox is set up using the best working extensions, but you can extend it to play music from other sources, such as SoundCloud, Google Music, and Beets Music.

Adding these extensions is beyond the scope of this hack, but you can find additional resources and documentation at *Mopidy's website* (*http://www.mopidy.com*) and reach the developers on the *Mopidy mailing list* (*https://groups.google.com/forum/? fromgroups=#!forum/mopidy*) or via IRC on the #mopidy channel on Freenode.

rc.local

The /etc/rc.local file is another important piece of Pi MusicBox. It's a shell script where the sound hardware is set up and the configuration is done. For example, the configuration file of Mopidy is created from rc.local. Edit this file is you want to add, change, or remove features.

Working at Midnight

For Linux novices, a nice utility called Midnight Commander could be useful for browsing the filesystem and editing files. It works like the age-old DOS-utility Norton Commander and it's included in MusicBox. Start it using the command mc.

Static network

To use MusicBox in a network with static IP addresses, you have to edit `/etc/network/interfaces`. The lines that configure the wired network look like this:

```
allow-hotplug eth0
iface eth0 inet dhcp
```

For a static wired network, you should change it to something like this:

```
iface eth0 inet static
address 192.168.1.5
netmask 255.255.255.0
gateway 192.168.1.1
```

Change the IP addresses as applicable for your network. For more about finding and setting your IP address, see Hack #13.

Updating

When a new version of MusicBox is released, the only way to update it is to do a new installation. Note that if you update the kernel or other packages on the system manually without a new MusicBox installation, it could eventually break things, so a fresh installation is preferred.

—Wouter van Wijk

HACK 49 Turn Your Pi into a Radio

Sure, it's easy to play an entire library of music files from your Raspberry Pi. But how about using the Pi itself (which doesn't have any sort of built-in radio transmitter) as a radio?

The PiFM project, created by Oliver Mattos and Oskar Weigl, was designed to turn your Raspberry Pi into a radio. By switching a GPIO pin from on to off at a high frequency, you'll build yourself a makeshift Rapberry Pi FM transmitter.

To get started, download the PiFM files from *http://www.icrobotics.co.uk/wiki/images/c/c3/Pifm.tar.gz* to your Raspberry Pi and extract the tarball in the Pi's home folder. You'll have four files there:

- `sound.wav`
- `PiFm.py`
- `pifm.c`
- `pifm`

Tune a radio to 103.3 FM and put it near your Pi. Then open a terminal and enter:

```
$ sudo python
  >> import PiFM
  >> PiFm.play_sound("sound.wav")
```

If you want to play your own sound, convert it to WAV format (16 bit mono, 22 Khz is best) and put it in your home directory.

This will work only with the radio next to the Raspberry Pi. To get a little more range, you can connect any 50 cm wire to GPIO4 to act as an antenna. Pointing it straight up works well and should get you around 50 m of range.

You might need a license to transmit radio in some countries, so if you're unsure, it is best to leave the antenna disconnected. It will still work, but with a very short range.

Compile the code for `pifm.c` using the following command:

```
$ gcc -lm -std=c99 pifm.c -o mypifm
```

To broadcast your WAV file, just run:

```
$ ./mypifm myaudio.wav
```

How It Works

FM stands for *frequency modulation*, which is how it sends sounds over the air. Frequency modulation works by having a signal (called a *carrier signal*) that regularly changes from positive to negative and back again very quickly (in the case of the PiFM radio, it changes and changes back again 103.3 million times every second!). When you vary speed of this change to be just a bit faster or slower, the radio on the other end can detect the changing speed and makes sound based on how it changes.

But how do you make the Raspberry Pi change something so quickly and accurately? The Pi has an on-board clock manager that can accurately produce any clock frequency you want by dividing the system processor clock (which is normally around 500 Mhz) down to any other rate you want. To tell it what to do, you set a register (a special piece of memory) to a number saying what you want the system clock divided by to make the FM radio clock. For example:

- System Clock = 500 Mhz
- Divider Register = 5.000
- FM radio clock frequency = 500/5 = 100 Mhz

This divider can be a fractional number and adjusted up and down by tiny bits to make your sound.

Alas, it turns out that to keep your sound playing smoothly, you need to regularly adjust the rate, and the Raspberry Pi isn't very good at that. The Pi can run more than one program at a time, but it has only one processor. It does this by quickly switching between running programs (multitasking). This normally works well, but in this case, if another program is running when the clock rate needs adjusting, there will be a glitch in the sound.

To combat this problem, you can use the Direct Memory Access (DMA) controller. You can give the DMA controller a list of things to do (e.g., what rate to adjust the sound to at each point in time), and then it does it in the background, even if the main processor is busy running other programs. The PiFM program just makes a list of things for the DMA controller to tell the clock generator to do and then gets it going.

Accessing Hardware

The Python library calls a C program (provided both precompiled and in source form). The C program maps the peripheral bus (`0x20000000`) in physical memory into virtual address space using `/dev/mem` and `mmap`. To do this, it needs root access, hence the `sudo`.

Next, it sets the clock generator module to enabled and sets it to output on GPIO4 (no other accessible pins can be used). It also sets the frequency to 103.3 Mhz (provided from *PLLD@500Mhz*, divided by 5), which provides a carrier. At this point, radios will stop making a "fuzz" noise and become silent.

Modulation is done by adjusting the frequency using the fractional divider between 103.325 Mhz and 102.275 Mhz, which makes the audio signal. The fractional divider doesn't have enough resolution to produce more than ~6 bit audio, but since the Pi is fast, you can do PWM to provide about 10 additional bits, giving a total resolution of 16 bits, matching the audio input.

Fun with FM

Here are some ideas of things you might be able to try with PiFm:

Make a repeated playlist (easy)
> A simple loop in Python calling `play_sound` on different sound files should let you play an entire list of files one at a time.

Make a "mystery sound" game (medium)
> Play a sound, and the player must guess which household object makes the same sound. They can take their radio round the house to try to find a matching sound.

Make a Morse code program (medium)

If you make a sound file for "dot," another for "dash," and a third as a "gap," you should be able to play them in the right order to send Morse code.

Make a wireless network (hard)

As an extension of the Morse code idea, see if you can send any information (for example, an image file) via noises on the radio, and make a decoder program on your computer that can recognize the noises through a microphone and convert it to a file again. You now have a crude wireless network link and radio-modem that you have made entirely yourself!

—Oliver Mattos and Oskar Weigl

HACK 50 Control the Pi via Touchscreen

While the Raspberry Pi has native hardware support for two types of video output (HDMI and composite video), there are times where it would be helpful to be able to use it with a touchscreen monitor, such as those used for both display and input in tablet computers.

The Raspberry Pi Model B contains a Display Serial Interface (DSI) connector, which is a 15-way, flat flex connector labeled S2 next to the Raspberry Pi logo on the board. DSI is sometimes used to connect touchscreens in small-form-factor devices such as smartphones. Sadly, adding a touchscreen to your Pi is not as simple as disassembling an abandoned smartphone and reconnecting the screen to the DSI connector.

The GPU firmware that enables the native video output needs code to explicitly support any device connected to the DSI port. Since this firmware is not open source, it is not currently possible to add support for any DSI-connected screens, nor are there any known devices that the GPU firmware supports on the DSI connector. It is widely expected that, at some point, the Raspberry Pi Foundation will release official peripherals that can connect to the DSI connector, which will make this a much simpler task (assuming that one of those peripherals is a touchscreen). Until that point, however, we'll just have to hack around it.

Choosing a Touchscreen

The first step is to figure out which touchscreen to connect to the Raspberry Pi. There are quite a few touchscreen devices on the market, but the majority of them are extremely expensive, and the Linux support for them is haphazard at best. We chose the Mimo 720 touchscreen because it is small (7" x 5.25" x 1"), light (less than a pound), USB-driven, mountable with a bracket, and relatively inexpensive (MSRP $199 USD, but it is regularly on sale around $129).

The Mimo 720 is technically two devices in one unit: an 800 x 480 LCD DisplayLink monitor and an e2i Technology, Inc. USB touchpanel. Linux detects these devices separately, so it is important for your Raspberry Pi Linux kernel to support for both of them.

Installing and Enabling Drivers

You can make the Mimo 720 available as a monitor to Linux via two kernel drivers, either the USB Display Link Framebuffer Driver (`CONFIG_FB_UDL` in `Kconfig`-speak, `udlfb.ko` as a module) or the USB Display Link Kernel Mode Setting (KMS) driver (`CONFIG_DRM_UDL` in `Kconfig`-speak, `udl.ko` as a module). The UDL Kernel Mode Setting driver does not work as well for this use as the UDL Framebuffer Driver. The KMS driver is likely to eventually be the better choice, but in the interim, the Framebuffer Driver works great for our hacking needs.

The e2i Technology touchpanel portion of the device is driven by the USB Touchscreen Driver (`CONFIG_TOUCHSCREEN_USB_COMPOSITE` in `Kconfig`-speak, `usbtouchscreen.ko` as a module).

Neither the USB Touchscreen Driver nor the UDL Framebuffer Driver is enabled by default in the prebuilt kernels provided by the Raspberry Pi Foundation, and thus, almost never present in Raspberry Pi Linux distribution images, but this is easily remedied with a custom kernel, which you can build from source with the instructions in "Install a New Kernel" on page 85.

When you build your custom kernel for this hack, you will need to be sure that you configure it so that these additional drivers are also built. As a reminder, you can configure which drivers and options to build using `make menuconfig`.

To enable the framebuffer driver, go into the Device Drivers menu and select "Graphics support" → "Support for frame buffer devices." At this screen, you need to enable "Displaylink USB Framebuffer support." Since you will want to use this driver as a module, hit the M key when that item is highlighted in the TUI. When successful, your screen should look something like Figure 5-7.

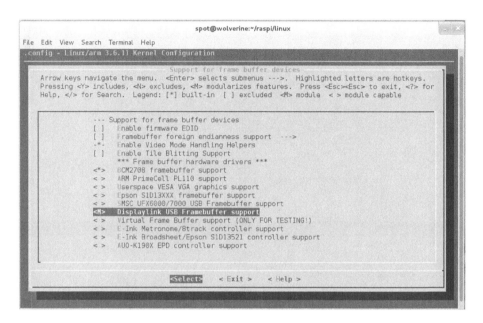

Figure 5-7.
Configuring Displaylink USB Framebuffer support as a module

Next, you need to enable USB touchscreen support. Exit to the Device Drivers menu (right arrow to Exit, then Enter). From there, go into the "Input device support" menu. You need to enable the "Touchscreens" option on this page (by hitting the spacebar when "Touchscreens" is highlighted), then press Enter to go into the Touchscreens menu.

In the Touchscreens menu, highlight the "USB Touchscreen Driver" option and press M to enable it as a module. By default, this enables all of the supported USB Touchscreens, but you should still scroll down and make sure that the "e2i Touchscreen controller (e.g., From Mimo 740)" option is enabled. You can confirm that is enabled by making sure that it has an asterisk beside it, as shown in Figure 5-8.

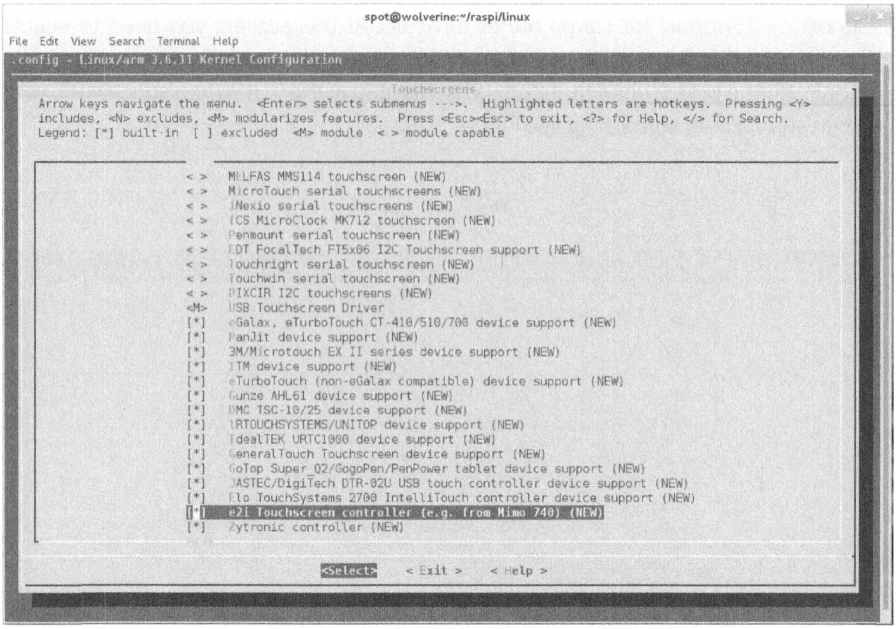

Figure 5-8.
e2i Touchscreen controller driver enabled

Once your kernel and modules are rebuilt, simply install them into the Raspberry Pi Linux distribution image. Reboot your Raspberry Pi with the Mimo 720 connected.

On the Mimo 720, the screen will cycle through several colors and patterns as the Raspberry Pi boots. This is the Mimo 720 initializing the frame buffer, and it means that the Mimo 720 works properly. At this point, it will stop at a green screen, which is fine, because you have not yet configured the Linux userspace to run the display.

Within the Raspberry Pi Linux instance, you should see kernel messages like this in the output of dmesg:

```
udlfb: DisplayLink MIMO - serial #101234567
udlfb: DisplayLink USB device /dev/fb1 attached. 800x480 resolution. Using
1504K framebuffer memory
```

There are a couple ways you can get this information from your Raspberry Pi:

- SSH into the Raspberry Pi (see Hack #12).
- Connect a monitor to the HDMI or composite video.

Later, you're going to reconfigure X to run the main display to the Mimo 720, but for now, the graphical X11 display should still be running on the directly connected monitor.

Linux Distributions Without Xorg/X11

OpenELEC makes a build of their XBMC-based Linux OS for the Raspberry Pi, but it does not use Xorg. Because OpenELEC relies entirely on the VideoCore output devices, this particular hack will not work on that distribution, unless you rebuild it entirely from source and enable Xorg support. You'll have the same problem if you try to use RaspBMC with this hack.

In the dmesg output, you're looking for the line that tells you which frame buffer device the Linux kernel has assigned to the Mimo 720. In the current example, the device is /dev/fb1. It is probably /dev/fb1 for you as well, unless you have other devices plugged into the Raspberry Pi that show up to the Linux kernel as frame buffers. Just make a note of this device name, as you will need it to write your Xorg configuration file later.

For the touch panel, look for messages like this in the output of dmesg:

```
input: e2i Technology, Inc. USB Touchpanel as /devices/platform/bcm2708_usb/
usb1/1-1/1-1.3/1-1.3.1/1-1.3.1.3/1-1. 3.1.3:1.0/input/input2
usbcore: registered new interface driver usbtouchscreen
```

These messages mean that the usbtouchscreen driver has been loaded and the e2i Technology USB Touchpanel in the Mimo 720 has been detected.

Now, look in the /dev/input/by-id/ directory. You should see a filename that looks something like:

```
/dev/input/by-id/usb-e2i_Technology__Inc._USB_Touchpanel_L000000000-event-
if00
```

Take a note of this filename, which you'll use to identify your touch panel device in the Xorg configuration file. You use this ID instead of using a /dev/input/event* device, because the ordering of those devices can (and does) change when you add things like USB mice and keyboards to the bus. Using the touchscreen's unique device identifier ensures that you always end up with a working X session.

Xorg Configuration

At this point, it is time to start writing your Xorg configuration file. Modern Linux distributions usually autodetect a working Xorg configuration for the present hardware, but in the case of the Raspberry Pi, it will result in a working X session for the GPU, not the Mimo 720. By making your own Xorg configuration file, you'll be overriding the autodetection and telling the Raspberry Pi Linux distribution to use the Mimo 720 as the primary graphical display and input device. You can still plug in a USB keyboard and mouse, and those will be auto-detected and used in addition to the Mimo 720 touchscreen as input sources.

Create a new file in your home directory called `xorg.conf.mimo` and open it in your favorite text editor. (If you don't care about the inner workings here, you can just download our `xorg.conf.mimo` from the *book's GitHub repository (https://github.com/spotrh/rpihacks*).)

Your Xorg cofiguration file needs five sections: Device, Monitor, Screen, ServerLayout, and InputDevice:

```
Section "Device"
        Identifier "DisplayLinkDevice"
          driver "fbdev"
          Option "fbdev" "/dev/fb1"
          Option "ShadowFB" "off"
    EndSection
```

This defines a video device named `DisplayLinkDevice` that uses the `fbdev` driver across the Mimo's framebuffer device (`/dev/fb1`). If your framebuffer device is different, adjust it accordingly.

We also disable the ShadowFB feature. ShadowFB causes the `fbdev` driver to force the CPU to do each drawing operation first into a shadow frame buffer in system virtual memory and then copy the result into video memory. While this behavior is good for most cases, for our DisplayLink device, you need the CPU to draw directly into video memory:

```
Section "Monitor"
        Identifier "monitor"
        Option "DPMS"
    EndSection
```

This section defines a Monitor device, which we have uncreatively named `monitor`. The only other setting here is to enable Display Power Management Signaling (DPMS), which allows power saving behaviour of the touchscreen when you are not using your Raspberry Pi:

```
Section "Screen"
        Identifier "screen"
        Device "DisplayLinkDevice"
        Monitor "monitor"
    EndSection
```

The third section defines a `Screen` device that ties our `DisplayLinkDevice` video device to our `monitor` device. This is how Xorg works; it draws to a screen device. Xorg supports multiple devices, including multiple screen devices, but for this hack, we're keeping it simple:

```
Section "ServerLayout"
        Identifier "default"
```

```
Screen 0 "screen" 0 0
InputDevice "touchscreen" "CorePointer"
Option "BlankTime"      "0"
Option "StandbyTime"    "0"
Option "SuspendTime"    "0"
Option "OffTime"        "0"
    EndSection
```

The `ServerLayout` section tells Xorg how to layout any screens that you wish to use. This is simple, because you have only one screen device, so just put it in position `0,0` (the numbers correspond to a horizontal and vertical ordering, where 0 is the first position).

You'll also tell it that, for your `ServerLayout`, you want to use the `touchscreen` input device as your mouse device. By passing it as `CorePointer`, it tells Xorg to use it as the default mouse device. The other options are for the DPMS timeout settings:

`BlankTime`

The time in minutes to let the screensaver (if any) run before blanking the screen

`StandbyTime` *and* `SuspendTime`

Define the inactivity period (in minutes) before going into standby and suspend mode, respectively

`OffTime`

Defines the inactivity period before turning the monitor device off entirely

In this example config, these options are all set to `0`, which effectively disables power saving on the device, but you should customize them for your needs.

When setting these, you should stagger them out, in the order presented, so that your monitor device goes blank, then to standby, then to suspend, then turns off entirely. If you do not want your monitor to go into one of those states (or it does not support that state), you can always disable it by passing a `0` value to it:

```
Section "InputDevice"
        Identifier "touchscreen"
        Driver "evdev"
        Option "Device" "/dev/input/by-id/usb-
e2i_Technology__Inc._USB_Touchpanel_L000000000-event-if00"
        Option "DeviceName" "touchscreen"
        Option "ReportingMode" "Raw"
        Option "SendCoreEvents" "On"
        Option "Calibration" "449 31910 31857 988"
    EndSection
```

The last section defines the input device for the touchscreen component of the Mimo. The touchscreen device uses the `evdev` driver, pointing to the e2i input device node identified earlier:

```
/dev/input/by-id/usb-e2i_Technology__Inc._USB_Touchpanel_L000000000-event-
if00
```

Continuing our less-than-creative naming scheme, it is named `touchscreen`. We need to have the Mimo touchscreen in `Raw` reporting mode to work properly, and since we are using it as the main input pointer, we want it to have the `SendCoreEvents` option enabled.

The last option is a calibration option, which is how the Mimo touchscreen knows how to properly report touch events. The calibration values should be correct for your device, but if they are not, you may need to determine them for yourself. There are a few ways to do this, but the tool that exists for most of the Linux distributions is called `evtest`. To install it on Pidora, run:

```
$ su -c 'yum install evtest -y'
```

Or on Raspbian/Occidentalis:

```
$ sudo apt-get install evtest
```

`evtest` is intended as a debugging tool, to see all of the input that is being generated from an evdev-compatible input device. For calibration purposes, we need to know the minimum and maximum values being reported along the X and Y axes of the touchscreen. Run `evtest` on the Mimo touchscreen device node:

```
$ sudo evtest /dev/input/by-id/usb-
e2i_Technology__Inc._USB_Touchpanel_L000000000-event-if00
```

Using the Touchscreen

Now, every time you touch the screen, `evtest` will output debugging information about the event. For example, when you touch near the center of the screen, it generates an event that looks like this:

```
Event: time 1378951053.759441, type 1 (EV_KEY), code 330 (BTN_TOUCH), value
1
Event: time 1378951053.759452, type 3 (EV_ABS), code 0 (ABS_X), value 17165
Event: time 1378951053.759456, type 3 (EV_ABS), code 1 (ABS_Y), value 17217
Event: time 1378951053.759460, ------------- SYN_REPORT ------------
Event: time 1378951053.766434, type 3 (EV_ABS), code 0 (ABS_X), value 17191
Event: time 1378951053.766442, type 3 (EV_ABS), code 1 (ABS_Y), value 17259
Event: time 1378951053.766446, ------------- SYN_REPORT ------------
Event: time 1378951053.773442, type 3 (EV_ABS), code 0 (ABS_X), value 17208
Event: time 1378951053.773452, type 3 (EV_ABS), code 1 (ABS_Y), value 17422
```

```
Event: time 1378951053.773456, -------------- SYN_REPORT ------------
Event: time 1378951053.826439, type 1 (EV_KEY), code 330 (BTN_TOUCH), value
0
Event: time 1378951053.826456, -------------- SYN_REPORT ------------
```

This is a single touch (BTN_TOUCH), but you can see it gets three distinct X (ABS_X) and Y (ABS_Y) measurements. To determine the minimum and maximum X and Y calibration values, you will need to touch the upper-left, upper-right, lower-left, and lower-right corners of the screen (as close to the edge as you can). Then, write down the smallest and largest values for ABS_X and ABS_Y that appear in the evtest output. These make up the values that go into your xorg config file, with this option syntax:

```
Option "Calibration" "<MIN_X> <MAX_X> <MIN_Y> <MAX_Y>"
```

Substitute in your discovered values for <MIN_X>, <MAX_X>, <MIN_Y>, and <MAX_Y>.

With your xorg.conf.mimo complete, you can now make the Mimo touchscreen into your primary device by copying it to /etc/X11/xorg.conf as root:

```
$ sudo cp -a xorg.conf.mimo /etc/X11/xorg.conf
```

When you reboot (assuming that your Linux instance is configured to boot into a graphical mode), you should see your desktop display out to your Mimo touchscreen.

Keep in mind that if you have something connected to the "normal" video output of the Raspberry Pi (e.g., HDMI), you will still see the Linux kernel and boot messages go to that device, because the DisplayLink device is not the main target for that output. Also, because it is not using the VideoCore GPU at all, you will not be able to playback videos using the hardware video codecs, and they will be *slow*.

HACK 51 Emulate Classic Video Game Consoles

Relive the golden era of home video gaming by letting your Raspberry Pi pretend to be the gaming systems of yesteryear. Hey, you kids, get off our lawn. We're hacking here!

We both have fond memories of the original Nintendo Entertainment System (NES). (For Tom, it was his first dedicated gaming console. Ruth was still playing with an Atari 2600 and stuck with whatever could be found on 5.25-inch floppies.) Now, although we both have kids who think of video games as something much more complicated than *Duck Hunt* could have dreamed to be, those old 8-bit (and later, 16-bit) games still have a lot of play left in them.

It's not surprising to see the retro trend in a lot of new independent video games, but what about going straight to the source? Those old games from the 1980s and 1990s were good enough for us then. We're certainly not too good for them now. You could spend a lot of money buying a working system and all of your old games on eBay, but let's assume for a moment that you're not independently wealthy. Your Raspberry Pi can emulate most of these old gaming consoles for you!

The original video game consoles were good for their time, but by today's standards, they're nothing but slow and weak. The NES had a 1.79 MHz CPU (that's an M, not a G), with 2 KiB of onboard memory. Today, most of these hardware consoles have been fully reverse-engineered, and pure software implementations have been written that can emulate them almost perfectly.

All that's left to worry about is the games. Even if you still have the media lying around, your Raspberry Pi didn't arrive with any slots designed for those old game cartridges and discs. Instead, those software emulators are written to read ROM files, which are imaged copies of the games, taken from their original media and saved to a file.

Downloading the ROM files from the Internet for the games that you want to play is the simplest way to get started; however, its legality is questionable in a lot of jurisdictions. There are other alternatives, such as the *Retrode gaming adapter* (*http://www.retrode.com*), which is a USB device that has native slots for Sega Genesis and Super Nintendo (SNES) games, as well as native connectors for the controllers of both systems.

This hack assumes that you have ROM image files for your games. Depending on where you are, ROMs may have some legal issues. For the purposes of this hack, we will simply assume that you possess legal ROMs.

As for controllers, Linux supports almost any USB joystick that you can find. For the full nostalgia experience, you can purchase original gaming controllers converted to use USB connectors and USB connectors that will provide a native port for the original controller.

Using an NES/SNES Controller Through the GPIO

It is possible to connect an NES or SNES controller directly through the Raspberry Pi GPIO, but you'll need to build and use a RetroPie GPIO Adapter. There is a complete writeup (with hardware specifications, schematics, and software) here: http://blog.petrockblock.com/2012/10/21/the-retropie-gpio-adapter/

First you need to turn your Raspberry Pi into a gaming supercomputer. Start with a fresh Raspbian install, which works best for this purpose. Update all of the components:

```
$ sudo apt-get update
$ sudo apt-get upgrade -y
```

While there are quite a few game console emulator software choices out there, because the Raspberry Pi is an ARM-based system (as opposed to x86-based), the best option is called RetroArch. Although building RetroArch for the Raspberry Pi was initially complicated, Florian Müller has created a tool called RetroPie that automates almost the entire process.

Florian also provides prebuilt images containing finished RetroPie setups (http://blog.petrockblock.com/retropie).

RetroPie needs to have some additional software installed on top of the Raspbian image to work properly, so you should start off by running:

```
$ sudo apt-get install -y git dialog
```

Then you can pull down a copy of the latest RetroPie setup software from GitHub:

```
$ git clone --depth=0 git://github.com/petrockblog/RetroPie-Setup.git
```

This will create a directory called `RetroPie-Setup`. Change into that directory, set the main setup script to be executable, then run it as root:

```
$ cd RetroPie-Setup
$ chmod +x retropie_setup.sh
$ sudo ./retropie_setup.sh
```

This will load a clean text interface to set up the RetroPie suite. You can install either from prebuilt binaries or from source. Installing from source (option 2) will give you the absolute latest versions of all of the emulators and game runtimes, but it will take quite a bit longer (and is a bit more complicated to do). Installing the binaries (option 1) is faster (though it still takes a while), so we recommend you go down that path. It will go out and download all of the files it needs to setup the various supported emulators and runtimes, and when it finishes, it will write out a debug log of everything it did.

When this finishes successfully, you need to select the SETUP option from the main menu (option 3). If you plan on using this as a dedicated video gaming station, you should consider starting the Emulation Station on boot (option 4), as that will provide a nice frontend to all of the gaming options. You can also enable a nice splash screen to display on boot (option 6), but that is entirely eye candy.

Option 7 might be useful to you. You can configure the sound output from the emulators to go over the HDMI connection, the analog audio connection, or automatically detect what is in use.

If you enable the Emulation Station on boot, you can reboot, and the system will boot directly into the Emulation Station GUI. You can also launch this GUI manually by running:

```
$ emulationstation
```

On its first run, Emulation Station will prompt you to configure your joystick. It uses the joystick to navigate through the GUI interface (though it does not pass those joystick settings to every emulator). You can choose from the emulated systems using the left and right buttons on your joystick controller.

If you do not have ROMs installed for an emulated system, Emulation Station will not display that system as a choice. To install ROMs for a system, put the files in `/home/pi/RetroPie/roms/<systemname>/`. If your ROM files are compressed, you might need to uncompress them before Emulation Station will recognize them.

HACK 52 Connect a DSLR

> The official Raspberry Pi camera is tiny and mighty, but there are times you'll want the control and interchangeable lenses of your DSLR. The Pi can handle that, too.

Although the Raspberry Pi was designed for a camera (that didn't even exist until more than a year after the Pi itself launched!), that camera doesn't have nearly the power of your DSLR. We used one to create a portable photobooth (along with a Tux the penguin mascot costume!) to take to open source conferences (see Hack #53).

Tethering a computer to your DSLR can offer you some big additional capabilities, including in-the-moment settings adjustments for rapid subsequent exposures, nearly instant backups, and remote camera control from anywhere. The fact that the Pi is so small makes the whole setup a lot more feasible.

Geting Started with gPhoto

The quickest way to get started on any of those projects or whatever else you can imagine doing with a Pi-controlled camera is with gPhoto, which is a set of software and libraries for doing just that. gPhoto supports more than 1,600 cameras, so there's a good chance that unless you have either an exceptionally old or exceptionally new piece of equipment, it's on the list. For example, if you own a Pi because you love tiny things, that *supported list (http://gphoto.sourceforge.net/proj/libgphoto2/*

support.php) even includes the absurdly small, 1.2-ounce, 2.36" x 1.52" Che-ez SPYZ camera!

Camera Protocols

gPhoto is not intended for controlling webcams, but there is one other reason your camera might not be on the supported list. Most cameras with USB ports use either (or both) Picture Transfer Protocol (PTP) or USB Mass Storage protocols. USB Mass Storage doesn't allow remote control of a device and very much limits what else you can do through the protocol and thus is fairly useless to us here. Many modern cameras (post 2003) have used PTP as well. Nikon cameras often default to USB Mass Storage, but you can switch them to PTP through the on-camera settings menus.

In addition to your Raspberry Pi, your camera, and a USB cable to connect the two, you'll need `libgphoto2`, a `libgphoto2` frontend (such as `gphoto2,gtkam`, `kamera`, or `digi kam`) and `libusb` on your Pi. To get everything running on Pidora, run the following command:

```
$ su -c 'yum install libgphoto2 gphoto2 libusb'
```

Here's how to get what you need on Raspbian:

```
$ su -c 'apt-get install libgphoto2-2 gphoto2 libusb'
```

If you'd like to see whether your camera is supported before trying this out, run gphoto2 --list-cameras, *but the list is quite long, and unless you have an odd or new camera, it's almost certainly in there.*

Now, let's test them! Plug your camera into your laptop via USB cable and enter:

```
$ gphoto2 --capture-image-and-download
```

You might get the following error:

```
*** Error ***
Out of Focus
ERROR: Could not capture image.
ERROR: Could not capture.
```

Fortunately, the error generally tells you where you went wrong. But preferably, you'll capture a photo:

```
New file is in location /capt0000.jpg on the camera
Saving file as capt0000.jpg
```

```
Deleting file /capt0000.jpg on the camera
Deleting 'capt0000.jpg' from folder '/'...
```

You can even capture video this way by specifying the number of seconds you'd like to record:

```
$ gphoto2 --capture-movie=5
Capturing 5 preview frames as movie to 'movie.mjpg'.
Movie capture finished (6 frames)
```

That's a "motion jpeg," in case you were wondering what a .mjpg *file is.*

Basic Capture Commands and Variables

What you do with your new camera+Pi powers is up to you. These are the three main capture commands:

`--capture-image`

Capture an image and keep it on the camera.

`--capture-movie`

Capture a movie file (depends on camera).

`--capture-sound`

Capture an audio clip.

You can also add `-and-download` to image capture, so `--capture-image-and-download` will take a photo and immediately download it to the computer.

These few commands should be enough to get you started, but explore gphoto2 `--help` *to learn even more.*

You might also want to include some of the following variables:

`--filename` *NAME*

Specifies a filename, where NAME is the desired filename. You can create a default value for this in `~/.gphoto/settings`. It accepts additions, including %n: (for incrementing numbers), + (for date and time information), and +% (to keep the filename in lowercase).

`-F`

The number of frames to capture in a row.

`-I` *N*

The time to wait between frames in seconds, specified by *N*.

`--force-overwrite`

Overwrite files without asking.

Finding More About Your Camera

To discover a stunningly large amount of information about your camera, from the serial number to how charged the battery is to whether the flash is on, and probably quite a few things that you aren't even entirely sure what they mean, run the `summary`:

```
$ gphoto2 --summary
```

Some cameras will take photos at regular intervals for you. Some will only do it for a few shots and then stop. You can use `gphoto2` to do so at an interval you specify. This is great for everything from science fair project displays to making composite photos to time-lapse videos of all sorts of things. To take photos at continuous intervals:

```
$ gphoto2 --capture-image --I 30
```

The `I` stands for "interval," and the number after it is the count in seconds between photos. It will continue indefinitely (or until the battery dies). Put your camera on a tripod and let it go. If you would rather it stop after a certain number of photos, add `--frames 5` and specify the number of shots you'd like it to take.

You can also adjust most of your camera's settings from gPhoto. This is one way to capture a long series of bracketed photos (for HDR photography, for example). Create a file called `bracket.sh` with the following contents:

```
$ gphoto2 --set-config-value /main/capturesettings/shutterspeed=.1\
  --capture-image\
  --set-config-value /main/capturesettings/shutterspeed=.5\
  --capture-image\
  --set-config-value /main/capturesettings/shutterspeed=1\
  --capture-image\
```

Turn on your camera, connect it to the Pi, and enter `./bracket.sh` to run the commands. Your camera will take three photos with shutter speeds of .1, .5, and 1 second and save them to the camera.

You can do the same thing with exposure compensation, for example:

```
$ gphoto2 --set-config-value /main/capturesettings/exposurecompensation=-3 \
  --capture-image \
  --set-config-value /main/capturesettings/exposurecompensation=0 \
  --capture-image \
  --set-config-value /main/capturesettings/exposurecompensation=3 \
  --capture-image
```

Experiment with various settings and image capture options. Remember that your camera will take all of these photos starting in the mode in which it is set. The best approach is to set it to full manual, focus on your subject, and switch to manual focus to lock it before running these scripts.

HACK 53 Set Up a Photobooth

Now that you know how to connect a camera (see Hack #52), you're ready to be the hit of your next party. Set up a fun backdrop, gather some props, and set up your Raspberry Pi photobooth.

We first set up this photobooth at the SXSW Interactive festival for a Fedora booth in the exhibit hall and then at several other conferences thereafter. It's a fun way to get people to come into the booth and hang out for a minute, even if you don't have one of us in a Tux costume there to amuse your visitors. It's also a great setup for something like a Halloween party (costumes!) or company event. All you have to do to is run one command (press Up and Enter to repeatedly do so from the command line), and you can keep the photo fun going all night.

You'll need a camera on a tripod connected via USB cable to the Raspberry Pi, as well as a monitor and peripherals. It's handy to have a fairly lengthy USB cable, depending on your setup and space, but particularly long USB cables can cause problems ranging from slowness to just plain not working.

Figure 5-9 shows the photobooth we set up in the Fedora booth at OSCON. You can see the backdrop and Tux on the left, with Ruth checking the Pi setup on the monitor in the foreground.

Figure 5-9.
Oscon photobooth (photo by Sarah White)

We've tested this with several cameras, including a Nikon D90, Nikon D5100, and a Canon EOS Rebel XSi (450D). However, any of the cameras listed as *supported by libgphoto2* (*http://gphoto.sourceforge.net/proj/libgphoto2/support.php*) should work.

Once you have the hardware set up, you need to install four packages on your Raspberry Pi. On Pidora:

```
$ su -c 'yum install python-imaging qrencode gphoto2 surl'
```

On Raspbian, the first three packages have the same names:

```
$ su -c 'apt-get install python-imaging qrencode gphoto2'
```

The last one, surl, is a URL shortener. It is packaged for Fedora (and thus Pidora), but it is not available via apt-get. If you're using Raspbian or some other Debian-based distribution, you'll need to acquire it for yourself from *https://launchpad.net/surl*. It's a normal Python module, so all you have to do is download the latest source and unpack it. Then, build it:

```
$ python setup.py build
```

To install it, run the following command from within the source directory:

```
$ su -c 'python setup.py build install -O1 --skip-build'
```

Finally, save the following Python script as photobooth.py, and you're ready to go (we've broken it up to explain the various sections and how you can adapt it to your purposes):

```python
#!/usr/bin/python
# photobooth.py - version 0.3
#
# Copyright (C) 2011 Luke Macken <lmacken@redhat.com>


# This program is free software: you can redistribute it and/or modify
# it under the terms of the GNU General Public License as published by
# the Free Software Foundation, either version 3 of the License, or
# (at your option) any later version.
#
# This program is distributed in the hope that it will be useful,
# but WITHOUT ANY WARRANTY; without even the implied warranty of
# MERCHANTABILITY or FITNESS FOR A PARTICULAR PURPOSE.  See the
# GNU General Public License for more details.
#
# You should have received a copy of the GNU General Public License
# along with this program.  If not, see <http://www.gnu.org/licenses/>.
#
# Requires: python-imaging, qrencode, gphoto2, surl


import os
import surl
import Image
import subprocess


from uuid import uuid4
from os.path import join, basename, expanduser
```

The script goes through a series of steps:

1. Uses gphoto2 to detect the camera.
2. Asks you to press Enter, and when you do, it tells the camera to take a photo, which it saves locally.
3. Applies a watermark to the lower-right corner of the photo.
4. Uploads the photo to the server you specify.
5. Generates a QR code that points to the image's URL so that your subjects can download their photos easily by scanning the QR code with their phones.

6. Generates a shortened URL for the image using the URL-shortening service you specify.

7. Creates and displays on the monitor an HTML page that shows the photo, the QR code, the shortened URL, and any other information you want it to show.

Figure 5-10 shows the output from the complete script: a web page with the photo and QR code for visitors to download it.

Figure 5-10.
Output of photobooth.py

Choose a location to store the assorted data that goes along with your photo:

```
# Where to spit out our qrcode, watermarked image, and local html
out = expanduser('~/Desktop/photodata')
```

You can add a watermark to your images, such as a project name (you can also exclude this line if you don't want the photos watermarked):

```
# The watermark to apply to all images
watermark_img = expanduser('~/Desktop/fedora.png')
```

You'll need to have a place you can upload the pictures to. You'll also need a stable Internet connection, which can be problematic if you're setting up a photobooth at an event like a conference. If that's the case, be sure to get a wired connection and not try to do this over WiFi:

```
# This assumes ssh-agent is running so we can do password-less scp
ssh_image_repo = 'fedorapeople.org:~/public_html/photobooth/'

# The public HTTP repository for uploaded images
http_image_repo = 'http://lmacken.fedorapeople.org/photobooth/'
[source, python]
```

Define the size of the QR code you want to display:

```
# Size of the qrcode pixels
qrcode_size = 10

# Whether or not to delete the photo after uploading it to the remote server
delete_after_upload = True
[source, python]
```

People will scan the QR code to visit your web page and download their photos. Then choose whether to save photos after they've been uploaded. If you're doing this at a conference, that directory can fill up quickly if you save them!

When you want to change picture quality and size or are having trouble with the photo, you'll want to consult the gphoto2 configuration options, which you can set here:

```
# The camera configuration
# Use gphoto2 --list-config and --get-config for more information
gphoto_config = {
    '/main/imgsettings/imagesize': 3, # small
    '/main/imgsettings/imagequality': 0, # normal
    '/main/capturesettings/zoom': 70, # zoom factor
}
```

Choose which service to use to create your short URLs (options include a.gd, bit.ly, burnurl.com, cli.gs, decenturl.com, digg.com, is.gd, kl.am, liip.to, metamark.net, sn.im, snipr.com, snipurl.com, snurl.com, tinyurl.com, tr.im, turl.ca, ur.ly, and zz.gd):

```
# The URL shortener to use
shortener = 'tinyurl.com'
```

The Photobooth class includes most of the hard work for this setup:

```
class PhotoBooth(object):

    def initialize(self):
        """ Detect the camera and set the various settings """
        cfg = ['--set-config=%s=%s' % (k, v) for k, v in gphoto_con
fig.items()]
        subprocess.call('gphoto2 --auto-detect ' +
                        ' '.join(cfg), shell=True)
```

```
def capture_photo(self):
    """ Capture a photo and download it from the camera """
    filename = join(out, '%s.jpg' % str(uuid4()))
    cfg = ['--set-config=%s=%s' % (k, v) for k, v in gphoto_con
fig.items()]
    subprocess.call('gphoto2 ' +
                    '--capture-image-and-download ' +
                    '--filename="%s" ' % filename,
                    shell=True)
    return filename

def process_image(self, filename):
    print "Processing %s..." % filename
    print "Applying watermark..."
    image = self.watermark(filename)
    print "Uploading to remote server..."
    url = self.upload(image)
    print "Generating QRCode..."
    qrcode = self.qrencode(url)
    print "Shortening URL..."
    tiny = self.shorten(url)
    print "Generating HTML..."
    html = self.html_output(url, qrcode, tiny)
    subprocess.call('xdg-open "%s"' % html, shell=True)
    print "Done!"
```

If you choose not to watermark, you'll want to delete this section:

```
def watermark(self, image):
    """ Apply a watermark to an image """
    mark = Image.open(watermark_img)
    im = Image.open(image)
    if im.mode != 'RGBA':
        im = im.convert('RGBA')
    layer = Image.new('RGBA', im.size, (0,0,0,0))
    position = (im.size[0] - mark.size[0], im.size[1] - mark.size[1])
    layer.paste(mark, position)
    outfile = join(out, basename(image))
    Image.composite(layer, im, layer).save(outfile)
    return outfile
```

The script continues by uploading the image, creating the QR code and the web page, and offering a shortened URL:

```python
    def upload(self, image):
        """ Upload this image to a remote server """
        subprocess.call('scp "%s" %s' % (image, ssh_image_repo), shell=True)
        if delete_after_upload:
            os.unlink(image)
        return http_image_repo + basename(image)

    def qrencode(self, url):
        """ Generate a QRCode for a given URL """
        qrcode = join(out, 'qrcode.png')
        subprocess.call('qrencode -s %d -o "%s" %s' % (
            qrcode_size, qrcode, url), shell=True)
        return qrcode

    def shorten(self, url):
        """ Generate a shortened URL """
        return surl.services.supportedServices()[shortener].get({}, url)

    def html_output(self, image, qrcode, tinyurl):
        """ Output HTML with the image, qrcode, and tinyurl """
        html = """
            <html>
              <center>
                <table>
                  <tr>
                    <td colspan="2">
                        <b><a href="%(tinyurl)s">%(tinyurl)s</a></b>
                    </td>
                  </tr>
                  <tr>
                    <td><img src="%(image)s" border="0"/></td>
                    <td><img src="%(qrcode)s" border="0"/></td>
                  </tr>
                </table>
              </center>
          </html>
        """ % {'image': image, 'qrcode': qrcode, 'tinyurl': tinyurl}
        outfile = join(out, basename(image) + '.html')
        output = file(outfile, 'w')
        output.write(html)
        output.close()
        return outfile


if __name__ == "__main__":
```

```
photobooth = PhotoBooth()
try:
    photobooth.initialize()
    while True:
        raw_input("Press enter to capture photo.")
        filename = photobooth.capture_photo()
        photobooth.process_image(filename)
except KeyboardInterrupt:
    print "\nExiting..."
```

Change the various settings to meet your needs, and your photobooth party is all set up. (Tux costume optional and not included with this book.)

HACK 54   Turn Your Pi into a Tiny Media Center

> The first thing that many people want to do with their new $35 computer is turn it into a tiny media center, so we'd be remiss in not helping you out.

This hack is going to veer off a bit from what you've read so far, as far as distro. We've been telling you how to do things in Pidora and Raspbian, two of the most common Raspberry Pi Linux distributions. Since we both work on Fedora, you can imagine we have an inclination toward Pidora. But you can also see that we've been giving you instructions throughout this book for Raspbian as well, and occasionally only one or the other. That's because sometimes one distro simply is the right one for the job, and in this case, it's *Raspbmc (http://www.raspbmc.com/)*.

If you're going to set up a media server, you want it to work as well as possible, becase it's standing between you and [insert your favorite show here]. That means you might as well use *XBMC (http://xbmc.org/)* (regardless of how you feel about the Xbox—see "XBMC" sidebar), as it's commonly used, which means it has a significant community waiting with answers to any problems you encounter. And because it's so popular, a distro has sprung up specifically intended for it. That's Raspbmc.

XBMC

XBMC was originally created for the Xbox and stood for Xbox Media Center. It's now available for Linux as well as Windows, OS X, and even Android and iOS. Their release names are all allusions to popular media. Releases so far have been Atlantis, Babylon, Camelot, Dharma, Eden, Frodo, and Gotham.

You can *download the Raspbmc image (http://www.raspbmc.com/download/)* and set up your SD card like you would with any other distribution, but the Raspbmc folks have also made an interactive installer to make it easier for you. Note that if you use the installer, you will need a network connection to the Pi at first boot for setup.

First, get the installer:

```
$ wget http://svn.stmlabs.com/svn/raspbmc/release/installers/python/
install.py
$ chmod +x install.py
$ sudo python install.py
[source, bash]
```

These three commands will then start the installer, as shown in Figure 5-11.

```
rsuehle@localhost:~                                         _ □ x

 File  Edit  View  Search  Terminal  Help
Raspbmc installer for Linux and OS X
http://raspbmc.com
----------------------------------------
Please ensure you've inserted your SD card, and press Enter to continue.

Enter the 'Disk' you would like imaged, from the following list:
Disk /dev/sda: 320.1 GB, 320072933376 bytes, 625142448 sectors
Disk /dev/mapper/vg-lv_swap: 6073 MB, 6073352192 bytes, 11862016 sectors
Disk /dev/mapper/vg-lv_root: 53.7 GB, 53687091200 bytes, 104857600 sectors
Disk /dev/mapper/vg-lv_home: 259.8 GB, 259778412544 bytes, 507379712 sectors
Disk /dev/mmcblk0: 7822 MB, 7822376960 bytes, 15278080 sectors

Enter your choice here (e.g. 'mmcblk0' or 'sdd'): mmcblk0
It is your own responsibility to ensure there is no data loss! Please backup you
r system before imaging
You should also ensure you agree with the Raspbmc License Agreeement
Are you sure you want to install Raspbmc to '/dev/mmcblk0' and accept the licens
e agreement? [y/N]
y
Downloading, please be patient...
Downloaded 6.36 of 16.22 MiB (39.15%)
```

Figure 5-11.
Raspbmc installer

Once installation is complete, you will be asked:

```
Would you like to setup your post-installation settings [ADVANCED]? [y/N]
```

If you say yes, you will be asked two questions:

```
Would you like to install Raspbmc to a USB stick or an NFS share?
Note that this still requires an SD card for booting. [y/N]


Would you like to configure networking manually? This is useful if you are
configuring WiFi or a non-DHCP network [y/N]
```

Once you have answered them, you will be told:

```
Raspbmc is now ready to finish setup on your Pi, please insert the SD card
with an active internet connection
```

Connect your Ethernet, keyboard, and mouse to the Pi. Insert the SD card and plug it in for first boot. If you don't have a network connection, you'll get an error on a blue screen:

```
Sorry, I couldn't connect to the update server. Please verify you have a
wired network ocnnection or properly configured wireeless connection and dis
able any proxy servers on your network.

After you have done this, unplug your Raspberry Pi for 60 seconds before try
ing again.
```

Assuming it does find the network connection, you'll get a message telling you that this is going to take 15–20 minutes.

Once it's finished, XBMC is ready to go. Restart the system, and you can start using your new media center. Periodically, XBMC will offer helpful tips when you do something for the first time (it's quite user-friendly). All that's left is to decide what to entertain yourself with!

XBMC supports just about any format you want to throw at it. You can watch DVDs and unencrypted Blu-ray discs. You can play CDs. For files you have on a drive, you can play, watch, or listen to more file types than you can name off the top of your head, including all the standard video formats—even the open Ogg format.

If you doubt the thoroughness of the options, acceptable audio files include NSF (NES Sound Format), SID (Commodore 64), and YM (Atari ST). The *XBMC wiki* (*http:// bit.ly/1eQ8yjh*) has a complete list of supported types for reference.

XBMC will communicate over all sorts of networking protocols, including AirPlay, UPnP, SMB/SAMBA/CIFS, NFS, NTP, and WebDAV. (And that's just a start.)

Decode MPEG-2 and VC-1

The Raspberry Pi doesn't include a license to decode MPEG-2 or VC-1. That decision was made to keep the price of the device as low as possible. Then everyone wanted to use the Pi for a media center with their existing libraries that included MPEG-2 encoded files.

If that includes you, you can purchase an inexpensive *MPEG-2 license* (*http:// www.raspberrypi.com/mpeg-2-license-key/*) from the Raspberry Pi store. Microsoft's *VC-1 license* (*http://www.raspberrypi.com/vc-1-license-key/*) is also available. Unfortunately, this isn't instant gratification, so plan ahead. The licenses are generated offline and sent to you within 72 hours of purchase.

To purchase one, you'll need your serial number, which you can find easily:

```
$ cat /proc/cpuinfo

Processor    : ARMv6-compatible processor rev 7 (v6l)
BogoMIPS     : 795.44
Features     : swp half thumb fastmult vfp edsp java tls
CPU implementer   : 0x41
CPU architecture: 7
CPU variant    : 0x0
CPU part     : 0xb76
CPU revision    : 7

Hardware      : BCM2708
Revision      : 000e
Serial        : 0000000011185abc
```

The last line, Serial, is the part you'll need in order to purchase a license. When you receive your license, it will be a text file with one line that says something like decode_MPEG2=0x8675309. Edit the config file on your Raspberry Pi:

```
$ sudo vi /boot/config.txt
```

Add the license information as a new line at the bottom, save, and exit. Reboot your Pi, and you're ready to go. Because this is in the configuration file on the distribution, if you change distributions or reinstall your card, you will need to add the license again. Because the code is linked to the serial number of the Pi, however, you will need to purchase a separate license for each physical Raspberry Pi you want to use it on.

Add a Remote Control

Once you've been using your new Pi media center and decided you like it, you might feel it's missing one familiar piece: a remote control. *Flirc (http://www.flirc.tv/)* is a small USB dongle that turns whatever remote control you have lying around the house into your new XBMC remote control. You can buy it from Flirc directly or one of their distributors, including The Pi Hut and ModMyPi.

Bonus: a portion of the profits go to the USC Cancer Research Facility (http://www.flirc.tv/fundraising/).

You can set up Flirc on your PC (Windows, Mac, or Debian/Ubuntu) with a simple .exe, .dmg, or by adding Flirc to your apt-get sources list. Instructions and downloads for each are available at *http://www.flirc.tv/downloads*.

Once you install the software and start it, you'll see the screen shown in Figure 5-12.

Figure 5-12.
Flirc setup screen

Plug in the Flirc dongle and let it run its automatic setup. Then you're ready to connect it to your remote control.

As each button on the on-screen Flirc remote flashes, press a button on your remote control to associate with that button. A few presses later, your remote control is now your XBMC remote control. You can unplug the Flirc dongle and plug it into your Raspberry Pi.

At this point, it is safe to unplug the mouse and keyboard, since you'll be using the remote control you just set up. (And unless you have a hub handy, you'll need one of those USB ports for it!) Flirc does offer some options specifically for XBMC—click Controllers, and choose XBMC from the drop-down.

If you'd like to explore other options for remote controls with XBMC, the *XBMC wiki offers several other options (http://wiki.xbmc.org/index.php?title=Remote_controls)*. This is particularly useful if you'd like to use a Media Center Edition (MCE) remote, which is meant to work with Microsoft Windows and Windows Media Center. These may not function well with Flirc.

Shortcut for Cord Cutters

One of the downsides to cutting the cord and ridding yourself of a cable or satellite service is that things don't *just come on*. You have to turn on your TV and wait for your Playstation 3 or Roku or whatever device you're using (now a Raspberry Pi!) to start as well. You can plug the Pi into a separate power outlet and leave it running all the time so that when you turn on your TV, you don't have to wait for it to boot. Or, if you'd rather not consume power and keep the Pi running when you're not watching TV, there's another option.

If your TV has a USB port, try connecting it to your Raspberry Pi for power. It might not work, but sometimes it does. And if it does, your Pi will boot when you turn on the TV, and you're one step closer to your favorite shows. We still can't make whatever you were hoping to watch magically appear when you turn on your TV, but maybe this will cut out one extra step. The downside to this approach is that most TVs cut the power to the USB port when the TV is turned off. This leads to a regular pattern of abrupt OS shutdown, which may shorten the life of your SD card in your Raspberry Pi, or at the very least, require the filesystems on it to be repaired with fsck more often.

Add Some Content

Now that you have a media center, what are you going to watch? If you're like us, you'd like to be able to get your Hulu and Netflix subscriptions in there. The easiest way to do so is with one more paid service: *PlayOn (http://www.playon.tv/)*.

PlayOn combines content from a wide source of online providers and makes it easy for you to find and consume. We've been using it for some time now and can genuinely recommend that it's worth the cost. The price varies with changing sales, but even a lifetime subscription is probably half or less of one of your monthly cable bills.

PlayOn is a really handy server for a Windows machine (that's the one downside: you need an extra machine, and only Windows will do) that streams your video content to just about any device. To get content to your TV, however, it needs a helper friend, like your new Raspberry Pi with XBMC. You can use it to play your subscription services, including Netflix, Hulu, and Amazon Instant Video. There are also plenty of free channels. If you want to be sure that the stuff you watch is available before you sign on, you can use the *PlayOn Show Finder* (*http://www.playon.tv/showfinder*).

Once you purchase your PlayOn subscription and install it on your Windows computer, you'll need to enter your registration license in the PlayOn Settings (Start → All Programs → PlayOn → PlayOn Settings) on the Registration tab, as shown in Figure 5-13.

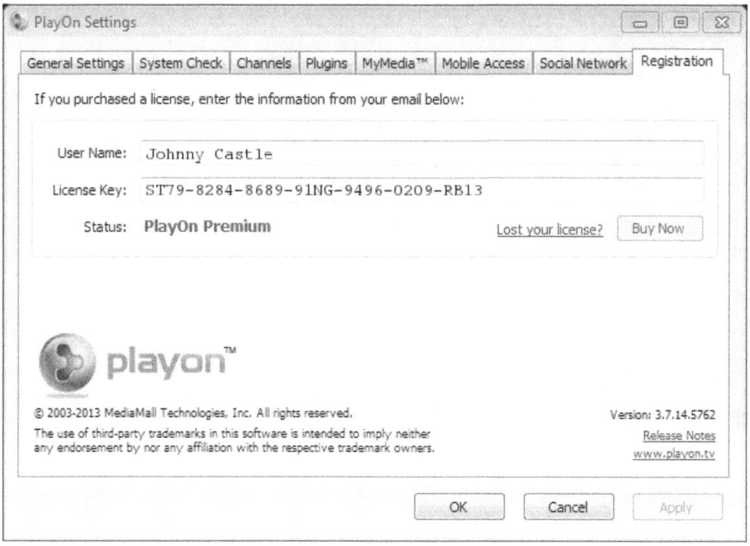

Figure 5-13.
PlayOn registration dialog

Once you've done that, go to the Videos menu on your XBMC setup to tell it about the PlayOn share.

Click the Files tab under Videos. From that screen, select Files → Add Videos. Click Browse → UPnP Devices. In that list, you should see PlayOn. Click it, and click OK, and XBMC will list it by it UPnP address (Figure 5-14).

Click OK to confirm, and you'll see the list of available services and channels (Figure 5-15).

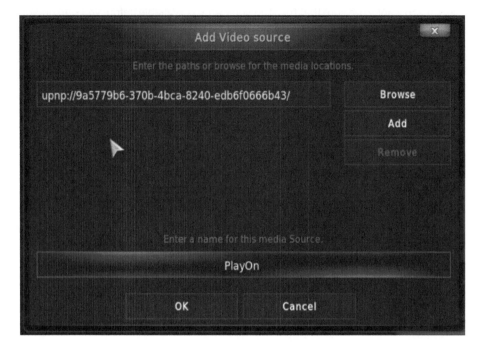

Figure 5-14.
PlayOn setup screen in XBMC

Figure 5-15.
PlayOn channel list in XBMC

Enjoy all of your favorite shows... right after you finish reading this book.

HACK 55 Watch Movies in the Backseat of Your Car

If you're a parent, you know that long trips in a car with children can be... trying. Why not build a relatively inexpensive, in-car media player?

The idea of a TV screen in the car is not at all new. In fact, you can right now drop a few thousand dollars and have one installed that plays DVDs from your dashboard. Or, you can spend significantly less and build something yourself that plays practically anything you can think of.

Our good friend, the Raspberry Pi, is small, efficient, and it plays movies very, very well, thanks to its dedicated hardware support for video codecs. Here's what you need to hack it together for those long car trips that need a little entertainment.

Your Reliant (in Terms of Power) Automobile

Really, any make or model of car should work for this, with one caveat: power. A bit of a history lesson is probably appropriate here.

Once upon a time, it was cool to smoke cigarettes, and car manufacturers felt like they were doing their customers a major service by providing an on-demand heat source that they could use to light their smokes. This device works by connecting a thin coil of nichrome wire to a high current from the car's electrical system. You'd push the handle in, the current would heat up the coil, and in a few seconds, the lighter would heat up (it would actually glow orange/red hot) and then the handle would pop out. You could then press the tip to your cigarette and enjoy the act of giving yourself lung cancer on the go.

Today, most people choose not to use those cancer sticks, but these "cigarette lighter" receptacles remain. Why? Because these ports provide 12 volts of electricity, and we have a lot of power-hungry gadgets that need juice. While some new vehicles provide dedicated USB (or even pronged power outlets), most of them still provide these standard, 12 V "cigarette lighter" plugs. In fact, a lot of cars that have them available intend for them to power *only* compatible accessories and don't actually include the actual lighter (many even include an explicit message that states "this is not a cigarette lighter").

These 12 V receptacles will power the parts for this hack. You'll need three of them to do it the way described here. You might be able to get away with using only two, but you'd have to power your Raspberry Pi from a powered USB hub that also powers devices connected to the same Raspberry Pi, and that isn't usually very reliable.

If you need more receptacles than your car has available, there are a few ways to hack around that. You can get a socket splitter, which will expand a single socket out to two. Some socket splitters even add a USB port in addition to the two sockets. With that setup, you could run everything that this hack needs off one 12 V receptacle. Other ways to get the power to your devices involve more complicated hardware setups or custom electrical wiring, so we're not going to cover them here.

Your Car Is a Special Snowflake

Keep in mind that some cars might have these receptacles wired up differently. For example, on the Dodge Caravan, some of the 12 V ports are wired to the ignition and provide power only when the car is turned on. Other ports provide power directly from the battery and will have juice even when the engine isn't running. Every make, model, year, and variant of vehicle will have its own eccentricities in this regard, so you should consult your owner's manual to understand the ground rules.

Assuming you don't have a USB power port available (either via a splitter or included in your car), you'll need to get a 12 V-to-USB converter. These are a lot more commonly available (and a lot less expensive) than they used to be, but the fact is that you get what you pay for with these converters. A good rule of thumb is that if they're free, they're junk.

Let us elaborate on that a little bit before you go off to rage-trash your free converters that you picked up as swag at your last tech conference. Most of these converters assume that you are plugging in a phone or a tablet into them. In fact, they even assume you're plugging in an Apple phone or tablet. Apple devices charge over USB at 1 amp of current, so these cheap/free converters often don't offer up more than 1 amp of current, nor do they try very hard to make that current very clean or regular.

This results in a slow charge for most other devices. Although other devices (such as your Android phone or tablet) will take 1 amp, they generally prefer 2.1 amps of current or even more, depending on the device, and as a result, can charge faster. These cheap converters also have a nasty tendency to be assembled poorly, resulting in a quick converter death if it overheats (or just has pieces fall off).

As a result, we recommend that you connect your Raspberry Pi to a high-quality converter that provides 2.1 amps of current. We've seen good results from the *Mediabridge High Output Dual USB Car Charger* (*http://www.amazon.com/Mediabridge-Output-Charger-iPhone-Design/dp/B007TV88F2*) on the 2.1AMP port, but anything with a dedicated 2.1AMP port (and a total rating of at least 3.1 amps) should do the trick.

We do not recommend that you use a 12 V converter cable designed for charging a phone (especially not a third-party provided cable), because they often have the same problems as the cheap converters do. Acceptably poor for a phone, but no good for an "always-on" Raspberry Pi. As always, your mileage may vary (YMMV), so don't rush to post an angry *but it works for me* rebuttal online. Things that shouldn't work sometimes do.

The touchscreen used in this hack (more about that in "Touchscreen" on page 280) comes with a power cable to connect directly to a 12 V receptacle, so you won't need to worry about it. However, because you need a powered USB hub to prevent the Raspberry Pi from using too much power (and simply turning off or behaving erratically), you will need to get an *inverter*.

In this context, an inverter is a device that takes the 12 V DC power coming from the "cigarette lighter" and changes it to an AC power outlet (the amount of wattage provided varies by the unit). These inverters vary in quality (and functionality), but because you need to plug only one thing into it, 200 watts should be enough.

We have successfully used a number of 300-watt inverters on the market. If you want to spend the money, you can get a pure sine-wave inverter that provides an exact replica of AC household power with two ground fault protected outlets and will likely work for *years* reliably and silently. This comes with a cost, though, as they run about $175.

Instead, you can get a modified sine-wave inverter for $20–30. These do not work as reliably, but they should work to power a USB hub. They're also a lot louder and hotter, usually with fans running all the time.

Storage for Your Movies

The next thing you're going to need is a place to put your digital video files. While you could put a few of these onto the SD card running the Raspberry Pi, that space will fill up quickly (and these files are usually quite large).

You'll also need to factor in the fact that you're installing this in a moving car. That rules out a traditional portable hard drive, because it has moving parts and is not usually very tolerant of a lot of bumps.

Instead, you're going to use a solid state drive (SSD). The technologies behind SSDs have been around since the 1950s, but since then, they've gotten much bigger (in capacity), much smaller (in size), and much cheaper (in cost). SSDs are basically big blocks of memory without any mechanical moving parts. This makes them very fast, but more importantly for this hack, they work perfectly through every bump and bounce of your car.

You can connect an SSD to the Raspberry Pi over USB. Purchase a drive that is designed to be external, or buy an internal SSD and put it in an external USB chassis. At this point, the majority of these USB chassis units are USB 3.0, due to the high speed (up to 5 Gbit/s at half duplex, twice that at full duplex). This is fine, but the Raspberry

Pi can only communicate across its USB bus at USB 2.0 speeds (up to 480 Mbit/s), and USB 2.0 is limited to half-duplex rates. Because USB 3.0 is backward-compatible to USB 2.0, this is not a problem, but you won't get USB 3.0 speeds out of the drive.

Whether you buy a premade external drive or use a separate chassis, you want to make sure it draws its power from the USB port, not from an external adapter. If it did that, you'd have something else you needed to plug into the inverter, and that really isn't necessary.

You should also remember that you cannot boot your Raspberry Pi from this SSD. You'll just be mounting it as a storage partition where you will put your movies.

Touchscreen

You could use a TV or a monitor that connects to the Pi's video outputs (either HDMI or composite), but then you'd have to interface with the Raspberry Pi through a keyboard or a mouse, and that's not ideal in a moving car (definitely not if you want your kids to use this setup from the backseat).

Instead, this hack uses a touchscreen. If you've been looking through this book, you may have noticed we have a separate hack (Hack #50) that covers how to add a touchscreen to a Raspberry Pi, but that particular type of touchscreen is not a good choice here. It is a DisplayLink device, which means it doesn't use the HDMI or composite outputs on the Raspberry Pi. Since the Raspberry Pi can decode hardware video using only those output devices, you'll need a touchscreen that is connected to them (instead of just over USB).

The part we found for this came from a company called Chinavasion, with the highly descriptive name of *7 Inch HD Touchscreen Car Monitor* (*http://www.chinavasion.com/china/wholesale/Home_Audio_Video/LCD_Monitors_TV/7_Inch_Touch_Screen_Car_Monitor*). This nifty little unit supports HDMI input at 1720x1440 (not quite 1080p, but still, not shabby), but it also has an integrated touchscreen with Linux support. It is not super cheap (about $150 at the time of this writing), but it is designed for use in a car, so it comes with a native 12 V power cable.

Powered USB Hub

You'll need a powered USB hub. Hypothetically, you could try to get away with just plugging your touchscreen and SSD into the Raspberry Pi directly, but practically, we're telling you not to try that. Your Pi is far more likely to simply turn off when you try that, and you won't be able to attach any other components, like a keyboard or mouse (for debugging the setup) or a wireless network controller (for downloading files or connecting to the Internet from a coffee shop on the road).

The brand or model doesn't matter so much here. The most important detail is this: it needs to be externally powered. You need to be able to plug it into the wall, or in this case, into the inverter plugged into the 12 V receptacle. Many inexpensive USB hubs are not externally powered and draw their power from the USB cable that it uses to connect to your computer (in this case, the Raspberry Pi). Since you're trying to work around the power limitations of the Raspberry Pi, this really will not work. If you want more of the gory details about why, see Hack #08.

You will be connecting two devices to the USB hub: your touchscreen and your portable SSD, so make sure your hub has enough juice coming from its power adapter to provide .5 A to two ports.

Software

Technically, you could use almost any Linux distribution here, but we strongly recommend using RaspBMC for this purpose. This customized version of Debian with XBMC preinstalled is ideal for the needs of this hack. XBMC is a robust and featureful suite of software that provides a GUI interface for a media center. RaspBMC has been customized specifically to support the hardware decoding and output features of the Raspberry Pi.

Connect your Raspberry Pi to your touchscreen (video to the HDMI port) and your external USB hub. Plug the touchscreen's USB cable into the USB hub, along with a normal keyboard and mouse. You'll need these input devices at first, because the touchscreen won't work yet. Then insert a new SD card into your Linux laptop and install RaspBMC onto it. We have a whole hack on how to install RaspBMC to the Pi, so flip over to Hack #54 and follow those instructions. Come back when you're done; we'll wait.

What About OpenELEC?

If you want to use something other than RaspBMC, OpenELEC will probably work, but you'll need to build a custom kernel for it that has support for touchscreens. If you follow the instructions in Hack #22, it should work.

Welcome back! You should now have a shiny (and Raspberry-tinted) RaspBMC session displaying on your touchscreen.

Enabling Touchscreen Support

If you touch the touchscreen now, you will probably notice that it does respond, but not properly. The mouse cursor will jump around, seemingly at random. It isn't really random, though; it just isn't properly calibrated yet. The good news is that it is already detected, and the proper Linux kernel drivers are loaded (RaspBMC is very clever).

To calibrate the touchscreen, you will need to SSH into the RaspBMC session to enable the touchscreen. To determine the IP address of your Raspberry Pi, navigate (with the mouse) over to to the System menu (it is the farthest item to the right), then to the System info tab. It will print out a page of system information details, including a field labeled "IP address."

From your Linux laptop, SSH into that IP address as the pi user. We'll assume the IP address is 192.168.5.128 in these examples, but you should of course replace it with your actual IP address:

```
$ ssh pi@192.168.5.128
```

The default password is raspberry. Once you successfully SSH in, RaspBMC will prompt you to set your locale and keyboard settings. For Americans, it's en_US.UTF-8 UTF-8. If you don't know your locale setting, you can enable "All locales" at the top, but it will eat up space on the SD card.

After this finishes, you can set the timezone, and finally, it will drop you to a shell prompt, where you can get down to the business of calibrating the touchscreen. First, go ahead and stop XBMC:

```
$ sudo stop xbmc
```

Download and install the touchscreen library and calibration script:

```
$ wget --no-check -O tslib_1-1_armhf.deb "https://docs.google.com/uc?
export=download&id=0B4lrG9aRe-8MUlRaRW5LcXNDaDA"
$ sudo dpkg -i tslib_1-1_armhf.deb
$ wget --no-check -O ts_calib.sh "https://docs.google.com/uc?
export=download&id=0B4lrG9aRe-8MOV94Nl90SExsVE0"
$ chmod +x ts_calib.sh
```

You'll need to configure the ts_calib.sh calibration script before it will work properly. Specifically, you need to know the device name for the touchscreen's event device. The easiest way to determine this is to run ls -l /dev/input/by-id:

```
$ ls -l /dev/input/by-id
total 0
lrwxrwxrwx 1 root root 9 Sep 12 21:19 usb-Logitech_USB_Keyboard-event-if01 -
> ../event3
lrwxrwxrwx 1 root root 9 Sep 12 21:19 usb-Logitech_USB_Keyboard-event-kbd -
> ../event2
lrwxrwxrwx 1 root root 9 Sep 12 22:23 usb-Logitech_USB_Optical_Mouse-event-
mouse -> ../event4
lrwxrwxrwx 1 root root 9 Sep 12 22:23 usb-Logitech_USB_Optical_Mouse-mouse -
> ../mouse2
lrwxrwxrwx 1 root root 9 Sep 12 21:19 usb-eGalax_Inc._Touch-event-mouse -
```

```
> ../event1
lrwxrwxrwx 1 root root 6 Sep 12 21:19 usb-eGalax_Inc._Touch-mouse -> ../js0
```

The touchscreen in this example is an "eGalax Inc." touchscreen, so the event device is event1. Edit ts_calib.sh with your favorite text editor, and change the TSLIB_TSDE VICE line to reflect the proper event device. For the setup in this example, it should look like this:

```
export TSLIB_TSDEVICE=/dev/input/event1
```

Save it to disk, and then run it (as root):

```
$ sudo sh ./ts_calib.sh
xres = 1280, yres = 720
```

The touchscreen display should flash, then display a calibration screen with a cross-hair. Carefully tap the crosshair with the included stylus (or, if you've already lost the stylus, the tip of a click pen with the ink tip not pushed out). It will move around the screen to all four corners, then to the center. When you finish, it will print the calibration values out to the terminal, and the calibration is done.

Now you need to use uinput-mapper to map the touchscreen input to an input device that xbmc finds friendlier. To be specific, it lets you map specific touch behaviors to various mouse click types. Download the software and the configuration, and install it into the /scripts directory:

```
$ wget --no-check -O uimapper.tar.gz "https://docs.google.com/uc?
export=download&id=0B4lrG9aRe-8Malg2VkM0YW1CT28"
$ wget --no-check -O uimapper.conf "https://docs.google.com/uc?
export=download&id=0B4lrG9aRe-8MM2RIWFh1WjJWUW8"
$ sudo mkdir -p /scripts
$ sudo tar -xf uimapper.tar.gz -C /scripts
```

Edit uimapper.conf with your favorite text editor, and correct the UIMAPPER_DEV line to reflect the event device you found earlier:

```
env UIMAPPER_DEV="/dev/input/event1"
```

Save out the file, and move it (as root) into position inside /etc/init. This will allow uinput-mapper to start when the RaspBMC instance boots:

```
$ sudo mv uimapper.conf /etc/init
```

You need to tweak the internal uinput_mapper configuration a bit before it will work properly. Open /scripts/uinput_mapper/configs/touchscreen.py in a text editor (as root) and change this line:

```
sres = subprocess.check_output("tvservice -s", shell=True)
```

to look like this:

```
sres = subprocess.check_output("/opt/vc/bin/tvservice -s", shell=True)
```

Without that change, the `uinput_mapper` upstart service will fail to find the `tvservice` binary and silently fail.

Your touchscreen should be ready. Reboot your Raspberry Pi to test it:

```
$ sudo shutdown -r now
```

When it comes back up, try touching the screen. The cursor should move to where you touched. If you want to "touch" a click, touch and hold for a half-second and then release. It will take some getting used to. This setup should work simultaneously with any other attached input devices (such as a keyboard and mouse), so if you want to have an "override" console, you can add that easily.

If you need to debug the `uinput_mapper` service, first stop the `xbmc` service:

```
$ sudo stop xbmc
```

If you do not do this, XBMC will hold the `uinput_mapper` device, and you won't be able to access it with anything else for debugging. You can install the `evtest` utility from the Raspbian repository and use it to debug the events that the touchscreen is registering:

```
$ sudo apt-get install evtest
$ evtest
No device specified, trying to scan all of /dev/input/event*
Not running as root, no devices may be available.
Available devices:
/dev/input/event0:    eGalax Inc. Touch
/dev/input/event1:    eGalax Inc. Touch
/dev/input/event2:      Logitech USB Keyboard
/dev/input/event3:      Logitech USB Keyboard
/dev/input/event4:      Logitech USB Optical Mouse
/dev/input/event5:      uimapper - touchscreen
Select the device event number [0-5]: 5
Input driver version is 1.0.1
Input device ID: bus 0x3 vendor 0x42 product 0xbebe version 0x1
Input device name: "uimapper - touchscreen"
Supported events:
  Event type 0 (EV_SYN)
  Event type 1 (EV_KEY)
    Event code 106 (KEY_RIGHT)
    Event code 273 (BTN_RIGHT)
    Event code 320 (BTN_TOOL_PEN)
    Event code 330 (BTN_TOUCH)
  Event type 3 (EV_ABS)
    Event code 0 (ABS_X)
      Value     0
```

```
            Min        0
            Max      2047
        Event code 1 (ABS_Y)
            Value      0
            Min        0
            Max      2047
      Event type 4 (EV_MSC)
        Event code 4 (MSC_SCAN)
    Properties:
    Testing ... (interrupt to exit)
```

When `evtest` prompts you to select the device, choose the `uimapper` device and then touch away (and hold touch and double-touch). You will see the different signals that `uinput_mapper` is generating as a result of your touches. If you do not see a `uimapper` device at this screen, it means that the `uinput_mapper` service is either stopped or not running properly.

Adding Videos

If you have not already done so, put your videos on your SSD. The SSD can be formatted for any filesystem that RaspBMC understands (NTFS, FAT, ext2/3/4, etc.), and your video files can be in any directory or folder hierarchy that you want. Just be aware that XBMC will force you to navigate through those folders to play your videos, so we recommend keeping it as shallow as possible. You can also add music or pictures in this same way.

Supported Encodings

By default, the Raspberry Pi hardware supports hardware decoding of only H264/MPEG-4 video encoding. RaspBMC will try to play files that are encoded with other video codecs, but it might have to fall back to software decoding to do so, and the performance of that will be poor. For more details on how to add additional hardware video codecs, see Hack #47.

When you plug the SSD into the USB hub, if RaspBMC is running, it will automatically detect the additional drive, and you will be able to select that source for your videos (or music/pictures). You should test it out now to make sure you can successfully playback videos. The touchscreen has small speakers that will play the HDMI audio being output by the Raspberry Pi.

Putting It All Together

Now that everything works properly, you just need to put it in your car. Plugging in the power should be straightforward: you plug the touchscreen into one 12 V receptacle, your power inverter (to household AC power plug) into another, and then plug the Raspberry Pi into a third one (or a USB port if it is available). The SSD and the touchscreen USB connectors should be plugged into the USB hub, and the USB hub should have its interconnect hooked to the Raspberry Pi. The touchscreen HDMI connector should be connected directly to the Raspberry Pi.

The touchscreen includes mounting plates, so you can mount it directly to the car seat, but if you are crafty, you can make a container that will hang over the back of the headrest of a front seat that encapsulates all of this loose hardware.

It is also possible for you to hide it all away in your car by hacking it into the empty spaces (or carving out empty spaces). There is no one right way to do this, and it's dependent on your vehicle's design, so we leave it up to you to figure out what works best for your car.

6

Extend Your Pi

The real magic of the Raspberry Pi happens when you make it a part of something else. Use the GPIO to connect it to new devices (Hack #56). Connect Arduino shields (Hack #58). Add a tiny screen (Hack #57), numeric keypad (Hack #60), or heat sink (Hack #61). Do all of them, and make something amazing. This chapter is to help get you started taking the Pi beyond mere Linux computer into something more.

HACK 56   Control GPIO from a Web Browser

> Your Raspberry Pi GPIO interface is a gateway to an entire Internet of Things. Here is a simple way to access it from a web browser.

Every day, more and more devices become network-aware, either intentionally or as a result of clever hacks. This phenomenon has many names, but the most common seems to be "Internet of Things." You can use your Raspberry Pi to help your dumb devices get smart and join the Internet of Things.

The best way to connect your Pi to other devices is via the GPIO expansion ports. If you're not sure what that means, go take a quick read through Hack #14. These digital pins will let you wire almost anything into your Raspberry Pi, but once the physical connection is made, you'll want a framework in place to actually *do* something.

Eric PTAK created a REST framework and web app to control the Raspberry Pi and its GPIO through the Web. Called *WebIOPi* (*http://code.google.com/p/webiopi/*), this framework allows you to use and control your Pi's GPIO over the Internet (or through a number of language bindings and APIs).

To install it, start with a current image of Raspbian. Then, from the running instance of Raspbian, download and install the WebIOPi code:

```
$ wget http://webiopi.googlecode.com/files/WebIOPi-0.6.0.tar.gz
$ tar xvzf WebIOPi-0.6.0.tar.gz
$ cd WebIOPi-0.6.0
$ sudo ./setup.sh
```

You might want to check the WebIOPi website to make sure that 0.6.0 is still the latest version before proceeding. If it has been updated, adjust appropriately.

The setup script (`setup.sh`) will download and install the necessary WebIOPi dependencies from the `apt-get` repositories in Raspbian, then build the code and install it into the proper locations.

When this finishes, you'll have a WebIOPi service that you can run and access via a web browser. To turn it on, run:

```
$ sudo /etc/init.d/webiopi start
```

You can then connect to it from within the Raspbian session by opening a web browser and navigating to *http://localhost:8000/*. If you want to connect to it from a remote system, you can replace `localhost` with either the IP address or fully qualified hostname of the Raspberry Pi. For login credentials, the user is `webiopi` and the password is `raspberry`.

Once connected, you will be able to view a graphical representation of the Raspberry Pi GPIO header (click on the "GPIO header" link), as shown in Figure 6-1. From this page, you can swap the direction on the Input/Output pins (not on the power or Ground pins, for what are hopefully obvious reasons).

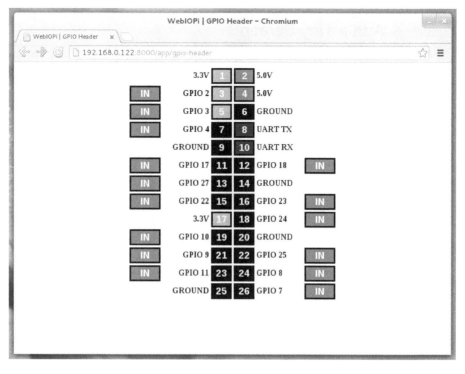

Figure 6-1.
WebIOPi browser showing GPIO view

WebIOPi is capable of doing a lot more than this though. It provides a Python library that contains support for all kinds of GPIO interactions, including explicit support for digital-to-analog converters (DAC), analog-to-digital converters (ADC), common sensors, I2C, serial, and SPI devices.

Additionally, the web application itself allows you to monitor and debug these same devices and connections. It also includes Java and Javascript libraries that will enable you to make custom web (and Android) clients to interface with and remotely control devices that are connected through the Raspberry Pi GPIO.

Finally, because WebIOPi talks REST, you can interface to it through any other language that you choose, but the native libraries are a bit more friendly.

Add a Tiny Screen

Sometimes it's just not convenient to carry around a full-sized monitor. Maybe you want to build a tiny, portable computer. There are screens for you!

When we decided to start working on portable Raspberry Pi projects, we chose *Adafruit's 2.5" NTSC/PAL display* (*http://www.adafruit.com/products/912*), partly for the quality and partly because it was one of the few options at the time. It has RCA connections, 32 levels of backlight brightness you can adjust with buttons, and a switch that changes it from portrait to landscape display.

The one downside for connecting this piece to your Raspberry Pi is that it has a female RCA jack, just like your Pi. There are male-male RCA connector pieces, which is what we've used here to connect them, but that adds about an inch and a half of inflexible metal bulk to your project.

OK, we lied. There's a second downside. The ribbon that connects the display to the board in this little TFT setup is pretty fragile. Be extremely careful with it when you're getting your project together, and take this into account when you decide how to build it a housing, especially if it's a portable project.

Perhaps you've noticed that we like to tell you to do things that are generally considered a bad idea. (To some degree, that's the nature of a *hack*, isn't it?) Here's another one. Officially, you can't power this TFT through the GPIO. It doesn't even make a lot of sense to try if you read the description for the board, which states:

- Power with 6-15VDC only into onboard buck converter
- 80 mA power draw at 12 V, 150 mA at 6 V

Conveniently, we're not the kind of people who read instructions (or requirements, or even good advice sometimes). And thus we didn't notice that at all before connecting it to the GPIO in a prototype miniature game center. (If you'd like to do so, combine this hack with Hack #51.)

And it worked. We wired the red to pin 2 (5 v) and the black one to pin 4 (ground), as shown in Figure 6-2.

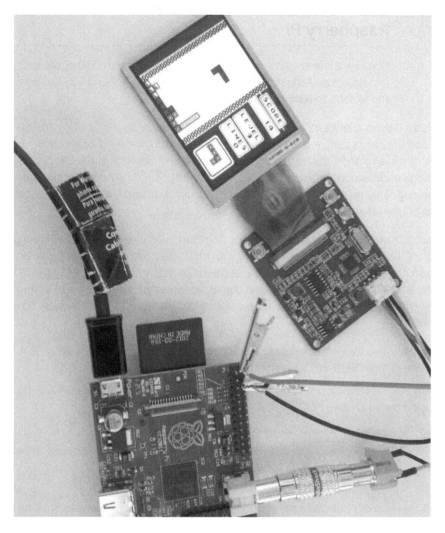

Figure 6-2.
Prototype handheld gaming system

The correct thing to tell you is that it's probably not very stable or a good way to run long-term. The truth is that we played Tetris this way for longer than we'd like to admit, given the number of full-sized modern gaming devices at our disposal. If you don't want to build in a second power supply, this appears to work out just fine, at least for an afternoon of Tetris.

A better way, however, is to purchase a *female DC power adapter* (*https:// www.adafruit.com/products/368*). Unscrew the side marked +, insert the red wire, and screw it back down. Insert the black wire on the other side, and you're set to connect the screen to any power supply with a 2.1 mm DC connection.

Connect Arduino Shields to Your Raspberry Pi

Because there are already many available shields for extending the functionality of an Arduino, Raspberry Pi hackers have found ways to bring those parts to Raspberry Pi.

The idea behind the *Raspberry Pi to Arduino shields connection bridge* (*http://www.cooking-hacks.com/index.php/Raspberry-pi-to-arduino-shield-connection-bridge.html*) is to allow the Raspberry Pi to make use of any of the shields, boards, and modules designed for Arduino. It also includes the possibility of connecting digital and analog sensors, using the same pinout of Arduino but with the power and capabilities of the Raspberry Pi.

In order to make the compatibility complete, Cooking Hacks created the arduPi library, which allows you to use the Raspberry Pi with the same code used with an Arduino. To do so, they implemented conversion functions so that you can control all the I/O interfaces (I2C, SPI, UART, analog, and digital) in the same way you would control them with the Arduino. Options with this shield and the arduPi library include connecting:

- Any Arduino wireless module to the Raspberry Pi, such as the XBee 802.15.4/ XBee ZigBee, RFID, NFC, Bluetooth, Bluetooth Pro, WiFi, GPRS, or 3G
- Any sensor (analog 0-5 V, digital) to the Raspberry Pi with a precession of 16b using the integrated ADC.
- Complex sensors through I2C and UART buses
- Arduino-specific shields, like the radiation sensor shield, CanBus, and relay shield
- Any electronic module or actuator that works over I2C, SPI, UART

The bridge board connects to the Raspberry Pi's GPIO pins from below. As shown in Figure 6-3, the top includes the following items:

- 8 digital pins
- Socket for wireless modules
- RX/TX pins
- I2C pins (SDA, SCL)
- SPI pins (SCK, MISO, MOSI, CS), which can be used also as GPIO
- 8-channel analog-to-digital converter
- Switch to enable external power supply

Figure 6-3.
Cooking Hacks' Raspberry Pi to Arduino shields connection bridge

Cooking Hacks includes the *schematic as a PDF download* (*http://www.cooking-hacks.com/skin/frontend/default/cooking/images/catalog/documentation/rasp-berry_arduino_shield/arduino2raspberryPi_sch.pdf*) on its website.

Using the arduPi Library

arduPi is a C++ library that lets you write programs for Raspberry Pi as if you were writing an Arduino program. All the functions that control serial port communications, I2C, SPI, and GPIO pins are available using the Arduino syntax. The available library functions are listed in Table 6-1.

To get started, first *download the arduPi library* (*http://www.cooking-hacks.com/skin/frontend/default/cooking/images/catalog/documentation/raspberry_ardui-no_shield/arduPi_1-5.tar.gz*). In the library folder you will find three files: `arduPi.cpp`, `arduPi.h`, and `arduPi_template.cpp`. The `arduPi_template.cpp` file is meant to be used as a starting point to create programs with the same behavior as an Arduino program.

Table 6-1. ArduiPi library functions

SERIAL LIBRARY FUNCTIONS	WIRE LIBRARY FUNCTIONS	SPI LIBRARY FUNCTIONS
available()	begin()	begin()
begin()	requestFrom()	end()
end()	beginTransmission()	setBitOrder()
flush()	endTransmission()	setClockDivider()
peek()	write()	setDataMode()

SERIAL LIBRARY FUNCTIONS	WIRE LIBRARY FUNCTIONS	SPI LIBRARY FUNCTIONS
print()	read()	transfer()
println()		
read()		
readBytes()		
readBytesUntil()		
find()		
findUntil()		
parseInt()		
parseFloat()		
setTimeout()		
write()		

The arduPi template looks like this:

```
//Include arduPi library
#include "arduPi.h"

/************************************************************
 *   IF YOUR ARDUINO CODE HAS OTHER FUNCTIONS APART FROM    *
 *   setup() AND loop() YOU MUST DECLARE THEM HERE          *
 *  ********************************************************/

/*************************
 * YOUR ARDUINO CODE HERE *
 *  *********************/

int main (){
    setup();
    while(1){
        loop();
        }
        return (0);
    }
```

As you can see in the main() function, the setup() function is called once, and then the loop() function is called continuously until the program is forced to finish.

Whether you're writing a new program or already have an Arduino program written that uses the ported functions, you can use the template (ardupi_template.cpp) and put your Arduino code where it says YOUR ARDUINO CODE HERE. Remember that the program you are writing is a C++ program, so you can use all the C++ libraries. Here are the available Arduino functions:

- delay()
- delayMicroseconds()
- millis()
- pinMode()
- digitalWrite()
- digitalRead()
- analogRead() (on pins from A0 to A7—for example, analogRead(5) will read from A5)
- shiftIn()
- shiftOut()
- attachInterrupt()
- detachInterrupt()

You can detect RISING and FALLING interrupts. Any digital pin (from 2 to 13) can be used in attachInterrupt(). For example, if you want to be aware of RISING events on pin 6, you can use attachInterrupt(6,function_to_call,RISING).

Enable the UART port

On the Raspberry Pi, make a backup of /boot/cmdline.txt and open it for editing:

```
$ sudo cp /boot/cmdline.txt /boot/cmdline_backup.txt
$ sudo vi /boot/cmdline.txt
```

Here's what this file contains:

```
dwc_otg.lpm_enable=0 console=ttyAMA0,115200 kgdboc=ttyAMA0,115200 con
sole=tty1 $
```

Remove the parameters that reference the UART serial port (ttyAMA0) so that it says only this:

```
dwc_otg.lpm_enable=0 console=tty1 $
```

Open /etc/inittab and comment out the following line:

```
T0:23:respawn:/sbin/getty -L ttyAMA0 115200 vt100
```

Then reboot the Raspberry Pi.

Compile the arduPi library and a program using it

As arduPi is a C++ library, we will use g++ to compile it. You can compile the arduPi library to obtain an object file (`.o`) and use this file to link your program: `g++ -c arduPi.cpp -o arduPi.o`.

Once you have already compiled the arduPi library, you can run:

```
$ g++ -lrt -lpthread my_program.cpp arduPi.o -o my_program
```

If the arduPi library is not yet compiled, you can compile both it and your program and link them in a single step:

```
$ g++ -lrt -lpthread my_program.cpp arduPi.cpp -o my_program
```

The `-lrt` flag is necesary because the library uses the function `clock_gettime` (`time.h`). The `-lpthread` option is needed because `attachInterrupt()` and `detachInterrupt()` functions use threads.

Run your program

Now, to run your program, you must have the right permissions in order to use GPIO so that `/dev/mem` can be accessed on the Raspberry Pi. Then you simply run the following command:

```
sudo ./my_program
```

GPIO input

GPIO peripherals vary quite widely. In some cases, they are simple: a group of pins that can be switched as a group to either input or output. The input and output voltages are typically, though not universally, limited to the supply voltage of the device with the GPIOs on and may be damaged by greater voltages.

Some GPIOs have 5 V tolerant inputs, and even on low-supply voltages the device can accept 5 V without damage. For the Raspberry Pi, you must adapt the voltage level of a 5 V sensor to prevent possible damage. If you don't have an assortment of parts readily available, you can reproduce these instructions with the contents of Cooking Hacks' *Starter Kit for Raspberry Pi, A/V Edition* (*http://www.cooking-hacks.com/index.php/starter-kit-for-raspberry-pi-a-v-edition.html*).

GPIO voltage levels are 3.3 V and are not 5 V tolerant. There is no over-voltage protection on the board. Digital inputs use a 3.3 V logic level and are not tolerant of 5 V levels, such as you might find on a 5 V powered Arduino. Use extreme caution when working with GPIO. You might damage your Raspberry Pi or your other equipment and potentially shock yourself.

When a GPIO pin is set as an input, such as with a basic push-button example, you can have these voltage incompatibility problems. The circuit in Figure 6-4 is wrong, because when you press the button, the GPIO input is connected to 5 volts, which might damage the device.

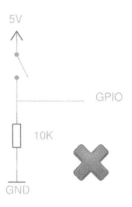

Figure 6-4.
Incorrect circuit

You can avoid damage by using a resistor in the push-button cable. The value of the resistor is determined by the leakage current of the GPIO pin (the current used by the circuit to read the pin) and the amount of voltage drop it creates as a result. With the 5K resistor, you obtain 3.3 V in the GPIO input because Vgpio = 5 V·(10K/(10K+5K)) = 3.3 V. Figure 6-5 shows a correct circuit.

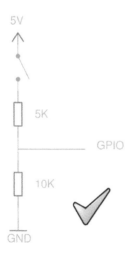

Figure 6-5.
Correct circuit

You will have the same problem if you use a sensor operating at 5 volts. Figure 6-6 shows an example using a PIR sensor, using the same resistive divider that we used to adapt voltage level.

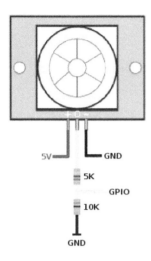

Figure 6-6.
Adapting voltage with resistors

Analog-to-Digital Conversion

The shield includes an Analog-to-Digital Converter (ADC) of 12 bits of resolution, which allows you to connect any sensor to the Raspberry Pi with higher precision than an Arduino does. The communication between the Raspberry Pi and the ADC of the shield is made via I2C.

The information of each channel can be obtained reading two bytes from I2C, but first, one byte (corresponding to the channel address) should be sent through I2C, depending on the channel you want to select. Table 6-2 shows a list of the channel addresss.

Table 6-2. Channel addresses

CHANNEL	ADDRESS
0	0xDC
1	0x9C
2	0xCC
3	0x8C
4	0xAC
5	0xEC
6	0xBC
7	0xFC

The following example program reads every channel continuously, waiting five seconds between iterations. With a wire connecting the 5 V pin with some of the pins of the ADC, it should read a value close to 5.000000:

```
//Include arduPi library
#include "arduPi.h"

unsigned char val_0 = 0;
unsigned char val_1 = 0;
byte address = 0x08;

int channel_0 = 0;
int channel_1 = 0;
int channel_2 = 0;
int channel_3 = 0;
int channel_4 = 0;
int channel_5 = 0;
int channel_6 = 0;
int channel_7 = 0;

float analog_0 = 0.0;
float analog_1 = 0.0;
float analog_2 = 0.0;
float analog_3 = 0.0;
float analog_4 = 0.0;
float analog_5 = 0.0;
float analog_6 = 0.0;
float analog_7 = 0.0;

void setup()
{
```

```
  Wire.begin(); // join I2C bus (address optional for master)
}

void loop()
{
  // channel 0
  Wire.beginTransmission(8);
  Wire.write(byte(0xDC));

  char val[2];
  val_0 = Wire.read();   // receive high byte (overwrites previous reading)
  val_1 = Wire.read();
  channel_0 = int(val_0)*16 + int(val_1>>4);
  analog_0 = channel_0 * 5.0 / 4095.0;


  printf("Channel 0: digital value = %d", channel_0);
  printf(" analog value = %f\n", analog_0);

  // channel 1
  Wire.beginTransmission(8);
  Wire.write(byte(0x9C));


  val_0 = Wire.read();   // receive high byte (overwrites previous reading)
  val_1 = Wire.read();
  channel_1 = int(val_0)*16 + int(val_1>>4);
  analog_1 = channel_1 * 5.0 / 4095.0;


  printf("Channel 1: digital value = %d", channel_1);
  printf(" analog value = %f\n", analog_1);

  // channel 2
  Wire.beginTransmission(8);
  Wire.write(byte(0xCC));


  val_0 = Wire.read();   // receive high byte (overwrites previous reading)
  val_1 = Wire.read();
  channel_2 = int(val_0)*16 + int(val_1>>4);
  analog_2 = channel_2 * 5.0 / 4095.0;

  printf("Channel 2: digital value = %d", channel_2);
```

```
printf(" analog value = %f\n", analog_2);

// channel 3
Wire.beginTransmission(8);
Wire.write(byte(0x8C));

val_0 = Wire.read();  // receive high byte (overwrites previous reading)
val_1 = Wire.read();
channel_3 = int(val_0)*16 + int(val_1>>4);
analog_3 = channel_3 * 5.0 / 4095.0;

printf("Channel 3: digital value = %d", channel_3);
printf(" analog value = %f\n", analog_3);

// channel 4
Wire.beginTransmission(8);
Wire.write(byte(0xAC));

val_0 = Wire.read();  // receive high byte (overwrites previous reading)
val_1 = Wire.read();
channel_4 = int(val_0)*16 + int(val_1>>4);
analog_4 = channel_4 * 5.0 / 4095.0;

printf("Channel 4: digital value = %d", channel_4);
printf(" analog value = %f\n", analog_4);

// channel 5
Wire.beginTransmission(8);
Wire.write(byte(0xEC));

val_0 = Wire.read();  // receive high byte (overwrites previous reading)
val_1 = Wire.read();
channel_5 = int(val_0)*16 + int(val_1>>4);
analog_5 = channel_5 * 5.0 / 4095.0;

printf("Channel 5: digital value = %d", channel_5);
printf(" analog value = %f\n", analog_5);

// channel 6
Wire.beginTransmission(8);
Wire.write(byte(0xBC));

val_0 = Wire.read();  // receive high byte (overwrites previous reading)
val_1 = Wire.read();
```

```
channel_6 = int(val_0)*16 + int(val_1>>4);
analog_6 = channel_6 * 5.0 / 4095.0;

printf("Channel 6: digital value = %d", channel_6);
printf(" analog value = %f\n", analog_6);

// channel 7
Wire.beginTransmission(8);
Wire.write(byte(0xFC));

val_0 = Wire.read();   // receive high byte (overwrites previous reading)
val_1 = Wire.read();
channel_7 = int(val_0)*16 + int(val_1>>4);
analog_7 = channel_7 * 5.0 / 4095.0;

printf("Channel 7: digital value = %d", channel_7);
printf(" analog value = %f\n", analog_7);

printf("\n");



delay(1000);

}


int main (){
        setup();
        while(1){
                loop();
        }
        return (0);
}
```

Figure 6-7 shows the output of this program when connecting the 5 V pin of the Raspberry Pi to the analog input O.

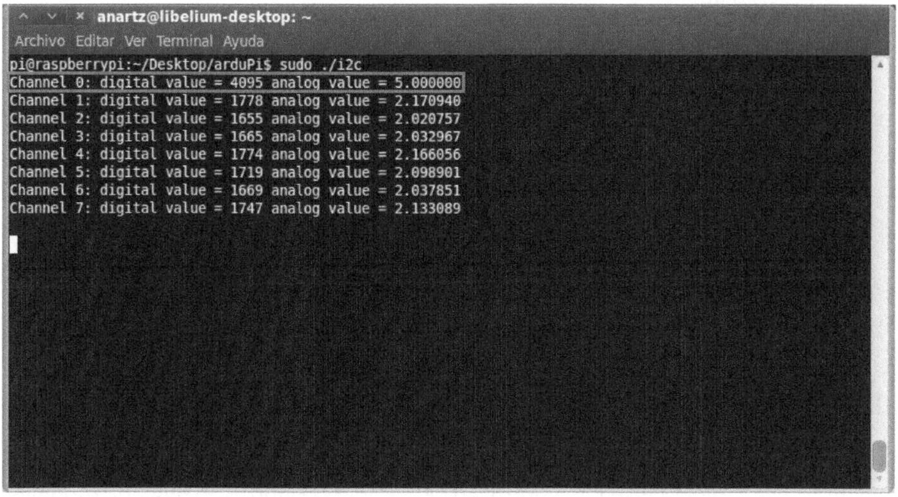

Figure 6-7.
Output of ADC program

UART

Accessing UART with the arduPi library is as simple as doing it with Arduino. You need to include `arduPi.h` in your code and create an instance of the `SerialPi` class, naming it `Serial`. Naming the instance as `Serial` allows you to use the Arduino syntax.

These steps are already done for you if you use the template to create your programs.

These are the available functions:

- `Serial.available()`
- `Serial.begin()`
- `Serial.end()`
- `Serial.flush()`
- `Serial.peek()`
- `Serial.print()`
- `Serial.println()`
- `Serial.read()`
- `Serial.readBytes()`
- `Serial.readBytesUntil()`

- `Serial.find()`
- `Serial.findUntil()`
- `Serial.parseInt()`
- `Serial.parseFloat()`
- `Serial.setTimeout()`
- `Serial.write()`

All of these functions have the same functionality as their Arduino counterparts, which you can read more about at *http://arduino.cc/en/Reference/serial*.

I2C

"Analog-to-Digital Conversion" on page 298 briefly discussed I2C. This example in this section uses a BlinkM RGB I2C-controlled LED. BlinkM (Figure 6-8) has a high-quality, high-power RGB LED and a small AVR microcontroller in one piece, allowing a user to digitally control an RGB LED over a simple I2C interface. In this example, you'll change the LED color both directly and using fade transitions.

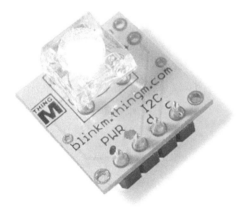

Figure 6-8.
blinkM module

More information about this part and the commands you can send to it can be found in the BlinkM datasheet (http://thingm.com/fileadmin/thingm/down-loads/BlinkM_datasheet.pdf).

To set up Blink FM, make the following connections:

1. Connect the (-) pin of the LED with the GND pin of the shield.
2. Connect the (+) pin of the LED with the 5V pin of the shield.
3. Connect the d pin of the LED with the SDA pin of the shield.
4. Connect the c pin of the LED with the SCL pin of the shield.

Then create and execute a file with the following code, which will alternate the LED's color from red to blue five times and then make some smooth transitions resulting in purples:

```
 *
 * Copyright (C) 2012 Libelium Comunicaciones Distribuidas S.L.
 * http://www.libelium.com
 *
 * This program is free software: you can redistribute it and/or modify
 * it under the terms of the GNU General Public License as published by
 * the Free Software Foundation, either version 3 of the License, or
 * (at your option) any later version.
 *
 * This program is distributed in the hope that it will be useful,
 * but WITHOUT ANY WARRANTY; without even the implied warranty of
 * MERCHANTABILITY or FITNESS FOR A PARTICULAR PURPOSE.  See the
 * GNU General Public License for more details.
 *
 * You should have received a copy of the GNU General Public License
 * along with this program.  If not, see .
 *
 * Version 0.1
 * Author: Anartz Nuin Jiménez
 */


//Include arduPi library
#include "arduPi.h"


void setup(){
        Wire.begin();
        Wire.beginTransmission(9);
        Wire.write('o'); //End the current light script
        Wire.endTransmission();
}

void loop(){
```

```
        for (int i=0;i < 5;i++){
                Wire.beginTransmission(9);
                Wire.write('n'); //Change to color
                Wire.write(byte(0xff)); //Red component
                Wire.write(byte(0x00)); //Green component
                Wire.write(byte(0x00)); //Blue component
                Wire.endTransmission();

                delay(500);

                Wire.beginTransmission(9);
                Wire.write('n'); //Change to color
                Wire.write(byte(0x00)); //Red component
                Wire.write(byte(0x00)); //Green component
                Wire.write(byte(0xff)); //Blue component
                Wire.endTransmission();

                delay(500);
        }

        for (int i=0;i < 10;i++){
                Wire.beginTransmission(9);
                Wire.write('c'); //Fade to color
                Wire.write(byte(0xff)); //Red component
                Wire.write(byte(0x00)); //Green component
                Wire.write(byte(0x5a)); //Blue component
                Wire.endTransmission();

                delay(150);

                Wire.beginTransmission(9);
                Wire.write('c'); //Fade to color
                Wire.write(byte(0x55)); //Red component
                Wire.write(byte(0x20)); //Green component
                Wire.write(byte(0x5a)); //Blue component
                Wire.endTransmission();

                delay(150);
        }
}

int main (){
        setup();
        while(1){
```

```
                loop();
        }
        return (0);
    }
```

SPI

It is possible to communicate with SPI devices using the functions provided by arduPi. The following example uses the SPI functions to print messages on a ST7920 LCD12864 (SPI LCD).

First put the switch of the LCD in SPI mode. Then proceed with the connection between the LCD and the Raspberry Pi to Arduino shield. Use jumper wires to connect the following, as shown in Figure 6-9:

- VCC of the LCD to 5 V of the shield
- GND of the LCD to GND of the shield
- SCK of the LCD to SCK of the shield
- SID of the LCD to MOSI of the shield
- CS of the LCD to 8 pin of the shield

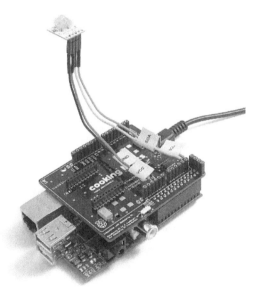

Figure 6-9.
LCD shield

For this project, we are using GPIO pin 8 on the Raspberry Pi shield as chip select. So, when you need to select the LCD as the target device for the SPI communication, you need to set pin 8 to HIGH.

Create and execute a file with the following code to show the messages "Cooking Hacks" and "SPI LCD for Raspberry Pi" with a delay of two seconds in between:

```
/*
 * Copyright (C) 2012 Libelium Comunicaciones Distribuidas S.L.
 * http://www.libelium.com
 *
 * This program is free software: you can redistribute it and/or modify
 * it under the terms of the GNU General Public License as published by
 * the Free Software Foundation, either version 3 of the License, or
 * (at your option) any later version.
 *
 * This program is distributed in the hope that it will be useful,
 * but WITHOUT ANY WARRANTY; without even the implied warranty of
 * MERCHANTABILITY or FITNESS FOR A PARTICULAR PURPOSE.  See the
 * GNU General Public License for more details.
 *
 * You should have received a copy of the GNU General Public License
 * along with this program.  If not, see .
 *
 * Version 0.1
 * Author: Anartz Nuin Jiménez
 */

//Include arduPi library
#include "arduPi.h"

int latchPin = 8;
unsigned char char1[]=" Cooking Hacks   ";
unsigned char char2[]="  SPI LCD for    ";
unsigned char char3[]="  Raspberry Pi   ";

void initialise();
void displayString(int X,int Y,unsigned char *ptr,int dat);
void writeCommand(int CMD);
void writeData(int CMD);
void writeByte(int dat);
void clear();

void setup(){
        SPI.begin();
```

```
        SPI.setBitOrder(MSBFIRST);
        SPI.setDataMode(SPI_MODE0);
        SPI.setClockDivider(SPI_CLOCK_DIV128);

        initialise();
}

void loop(){
        displayString(0,0,char1,16);
        delay(2000);
        clear();
        displayString(1,0,char2,16);
        displayString(2,0,char3,16);
        delay(2000);
        clear();
}

void initialise(){
        pinMode(latchPin, OUTPUT);
        digitalWrite(latchPin, LOW);

        delayMicroseconds(80);

        writeCommand(0x30);
        writeCommand(0x0c);
        writeCommand(0x01);
        writeCommand(0x06);
}


void displayString(int X,int Y,unsigned char *ptr,int dat){
        int i;

        switch(X){
                case 0:  Y|=0x80;break;

                case 1:  Y|=0x90;break;

                case 2:  Y|=0x88;break;

                case 3:  Y|=0x98;break;

                default: break;
        }
```

```
        writeCommand(Y);

        for(i=0;i < dat;i++){
                writeData(ptr[i]);
        }

}

void writeCommand(int CMD){
        int H_data,L_data;
        H_data = CMD;
        H_data &= 0xf0;
        L_data = CMD;
        L_data &= 0x0f;
        L_data <<= 4;
        writeByte(0xf8);
        writeByte(H_data);
        writeByte(L_data);
}

void writeData(int CMD){
        int H_data,L_data;
        H_data = CMD;
        H_data &= 0xf0;
        L_data = CMD;
        L_data &= 0x0f;
        L_data <<= 4;
        writeByte(0xfa);
        writeByte(H_data);
        writeByte(L_data);
}

void writeByte(int dat){
        digitalWrite(latchPin, HIGH);
        delayMicroseconds(80);
        SPI.transfer(dat);
        digitalWrite(latchPin, LOW);
}

void clear(){
        writeCommand(0x30);
        writeCommand(0x01);
}
```

```
int main (){
        setup();
        while(1){
                loop();
        }
        return (0);
}
```

You can find further *support and forums and purchase shields and sensors (http://cooking-hacks.com)* that work with these instructions.

If you're interested in further pursuing Raspberry Pi projects that integrate Arduino parts, you might also be interested in the *Alamode (http://www.seeedstudio.com/depot/alamode-arduino-compatible-raspberry-pi-plate-p-1285.html)* (shown in Figure 6-10), a development board that, like the Cooking Hacks board, makes your Raspberry Pi compatible with Arduino shields. The Alamode is voltage-safe, it has a built-in, bi-directional translator that makes the 3.3 V to 5 V conversion for you, and it also has a Micro-SD slot for storage and an RTC chip.

Figure 6-10.
Alamode board sitting on Raspberry Pi, showing GPIO connection

Although the Cooking Hacks Raspberry Pi to Arduino board and the Alamode are not identical, you might end up making a decision based partly on features and partly on which you find easier and more convenient to obtain based on where in the world you live. Cooking Hacks is based in Spain but has global distributors. In the United States, look to *MicroController Pros* (*http://microcontrollershop.com*) for their products. You can buy the Alamode *here* (*http://seeedstudio.com*), which has an American warehouse and *distributors around the world* (*http://www.seeedstudio.com/depot/index.php?main_page=distributors*).

—*David Bordonada*

HACK 59   Control a 3D Printer

> Home 3D printing is a relatively new possibility for most people, but as prices for printers continue to drop, you might find yourself happily printing plastic. Why not let your Raspberry Pi help?

A 3D printer is an amazing machine that lets you convert a 3D model that exists only in bits and bytes into something tangible. Until recently, the cost for this hardware was prohibitively high, both in price and space required to house it. In the last few years, however, they've gone from tens (or hundreds) of thousands of dollars to as little as a few hundred and from the size of a refrigerator to smaller than your toaster.

These increasingly common home 3D printers use an *additive* method, which means plastic (or other malleable materials) are driven through a heated extruder. This extruder is attached to a series of belts and motors, which allow it to move along the X, Y, and Z axes. The plastic is then extruded in layers onto a plate of glass (which may or may not be heated, depending on the plastic type in use), where it cools quickly. The printer repeats this process, printing layer upon layer (upward) until the object is completed.

There are many different types of these 3D printers, but the most common is known as the RepRap family of printers. These printers feature open hardware and are relatively easy to build from publicly available plans on the Internet, but they are also available in prebuilt commercial offerings. One such vendor is *Lulzbot* (*https://www.lulzbot.com/*), which produces and sells high-quality (and high-resolution) RepRap style printers.

For the purposes of this hack, we'll assume that you have a Lulzbot AO-101 (shown in Figure 6-11), but these instructions apply generally to any printer in the RepRap family.

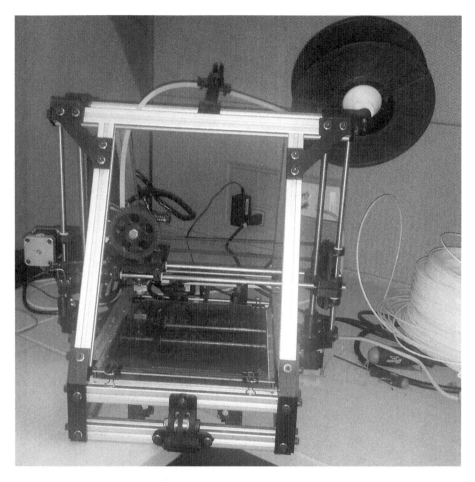

Figure 6-11.
Tom's Lulzbot AO-101

The Lulzbot AO-101 is powered by a RAMBo electronics board (Figure 6-12), which uses an Atmega processor, stepper motor drivers, and power management outputs to control the movement and temperature of the extruder and the heated plate glass bed. While this hardware does its job very well, it is not very smart. It knows only how to process a series of instructions called G-code.

Figure 6-12.
RAMBo electronics in Lulzbot AO-101

G-code is a computer language that tells the 3D printer exactly what to do, through a series of explicit instructions. It tells the printer where to move its extruder and bed, at what speeds, and through what paths. It is roughly analogous to PostScript for traditional 2D printers.

G-code has existed since the 1950s and is generally accepted as the standard language for interfacing with computerized machine tools. However, because each 3D printer is different, you cannot simply take a G-code file and send it to any printer. The G-code has to be generated with the specifications of your printer taken into account.

Replace the RAMBo with a Raspberry Pi?

You might wonder why we don't talk about replacing the RAMBo electronics with the Raspberry Pi. While the Raspberry Pi is a lot smarter than the RAMBo board and is capable of sending instructions to the 3D printer and manipulating and "slicing" models into G-code, the RAMBo board is specialized for performing real-time control of the stepper motors (and heating units) that make up the heart of the 3D printer. The Raspberry Pi would be a poor substitute for this without extensive (and complicated) modifications. Even when hacking, we prefer to let the Raspberry Pi and the RAMBo live in harmony, taking advantage of each other's strengths.

Using a 3D printer from Linux is a multiple-stage process. First, you need to have a 3D model that you want to print. This could be something that you built yourself using free software like Blender or OpenSCAD, or it could be something you downloaded off the Internet. *Thingiverse (http://www.thingiverse.com)* is dedicated to the sharing of user-designed files for 3D models, and it's a great starting point if you're looking for something to print.

Once you've got a 3D model that you want to print, the next step is to convert that model into the G-code for your printer. There are several available software packages that do this, but our favorite is *Slic3r (http://slic3r.org)*.

On Pidora, `slic3r` is packaged up, so you can install it with `yum`:

```
$ sudo yum install slic3r
```

On other distributions, you'll need to download and install `slic3r` from source:

```
$ git clone git://github.com/alexrj/Slic3r
$ cd Slic3r
$ sudo perl Build.PL
$ sudo perl Build.PL --gui
```

Once `slic3r` is installed, you can run it in GUI mode. It will prompt you to configure your printer. The Lulzbot website includes `slic3r` *configuration files for their printers (http://download.lulzbot.com/AO-101/software/current/slic3r/config/)*.

Add your 3D model to `slic3r` (scaling and copying as desired), then click the Export G-code button. This is a resource intensive process, so it will take quite a bit longer on your Raspberry Pi than it would on your laptop, but it will eventually complete.

When you have your `.gcode` file, you'll need to send it to the printer to print. The recommended printer control software for the Lulzbot AO-101 is called `Printrun`. Printrun is a set of Python applications for sending G-code instructions to the printer, including the instructions to print your 3D model, but also for moving the printer around and controlling the heated units.

On Pidora, `Printrun` is packaged up, so to install it, just run:

```
$ sudo yum install printrun
```

On other distributions, you'll have to download the `Printrun` source code from GitHub:

```
$ git clone https://github.com/kliment/Printrun.git
```

The Printrun source is Python, so no compilation is needed. To run the GUI interface for printrun (`pronterface`), simply run:

```
$ sudo ./pronterface.py
```

Pronterface Naming

Did we say `pronterface`*? Yes, we did. It isn't a typo. That's just what* `printrun` *calls their GUI application. The name is derived from their console utility,* `pronsole`*. The name looks funny, but the GUI works well.*

This will open a `wxPython` GUI interface. You will need to configure it to connect to the 3D printer (plugged into the Raspberry Pi via USB). The Lulzbot AO-101 looks like a USB serial device, so you will tell `Printrun` to connect to the `/dev/ttyACM0` port.

Make sure the port baud rate is set to 115200 in the pull-down menu to the right of the port selection. Then hit the connect button, and the 3D printer (assuming it is turned on) will connect and send a status message. You can then load up the `.gcode` file for your 3D model.

You will need to turn on the heated nozzle and bed to the proper temperatures for the type of plastic that is loaded into your printer (these buttons are in the lower left of the UI interface). Once the printer is at the proper heat settings, you click the Print button, and off it goes!

HACK 60   Add a Numeric Keypad

Thanks to the ubiquity of telephones and automatic teller machines, most people alive today are intimately familiar with a numeric keypad. Hacking one into your Raspberry Pi can open up a wide range of possible projects.

A numeric keypad doesn't seem like much—just a 3 x 4 grid of numbers and symbols (occasionally a 4 x 4 grid), right? And everyone who has ever dialed (a humorous leftover term, given that we're talking about keypads rather than rotary dials) a phone number or entered a PIN for an ATM withdrawal or debit purchase knows how to use it. But added to a Raspberry Pi, you could use a keypad as part of a locking mechanism or for any kind of numeric input. You could even use it to turn your Raspberry Pi into a Voice over IP (VoIP) phone, but with that old push-button feel.

In addition to your Pi, you'll need:

- Linux preinstalled with `python2` (any distribution should work).
- A matrix input numeric keypad. We used the *Membrane 3x4 Matrix Keypad* (*http://www.adafruit.com/products/419*) available from Adafruit, but you can adjust our instructions to work with other keypads.
- A breadboard and male-to-female jumper wires. These are just for prototyping the numeric keypad connection to the GPIO on the Raspberry Pi. For a more permanent setup, you should solder things together.

These instructions assume you're using a Raspberry Pi Model B, revision 2. If you're not, the GPIO pin numbers are different, and you'll need to adjust.

How the Matrix Keypad Works

The Membrane 3x4 Matrix Numeric Keypad is simple. It has three columns with four rows of buttons and one wire for each row and column, as shown in Figure 6-13.

Figure 6-13.
Membrane 3 x 4 Matrix Numeric Keypad

The wires from the numeric keypad run to seven pins (pins 1 and 7 are labeled). Use the jumper wires to connect these pins into your breadboard. By scanning the activity of the rows and columns, you can detect which button is being pressed on the keypad and translate it to the corresponding number.

The ordering of the pins might be logical from a layout perspective, but it took us a bit of trial and error to determine which rows and columns matched up to the keypad pins. See Table 6-3 for reference.

Table 6-3. Keypad pins and associated rows/columns

KEYPAD PIN NUMBER	ROW/COLUMN
7	Row 1
6	Row 2
5	Row 3
4	Row 4
3	Column 1
2	Column 2
1	Column 3

Obviously, if you're using a different numeric keypad, your pinouts may differ.

Connecting the Keypad to the Raspberry Pi

The simplest way to connect the numeric keypad to the Raspberry Pi is to connect each of the keypad pins to a dedicated GPIO pin. The code in this hack assumes that you have the pins connected as shown in Table 6-4.

Table 6-4. Keypad pins to GPIP pins

KEYPAD PIN NUMBER	ROW/COLUMN	GPIO PIN
7	Row 1	18
6	Row 2	23
5	Row 3	24
4	Row 4	25
3	Column 1	4
2	Column 2	17
1	Column 3	22

The simplest way to wire this is by connecting the female end of a jumper wire to a GPIO pin, then connecting the male end of that wire into the appropriate location on the breadboard. Remember, you want to have the GPIO-connected jumper wires lined up with the corresponding horizontal row that contains the keypad pin.

How to Use Fewer Pins

This configuration is the easiest to wire, but it does have the disadvantage of using up a lot of the GPIO pins on your Raspberry Pi. If you are feeling braver, you could cut back on the number of GPIO pins used by wiring a demultiplexer (demux) to the row pins, cutting them from four down to two.

You could also binary encode the column outputs with pull-down resistors on the GPIO input pins and diodes to generate and mix the binary signal, resulting in two column pins instead of three. If you do this, you'd need to write new code to handle the more complicated inputs, which is left as an exercise to the power hacker. (Credit goes to aTao on the Raspberry Pi forums for pointing this out.)

Installing the Software

To keep things simple here, we'll take advantage of the Python Raspberry Pi GPIO library. Pidora and Raspbian install this software by default, but if you do not have it already available in your Linux distribution, you can *download the source code (http:// code.google.com/p/raspberry-gpio-python/)*. A copy of this code is also included in *the GitHub repository for this book (https://github.com/spotrh/rpihacks)*.

Chris Crumpacker (http://www.chriscrumpacker.com/) wrote a Python library called `matrix_keypad` to interface the Raspberry Pi directly with the Adafruit Matrix numeric keypad, but unfortunately, it has some bugs which prevent it from working as is. We've taken *revision 1.0.4 of his library (https://pypi.python.org/pypi/matrix_keypad)* and cleaned up the bugs that were preventing it from working properly.

To install this library, first check out the fixed source code:

```
$ git clone https://github.com/spotrh/rpihacks
$ cd rpihacks/matrix_keypad-1.0.4-fixed
```

Next, build and install the fixed library:

```
$ python setup.py build
$ su -c 'python setup.py install --prefix=/usr'
```

Running the Program

Now you have a working copy of the `matrix_keypad` library installed on your Raspberry Pi. We have also included a demonstration script (derived from Chris's examples) so that you can test your setup. There is a file in the `matrix_keypad-1.0.4-fixed/` directory called `book-demo.py`. Make sure your numeric keypad is wired in correctly, then run:

```
$ chmod +x book-demo.py
$ su -c './book-demo.py'
```

This code will prompt you to enter your four-digit secret code into the numeric keypad. The code in this example is 8675. As you enter the digits, it will print out debugging details showing you the digit entered, the current stored value of your code to that point, the number of digits in your code that you have entered, and finally, after four digits have been entered, whether your code is correct.

Nifty, huh? But how does it work? book-demo.py uses the keypad function from the matrix_keypad_RPi_GPIO module in the matrix_keypad library. The matrix_key pad_MCP230xx module in the library it is only for when you have an I2C Port Expander in use. The code also imports the sleep and exit functions from the standard Python time and sys libraries so the code can sleep briefly if it's entered incorrectly and so that it can exit if it is entered properly:

```
from matrix_keypad.matrix_keypad_RPi_GPIO import keypad

from time import sleep
from sys import exit
```

Now, to silence the GPIO warnings. The Python Raspberry Pi GPIO library emits warnings whenever you have any GPIO pins configured as anything other than input. Since the matrix_keypad_RPi_GPIO library always configures the column pins as output (low), you'll get this warning every time you use it. You don't want to see that, so silence it by disabling the warnings:

```
import RPi.GPIO as GPIO
GPIO.setwarnings(False)
```

Now you need to initialize the keypad class from the matrix_keypad_RPi_GPIO module. This will create a kp variable you can use to read the keys from the physical numeric keypad. The matrix_keypad_Rpi_GPIO module supports both 3 x 4 and 4 x 4 numeric keypad devices, but because our hardware is a 3 x 4, we'll tell it that we have only three columns. We also set up variables to store code attempts, the passcode we are checking for, and a counter variable to track the progress of inputting the code:

```
kp = keypad(columnCount = 3)

# Setup variables
attempt = "0000"
passcode = "8675"
counter = 0
```

At this point, the program prints a friendly message to the user to tell her what to do (input the four-digit secret code) and start a loop:

```
```

```
print 'Enter your four digit secret code into the numeric keypad!'

# Loop while waiting for a keypress
while True:
    # Loop to get a pressed digit
    digit = None
    while digit == None:
            digit = kp.getKey()
```

The loop uses the getKey() function from the keypad class to continuously poll the numeric keypad device waiting for the user to press keys and input parts of her code. Once a key is pressed, the value of digit changes from None to the value of the key pressed, the value of the digit entered prints, the value for the code to that point (in the attempt variable) updates, and the code entered so far prints:

```
# Print the result
print "Digit Entered:      %s"%digit
attempt = (attempt[1:] + str(digit))
print "Attempt value:      %s"%attempt
```

Now the program checks to see if the code as entered so far matches the value set in passcode earlier. If it does, the program prints a happy message and exits:

```
# Check for passcode match
if (attempt == passcode):
        print "Your code was correct, goodbye."
        exit()
```

If it doesn't match the passcode (either because it is incorrect or because not enough digits have been entered), the program proceeds to the end of the loop, updating the number of digits entered. If the number of digits in the entered code is more than four, the program knows the user did not find the correct code in time it restarts the loop. If it is fewer than four digits, it simply loops again and waits for more digits:

```
    else:
        counter += 1
        print "Entered digit count: %s"%counter
        if (counter >= 4):
                print "Incorrect code!"
                sleep(3)
                print "Try Again"
                sleep(1)
                counter = 0
    sleep(0.5)
```

This example program plays a simple guessing game, but it illustrates how you can use the physical numeric keypad as an input device. You could easily modify this code to unlock a door when the correct code is entered, incorporate it as part of an alarm system, or use it to take numeric input for a Raspberry Pi-controlled thermostat.

HACK 61 Add a Heat Sink

> A heat sink for your Raspberry Pi? But it's so little! Tiny, but mighty. You may be surprised at just how warm it can get.

You've probably noticed that computers are hot. Not like "don't touch the stove" hot (most of the time), but "my smartphone is sometimes a hand warmer in the winter" hot. It's the integrated circuits (ICs) that make that toasty feeling (as well as make your electronics work), and assorted bad things happen when they get too toasty, ranging from warping the plastic case to (in extreme cases) burning laps of people who take "laptop" literally. Sometimes you'll learn your computer is too hot because it knows it's overheating and locks up or shuts down. It's unlikely your Raspberry Pi will overheat in average use, but it's not impossible with more intense use.

A heat sink could seem like a bit much for such a little device, but depending on what you're using the Pi for (have you read Hack #06?), it could extend the computer's life. And frankly, heat sinks look neat. Of course, if your goal is "as small as possible," this isn't the plan for you. If your goal is "naked electronics looking awesome," you're in the right place.

Not Safe for Kids?

The Raspberry Pi was designed for education, and that includes with safety in mind. It's exceptionally unlikely that in any normal use, the Pi is going to get so hot as to be unsafe to touch, so don't worry about giving it to your kids.

The Raspberry Pi produces heat from three ICs: the CPU, the Ethernet controller, and the power regulator. *Geektopia* (*http://www.geektopia.es*) used a thermal camera to study the Raspberry Pi's heat output (as shown in Figure 6-14. Simply plugged in and running, the three ICs had measured temperatures of, 48.7° C (119.66° F), 53° C (127.4° F), and 49.9° C (121.82° F), respectively.

Figure 6-14.
Thermal photo of Raspberry Pi running but at rest (courtesy of GeekTopia, *http://www.geektopia.es*)

The hottest test Geektopia ran was during video playback with Ethernet plugged in, which drove the Ethernet controller to 65.1° C (149.18° F). (The *full test results (http://www.geektopia.es/es/technology/2012/06/22/articulos/se-calienta-el-ordenador-raspberry-pi-estudio-de-sus-temperaturas-en-funcionamiento.html*) are available in Spanish.) You can read one method of measuring your own CPU's temperature in "Measure Temperature" on page 16.

Which heat sink you buy depends not only on your performance needs, but potentially on your aesthetic preferences and shipping location. Barch Designs sells a *Raspberry Pi case made from CNC-milled aircraft-grade aluminum (http://www.raspberry-pi-case.com*) that also acts as a heat sink. The case gives you access to all the ports and has visibility to the LEDs with engraving showing their purposes. As a bonus, you can have it etched with your words or design—perhaps the name of your project?

The Barch Design case (shown in Figure 6-15) comes with a thermal paste. The interior of the case has three raised pillars that contact the three IC chips on the Raspberry Pi. Apply the paste to each of these pillars to activate the heat sink properties of the case.

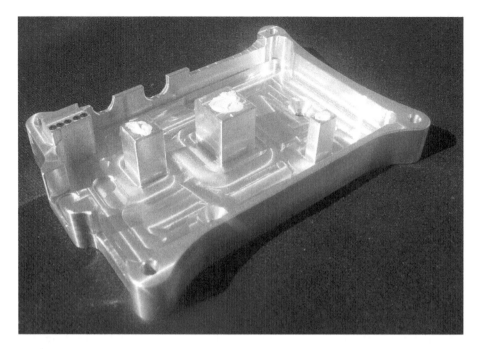

Figure 6-15.
Heat sink case (photo by Benjamin Barch)

Because we're based in the United States, we refer frequently in this book to parts available from Adafruit, but if you're not in North America, *ModMyPi* (*https:// www.modmypi.com*), a UK-based company that sells Raspberry Pi accessories and parts, might be a better bet for a lot of your needs. They deliver internationally with an expected wait of three to seven days, which isn't bad if they have something you can't find anywhere else.

ModMyPi sells a *more traditional-looking set of alumnium heat sinks* (*https:// www.modmypi.com/raspberry-pi-heat-sink-kit*) with a small piece for each of the three heat-producing areas. No glue required for this one—they attach with provided thermal tape.

A heat sink alone won't change everything, though. If you have it sealed up inside a case (other than ones like that above designed to be or complement a heat sink), you're just sending the heat a few extra centimeters away—not that useful. Make sure your chosen housing has appropriate air circulation.

Enable the Raspberry Pi Camera on Pidora

As of this writing, the Raspbery Pi camera module does not yet officially work with Pidora. That doesn't mean we can't make it happen anyway.

Using the Raspberry Pi camera module is well-documented online—if you're using Raspbian. To do so, you need to update the OS and use the built-in `raspi-config` tool to enable it. There are a few more steps, but that's the gist of it. Pidora doesn't use `raspi-config`, though, so it takes another step or two, but you can still use the camera module with it.

Mount the SD card in your laptop or other computer that isn't the Raspberry Pi. Mount the two partitions, replacing /dev/mmcblk0 with the location of your own SD card, which you can find with `df -h`:

```
$ sudo mnt /dev/mmcblk0p1 /mnt/raspi-boot/
$ sudo mnt /dev/mmcblk0p2 /mnt/raspi-root/
```

Then update all the boot firmware from the Pidora image to the latest version from GitHub and copy the firmware onto the SD card:

```
$ git clone https://github.com/raspberrypi/firmware
$ cp -a firmware/boot/*.bin firmware/boot/*.dat firmware/boot/*.elf /mnt/
raspi-boot/
```

Update the videocore libraries and binaries. With the Pidora SD card mounted, run:

```
$ sudo cp -a firmware/hardfp/opt/vc/bin /mnt/raspi-root/usr/
$ sudo cp -a firmware/hardfp/opt/vc/include /mnt/raspi-root/usr/
$ sudo cp -a firmware/hardfp/opt/vc/lib /mnt/raspi-root/usr/
$ sudo cp -a firmware/hardfp/opt/vc/sbin /mnt/raspi-root/usr/
```

Finally, add these two lines to /boot/config.txt on the SD card:

```
gpu_mem=128
start_x=1
```

As mentioned previously, the camera needs 128 MB of memory dedicated to the GPU to work correctly. The _x firmware variant is the one that the Pi needs to use the camera.

Shut down and connect the camera to the Raspberry Pi. The blue tape side of the ribbon cable should be facing toward the Ethernet jack, and the leads side should be facing toward the HDMI connector. Make sure none of the lead pins are bent.

Start the Pi, and you're ready to test the connection:

```
sudo raspistill -v -o temp.jpg
```

Of course, before performing that last step, you should be sure to slyly point it at family members doing something hilarious. That camera's so small, they'll never notice.

HACK 63 Build a Solar-Powered Lab

One of the benefits of the Pi is its low-power consumption, which makes it well suited to being the centerpiece of a solar-powered education lab.

Several rural labs around the world have taken advantage of RACHEL (*http:// www.worldpossible.org/rachel*). Short for *remote area community hotspots for education and learning*, RACHEL deployments are low-cost, scalable collections of open source software and educational content pulled from Creative Commons licensed sources such as The Khan Academy, Wikipedia, and CK-12.

RACHEL servers are specifically intended for remote locations with low-to-no Internet connectivity. Powering Potential uses the RACHEL educational software on the server that is then accessed through each student's unit. RACHEL is free to download, install, manage, and replicate and can be deployed in nearly any environment with minimal hardware, such as a Raspberry Pi lab.

In fact, one of the configurations available from RACHEL is designed specifically for the Raspberry Pi and called RACHEL-Pi. It's been used by *The Best of Both* (*http:// www.thebestofboth.org/*) initiative in Ghana and *Powering Potential* (*http:// www.thebestofboth.org/*) in Tanzania. Powering Potential also uses solar power to run the labs. Thanks to a low-power monitor and the Pi, each workstation consumes less than 10 watts over DC power.

Powering Potential's flagship program, Educating-Through-Technology, partners with government secondary schools in Tanzania to bring the Raspberry Pi and basic technology instruction to students. In 2013, they began rolling the program out to three schools in each of Tanzania's 30 regions.

Unlike many of the hacks in this book, these workstations require a Model B, revision 2 with 512 MB of RAM. (And because it is for educational purposes, Powering Potential houses the Pis in clear cases so that the students can see the components.) You'll also need a 4 GB or greater SD card, and they recommend a Class 10 or UHS-1 (Ultra High Speed) card (see Class 10 Too Classy? for notes on this).

Gather Hardware

For each station, the Raspberry Pis in their cases are mounted on the back of each monitor. Each workstation includes:

- Hanns-G Model HI161Abb 15.6" LED monitor. This choice is part of a goal to obtain low-wattage equipment that consumes only 10 watts of electricity between the monitor and the computer (and running on DC instead of AC power).

- Pi View HDMI to VGA Adapter.

- Keyboard, mouse, router, printer, and modem (for their work, Powering Potential sources these locally in Tanzania).

- Wi-Pi USB Wireless Adapter (originally used for communication between the student client and the servers, but due to intermittent connection issues, Powering Potential is exploring replacement solutions).

- Powered USB hub (optional).

- 12-volt-to-5-volt stepdown converter 3 A female USB (Figure 6-16), which is used to connect the Raspberry Pi to the 12 V solar power system, in addition to the Micro USB cable to power to Raspberry Pi.

- Headsets for sound.

Figure 6-16.
12-volt-to-5-volt stepdown converter

For the solar power system for the lab, they use a vendor configuration from *Ensol Tanzania Limited* (*http://ensol.co.tz*), which includes:

- 85 W solar module
- 108 Ah solar battery
- 45 A solar controller
- Mounting frame
- Battery box
- 180 watt DC-to-AC inverter (for printer)
- Lightning arrestor and earthing system

The hardware required for the RACHEL server is identical to the client/student configuration, except that it requires a larger SD card—32 GB for only RACHEL-Pi or 64 GB if KA-Lite is included. Because 64 GB cards are not well-suited to the purpose, only cards rated UHS-1 will work for that scenario. In addition, a router facilitates communication between student clients and the servers. The UHS-1 class 64 GB cards that have been tested and known to work with the Pi include:

- Kingston SD10G3/64GB UHS-I Elite
- Lexar Platinum II SDXC UHS-I Card
- SanDisk Ultra® SDXC™ UHS-I

Set Up the Raspberry Pi

Powering Potential uses Raspbian for the student Raspberry Pis. Emmanuel Ackerman, technical adviser at Powering Potential, offers configuration tips on the *World-Possible forums* (*http://worldpossible.org/forum/rachel-pi/34-access-rachel-pi-content*) under the handle mannyack.

Most importantly, he notes that the default sound configuration is "auto," which means that if you connect the monitor through the composite video port, the sound will be directed through the audio jack, and if you connect the monitor through the HDMI port, the audio will be directed to the HDMI audio. The monitor they use is an HDMI monitor that doesn't support audio. To tell Raspbian to use the headphones, you should be able to run:

```
$ sudo amixer cset numid=3 1
```

Mannyack recommends doing this manually through /var/lib/alsa/asound.state in a text editor instead, followed by pulling the power to force a shutdown.

The Raspberry Pi's GPU can be used for video decoding, including high-definition video. Raspbian includes a video player called omxplayer, which uses the GPU for processing. Powering Potential has adapted the *media-berry package* (*http://lin.jojen.de/?p=32*) that reroutes HTML5 video playback in Midori (the default Raspberry Pi web browser) for omxplayer to work with RACHEL videos.

The lab is powered by solar powers installed on the roof of the computer lab in a conventional arrangement (panels and batteries). Power cabling brings the 12 V power produced by the sun from the batteries to the computers. A 12-volt-to-5-volt stepdown converter brings that down to usable power for the Raspberry Pis. The monitors, however, are connected directly to the 12 V circuit, rather than using the supplied power cord (including brick/transformer) that come with the monitors.

In the lab, the tables each have three computers with two students per computer to encourage synergy and collaboration between students, as shown in Figure 6-17.

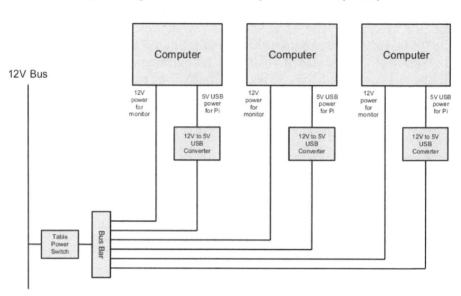

Figure 6-17.
Classroom diagram

RACHEL completes the setup. English and Spanish versions are available for download at *http://worldpossible.org/rachel/download*. They also offer installation instructions, or you can order preinstalled units.

—Emmanuel Ackerman

HACK 64 Build a MIDI Controller (on the Cheap!)

This hack helps you build a homemade MIDI controller, using the Raspberry Pi as a central controlling component, for a fraction of the cost of commercial devices.

The Alcyone, a Raspberry-Pi-based MIDI controller, was inspired by the Moog Taurus 2, including its astronomical name. However, if you're familiar with these machines, the Roland PK-6 is more of a direct equivalent to the Alcyone. The goal was to create a MIDI controller in the form of bass pedals. Building a foot pedal would be far less expensive than purchasing a Moog Taurus 3 (a full analog synthesizer in a foot pedal form factor) or even a PK-6 (a simple foot pedal controller, at roughly $900 USD).

For those less familiar with music production, MIDI stands for *musical instrument digital interface*, and it's an industry-standard protocol for electronic instruments. It is based on three types of events (note events, control events, and global events) and uses a serial connection at 31250 baud.

Why "Alcyone"?

The Moog Taurus was originally designed as a part of a synthesizer ensemble called the Constellation. The Taurus was the bass pedal of the ensemble; the other parts were the Lyra and the Apollo. The Lyra was never built; the Apollo's design found its way into the PolyMoog. The Taurus, however, became very popular, through its use in bands such as Rush, Genesis, ELP (from whom the explanation of the Constellation comes), and others.

When naming this project, various star names were considered. Alcyone is Taurus's second-brightest star and one of the Pleiades. The project Alcyone is pronounced "al-SEE-on-ee," though the star is "al-SIGH-on-ee." The warped pronunciation came from "halcyon," which is a variant of the mythological character Alcyone's name. "Halcyon" uses the "ee" form of the "y."

The Alcyone is "merely" a MIDI controller; it does not generate any sound in and of itself. The actual processing power is provided through a Raspberry Pi, and the Raspberry Pi's audio output is only 11 bits, which is better than, say, a Nintendo DS or some ancient digital synthesizers, but is far inferior to CD quality, and is nowhere near what you'd want for actual audio creation.

Hardware

The Alcyone uses a simple internal electronic design (shown in Figure 6-18). The pedals themselves are a 13-note chord, salvaged from an old Lowrey organ, purchased over eBay. They rely on a rocker switch that pulls a spring across a circuit to close it. You could build your own (or perhaps 3D-print your own) if organ salvage proves challenging.

Figure 6-18.
The Alcyone

In the Lowrey design, the pedals convert the circuit to a CV/Gate signal, which was a standard before MIDI was created. However, CV/Gate was never formally specified, so different manufacturers use different implementations. CV/Gate normally converts to a voltage: the first note might be +1 V, the second note +2 V, and so forth. However, this is a convention and not a standard, and the Raspberry Pi has neither analog inputs nor the capability to handle +13 V.

Thus it was simpler to use as little of the existing mechanism as possible, which meant relying solely on the rocker switch and wiring custom digital I/O. As the Pi has only a limited number of GPIO pins, the circuits for the rocker switches are wired to a set of I2C chips. These use a serial protocol to map GPIO pins. The MCP23008 offers eight individually addressable GPIO pins, and the MCP23017 offers 16.

The I2C chips can be wired such that seven of them are on a single serial connection. Thus, if you use seven MCP23008 chips in a series, you have 56 uniquely addressable pins. With the MCP23017, you could have 112. There are likely to be other I2C chips available, and you don't have to have a homogenous chain.

The physical electronic circuit is thus simple: three MCP23008s in series with two of them dedicated to pedal input and one driving three LEDs for runtime status.

The pedals are connected to power (+5 V) and wired to the MCP23008s. The digital inputs are also connected to pull-down resistors to clear out digital noise.

The Raspberry Pi is connected to the I2C series and also to a Din5 connector (the industry standard for MIDI connections). The Din5 is mounted on a Sparkfun MIDI shield kit, mostly chosen for availability and ease of use.

A powered USB hub is also part of the hardware installation. The hub has one device attached, a wireless networking dongle. The powered hub is necessary because the Raspberry Pi does not carry enough current to reliably power most wireless dongles (see Hack #08).

Why Wireless TCP/IP?

The wireless networking is part of a software choice made fairly early in the implementation cycle. Initial external control relied on the Raspberry Pi's onboard Ethernet connection, which implies a requirement for networking infrastructure. However, one facet of the Alcyone's potential use is stage work, and at many theaters, networking is spotty if existent at all.

The simplest solution involves the Alcyone serving as its own wireless access point, meaning that it provides its own networking infrastructure.

An alternative would be to avoid TCP/IP altogether. Bluetooth is another messaging protocol, one designed for device-to-device communications, particularly for short messages. Bluetooth devices can also be designed for low-power usage. However, this means writing a custom Bluetooth client for every possible client platform.

The wireless on the Raspberry Pi is configured as an access point so the Alcyone can serve as its own networking infrastructure. It has its own network SSID and security. The external client has to use this access point in order to control the Alcyone.

Not only does this avoid reliance on what might be inconsistent or nonexistent network services, it also limits the amount of traffic that competes for the client, and it also allows us to use a consistent IP for the Alcyone (as opposed to guessing what valid address the Alcyone happens to receive from the network infrastructure).

You need two packages to set this up: hostapd and udhcpd as described in *eLinux.org's RPI Wireless Hotspot page* (*http://elinux.org/RPI-Wireless-Hotspot*).

Software

The software for the Alcyone comes in two artifacts: the actual embedded code (the code running on the Raspberry Pi) and an external client app (currently targeted for Android).

The embedded platform runs a single application (called `alcyone` of all things), written in C. C was chosen because the original test program was written on an Arduino Uno, which tends to encourage the use of Arduino "sketches," which are themselves a form of C++ code (mostly with really odd library support).

C++ editing was largely done through Code::Blocks, easily installed for Fedora through:

```
$ su -c 'yum install codeblocks'
```

Interaction with the physical hardware is provided by Gordon Prescott's wiringPi library, an excellent utility with various language implementations.

It uses three threads, provided via boost::thread, to execute. All three threads are infinite loops. The Alcyone is a set of state machines, with the different machines able to affect the others.

The simplest thread is a "flare" machine. It loops through the output LEDs. The loop provides a timer value via an extern variable.

The second thread polls the digital inputs for changes in pedal state—in other words, when the pedals are pressed down and lifted up. The routine keeps track of two states: the "current state" based on a digital read, and the "previously read" state.

The current state is buffered to handle bounce.

Bounce is the natural tendency of an electrical current to fluctuate during changes. When a circuit is closed (or opened), electrons flow across it occasionally until the circuit settles in; the circuit appears to "bounce" open and closed for a short period of time. This makes consistent reads very difficult, unless you "debounce" the circuit.

There are two ways to debounce circuits. One hardware approach uses something called a *Schmitt trigger buffer*. Jack Ganssle has an excellent *guide to debouncing* (*http://www.eng.utah.edu/~cs5780/debouncing.pdf*) that describes a few different ways to handle bounce in hardware and software (including code).

Alcyone uses a similar approach with a class that examines the input and counts the "open" and "closed" states. It's possible that the debouncing mechanism could be fooled if the user plays quickly enough (pressing and releasing pedals much faster than the human eye can blink), but the sample frequency is high enough that we haven't seen any incorrect results yet.

Through the process, on every loop, it reads the digital state of the pedals, and feeds that into the debouncing mechanism, yielding a result (biased toward the actual state).

If the current state is different from the "previously read" state, then we have a change; if the "current state" is "down," then the pedal was just pressed, and we need to send a "note on" event; otherwise, a "note off" event should be sent.

Which note is sent is based on an offset. The MIDI mechanism contains a reference to a "current octave" and a "current transposition" setting; the actual note used is determined by multiplying the octave by 12, then adding the transposition value.

Therefore, if the current octave is three, and the transposition setting is one (meaning that the farthest left pedal is now C# and not C, an offset of one half-step), and the third pedal is depressed, the actual note is calculated through the use of the pedal, plus the octave offset, plus the transposition. The pedals start at zero, so the pedal number is two:

```
2 + 3*12 + 1 = 39
```

This actually yielded a bug in the initial demonstration of the Alcyone. If the transposition settings were changed while a note was being played, the "note off" event would be for the wrong note! The reason should be fairly apparent.

Assume the "note on" event is for note 39 (as in the calculation above). Now let us set the transposition to zero (i.e., reset it). Now, when the pedal is released, the "note off" value is calculated... at 38, instead of 39.

The "note off" event thus doesn't correspond to the "note on" event, and therefore a receiver doesn't actually get the correct signal to release the note.

This is corrected by the use of another data element, the "last note sent by this pedal." Thus, note off events take the note value from this dataset, rather than recalculating the note value when the pedal is released.

Thus, the pedal press/release cycle follows this process:

1. Physically depress pedal (poor, sad pedal).
2. Calculate MIDI note by offset of pedal + 12*octave + transposition.
3. Store MIDI note in an internal array, index based on the offset of the pedal.
4. Send MIDI on.
5. Physically release the pedal.
6. Send MIDI off based on the note in the internal array.

MIDI actually required a number of changes to the Linux configuration for the Raspberry Pi.

The Pi's serial driver does not actually support 31250 baud, the baud rate required by the MIDI specification. Therefore, you must overclock the serial chip, by modifying /boot/config.txt:

```
init_uart_clock=2441406
init_uart_baud=38400
```

Next, you must disable the serial console, which uses the RX/TX pins needed for MIDI, through modification of /boot/cmdline.txt:

```
dwc_otg.lpm_enable=0 console=tty1 console=tty1 root=/dev/mmcblk0p2 /
rootfstype=ext4 elevator=deadline rootwait bcm2708.uart_clock=3000000
```

Lastly, you must disable the TTY that would normally get assigned to the RX/TX pins, as well, by modifying /etc/inittab:

```
#Spawn a getty on Raspberry Pi serial line
#T0:23:respawn:/sbin/getty -L ttyAMA0 115200 vt100
```

The last thread is a simple web server, based on CoralBits' *libonion* (*http://coralbits.com/libonion/*), which uses the C++ interface layer to map three request patterns (two with no-op responses for client performance). The Alcyone uses a simple web app written with *JQuery* (*http://jquery.com*) (and served via lighttpd) to call this service with a single parameter: message. This app has a series of buttons corresponding to control events: two kinds of channel changes, four kinds of transposition events, and three different kind of system resets.

The message is actually an encoded byte, based on Table 6-5.

Table 6-5. Messages and encoded bytes

MESSAGE	PAYLOAD	NOTES
MSG_MIDI_RESET	0001	Turns off all MIDI notes on every channel
	xxxx	
MSG_MIDI_CHANNEL_CHANGE	0010	
	vvvv	
MSG_MIDI_OCTAVE_CHANGE	0100	
	vvvv	MSG_MIDI_TRANSPOSITION_CHANGE
1000		
vvvv	MSG_RESET	1111
Resets the Alcyone's internal state to defaults		xxxx
MSG_REQUEST_STATUS	0011	Responds with three bytes: octave, transposition, channel

In Table 6-5, xxxx is an "ignored value" and vvvv is "down if zero."

The web service mechanism is a simple loop. It processes a request, has an internal switch/case that examines the upper nybble of the message value, and applies changes as required.

No matter what the requested operation is, the Alcyone responds with three integers in plain text, which correspond to the current octave, the current transposition setting, and the current MIDI channel. The JQuery-based request reads these three integers and populates the web page with the current instrument status.

Ergonomics

An implemented schematic and working software (both embedded and external) are all well and good, but they all ignore the actual aspect of playing the Alcyone.

The Alcyone is designed to be played by standing guitarists. It is not likely to be played delicately.

In order to be useful, it must be mounted in a case that offers the following qualities:

- Heavy enough to allow stability for the pedals. It would be unfortunate for the musician if the pedals moved during performance (as many stage configurations are laid out for the convenience of the performer, and often monitors are aimed in specific ways). It would be even less fortunate for an audience member if the Alcyone were to somehow be launched at him or her.
- Tough enough to handle being stepped on thousands of times, by a full-grown adult.
- Pedals low enough so that the musician's ankle is comfortable while playing the instrument.

All of the "white keys" were replaced with wooden keys made from wood meant for a picket fence cut down to size to match the existing pedals (roughly six inches long). These are more likely to be immediately durable as compared to the original organ pedals (which would be decades old).

As for the external container, the Alcyone has a wooden case built from 2 × 4 wood and shellacked fencing, giving it a rustic look (which has its own appeal, for various reasons) and is tough enough to handle rough treatment. With proper reinforcement, the Alcyone is strong enough for an adult to stand on, although you probably shouldn't jump on it. It's not a percussion instrument!

—Joe Ottinger

Build a Raspberry Pi Supercomputer

There seem to be two things people immediately want to do with their Pis: make a media server (see Hack #54) or make a cluster of Raspberry Pis. This hack is for those of you in the latter group.

Be þéos sceaft, sum clyster, nemnende for se eponymous ceorl fram... Just kidding. We're talking a Beowulf *cluster*, not the Old English stuff. And not Old English like the wood cleaner, like the epic poem. Either way, it doesn't matter. By the time we translated this whole hack into mediocre Old English, our grandchildren would be writing about installing Fedora 140 on the Lingonberry Muffin (all the rage in 2073—keep an eye out).

A Beowulf cluster is what happens when you connect some smaller computers (most likely some cheap bits somebody stuck in a storage closet a while back, or as Wikipedia more politely describes it, "commodity-grade") together to build a supercomputer. The term came from such a computer built at NASA in the mid '90s, so named because the eponymous character of *Beowulf* had "thirty men's heft of grasp in the gripe of his hand."

The following instructions are adapted from those written by Simon Cox in the Computational Engineering and Design Research Group at the University of Southampton for a *Raspberry Pi supercomputer with LEGO racking* (*http://www.southampton.ac.uk/~sjc/raspberrypi/*). It uses MPI (Message Passing Interface) to communicate between nodes.

These instructions assume you are using Raspbian. When you first boot the image, expand the image to fill the card. Don't forget to change the default password and refresh the list of packages in your cache (`sudo apt-get update`). Then you're ready to start supercomputing!

Background Reading

Parallel Processing on the Pi (*http://westcoastlabs.blogspot.co.uk/2012/06/parallel-processing-on-pi-bramble.html*) is an excellent post to read, if only for reassurance that you are going to make it by the end, but don't start following those instructions. You're going to build everything yourself in this hack.

You'll also want to look at the *MPICH Installer's Guide* (*http://www.mpich.org/documentation/guides*) to better understand some of the steps in this hack.

Build MPI to Run Code on Multiple Nodes

To begin, get Fortran:

```
$ sudo apt-get install gfortran
```

After all, what is scientific programming without Fortran being a possibility?

If you have Fortran, you are good to go without excluding anything. The packages here are for `armel`, *but you need* `armhf`, *so in this hack you'll build MPI yourself.*

Make a directory to put the MPI sources in:

```
$ mkdir /home/pi/mpich2
$ cd ~/mpich2
```

Next, get the MPI sources from Argonne National Laboratory. The MPI source continues to be updated, so you might need to visit *http://www.mpich.org/downloads/* to find the latest stable release version for MPICH2:

```
$ wget http://www.mcs.anl.gov/research/projects/mpich2/downloads/tarballs/
1.4.1p1/mpich2-1.4.1p1.tar.gz
```

Once you have it, unpack the file:

```
$ tar xfz mpich2-1.4.1p1.tar.gz
```

You will need to update this as the version of MPICH2 increments. Next, make a place to put the compiled stuff, which will also make it easier to figure out what you have put in new on your system:

```
$ sudo mkdir /home/rpimpi/
$ sudo mkdir /home/rpimpi/mpich2-install
```

You might end up building this a few times. Make a build directory (so you keep the source directory clean of build things) and then change into it:

```
$ sudo mkdir /home/pi/mpich_build
$ cd /home/pi/mpich_build
```

Now you're ready to configure the build:

```
$ sudo /home/pi/mpich2/mpich2-1.4.1p1/configure -prefix=/home/rpimpi/mpich2-
install
```

Again, you will need to update this as the version of MPICH2 increments. Now is a good time to go make a cup of tea. (We recommend Earl Grey, hot, but that part is up to you.) It will be waiting when you come back.

Make the files, have another cup of tea, install them, and have a third cup of tea:

```
$ sudo make
$ sudo make install
```

Add the place that you put the install to your PATH:

```
$ export PATH=$PATH:/home/rpimpi/mpich2-install/bin
```

Note that to put this on the path permanently you will need to edit .profile and add at the bottom these two lines:

```
# Add MPI to path
PATH="$PATH:/home/rpimpi/mpich2-install/bin"
```

Check whether things installed successfully:

```
$ which mpicc
$ which mpiexec
```

Now you're ready to test whether MPI works for you on a single node. Change directory back to home (cd ~), make a directory for testing (mkdir mpi_testing), and change into your testing directory (cd mpi_testing). Get your IP address (ifconfig if necessary) and put it into a single file called machinefile.

Then, test whether MPI works:

```
$ mpiexec -f machinefile -n <number> hostname
```

If you run:

```
$ mpiexec -f machinefile -n 1 hostname
```

The output should look like this:

```
raspberrypi
```

Now try a little C code. In the examples subdirectory of where you built MPI, you'll find the famous CPI example, which you will now use MPI on your Pi to calculate pi:

```
$ cd /home/pi/mpi_testing
$ mpiexec -f machinefile -n 2 ~/mpich_build/examples/cpi

Process 0 of 2 is on raspberrypi
Process 1 of 2 is on raspberrypi
pi is approximately 3.1415926544231318, Error is 0.0000000008333387
```

Take a break and celebrate getting this far! (Perhaps a fourth cup of tea is in order?)

Flash Me... Once

You now have a master copy of the main node of the machine with all of the installed files for MPI in a single place. It's time to clone the card. Shut down your Pi (sudo poweroff). Remove the SD card and write the image *from* your SD card *back* to your PC. In the following example, we'll call that file wheezy-raspbian_backup_mpi_master.img.

Eject the card and put a fresh card into your SD card reader. Write the `wheezy-raspbian_backup_mpi_master.img` image you just created to the SD card. Put this second card into your second Raspberry Pi and boot it. You should now have two Raspberry Pis on. Unless otherwise stated, all the commands that follow are typed from the Master Pi that you built first.

Use SSH Instead of Password Login Between the Pis

Using RSA will give you a much quicker login. Working on the master Pi node:

```
$ cd ~
$ ssh-keygen -t rsa -C "raspberrypi@raspberrypi"
```

This sets a default location of /home/pi/.ssh/id_rsa to store the key. Enter a passphrase (e.g., `myfirstpicluster`). If you leave this blank, you'll have bad security, but you won't have to type passphrases any more.

Next, copy the keys to the Raspberry Pi:

```
$ cat ~/.ssh/id_rsa.pub | ssh pi@192.168.1.162 "mkdir .ssh;cat >> .ssh/
authorized_keys"
```

Log on to your second Pi and enter:

```
$ ls -al ~/.ssh
```

You should see a file called `authorized_keys`. This file is your ticket to No-Login Heaven on the nodes. Now add the new Pi to `machinefile`. Log into it and get its IP address (`ifconfig`). Working on the Master Raspberry Pi (the first one you built), `machine file` should now have both of the IP addresses for your Raspberry Pis—for example:

```
192.168.1.161
192.168.1.162
```

Again it's time to run a little C code. Like before, you'll find the CPI example in the examples subdirectory of where you built MPI. The first time, you will need to enter the passphrase for the key you generated (unless you left it blank) and the password for the second Pi:

```
$ cd /home/pi/mpi_testing
$ mpiexec -f machinefile -n 2 ~/mpich_build/examples/cpi

Process 0 of 2 is on raspberrypi
Process 1 of 2 is on raspberrypi
pi is approximately 3.1415926544231318, Error is 0.0000000008333387
```

If you repeat this a second time, you won't need to type any passwords. Note that you have *not* changed the hostnames yet (so yes, the previous code *is* running on the two machines, but they both have the same hostname at the moment).

If you want to rename each machine, you can do it from the Master node:

```
$ ssh pi@192.168.1.162 'sudo echo "iridispi002" | sudo tee /etc/hostname'
$ ssh pi@192.168.1.163 'sudo echo "iridispi003" | sudo tee /etc/hostname'
$ ssh pi@192.168.1.164 'sudo echo "iridispi004" | sudo tee /etc/hostname'
```

You should then reboot each worker node.

If you put in the following command again:

```
$ mpiexec -f machinefile -n 2 ~/mpich_build/examples/cpi

Process 0 of 2 is on raspberrypi
Process 1 of 2 is on iridispi002
pi is approximately 3.1415926544231318, Error is 0.0000000008333387
```

This shows the master node still called raspberrypi and the first worker called iridis pi002, and you see each process running on the separate nodes.

Congratulations! You've built a two-node supercomputer! Continue to build up to 64 (or more!) nodes.

Build More Nodes

You now have a copy of the worker nodes of the machine with all of the installed files for MPI in a single place. You want to clone this card, because it has the SSH key on it in the right place. Shut down your Pi (sudo poweroff) and eject the card. Put it into your SD card reader and write the image *from* your SD Card *back* to your PC, naming it wheezy-raspbian_backup_mpi_worker.img.

Eject the card and put a fresh card into the machine. Write the wheezy-raspbian_backup_mpi_master.img image you created *from* the PC *to* your card. Repeat for each additional node you would like to add.

Use Python Bindings for MPI

Now that your supercomputer is set up, you have options for various Python bindings for MPI. These instructions will get one of them, mpi4py working (read more about it at *http://mpi4py.scipy.org*).

Start by installing the package:

```
$ sudo apt-get install python-mpi4py
```

You also want to run the demo, so get the source, too:

```
$ cd ~
$ mkdir mpi4py
```

```
$ cd mpi4py
$ wget http://mpi4py.googlecode.com/files/mpi4py-1.3.tar.gz
$ tar xfz mpi4py-1.3.tar.gz
$ cd mpi4py-1.3/demo
```

Now repeat these steps on each of your other nodes, as this hasn't been baked into the system image.

Run examples (on your master node):

```
$ mpirun.openmpi -np 2 -machinefile /home/pi/mpi_testing/machinefile python
helloworld.py

Hello, World! I am process 0 of 2 on raspberrypi.
Hello, World! I am process 1 of 2 on iridispi002.
```

Then:

```
$ mpiexec.openmpi -n 4 -machinefile /home/pi/mpi_testing/machinefile python
helloworld.py

Hello, World! I am process 2 of 4 on raspberrypi.
Hello, World! I am process 3 of 4 on iridispi002.
Hello, World! I am process 1 of 4 on iridispi002.
Hello, World! I am process 0 of 4 on raspberrypi.
```

Getting Pip for Raspberry Pi

Pip is a tool for installing and managing those Python packages, which will give you an easy way to do so with your cluster. Read more about it at *http://www.pip-installer.org/en/latest/index.html*.

Make a directory under your home called `pip_testing` and change into it. A prerequisite for `pip` is `distribute`, so let's get that first and then install `pip`:

```
$ curl http://python-distribute.org/distribute_setup.py | sudo python
$ curl https://raw.github.com/pypa/pip/master/contrib/get-pip.py | su
do python
```

Notes on Making MPI Shared Libraries for Raspberry Pi

MPI libraries can also be built "shared" so that they can be dynamically loaded. This gives a library file that ends in `.so`. not `.a`, and you can do that by building those MPI libraries again.

To do so, repeat the steps beginning with making a directory for your MPI sources, but with a suffix of _shared on the directory names:

- /home/pi/mpich2_shared
- /home/rpimpi_shared/
- /home/rpimpi_shared/mpich2-install_shared
- /home/pi/mpich_build_shared

Configure the build:

```
$ sudo /home/pi/mpich2_shared/mpich2-1.4.1p1/configure -prefix=/home/rpim
pi_shared/mpich2-install_shared --enable-shared
```

Follow the steps to make and install the files. Then add the place that you put the install to your PATH:

```
$ export PATH=$PATH:/home/rpimpi_shared/mpich2-install_shared/bin
```

Remember that to permanently put this on the path you will need to edit .profile and add at the bottom these two lines:

```
# Add MPI Shared to path
PATH="$PATH:/home/rpimpi_shared/mpich2-install_shared/bin"
```

Actually Read Beowulf While You Wait for make

If you don't like tea, you can spend those tea-drinking steps reading John Lesslie Hall's translation of Beowulf *with notes and additional information at* http://www.gutenberg.org/ebooks/16328 *or the 1337 version (straight-up translation-only) by Francis Barton Gummere at* http://www.gutenberg.org/ebooks/981

—*Simon Cox*

Index

A

AC power, changeing DC to, 279
Adafruit
    2.5 inch NTSC/PAL display, 290
    I2C Python module, 194
    LCD Pi Plate, 103
    Pi Cobbler, 40
    power supplies, 27
    Python library for LCD Pi Plate, 104
    Raspberry Pi Educational Linux Dis-
        tro (Occidentalis), 99
    Ultimate GPS Module, 185
    USB Micro B cables, 28
    USB-to-TTL Serial Cable, 48
Adafruit_DHT binary, 175
ADCs (Analog-to-Digital Converters),
    298
aerial photography, controlling, 204–
    219
    advantages of Raspberry Pi for, 204
    building the payload, 205
    components needed in addition to Pi,
        205
    gathering gas, balloon, and para-
        chute, 207
    installing software in Pi, 207
    preparing for launch, 217
    results from successful mission, 218
    tracking the payload, 217
aircraft transponders, listening to, 198–
    203
    getting a map that centers in your re-
        gion, 202

    materials for project, 198
    running Dump1090, 202
Alamode board, 311
alcyone application, 333
Alcyone MIDI controller, 330, 330
aliens, looking for, 158–164
AM2302 sensor, 173
    adding to Linux kernel, 174
    C code to read data from, 175
    wiring to Raspberry Pi, 174
Amateur Position Reporting System
    (see APRS)
Amazon Instant Video, 274
analog output of Pi for sound output,
    242
Android
    accessing Pi MusicBox, 235
    AndroBOINC, 163
    CSipSimple softphone, 124
    MPDroid, 238
        installing and using, 239
    running on Raspberry Pi, 107–109
Android_Pi_Wiki, 107
Answer( ) application, 126
antennas
    for aerial photography hack, 218
    included with NooElec R820T, 199
    wire connected to GPIO4, 245
Apache web server
    documentation and information re-
        sources, 128
    installing, 127
    starting, 128

We'd like to hear your suggestions for improving our indexes. Send email to index@oreilly.com.

Apple Airplay, 232
Apple Bonjour, 235
Apple Macintosh (see Mac OS X)
APRS (Amateur Position Reporting System), 204
　Trackuino, Arduino-based system, 206
APRS (Automatic Packet Reporting System), 217
　hand-held system to track signal in the field, 218
APT repository, ROSpbian, 135
Arduino
　connecting Arduino shields to Pi, 292–312
　　analog-to-digital conversion, 298
　　compiling arduPi and a program using it, 296
　　enabling the UART port, 295
　　GPIO input, 296
　　I2C, 304
　　options with shield and arduPi library, 292
　　SPI, 307
　　UART, 303
　　using arduPi library, 293
　Trackuino APRS system, 206
arduPi library, 292
　accessing UART, 303
　compiling, and a program using it, 296
　running your program, 296
　using, 293
ARM architecture revision of Raspberry Pi ARM, 70
ARM CPU (see CPU/GPU of Raspberry Pi)
ARM Installer (Fedora), 131
ARM Linux compilers, 67
ARM1176 core, 99
armor building, 150
　other materials for, 151
armor-building tools, 152
ARMv6 hard-float optimization, 13

ARMv6 soft-float optimization, 14
assimp (Open Asset Import Library), 139
Asterisk telephone system, 121–127
　installing, 121
　prompt for command line, 123
　setting up a softphone, 123
　　configuring SIP account, 123
　　registering SIP client, 124
　　setting up extension in dialplan, 125
　starting, 122
Atmel AT91SAM7S256 microcontroller, 134
Atmel ATmega48 microcontroller, 134
audio files accepted by XBMC, 271
audio set, 233
Automatic Packet Reporting System (see APRS)
Avahi, 235

B
backpower, 24
　avoiding when using USB hubs, 25
　providing reliably for Raspberry Pi, 26
backups
　critical firmware files in boot partition, 11
balloon photography project, 207
　(see also aerial photography, controlling)
　choosing the balloon, 207
　reasons to use Raspberry Pi, 204
BAM (BOINC Account Manager), 162
　(see also BOINC)
Barch Designs case, 323
batteries for aerial photography project, 206
battery packs, 57
baud, 47
　baud rate for MIDI specification, 335
BCM labeling (GPIO pins), 38
Beowulf, 337
　reading, 343

Beowulf clusters, 337

Berkeley Open Infrastructure for Network Computing (see BOINC)

Binary Utilities Options (crosstool-ng), 72

bison, 64

bit rate, 47

bitrate, 238
    setting Spotify bitrate for Pi, 239

Bitwizard B.V., USB prodder , 28

Black Sky Telemetry site, 218

Blink softphone for Mac and Windows, 124

BlinkM RGB I2C-controlled LED, 304

blogging
    setting up basic blog server, 127–131

Bluetooth, 332

BOINC, 158
    account managers, 162
    AndroBOINC, 163
    BOINC Account Manager (BAM), 162
    GridRepublic account manager, 163
    installing manager and client, 159
    setting up, 160

boot partition, SD card, 3
    alternative prebuilt kernel variants, 89
    copying new core Linux kernel image into, 86
    mounting manually, 6
    updating firmware on, 11

boot process, Raspberry Pi, 9

/boot/config.txt file (see config.txt file)

bootcode.bin file, 11

bounce, 333

bps (see bit rate)

bracketed photos, 261

breadboards
    connecting GPIO pins to, 39–47

bricks, programmable, 134, 134
    (see also NXT Intelligent Brick)

broadcast, finding with ifconfig, 35

Broadcom BCM2835 chip, xiv

broken Raspberry PI, fixing, 29

Brown, Ty, 194

buffer support within IIO, 191

bus-powered USB hubs, 22

byte encoding, MIDI message based on, 335

C

C code for AM2302 sensor, 175

C Compiler Options (crosstool-ng), 73

C-library options (crosstool-ng), 74

C6 capacitor, 29
    replacing, 30

Cacheberry Pi, 183–188
    hardware needed for, 184
    loading cache data, 187
    project website, 186
    software image for, 186
    wiring, 187

calibration option, Mimo touchscreen, 254
    determining max/min X and Y calibration values, 255

calibration script for in-car touchscreen, 282

cameras, 258
    (see also DSLR, connecting)
    enabling Raspberry Pi camera on Pidora, 325
    finding out more about, 261
    for aerial photography hack, 207
        gphoto to control Nikon camera, 207
    for cosplay project, 152
        ribbon cable, 153
        software and script to power it, 153
    for photobooth, 263
    getting configuration from gphoto2, 266
    Pi Raspberry camera, 258

capacitor 06 (see C6 capacitor)

capture commands, 260
    variables, 260

carrier signal, 245

case (water-resistant) for Pi, 177

case for Pi used as heat sink, 323

catkin tool, 138
  building catkinized ROS components, 140
  running catkin-make, 141
  running catkin_make to install files into /opt/ros/groovy/ ROS structure, 142

Celsius/Fahrenheit/Kelvin temperature conversions, 16

Class 10 SD cards, 2

clock frequency, FM radio, 245

clock generator module, 246

cmake_modules ROS component, 141

cmdline.txt file
  options to use GPU low- and high-water marks, 95

code examples from this book
  config file for Reasperry Pi Linux kernel, 79

Coder, using for your website, 131–133

COLLADA Document Object Model (DOM), 138

color sensor
  testing ROS sensor, 144

command-line interface (CLI), Asterisk, 123

Common UNIX Printing System (see CUPS)

compiled-in options, 82

composite video output, 247

config file, Linux kernel, 79

config.txt file
  booting file other than default kernel.img, 86
  memory allocation with, 93
    GPU low- and high-water marks, 95
    making file compatible with 256 or 512 MiB models, 94
  quick changes on mounted SD card, 6

configuration
  checking custom overrides, 16

checking value of specific, 17

configuration hacks, 1–62
  adding a Reset button, 54
  adding a USB serial console, 47–54
  adding memory with swap, 61–62
  choosing and formatting the SD card, 1–3
  connecting GPIO pins to a breadboard, 39–47
  connecting with SSH, 32–34
  decoding the LEDs, 7–8
  getting more USB ports, 22–24
  getting power to Pi on the move, 56
  going headless, 31
  learning GPIO, 36–39
  monitoring Raspberry Pi hardware, 13–17
  mounting the SD card, 3–7
  overclocking, 17–20
  overvolting, 20
  static IP address for Pi, 34–36
  troubleshooting power problems, 24–29
  unbreaking your Raspberry Pi, 29
  updating the firmware, 8–13

CONFIG_HWMON, 166

CONFIG_I2C_BCM2708, 166
  enabled as module, 170

CONFIG_I2C_CHARDEV, 166
  enabled as module, 170

CONFIG_IIO, 191

CONFIG_IIO_ST_HWMON, 192

CONFIG_SENSORS_TMP102 enabled as module, 166

CONFIG_SENSORS_TSL2563, 192

connectors, 36

console mode, starting Asterisk in, 122

consoles
  adding USB serial console, 47–54
    hack for the red wire, 48

Contiguous Memory Allocator (CMA), 95

controllers, 256
    using NES/SNES controller through
        GPIO, 256
converter board, 220
    connecting, 221
converters, 278
Cooking Hacks, Raspberry Pi to Arduino
    shields connection bridge, 292
core frequency, GPU processor, 19
    problems with overclocking, 19
core Linux kernel image, 88
cosplay, surviving gaping chest wound,
    150–158
    adding the battle wound, 152
    building the costume, 150
    finishing the custume, 155
    putting it all together, 157
costumes, building, 150
    other materials for armor building,
        151
    resources for, 151
CPU cores, number of, 84
CPU/GPU of Raspberry Pi, 18
    -cpu option in QEMU, 99
    decoding/encoding video files by
        GPU, 227
    GPU and DisplayLink technology,
        248
    GPU firmware, no support for DSI-
        connected devices, 247
    increasing ARM CPU frequency, 18
    increasing GPU frequency, 19
    monitoring memory split, 16
    overvolting, 21
    sharing memory automatically, 95
cross-compiler, building, 63–76
    adding crosstool-ng to PATH, 66
    beginning the build, 76
    configuring cross-compiler, 67–75
    configuring crosstool-ng, 65
    installing crosstool-ng, 63
    installing development tools, 64
crosstool-ng
    adding to your PATH, 66

configuration menu, 67
configuring, 65
configuring the cross-compiler, 67–
    75
    Binary Utilities Options, 72
    C Compiler Options, 73
    C-library options, 74
    Operating System Options, 71
    Paths and Misc. Options, 68
    Target Options, 69
    Toolchain Options, 71
    disabling CT_WANTS_STATIC_LINK,
        75
    installing, 63
    PPL bug fix, 65
CSV files for geocache data, 188
CT_WANTS_STATIC_LINK, disabling, 75
CUPS (Common UNIX Printing System),
    117
    Add Printer configuration page, 119
    administration web portal, 118
    editing configuration file, 117
    setting up another network comput-
        er to print, 120
current, defined, 60
CUSF Landing Predictor, 218
CV/Gate, 331
CyanogenMod, 107
    compiling to run on Raspberry Pi,
        109
    CyanogenMod 7.2 (based on Android
        2.3), 108

D

DACs (Digital Audio Converters), 242
DC power, changing to AC, 279
dd command, 186
debouncing circuits, 333
demultiplexer (demux), 319
device name
    finding for SD cards, 2
    for UART serial device, 49
Device section, Xorg configuration, 252
DHT22 temperature-humidity sensor,
    174

dialing plan (or dialplan), 123
    getting complete list of applications, 127
    setting up an extension, 125
Digital Audio Converters (DACs), 242
Display Power Management Signaling (DPMS), 252
Display Serial Interface (DSI) connector, 247
DisplayLink, 248
DIY culture, xii
DMA (Direct Memory Access) controller, 246
dmesg command, 4
    device name for UART serial device, 49
DNS server, sepcifying for static IP address, 36
dphys-swapfile, 62
DPMS (Display Power Management Signaling), 252
DSI (Display Serial Interface) connector, 247
DSLR, connecting, 258–262
    basic capture commands and variables, 260
    finding out more about your camera, 261
    getting started with gPhoto, 258
Dump1090, 199
    dependencies for building, installing, 199
    getting map centered on your region, 202
    preparing for use, 201
    running the script, 202
dynamic IP addressing, 34
dynamic voltage scaling to increase voltage, 20

E

e2i Technology touchpanel, 248
e2i Touchscreen controller option, 249
Einstein@Home, 159

electricity
    essential terms and relationships, 59
    mixing with water, hazards of, 178
elfutils package, 14
emulating Raspberry Pi, 97–99
Emulation Station, 257
    configuring your joystick, 258
enabling Raspberry Pi camera on Pidora, 325
encryption (for wireless networks), 234
Enigma@home, 158
Enzol Tanzania Limited, 327
error codes, common LED codes, 7
evtest tool, 254, 284
    output about touch events, 254
EXPERIMENTAL or DANGEROUS options, 84
extending your Pi, 287–343
    adding a heat sink, 322–324
    adding a numeric keypad, 316–322
        connecting the keypad to Pi, 318
        how the Matrix Keypad works, 317
        installing the software, 319
        running the program, 319
    adding a tiny screen, 290
    building a MIDI controller, 329–336
        ergonomics, 336
        hardware, 330
        software, 333
    building a solar-powered lab, 326
        gathering hardware, 326
        setting up Pi, 328
    building a supercomputer, 337–343
        building more nodes, 341
        building MPI to run on multiple nodes, 338
        making MPI shared libraries for Pi, 342
        using Python bindings for MPI, 341
        using SSH for login between Pis, 340

connecting Arduino shields to Pi,
  292–312
  analog-to-digital conversion, 298
  compiling arduPi library and a pro-
    gram using it, 296
  enabling the UART port, 295
  GPIO input, 296
  I2C, 304
  SPI, 307
  UART, 303
  using arduPi library, 293
controlling a 3D printer, 312–316
controlling GPIO from a web browser,
  287–289
enabling camera on Pidora, 325
extensions, setting up in dialplan, 125
external hard drives, using for shared
  file storage, 112
externally powered USB hubs, 22
  possible issues using with Raspberry
    Pi, 24
extraterrestrial intelligence, searching
  for, 158–164

F

FAA regulations on balloon-launched
  payload, 205
Fahrenheit/Celsius/Kelvin temperature
  conversions, 16
FAT formatted partition on SD card, 3
Fedora ARM Installer, 131
ffmpeg, 208, 228
  building from source, 229
filesystem, resizing, 241
filesystems, SSD formatting for, 285
firewalls
  getting SIP traffic through, 121
  permitting traffic to access CUPS
    server, 118
firmware
  home for Raspberry Pi firmware, 10
  updates on the Pi, 2
  updating for Raspberry Pi, 8–13
  updating the easy way, 96

version currently used by Raspbian
  Linux kernel, 10
fixup.dat file, 11
flex, 64
Flirc USB dongle, 272
FM (frequency modulation), 245
formatting SD cards, 2
Fortran, 338
four-port USB hub, 24
framebuffer driver support, enabling,
  249
free command, 62
frequency modulation (FM), 245

G

G-code, 314
  converting 3D model to, 315
  sending instructions to the printer,
    316
gateway, finding with ifconfig, 35
GCC compiler, 64, 175
  configuring gcc and gcc4.7 as defualt
    compilers, 229
  Linaro version, 67
gd module (PHP), 128
General Purpose Input/Output (see
  GPIO)
geocaching with Pi, 182–188
  Cacheberry Pi, 183
  gathering Cacheberry Pi hardware,
    184
  loading cache data into Cacheberry
    Pi, 187
  overview of geocaching, 183
  preparing Cacheberry Pi software im-
    age, 186
  wiring Cacheberry Pi, 187
getty, 52
git
  Adafruit-Raspberry-Pi-Python-Code,
    175
  checking out Raspberry Pi Linux ker-
    nel source tree, 77
  git binary in git package, 96

prebuilt Linux kernel images for Raspberry Pi, 88

using to update Raspberry Pi firmware, 10

GitHub

nxt codebase and fixes, 137

Python library for LCD Pi Plate, 104

ROS repository, multiple branches, 140

tarball of Linux kernel source tree, 78

GMP (GNU Multiple Precision Arithmetic Library, 65

GNU MP, 64

Google Docs, Adafruit_DHT, Python script for, 176

Gparted tool, 3

gperf, 64

gPhoto, 207, 258

gphoto2, 259

installing on Raspberry Pi, 263

GPIO, 24, 36–39

BCM labeling for pins, 38

connecting numeric keypad, 318

connecting pins to a breadboard, 39–47

GPIO quick reference, 45

connecting wire to GPIO4 to act as antenna, 245

controlling from a web browser, 287–289

getting power through safely, 26

header of GPIO pins, 36

input, 296

labeling your own pins, 38

libraries for aerial photography hack, 207

mapping of TMP102 breakout pins to, 168

one-wire support on GPIO 4, 100

pin-number labeling, 37

problems in using to power Pi, 25

Python Raspberry Pi GPIO library, 320

using NES/SNES/controller through, 256

GPS, 183

GPS receiver for Cacheberry Pi, 184

plugging into Raspberry Pi, 187

GPSd daemon to decode GPS data streams, 207

tracking aerial photography payload, 217

Trackuion APRS system, 206

graphics processing unit (GPU), 227

(see also CPU/GPU of Raspberry Pi)

GridRepublic, 163

Groovy ROS, 135

groovy-devel code branch (ROS repository), 140

Ground Fault Circuit Interruptor (GFCI), 182

GSAK (on Windows), 188

GY-80 module, 206

H

H.264/MPEG-4 video, 231

Hackerspaces in Space contest, 204

ham radio Automatic Packet Reporting System (APRS), 217

Hangup( ) application, 126

Hanns-G Model HI161Abb LED monitor, 327

hard float, checking for, 13

Hardware Monitoring support, 166

hardware monitoring, by IIO devices, 192

hardware video block frequency, 19

HDMI, 247

connecting Pi MusicBox to amplifier, 242

headless mode, running Raspberry Pi in, 31

headphones, 233

analog headphones jack of Pi, 242

telling Raspbian to use, 328

heat sink, adding to Pi, 322–324

thermal photo of heat output from Pi, 322

helium for aerial photography balloon, 207

high-power USB devices, 23

holiday lights display, 219–225
    connecting the hardware, 220
    installing the software, 222
    setup, 219

Holux M-215 GPS receiver, 184

hotplugging, 28

household projects, 111–164
    building a web server, 127–133
    controlling a LEGO robot, 134–150
    cosplay (costume play), 150–158
    looking for aliens, 158–164
    sharing files with Samba, 111–116
    using Raspberry Pi as remote print server, 117–120
    using Raspberry Pi Aterisk telephone system, 121–127

HPLIP (HP Linux Imaging and Printing project), 119

Hulu, 274

humidity, 173
    combined temperature and humidity sensor (AM2302), 173

Hynix RAM, Occidentalis and, 101

hysteresis limit value, 171

I

I2C (Inter-Integrated Circuit), 46
    Adafruit I2C Python module, 194
    attempt to install i2ctools and lm-sensors on default Raspbian, 170
    BlinkM RGB I2C-controlled LED, 304
    communication between Pi and ADC of Arduino shield, 298
    connection of TSL2561 to I2C bus on GPIO, 191
    defined, 166
    kernel support for, 166
    libraries for talking to GY-80 sensor board, 207
    TMP102 I2C sensor, 165

I2C support
    enabling in Linux kernel, 105
    in Occidentalis, 100
    kernel option, 82

i2c-tools, installing, 169, 193

i2cdetect command, 193

i2cdetect command line, 169

ifconfig command, 33, 201
    finding current IP address, netmask, and broadcast, 35

IIC/I2C/TWI SPI Serial LCD 1602 Module, 185

image sensor pipeline block frequency, 19

Industrial IO Support option, 191

input device for Mimo touchscreen, 254

Inter-Integrated Circuit (see I2C)

interactive_markers ROS component, 141

Internet of Things, 287

intervals for taking photos, specifying, 261

inverters, 279

iOS
    accessing Pi MusicBox, 235
    mPod and mPad for Pi MusicBox, 238

ip addr command, 33

IP address
    accessing Pi MusicBox by, 235
    blinking through LEDs, 8
    getting for Raspberry Pi, 201
    giving your Pi a static IP address, 34–36
        choosing unique address, 36
    headless mode and, 31
    monitoring for Raspberry Pi, 102–107
        building LCD Pi Plate, 103
        installing software to control LCD Pi Plate, 104
    network with static address, using Pi MusicBox in, 244
    router's default IP address, 33

ip-flash command, 32

ip-info package, 32

ip-read command, 32
iptables, editing for CUPS traffic, 118
IRC channel, #razdroid, on Freenode, 107
iTunes, 235

J
JQuery, 335

K
Kelvin temperature, 16
kernel
    building a custom kernel, 76–87
        building kernel image, 84
        configuring the kernel, 79
        downloading kernal source tree, 77
        installing new kernel, 85
        natively, on Raspberry Pi, 77
        post-installation tasks, 87
    updating prebuilt kernel easy way, 96
    updating to latest prebuilt kernal
        installing prebuilt kernel modules, 89
    updating to latest prebuilt kernel, 87–91
        distribution-specific features, 88
        getting prebuilt kernel, 88
kernel modules
    building for custom kernel, 85
    copying for new kernel image file, 86
    enabling feature or driver as, 82
kernel-qemu file, downloading, 97
kernel.img file, 8
    changing GPU firmware booting of, 86
kernel_cutdown.img, 89
kernel_emergency.img, 89
keypad class, 320
keypad for LCD Pi Plate, 103
Kondik, Steve, 108

L
LAMP, 127
    Apache web server, installing, 127

MySQL, PHP, and PHP gd module, installing, 128
Last.fm, playing music via, 232, 237
LCD Pi Plate, 103–107
    building, 103
    displaying IP address for Pi, 107
    installing software to control, 104
    library of Python functions to access, 106
    running LCD-pi-plate-demo.py script, 106
LCD screens
    DisplayLink monitor in Mimo 720, 248
    for Cacheberry Pi, 185
        connecting to Raspberry Pi, 187
    SPI LCD, printing messages on, using arduPi, 307
LCDtest.py script, 106
LEDs
    BlinkM RGB I2C-controlled LED, 304
    decoding, 7–8
        blinking your IP address, 8
        common LED error codes, 7
    flashing IP address, 32
    Hanns-G Model HI161Abb LED monitor, 327
    indicator LED for Cacheberry Pi, 186
        connecting to Raspberry Pi, 187
LEGO Mindstorms kits, 134
LEGO robot (see robot (LEGO), controlling)
LHC@home, 158
libgphoto2, 259
    cameras supported by, 263
libsensors library, 170
libusb, 259
license keys for video codecs, 232
light, monitoring, 189–198
    accessing TSL2561 sensor directly from Linux kernel, 197
    accessing TSL2561 sensor via Python, 194
    lux, 189

TSL2561 sensor, 189
lighthttpd web server, 207
lights display (see holiday lights display)
Linaro variant of GCC compiler, 67
Linux
    configuration for Raspberry Pi,
        changes required by MIDI, 335
    distribution images for use with
        Raspberry Pi, 9
    distribution on SD card for Raspberry
        Pi, 1
    distributions for Raspberry Pi, 3, 269
        hard float, 13
    flashing NXT Intelligent Brick firm-
        ware from, 135
    GMPC and Sonata to control Pi Mu-
        sicBox, 238
    hacking for Raspberry Pi, 63–109
        building a custom kernel, 76–87
        building cross-compiler toolchain,
            63–76
        emulating Pi, 97–99
        monitoring IP address for Pi, 102–
            107
        Occidentalis, 99–102
        splitting memory between GPU
            and Linux userspace, 91–96
        updating firmware and kernel
            easy way, 96
        updating to latest prebuilt kernel,
            87–91
    installing OpenSSH, 33
    making Pi MusicBox work on Linux
        computers, 235
    mounting SD card on Linux comput-
        er, 4
    mounting USB flash drive, 187
    not using to connect to serial port,
        50
    swapfile, 62
    video player software, 227
Linux, Apache, MySQL, and PHP (see
    LAMP)

lm_sensors, 166
    installing, 169
    reading data from TMP102 sensor,
        170
locale handling in Raspbian, 137
login console, using Raspberry Pi UART
    serial device as, 52
Lowrey organ pedals, 330
lpadmin group, 117
lsusb application, 54
Lulzbot AO-101 printer, 312
luminosity sensors, 189
lux (lx), 189
    Python script to calculate from
        TSL2561 readings, 194
    TSL2561 sensor readings and, 194

M

M3U files, 236
Mac OS X
    terminal software, 50
    Theremin, 238
    using to connect to serial port, 50
make clean command, 78
make mrproper command, 78
make package, 77
make utility, 175
    -j flag to speed up build, 84
    ARCH=arm CROSS_COMPILE=arm-
        rpi-linux-gnueabi- options, 80
    compiling Dump1090, 201
    making sure Linux kernel config file is
        current, 80
    menuconfig option, 81
    starting Linux kernel modules build,
        85
Makefile.include
    adding dbus header include flags,
        229
    bug in, 228
male header pins, 41
map_msgs ROS component, 140
Matrix Numeric Keypad
    connecting to Raspberry Pi, 318
    how it works, 317

matrix_keypad library, 319
    program using, 319
matrix_keypad_RPi_GPIO module, 320
maximum permitted current draw from
    5 V pins, 26
media center, turning Pi into, 269–277
    adding a remote control, 272
    adding content, 274
    decoding MPEG-2 and VC-1, 271
    shortcut for cord cutters, 274
    XBMC, 269
media-berry package, 328
Mediabridge
    High Output Dual USB Car Charger,
      278
    USB charging cables, 28
Membrane 3x4 Matrix Numeric Keypad,
    317
memory split, 91–96
    allocating memory with config.txt
      file, 93
    and optional versions of firmware
      files, 13
    automatically sharing memory, 95
    monitoring, 16
    setting up for ffmpeg code to com-
      pile, 228
    start.elf file corresponding to, 93
memory, adding with swap, 61–62
Message Passing Interface (see MPI)
MicroController Pros, 312
Microsoft
    Streets and Trips format, 188
    VC-1 license, 271
    Windows (see Windows systems)
MIDI (musical instrument digital inter-
    face), 330
MIDI controller, building cheaply, 329–
    336
    ergonomics, 336
    hardware, 330
    software, 333
Midnight Commander utility, 243
Miller, Florian, 257

Mimo 720 touchscreen, 247
    e2i Technology USB Touchpanel de-
      tected, 251
    frame buffer devices assigned by ker-
      nel to, 251
    kernel drivers for, 248
    rebooting Pi with it connected, 250
    using, 254
    Xorg configuration file for, 251
minicom, 50
MJPEG codec, 232
mkdosfs command, 3
MMC block device partitions, 4
    confirming correct device names, 5
Model A and Model B, xiv
    LEDs, 7
    maximum permitted current draw
      from 5 V pins, 26
    memory on Model B, 91
    peak current draw on Model B, 28
    revisions of Model B board, xiv
    USB ports on Model B, 22
ModemManager, 53
ModMyPi, 324
modular options, 82
modules, Linux kernel
    building for custom kernel, 85
    enabling feature or driver as, 82
    installing prebuilt modules, 89
    prebuilt Linux kernel modules, 88
monitoring Raspberry Pi hardware, 13–
    17
    checking custom configuration over-
      rides, 16
    checking for hard float, 13
    measuring component voltage, 15
    memory split, 16
monitors
    connecting to HDMI or composite
      video, 250
    Hanns-G Model HI161Abb LED moni-
      tor, 326
    Monitor section, Xorg configuration,
      252

operating Raspberry Pi without a
monitor, 31
Monk, Simon, 38
Moog Taurus, 330
Mopidity, 243
Morse code program, 247
mounting the SD card, 3–7
movies, watching in your car, 277–286
adding videos, 285
power source, 277
powered USB hub, 280
putting it all together, 285
software, 281
storage for movies, 279
touchscreen, 280
MPD (Music Player Daemon), 238
MPDroid, 238
installing and using, 239
MPEG-2 codec, 231
decoding, 271
enabling in config.txt, 231
MPI (Message Passing Interface), 337
building to run code on multiple nodes, 337
making shared libraries for Pi, 342
using Python bindings for, 341
writing master image onto SD card,
339
MPICH Installer's Guide, 337
multi-room audio, 238
multimedia hacks, 227–286
building Pi MusicBox, 232–244
connecting a DSLR, 258–262
controlling Pi via touchscreen, 247–
255
emulating classic video game consoles, 255–258
enabling additional video codecs,
231–232
playing video files, 227–231
setting up a photobooth, 262–269
turning Pi into a radio, 244–247
turning Pi into media center, 269–
277

watching movies in your car, 277–
286
multimeter
testing USB cable's resistance, 28
testing voltage on Raspberry Pi, 59
testing your power supply, 30
music player, Pi MusicBox, 232–244
getting and configuring software, 233
editing Pi MusicBox settings, 233
network connections, 234
Midnight Commander utility, 243
Mopidity, 243
more options to explore, 243
MPD (Music Player Daemon), 238
multi-room audio, 238
networked music, 240
playing local music, 241
playing music, 234
search function, 235
selecting songs and adding to
queue, 235
streams from web radio stations,
236
rc.local file, 243
security, 242
sound configuration, 242
updating, 244
using in network with static IP address, 244
musical instrument digital interface
(MIDI), 330
MySQL
creating database and user for Word-
Press, 129
in LAMP, 127
setting up installation, 128
starting, 128
mystery sound game, 246

N

native compiler, 64
nav.csv file, 188
NC (Normally Closed) wires, 221
NC Near Space Research Group, 204
ncurses, 64

ncurses-dev package, 77
ncurses-devel package, 77
NES (Nintendo Entertainment System), 255
  using NES/SNES controller through GPIO, 256
Netflix, 274
netmask, finding with ifconfig, 35
network connections (Pi MusicBox), 234
network interfaces
  configurations, 34
  editing to use Pi MusicBox in static network, 244
network interfaces file, wireless connection for Occidentalis, 102
networked music, playing on Pi MusicBox, 240
networking protocols used with XBMC, 271
NeverWet coating, 179
  painting Raspberry Pi and components with, 180
Nikon Coolpix, 207
nmap tool, 33
nmbd, 112
NO (Normally Open) wires, 221
NOOBS (New Out-Of-Box Software)
  installing/copying directly onto SD card, 3
  SD cards preloaded with, 2
NooElec R820T, 198
numeric keypad, adding to Pi, 316–322
  connecting the keypad, 318
  how the Matrix Keypad works, 317
  installing the software, 319
  other uses for keypad, 321
  running the program, 319
nxt family of modules, 136
NXT Intelligent Brick, 134
  firmware, 135
  permission for Pi user to communicate with, 137
  testing ROS connection to, 143

udev rules for lego group users to access, 137
using NXT Python bindings for simple robot, 148

O

Occidentalis, 99–102
  download site for most recent version, 101
  features of Version 0.1 and 0.2, 100
  I2C and TMP102 sensor support, 166
  origin of the name, 101
  raspi-config options, 101
  wireless connection, setting up, 102
Ogg Theora codec, 232
Ohm's law, 60
omxplayer, 227, 328
  building on Raspbian, 228
  control keys for video playback, 230
  documentation, 230
  installing on Raspbian, 228
  installing system-wide, 230
  running as user other than root, 230
  watching videos with, 230
1-Wire sensors, 173
Open Asset Import Library (assimp), 139
Open Cache Manager (Linux/OSX), 188
OpenELEC, 251, 281
OpenSSH, 32
Operating System Options (crosstool-ng), 71
OS distributions for Raspberry Pi, 3
outdoors, hacking, 165–225
  checking on your plants, 172–176
  controlling aerial photography, 204–219
  geocaching with Pi, 182–188
  holiday lights display, 219–225
  light-monitoring, 189–198
  listening to aircraft transponders, 198–203
  making Pi water-resistant, 176–182

overclocking, 17–20
  causing errors with Class 10 SD
    cards, 2
  increasing ADRAM frequency, 18
  increasing ARM CPU frequency, 18
  increasing GPU frequency, 19
  pretested overclock presets, 20
  warnings about, 18
overvolting, 20

P

package on package (PoP), 91
parachute for aerial photography, 207
parallax, 152
Parallel Processing on the Pi, 337
Parma Polyhedra Library (PPL), bug fix,
  65
partitioning SD cards, 3
  adjusting partitions and their sizes, 3
  boot and root partitions, Linux distri-
    butions, 3
  resizing filesystem, Pi MusicBox, 241
Paths and Misc Options (crosstool-ng
  menu), 68
payload for balloon photography, 205
  components included in, 206
  container for, 206
  FAA regulations on, 205
  tracking, 217
pedal press/release cycle, MIDI controller, 334
Pepakura, 151
performance optimization, 17
  (see also overclocking)
  overvolting, 20
photobooth, setting up, 262–269
  camera configuration, examining,
    266
  choosing URL shortener, 266
  materials required for, 262
  packages to install on Raspberry Pi,
    263
  Photobooth class, 266
  photobooth.py script, 264
  QR code, 266

stable Internet connection for uploading pictures, 265
  watermark for images, 265
photography, aerial (see aerial photography, controlling)
PHP
  in LAMP, 127
  installing PHP and gd module, 128
Pi Cobbler, 40, 169
  versions, 41
Pi MusicBox (see music player, Pi MusicBox)
Picture Transfer Protocol (PTP), 259
Pidora
  building omxplayer, 228
  enabling Raspberry Pi camera on,
    325
  giving your Pi a static IP address, 34
  headless configuration option, 31
  pidora-18-r1c.img, 98
    starting in QEMU, 98
  swap configuration, default, 62
  systemd service file for camera
    script, 154
PiFM, 244–247
  accessing hardware, 246
  downloading and extracting files, 244
  fun with, 246
  how it works, 245
PIHUB, 24
pin-number labeling (GPIO), 37
PinMux control, 82
Pip, 342
PL2303HXA drivers, 50
plants (outdoor), checking on, 172–176
  requirements for plants, 172
Playback( ) application, 126
playlist, creating, 246
PlayOn, 274
PLS files, 236
plus sign (+), appended to Raspberry Pi
  kernel builds, 90
polyfuse, 60
  testing for problems, 61

PoP (package on package), 91
power
    essential terms in electricity, 59
    getting to Pi on the move, 56
    in cars, 277
    less-than-recommended power options, 56
power cord for Cacheberry Pi, 185
power problems, troubleshooting, 24–29
    avoiding backpowering Pi over USB, 25
    considerations in using GPIO to power Pi, 25
    getting a better Micro USB cable, 27
    getting a better power supply, 27
    getting power through GPIO safely, 26
    symptoms of power problems, 27
    testing USB cable's resistance, 28
power source for Raspberry Pi, 24
power supplies
    getting a better one, 27
    irregularities in voltage supplied, 25
    testing, 30
Powering Potential, 326
print server, remote, using Raspberry Pi as, 117–120
printed circuit boards (PCBs), 40
Printrun, 316
project box for Cacheberry Pi, 186
pronterface, 316
PTP (Picture Transfer Protocol), 259
Pulse-Width Modulation (PWM), 46
PuTTY, 50
PWM (Pulse-Width Modulation), 46
Python
    accessing TSL2561 sensor via, 194
    bindings for MPI, 341
    holiday lights project tools, 222
    library for LCD Pi Plate, 104
    matrix_keypad library, 319
    NXT Python bindings for simple robot, 148

photobooth.py script, 264
python-imaging package, 263
python-smbus library, 194
Raspberry Pi GPIO library, 319
ROS script to test color sensor, 144
ROS script to test touch sensor, 144
script to run Adafruit_DHT binary, 175
scripts for aerial photography project, 207
System Management Bus (SMBus) support modlue, 105

Q
QEMU (Quick EMUlator), 97–99
    documentation of other options, 99
    installing, 97
    starting Pidora in, 98
QR code, size of, 266
qrencode package, 263

R
RACHEL, 326
    hardware required for server, 328
RACHEL-Pi, 326
radio
    finding web radio stations, 237
    license requirements in some countries, 245
    playing streams from web radio stations on Pi MusicBox, 236
    turning your Pi into (PiFM), 244–247
rain gauge sensors, 173
rainbow screen, 12
RAMBo electronics boards, 313
Raspberry Leaf, 39
Raspberry Pi
    determining which version you have, 92
    emulating, 97–99
    Linux kernel source tree, 77
    merging changes into upstream Linux kernel source, 90
    prebuilt Linux kernel, 88
        alternative or variant versions, 88

Raspberry Pi to Arduino shields connection bridge, 292

Raspbian
  enabling I2C support in Linux kernel, 105
  static IP address for Pi, 35

Raspbian Wheezy, 100

Raspbmc, 269
  for in-car movie watching, 281
  interactive installer for, 269
  post-installation settings, 270

raspi-config file, options for Occidentalis, 101

raspi-config tool, 20

raspivid utility, 153
  script to run it, 154

rc.local file, 243

readelf
  checking for ARMv6 hard-float support, 14
  in binutils package, 96

Realtek RTL8188CUS USB module, 100

RealTek Software Defined Radio (see RTL-SDR)

regulated voltage, 25

relay board, 220
  connecting, 221

remote control, adding to Pi media center, 272

rep-update script, warnings about use of, 96

RepRap family of printers, 312

Reset button, adding, 54

resistance
  defined, 60
  testing for USB cables, 28
  USB cables, 27

resistors, adapting voltage with, 297

resolution, parallax, and battle wound effect, 152

REST, WebIOPi framework, 287

RetroArch tool, 257

Retrode gaming adapter, 256

RetroPie tool, 257

robot (LEGO), controlling, 134–150
  installing ROS and dependencies, 135–143
  testing ROS connection to NXT Brick, 143
  using NXT Python bindings, 148

The Rocketman, 207

ROM files for video games, 256
  Emulation Station and, 258

root partition, SD card, 3
  Linux kernel modules on, 86
  mounting manually, 6

root user
  changing root password, 31
  su versus sudo command, 11

rootfs-resize, 31

ROS (robot operating system), 135
  information resources on robot building, 148
  installing ROS and dependencies, 135–143
    assimp library, 139
    building catkinized ROS components, 140
    building legacy ROS stacks, 142
    COLLADA DOM, 138
    nxt codebase, 136
  testing connection to NXT Brick, 143

roscore command, 143

roslaunch command, 146

ROSpbian repository, 135

rosrun command, 144

routers, default IP address, 33

rpi-3.6.y kernel source tree, 77

rpi-update script, 96
  in Occidentalis, 100
  putting on SPATH and making it executable, 96

RPM Fusion project, 208

RS-232 serial ports, 48

RTL-SDR (RealTek Software Defined Radio), 199
  drivers, building and installing, 199
  plugging into Pi and rebooting, 200

Rustoleum, NeverWet, 179
rviz ROS component, 141

S

Sainsmart 1602 ICD LCD unit, 185
Samba, 111–116
    connecting to share from another
        machine, 115
    GUI configuration tool, 115
    installing on Raspberry Pi, 114
    Samba/Winbind for Pi MusicBox,
        235
Samba Server Configuration Tool, 115
SCAN_ONCE and SCAN_ALWAYS set-
    tings, 241
Schmitt trigger buffer, 333
screen, 50
    installing and connecting to Raspber-
        ry Pi UART serial device, 52
screens, 307
    (see also LCD screens; monitors)
    screen device, Xorg configuration,
        252
    tiny screen for Raspberry Pi, 290
SD cards
    choosing and formatting, 1–3
    copying files onto for new Linux ker-
        nel, 85
    flashing Coder image onto, 131
    hazards of adding swap to, 61
    image-flashing tool, 131
    loading CyanogenMod 7.2, 108
    mounting, 3–7
    music files stored on, 241
    playing music via, 232
    putting musicbox0.4 image on, 233
    writing Cacheberry Pi image onto,
        186
SDHC Class 4 cards, 1
SDRAM
    increasing frequency, 18
    voltage settings, 21
Search for Extraterrestrial Intelligence
    (see SETI project)

sed, 64
    disabling CT_WANTS_STATIC_LINK,
        75
Sega Genesis video games, 256
sensors
    combined temperature and humidity
        sensor (AM2302), 173
    confirming active sensor with rostop-
        ic list command, 147
    for aerial photography hack, 208
        downloading libraries, 208
        main control loop of 10DOFd.py
            program, 208
    luminosity, 189
    reading data from, 170
    ROS script to test color sensor, 144
    running ROS script to test touch sen-
        sor, 144
    support in Occidentalis, 100
    temperature sensor, 165
    touch sensor on test robot, 146
serial connections
    clients supporting, 50
    weird noise (or missing signal) on, 53
serial consoles
    for Cacheberry Pi, 185
    trivia, 52
Serial Peripheral Interface Bus (see SPI)
Server Message Block protocol (see
    SMB)
ServerLayout section, Xorg configura-
    tion, 253
servos, adding servo motor to robot, 148
SETI project, 158
SETI@Home, 158
7 Inch HD Touchscreen Car Monitor,
    280
seven-port USB hub, 24
shares on Windows networks, 241
signal decoding script (see Dump1090)
silica gel packets, 177
sine-wave inverters, 279

SIP, 121
    configuring account for SIP soft-
        phone, 123
    registering your SIP client, 124
Slic3r, 315
SMB (Server Message Block), 111
smb.conf file, editing, 114
smbd, 112
SMBus, Python module for, 105
SNES (Super Nintendo) video games,
    256
socket splitters, 278
softphone application, 121
    setting up a softphone with Asterisk,
        123
        configuring SIP account, 123
        registering your SIP client, 124
        setting up extension in dialplan,
            125
solar-powered lab, building, 326
    gathering hardware, 326
    setting up Raspberry Pi, 328
    solar power system, 327
soldering
    connecting Pi Cobbler PCB to GPIO
        pins, 42
    reminders about, 42
solid state drives (SSDs), 279
    storing videos on, 285
sound configuration, Pi MusicBox, 242
sound module on Pi, 204
SoundCloud, 237
speakers (USB), 233
SPI (Serial Peripheral Interface Bus), 46
    communicating with, using arduPi
        functions, 307
    support in Occidentalis, 100
SPOT Satellite GPS Messenger device,
    217
Spotify, 232
    account information, 233
    levels of quality for music, 238
    limitation on playing different music
        on multiple devices, 238

playlists on Pi MusicBox, 235
sqllite database, 207
SSDs (solid state drives), 279
    storing videos on, 285
SSH
    connecting to Raspberry Pi, 32–34
        launching GUI interfaces, 34
    enabling for Pi MusicBox, 243
    ready-to-go sshd in Occidentalis, 100
    using instead of password login be-
        tween Pis, 340
start.elf file, 8, 11
    corresponding to memory splits, 93
static IP address (see IP address)
stationid.py script, 215
status LEDs on Model B, 7
stepdown converter, 327
stream URL for web radio, 236
su versus sudo command, 11
subscription services, 274
subversion, 64
super settings
    gpu_freq, 19
    over_voltage, 21
supercomputer, building, 337–343
    building more nodes, 341
    building MPI to run on multiple no-
        des, 338
    making MPI shared libraries for
        Raspberry Pi, 342
    using Python bindings for MPI, 341
    using SSH for login between Pis, 340
surl package, 263
swap, 61–62
    hazards of, 61
    setting for headless mode, 31
sync command, 12
    ensuring image is written onto SD
        card, 186
    running after installing new kernel, 87
system board voltage, 15
System Management Bus (SMBus) sup-
    port, Python module for, 105

T

TAOS light sensors device driver, 192
Taos TSL2561 luminosity sensor, 189
  (see also TSL2561 luminosity sensor)
tar command, unpacking Linux kernel
  tarballs, 78
Target Options (crosstool-ng menu), 69
telephone system (see Asterisk telephone system)
teletype, 52
television
  connecting to Raspberry Pi for pow-
    er, 274
  getting content to, 274
temperature
  converting to different scales, 16
  measuring for BCM2835 system-on-
    chip, 16
  monitoring without going outside,
    165
  plant hardiness zones, 172
temperature hysteresis limit, 171
temperature sensors, 169
  (see also TMP102 sensor)
  combined temperature and humidity
    sensor (AM2302), 173
  Texas Instruments TMP102 I2C sen-
    sor, 165
test point locations, 57
Texas Instruments TMP102 I2C temperature sensor, 165
texinfo, 64
Text User Interface (TUI) menu configuration system, 81
TFT LCD screen, 152
  mounting on costume and running it,
    157
  preparing for armor costume, 155
  resolution, 152
Theremin, 238
Thingiverse, 315
3D block frequency, 19
3D file formats, support for (assimp),
  139

3D models to print, 315
3D paper models, 151
3D printer, controlling, 312–316
TMP102 sensor, 165
  connecting to Raspberry Pi, 169
  finding on Pi I2C Bus, 169
  labels, 167
  mapping of breakout pins to GPIO,
    168
  reading data from, 170
Toolchain Options (crosstool-ng), 71
touch events, determining, 254
touch sensor
  confirming active sensor with rostop-
    ic list command, 147
  ROS script to test, 144
  test robot with, 146
touchscreen, controlling Pi via, 247–255
  choosing a touchscreen, 247
  installing and enabling drivers, 248
  using the touchscreen, 254
  Xorg configuration file, 251
touchscreens
  enabling USB touchscreen support,
    249
  for use in cars, 279, 280
    connecting Raspberry Pi to, 281
    enabling support, 281
    mounting, 286
Trackuino, 206
transient voltage suppression (TVS) diode, 25
transistor-transistor logic (TTL) serial,
  47
triggered sampling support in IIO, 191
TSL2561 luminosity sensor, 189
  accessing directly from kernel, 197
  accessing readings via Python mod-
    ule, 194
  connecting to Raspberry Pi GPIO,
    190
ts_calib.sh script, 282
TUI (Text User Interface) menu configuration system, 81

turbo mode, disabled by changes to comline.txt, 95

turbo presets, 20

Twinkle SIP softphone on Linux, 124

2.5 inch NTSC/PAL display, 290

U

UART (Universal Asynchronous Receiver/Transmitter), 46
  accessing with arduPi library, 303
  connecting Raspberry Pi UART serial port to computer USB, 48
  enabling the UART port, 295
  Raspberry Pi UART serial device data rate, 47
    using as login console, 52
  serial communication over, 47

udev rules
  access to NXT Intelligent Brick by lego group users, 137
  blacklisting connector device, 53
  for RTL-SDR device, 200

UDL Framebuffer driver, 248

UDL Kernel Mode Setting driver, 248

uimapper.conf file, 283

uinput_mapper, 283

unbreaking your Raspberry Pi, 29
  replacing the C6 capacitor, 30
  testing the power supply, 30

unit loads, 22

Universal Asynchronous Receiver/Transmitter (see UART)

Universal Standard Bus (see USB)

unmounting boot and root SD partitions, 6, 12

update-alternatives command, 229

urdf component source, 140

URL shortener (surl), 263

URLs (short), services that create, 266

USB
  12 V-to-USB converters, 278
  Display Link Framebuffer Driver, 248
  Display Link Kernel Mode Setting (KMS), 248
  flash drive for geocache data, 187

flash drive for shared storage, 113

getting a better Micro USB cable, 27

getting more USB ports, 22–24

interconnect cable, hubs sending power across, 24

serial console from Raspberry Pi, 47–54

sound cards, speakers, or headphones for Pi MusicBox, 242

speakers, 233

SSD connected to Pi over, 279

testing cable's resistance, 28

touchpanel in Mimo 720, 248

Touchscreen Driver, 248

USB devices causing Pi to reboot, 28

USB Mass Storage protocol, 259

USB Digital Audio Converter/DAC, 242

USB hubs, 22
  4-port USB hub, 24
  7-port hub for Raspberry Pi, 24
  determining if a good choice, 23
  PIHUB, 24
  powered, for use in cars, 280
  reliable backpower for Raspberry Pi, 26

USB-to-TTL Serial Cable, 48
  female jumper connectors, hack for red wire, 48

usbutils package, lsusb application, 54

V

VC-1 codec
  decoding, 271
  enabling, 231
  license for, 231

vcgencmd tool, 14
  get_config command, 16
  get_mem command, 16
  measure_temp command, 16
  measure_volts command, 15
  source code, 17

versions
  prebuilt Linux kernel and modules, matching, 89

printing version of running Linux kernel, 87

video

adding videos to in-car entertainment, 285

capturing with gphoto, 260

DisplayLinkDevice in Xorg configuration, 252

enabling additional video codecs, 231–232

videocore accelerated video codecs, 232

Pi native hardware support for HDMI and composite video output, 247

playing video files on Raspberry Pi, 227–231

RACHEL videos, omxplayer working with, 328

video codecs, supported encodings, 285

video codec license keys, store to sell, 231

video game consoles (classic), emulating, 255–258

using NES/SNES controller through GPIO, 256

video stream, creating from aerial photo hack, 208

videocore accelerated video codecs, 232

Videocore IV GPU (see CPU/GPU of Raspberry Pi)

VideoCore libraries, 227

VideoCore SDK libraries, updating, 96

VoIP (voice over IP), 121

SIP protocol, 121

voltage

checking for Raspberry Pi, 57

defined, 60

measuring component voltage, 15

overvolting, 20

VP6, VP8, MJPEG, and Ogg Theora video codecs, 232

W

water

humidity, 173

mixing with electricity, hazards of, 178

requirements for plants, 172

water-resistant Pi, 176–182

building water-resistant case for Pi, 177

without a case, 178

immersing Pi in water, 182

requirements for hack, 179

WAV file format, 245

web browsers

controlling GPIO from, 287–289

for Pi MusicBox, 234

web pages for aerial photography hack, 207

downloading, 208

script generating main station ID page, 215

Web Radio, 232

web servers

building your own, 127–133

setting up basic blog server, 127–131

lighthttpd web server, 207

WebIOPi, 287

Python library supporting GPIO interactions, 289

websites, using Coder for, 131–133

WiFi

equipment for aerial photography hack, 218

network connection for Pi MusicBox, 234

Occidentalis support for, 100

playing music via, 232

winbindd, 112

Windows systems

LEGO Mindstorms software, 135

making Pi MusicBox work, 235

Music Player Daemon (MPD) clients, 238

networked music, playing on Pi Mu-
    sicBox, 240
PlayOn, 274
putting music files on Pi using Win-
    dows network, 242
terminal software, 50
using to connect to serial port, 50
wire strippers, 175
wireless networking
    creating wireless network with PiFM,
        247
    setting up connection for Occidenta-
        lis, 102
    support added to Raspberry Pi, 107
    TCP/IP wireless for MIDI controller,
        332
wiring, holiday lights project, 221
wiringPi library, 333
WordPress, 127
    configuring, 129
    database and user for, 129
    downloading and installing, 129
    web-based setup, 130
World Community Grid, 159

WorldPossible forums, 328

X

X forwarding, 34
XBMC, xi, 269
    networking protocols, 271
    Raspbmc for in-car movies, 281
    remote controls, 272
    support for many formats, 271
    uinput_mapper device, 284
    Videos menu, PlayOn share, 275
XBMC-based Linux OS for Raspberry Pi,
    251
Xbox, 269
Xorg configuration file for Mimo 720,
    251
Xorg/XII, Linux distributions without,
    250
XSPF files, 236

Z

zImage binary file, 85
ZOC, 50

About the Authors

Ruth Suehle manages the Community Leadership team in Red Hat's Open Source and Standards group, which supports upstream open source software communities. She also leads the Fedora Project's marketing team. Previously an editor for *Red Hat Magazine*, she now leads discussions about open source principles as a moderator at opensource.com. Ruth is also a senior editor at GeekMom.com, where she covers the adventures of motherhood alongside technology and sci-fi.

Tom Callaway is the Fedora engineering manager at Red Hat, where he has worked since 2001. He has been active with Fedora since its creation and currently serves as the Fedora packaging committee chair, responsible for defining the standards that Fedora uses to keep its package quality high. He also maintains 300+ packages in Fedora, which may also mean he is legally insane. He enjoys pinball, gaming, sci-fi, frogs, geocaching, traveling, and causing trouble with his wife, Pam, and son, Jimmy.

Colophon

The cover fonts are URW Typewriter and Guardian Sans. The text font is Benton Sans; the heading font is Benton Sans; and the code font is Dalton Maag's Ubuntu Mono.

Get even more for your money.

Join the O'Reilly Community, and register the O'Reilly books you own. It's free, and you'll get:

- $4.99 ebook upgrade offer
- 40% upgrade offer on O'Reilly print books
- Membership discounts on books and events
- Free lifetime updates to ebooks and videos
- Multiple ebook formats, DRM FREE
- Participation in the O'Reilly community
- Newsletters
- Account management
- 100% Satisfaction Guarantee

Signing up is easy:

1. **Go to: oreilly.com/go/register**
2. **Create an O'Reilly login.**
3. **Provide your address.**
4. **Register your books.**

Note: English-language books only

To order books online:
oreilly.com/store

For questions about products or an order:
orders@oreilly.com

To sign up to get topic-specific email announcements and/or news about upcoming books, conferences, special offers, and new technologies:
elists@oreilly.com

For technical questions about book content:
booktech@oreilly.com

To submit new book proposals to our editors:
proposals@oreilly.com

O'Reilly books are available in multiple DRM-free ebook formats. For more information:
oreilly.com/ebooks

Spreading the knowledge of innovators   oreilly.com

Have it your way.

CPSIA information can
Printed in the USA
LVOW01s1609141014

408715LV000

362348